THE HEALTH OF THE
INDUSTRIAL WORKER

THE HEALTH OF THE INDUSTRIAL WORKER

BY

EDGAR L. COLLIS,

B.Ch., M.A., M.D. (Oxon.), M.R.C.P. (Lon.), M.R.C.S. (Eng.)

Mansel Talbot Professor of Preventive Medicine, Welsh National School of Medicine; Member of Industrial Fatigue Research Board; Late H.M. Medical Inspector of Factories; Member of Health of Munition Workers Committee; Milroy Lecturer, R.C.P. (1915); Director of Welfare and Health, Ministry of Munitions

AND

MAJOR GREENWOOD,

M.R.C.P. (Lon.), M.R.C.S. (Eng.)

Member of Industrial Fatigue Research Board; Reader in Medical Statistics, University of London; late Statistician to Lister Institute; Head of Medical Research Branch, Ministry of Munitions; Arris and Gale Lecturer, R.C.S. (1908)

CONTAINING A CHAPTER ON

RECLAMATION OF THE DISABLED

BY

ARTHUR J. COLLIS,

M.A., M.D. (Cantab.), M.R.C.S. (Eng.), D.P.H. (Durh.)

Medical Superintendent, Ministry of Pensions Hospital, Leicester; late Temp. Lieut.-Col. R.A.M.C.

WITH AN INTRODUCTION BY

SIR GEORGE NEWMAN,

K.C.B., D.C.L., M.D., F.R.C.P

LONDON
J. & A. CHURCHILL
7 GREAT MARLBOROUGH STREET
1921

" The best way of arriving at a theory of disease is by beginning with the theory of health."

(H. T. BUCKLE, *History of Civilisation in England*, Vol. 2, Ch. 1.)

THIS BOOK IS

𝔇𝔢𝔡𝔦𝔠𝔞𝔱𝔢𝔡

BY PERMISSION

TO

THE FIRST MINISTER OF HEALTH

THE RIGHT HON. CHRISTOPHER ADDISON,

M.D., F.R.C.S., M.P.

AUTHORS' PREFACE

MANY and valuable books exist which describe diseases peculiar to certain occupations and the means by which these diseases may be prevented or relieved ; the literature of the general hygiene of industry is less satisfying. No book is known to us which deals at all adequately from the standpoint of hygiene with the profound changes in the lives of civilised people during the past century and a half consequent upon the rise and development of modern industry.

Vast and varied erudition is needed to rise to the height of so great an argument, vaster and more varied than is at our command ; we do not suggest that the present volume fills the gap which exists. Nevertheless, each of us has had to deal with problems of industrial hygiene from his particular point of view and has used methods of investigation which his particular way of life or habit of mind rendered accessible. We hope, therefore, we may not be too presumptuous in thinking that our joint work may suggest to others lines of fruitful inquiry and perhaps be of value to the novice.

We believe that at least we have made plain how great is the influence of employment upon general health ; how many are the opportunities presented in industry for studying conditions which lead up to divergencies from health, divergencies which when neglected pass into diseases ; how ready to hand are means for improving the workaday life of the productive classes ; and how important to the whole of preventive medicine are lessons learnt in the school of industrial hygiene.

Valuable information has been published in recent years in Government publications and scientific papers which for the most part are not readily accessible to those for whom this book has been prepared ; the extent to which these sources of information have been freely laid under contribution is indicated in the text.

We take this opportunity of expressing our thanks and gratitude to the Right Hon. Christopher Addison, the first Minister of Health, for accepting the dedication of this book ; to Sir George Newman, Chairman of the Health of Munition Workers Committee and the first Chief Medical Officer of the Ministry of Health, for writing the introduction ; and, for valuable help and assistance, to Miss A. M. Anderson, Principal Lady Inspector of Factories, Mr. G. Bellhouse, Deputy Chief Inspector of Factories, Dr. A. J. Collis (author of the last chapter), Mr. Leon Gaster, Mr. R. E. Graves, Chief Inspector of Factories, Dr. H. S. Hele Shaw, Mr. Higgins, Canteen Committee, Central Control Board (Liquor Traffic), Dr. C. S. Myers, Mr. E. A. Rusher, Investigator to Industrial Fatigue Research Board, Mr. G. Stevenson Taylor, Inspector for Dangerous Trades, Mr. W. W. Ware, Mines Department, Home Office, and Mr. D. R. Wilson, Secretary to Industrial Fatigue Research Board.

E. L. C.
M. G.

CONTENTS

PART I

CHAPTER I

INDUSTRY AND HEALTH—A RETROSPECT

CHAPTER II

REVIEW OF INDUSTRIAL LEGISLATION

CHAPTER III

THE UTILISATION OF STATISTICAL METHODS IN INDUSTRIAL PREVENTIVE MEDICINE

CONTENTS

CHAPTER IV

THE EFFECTS OF INDUSTRIAL EMPLOYMENT UPON HEALTH AS INDICATED BY VITAL STATISTICS

PART II

CHAPTER V

INDUSTRIAL ACTIVITY AND FATIGUE

CHAPTER VI

TUBERCULOSIS AND INDUSTRY

CONTENTS

PART III

CHAPTER X

THE FEEDING OF THE INDUSTRIAL WORKER

CHAPTER XI

FOOD AT THE FACTORY

CHAPTER XII

THE USE OF ALCOHOLIC BEVERAGES BY THE INDUSTRIAL WORKER

CHAPTER XIII

REASONS FOR AND METHODS OF VENTILATION

CHAPTER XIV

LIGHTING

CONTENTS

CHAPTER XV

WASHING ACCOMMODATION—SANITARY ACCOMMODATION—DRINKING WATER—WORKING CLOTHES—CLOAK ROOMS—SEATS

PART IV

CHAPTER XVI

LABOUR TURNOVER OR INDUSTRIAL WASTAGE

CHAPTER XVII

SUPERVISION OF INDUSTRIAL HEALTH

CHAPTER XVIII

RECLAMATION OF THE DISABLED

CONTENTS

INTRODUCTION

IN recent years we have learned that the public health is not only a matter of the postponement of mortality and the prevention of sickness, but of the positive side of health—the increase of vitality, capacity and efficiency of the human body. Our aim is not only to oppose disease but to advance and develop physical fitness and well-being. To secure this end we must have regard to the whole life of man—his heredity and upbringing, his work and rest, his food, his habits, his environment. We must pay attention not only to his actual ailments and diseases, but to the conditions making for a maximum degree of personal health. Thus it comes about that a new relation is found to exist between occupation and health. In a word, the health of the industrial worker forms an integral and inseparable part of the health of the community.

When we come to consider in what way and to what degree we can improve the health of the industrial worker we shall find that a fourfold problem awaits us. Accidents loom large in the laymen's view of industrial disability, and well they may, for in sum total they are extremely numerous and many of them are serious ; then every one knows that certain occupations, apart altogether from the so-called " dangerous trades," lead to a liability to poisoning, disease and high mortality ; in the third place, not a few workmen, in adolescence or early adult life, are found to lack the physical capacity to undertake particular branches of labour ; and lastly, it is common knowledge that much " broken time " and absence from work occurs due to sickness, fatigue or invalidity—due in their turn to a complex set of factors, most of which are controllable. Here then we have the outward sign of the health problem of the industrial worker. Whilst at first sight accidents, poisoning and a high occupational death rate are impressive, it cannot, I think, be doubted that the less dramatic side of the problem is, in fact, the more important—namely, the lost time and incapacity due to ill-health. For this is so widely prevalent as to be almost universal, in all districts, at all ages, in all trades, there is this vast mass of wasted life and energy due for the most part to preventable maladies—in their turn largely attributable to remediable conditions of industry or to the neglect of hygiene.

In this book, Professor Collis and Dr. Greenwood have furnished us with something of an interpretation and philosophy, something of a new foundation, of the science and art of preventive medicine as applied to the industrial worker. They have brought together in small compass the principal items of the accumulated evidence of the many years' experience which this country has now had of the working of the Factory Acts, and their pages are full of practical suggestion and sound method not only for improving the health of the worker but for enabling him to render a fuller measure of industrial service to the community. Both are fundamental issues, and it would be difficult to say which is the more important at the present juncture. It is certain we need to raise the whole standard of the health of the people—to prevent disease and to develop the physique and well-being of the individual. It is not less certain that one of the supreme requirements of this country at the present time is a re-establishment of industry itself—not alone with the object of increasing production, though that is imperative, but in the interest of the worker himself. We need not only more " goods " but better men and women—more competent and efficient, with more energy, with greater love of their craft, with an ever-expanding capability of enjoyment in their labour. That is the general case for this book.

But I have a further and more particular reason for commending it. I am convinced not only of the urgent necessity of its message, but, as it seems to me, the method of approach is significant. In the first place, I think we shall only obtain a true understanding of the facts and findings of industrial hygiene as they are presented to us in relation to the whole history of the evolution of this subject in England. Our record is a remarkable one from the beginning of the Industrial Revolution to the present day. It is a longer chapter of experience and experiment in State aid than that of any other country, and we can only reach sound conclusions if we give them the correct historical setting. Again, the crucial matters—hours of labour and their distribution, the effect of personal welfare, the effect of the occupation itself, and nutrition—find a place in the front rank of the subjects dealt with in this book, and thus the approach is personal rather than by external sanitation, important though that is. Thirdly, there is brought into bold relief the place, socially and economically, of the employment of women ; and lastly, this book almost breathes with the spirit of the solidarity of industrial society, the interdependence between employer and employee, the status, wages, equipment and surroundings of the worker in relation to his health and that of his fellow men. Nor must we allow ourselves to forget that true solidarity has an immensely important psychological aspect. We are always brought back, as I think we should be, to the broad fact that the most economical production is obtained by employing a man only while he is at his best in mind and body, and under circumstances in which he can yield his maximum output of both. We have been, and still are, wasteful of our workers. We do not seem to see that it is sound business, what is called a commercial proposition, to safeguard the health and capacity of the workman neither by fussy regulation nor pampering, but by sensible observance of the facts and teachings of physiological science. In short, physical health is the fundamental basis. In their report on *Industrial Health and Efficiency*, the Health of Munition Workers Committee laid their emphasis on this point. " There must be," they said, " a proper distribution of function of labour, a correct understanding of the part played by nutrition, by rest, by fatigue, by health conditions, if waste is to be avoided and maximum energy attained. The human being is a finely adjusted physiological instrument, which must no longer be wasted, much less destroyed, by ignorant or wilful misuse. A working man's capital is, as a rule, his health and his capacity to perform a full day's work. Once that is impaired or damaged beyond recuperation two things happen. First, his whole industrial outlook is jeopardised and he becomes by rapid stages a liability and even a charge on the State. Secondly, if the bodily defence is undermined by stress and strain the man falls a ready prey to disease." Hence the result of neglect is a double loss, we lose the man to industry and he becomes a burden to others and not infrequently to the community ; and the effect of the double loss is impairment of the industrial and physical efficiency of the nation. There is great loss in treasure and national wealth ; there is greater loss still in national health.

We have been the witnesses of much advance in public appreciation of these matters during the War and also some noteworthy progress in practice and application. We must now seek to secure the full advantage of these forward steps, and consolidate our gains and make them permanent. This book is an instrument to that end.

GEORGE NEWMAN.

PART I

CHAPTER I

INDUSTRY AND HEALTH—A RETROSPECT

I. Introduction.

WHAT industry is and what it means, what it exists for, and what its responsibilities are, will be explained differently according to the aspect from which it is viewed. A row of observers may declare—and declare truly—that a prism upon which light is falling appears to this one to be blue, to the next to be green, to another to be yellow and to a fourth red. Each observer may differ stoutly from his neighbour even to the point of quarrelling ; yet each is right from his limited outlook. So industry bears a different aspect as seen from economic, social or medical points of view. This book is frankly concerned only with the medical aspect ; if economists and socialists should happen to read and disagree with the views presented, then let them recall the simile of the prism and the possibility of the medical aspect being correct as well as their own.

Some grasp of what industry means for mankind and of its relation to civilisation is required before its relation to the health of the community can be seen in true perspective. " Industry " is a word to-day generally applied only to physical work connected with some particular form or branch of productive labour or with some trade or manufacture. Productive labour and manufactures represent man's effort to modify his environment to his needs ; they represent the activities which distinguish man from other animals—activities which are one of the products of his intelligence. Man's intelligence is manifested in other ways, but in no other way do its manifestations so differentiate man from the rest of the animal kingdom. Huxley, it is true, maintained that " other things being alike, the tribe of savages in which order was best maintained, in which there was most security within the tribe and most loyal support outside it, would be the survivors " in the struggle for existence.

But such mutual protection, evidence though it is of intelligence, can be paralleled in the wolf-pack, the bee-hive or ant life. Valuable indeed though mutual protection is, especially when directed by intelligence, it is not the fundamental difference between man and other animals, it is not that distinctive value of intelligence which distinguishes industrious man from the busy politicians of the Bandarlog, and has raised the more intelligent races above their competitors. That value depends upon the capacity his intelligence has conferred upon man for carrying on productive labour and manufacture. These are man's distinctive activities ; as they have multiplied simultaneously with his developing intelligence, so do we find his social organisation becoming more complex.

The mental capacity ascribed to different races of pre-historic man has been classified according to the evidence of manufacturing skill which have come down to us chiefly in the form of flint instruments. Mortillet, applying this rule to palæolithic man claims that these instruments, at first few in number and rude in workmanship, became more varied in form and of finer finish as the human skulls with which they are found associated had a greater brain capacity and more closely conformed in shape to those of historic man. Industry may be considered as an outward and visible sign of the progress of human intelligence ; and the milestones along the road—the stone age, the bronze age, the iron age, the machinery age—gather additional interest when considered as stages in the evolution of mind.

At each step the value of industry to the race has been the provision of better and better means for ensuring increased safety and a healthier life ; increased safety through the production of weapons of offence or defence for dealing with wild animals, or for conducting warfare with other human beings ; a healthier life through the production of food or of other means, such as clothes, for combating the forces of nature. The statement may be made that the intelligence of a race is measured by its industry, and that the primary *raison d'être* of industry is safety and health. In other words, industry is the means human intelligence employs to ensure the existence of the race ; and we may pause to ask with Berkeley, that greatest of querists, " whether the drift and aim of every wise state should not be to encourage industry in its members ? And whether those who employ neither heads nor hands for the common benefit deserve not to be expelled like drones from a well-governed state ? "

The anthropologist is interested in the way in which industry has influenced the race, and will recall Herbert Spencer saying that the starting point of human progress was " localisation of human industries "; and that Sir Charles Lyell and Dr. Isaac Taylor have described such localisation in pre-historic factories for the manufacture of flint implements. From one of these factories, Grime's Graves, near Brandon, ascribed by Reginald Smith to the palæolithic period, human remains are to-day in the museum of the Royal College of Surgeons. By some irony of fate that earliest of industries was probably associated with the occurrence of disease among our pre-historic ancestors, as it is to-day among the flint knappers at Brandon; these men suffer from silicosis, caused by inhaling flint dust, associated with a terrible mortality from tubercular silicosis (1). Localisation of industries, which in nearly every case has been determined by geological considerations, has intimately affected the distribution of the race on the globe. The flint knapper established himself where suitable flints were to be found in abundance; the shepherds and herdsmen naturally frequented the grassy upland pastures; the corn and rice grower favoured the rich alluvial deposits of river lands; the smelter of metals went where metallic ores and fuel occurred in association. Man, indeed, is found converting to his use what is of value in each locality for his industries; but the way in which the climatology of each locality has reacted on his mentality, stimulated or retarded his activities, necessitated the development of industries or permitted sloth, promoted or inhibited the course of progress, has been displayed by Buckle in his *History of Civilisation* (2).

At a later stage—indeed, not until within historic times—man discovered how to employ mechanical power. First, he made use of water power; but this was sufficiently new even in the time of Cicero to cause Antipater to write this epigram: " Set not your hands to the mill, O women that turn the millstone! Sleep sound though the cock's crow announce the dawn, for Ceres has charged the water-nymphs with the labours which employed your arms. These, dashing from the summit of a wheel, make its axle revolve, which, by the help of moving radii, sets in action the weight of four hollow mills. We taste anew the life of the first men, since we have learnt to enjoy, without fatigue, the produce of Ceres."* In the later Middle Ages in England " we hear occasionally of fulling mills, and of leases of mill-streams, which prove that the value of water-power was beginning to be realised. The mill-wheel of the forge in Bishop Langley's iron works (Durham) was worked by water-power; ' the stream was dammed and the water led up to a water-wheel by means of a stone trough or channel and wooden

* Antipater of Thessalonica, ap. *Bruck. Analecta Græca*, tom. ii., p. 119.

pipes ' " (19). . The factorial development of the textile industry depended primarily on water power ; and we find that " during the last twenty years or so of the eighteenth century, whilst the cotton industry was increasing by leaps and bounds, there were large mills or factories, built where water power was plentiful on country rivers, producing warp by means of Arkwright's water frames, whilst jennies and mules were producing the weft in dwelling houses or small establishments. Larger businesses, however, were gradually replacing the smaller, and steam power was also beginning to supplant water power " (24). Even to-day the influence of water power is still increasing. In this country the instance of great works for smelting aluminium at Kinlochleven can be quoted, while in America Niagara Falls have been harnessed to produce electric power ; and in Norway water power is similarly being used.

The industrial utilisation of wind power was later than the exploitation of water, and never influenced the course and localisation of industry to the same extent ; its indirect importance in facilitating transport was no doubt great, but this subject is beyond our scope.

The most important modern changes have been associated with the use of coal as fuel ; and with what practically sprang out of the getting of coal, namely, the invention of the steam engine, evolved by James Watt from Newcomen's original water pump invented for draining coal mines. The progress of industry from this time forward is touched on later ; but sufficient has been said to establish the influences which throughout the ages industry has exerted upon human civilisation, in addition to that aspect with which we are particularly concerned, namely, safety and health.

II. The State and Industrial Health.

Industries exist from the State's point of view to promote the safety and health of the community. The State, that is to say, organised Government, exists for the same ends ; and industries are instruments for attaining these ends. Normally the margin of industrial elasticity is such that the existence of an intimate association is hardly appreciated, and industries may appear to be self-contained or individually controlled ; but during the great War when industrial activities became curtailed, the necessity became clear to all for the State, in the interests of the nation's safety and health, to assume definite control.

Those who are employed in various industries are part of the community, for which collectively and individually the State is responsible. The State has, therefore, to consider how the conditions of life necessitated by industries affect them ; and at the same time to estimate the value to the safety and health of the community as a whole of the products of their labour. Some industries expose the workers to risk of life and limb, and the State has to balance this risk to the individual against the benefit accruing to the whole community from the results of his work.

The success of industries, the State's instruments for good, must depend in no small measure on the health of the workers ; for the productive labour of unhealthy workers is inferior to that of healthy workers ; yet the safety and health of all depend upon productive labour. The maintenance of healthy industries is then the State's first duty. As we shall now see, the duty has only been recognised within a period more than covered by the lives of many still living.

III. Industrial Conditions preceding the Eighteenth Century.

The Romans, during their occupation of Britain, established the manufacture of woollen clothing for their troops, of pottery, and also at least one military iron forge or fabrica (22, p. 7) ; but on their departure all was swept away, and for 900 years no great centres of industry and no factories existed. Now and again sprang up a very few notable, and apparently temporary, exceptions, such as the great clothier, "Jack of Newbury," who is said to have employed over 1,000 persons in the reign of Henry VII. ; but before the eighteenth century, industry as we know it did not exist in England. The only factories were the parish water-mills or wind-mills where corn was ground between stones brought from near Paris or Anderach on the Rhine. Craftsmen and artisans existed who followed definite occupations ; but the carpenter, mason and smith, acting for several neighbouring villages, appear to have manipulated materials entrusted to them for the purpose ; brickmaking was a lost art till the middle of the fifteenth century ; coal mining awaited the coming of Watt. Only here and there was there any local industry ; in the thirteenth century "manufactures of cloth are noted :—scarlet at Lincoln ; blanket at Bligh ; burnet at Beverley ; russet at Colchester (eight weavers are enumerated at this town in the rolls of Parliament under the year 1301) ; produce of linen fabrics at Shaftesbury, Lewes and Aylesham ; of cord at Warwick and Bridport, the latter being also quoted for its hempen fabrics ; of fine bread at Wycombe, Hungerford, and St. Albans ; of knives at Maxstead ; of needles at Wilton ; of razors at Leicester. . . . On the other hand, the most populous and busy districts of our day were the fens and moors, scantily peopled by a rude race. Lancashire was one of the poorest English counties, as was also the West Riding of York. As late as the end of the seventeenth century, these two counties were nearly at the bottom of the list in opulence. Population was scanty in them, and wages low. The Mersey was still a silent estuary ; the Irwell a mountain stream. There were forges and cutlery works in Hallamshire, and Bradford was a cloth mart in early times. But the greater part of the district, now so densely inhabited, which lies within the circuit of twenty miles from Leeds, was occupied by wild animals and lawless men, the latter hardly kept in order by swift justice " (3).

Our knowledge of the industries of the country in these later Middle Ages depends largely on the history of the Trade Guilds, from which capital and labour as they exist to-day evolved. We are not immediately concerned with this social and economic development, but only with the environment to which workers were then exposed ; probably the words of the simple but optimistic divine, Traherne,

" Even trades themselves seen in celestial light,
And care and sins and woes are bright,"

indicate the existence of a need at that time for some supernal interposition to render occupations acceptable to humanity.

Even what industries existed were primitive, as may be gathered from the following pen picture (taken from *The Tour of the Don*, published in 1836) of the famous cutlery industry of Sheffield :—" They (the grinders) are nearly the only inhabitants of the valley, and they do not reside in it. There is scarcely a dwelling-house throughout the whole length of it. They are a rough, half-civilised class. Removed thus from the restrictions of society, and the observation of all authority, they associate only with each other. In summer, when the mountain streams which feed their infant river are almost dried up, they have not a supply of water to employ them half their time. As, however, it is uncertain when the uppermost dam will be sufficiently filled to enable the wheel to work, and to dismiss the fluid element to the expecting wheels below, they are under the necessity of being upon or near the place, to take advantage of the supply when it does arrive. At those times, groups of human beings may be seen near every wheel, which, taken with the surrounding scenery, form such subjects as are well fitted for the pencil of a Salvator. Athletic figures, with brown paper turbans, the sleeves of their shirts rolled high up, exposing their brawny arms, bare almost to the shoulders, their short jackets unbuttoned

and their shirt collar open, displaying their broad, dark, hairy
chests ; their short leather aprons, their breeches knees unbuttoned, and their stockings slipped down about their ankles,
the whole tinged with ochre-coloured dust, so as to leave the
different colours and materials faintly discoverable—form a
figure, when taken singly, sufficiently picturesque ; when
grouped, and they generally are, they become strikingly so. You
there see them, some seated on the stone-raised, turf-covered
bench at the door, with their copious jug and their small pots,
handing round the never-cloying English beer ; others reared
up against the large round grinding-stones supported by the
walls of the building ; others, again, seated on the same kind of
stones, lying upon and against each other on the ground, whilst
some are stretched at their length, dozing or contemplating, in
the verdant sloping banks of the mill-dam ; some are amusing
themselves with athletic exercises, and others are devising, or
slyly engaged in executing, some rude practical jokes."

Industries as we know them were non-existent ; factories and
mines were yet to be ; and, " for five centuries and a half," says
Thorold Rogers, " for fifteen or sixteen generations, there was no
appreciable alteration in the conditions of these people. . . .
The village weaver made homespun cloth from the hempen or
woollen yarns a century ago as he did six centuries ago. The
year witnessed the same unvaried round of occupation that it
was when the third Henry was king. . . . Changes of dynasty,
civil wars, changes in religion, had occurred without making a
break, or leaving a memory in the routine of rural existence " (3).
This statement may be accepted if the effect in the fourteenth
and still more in the fifteenth century of England's success in
producing and working up wool is not forgotten ; at that time
she held the markets of Europe, especially Flanders and Italy.
The price of agricultural labour had risen, and farmers found
greater profit in pasturing sheep than growing wheat ; for as a
proverb then went : " The foot of the sheep turns sand into
gold." The result was that arable land was converted into
pasture on a vast scale, the villages were depopulated and the
tenants turned adrift (18). No information has come down to us
as to the result upon the health of the community of this agrarian
revolution ; but we can safely conclude that this increase of
sheep meant a decrease of cereals and a corresponding decrease
in population. Certainly, industry, as apart from agriculture,
had no appreciable influence upon the health of the nation, and
England down to the beginning of the eighteenth century was
overwhelmingly, and as late as 1770 mainly, devoted to agriculture ; in the latter year the income of the agricultural part

of the nation was estimated by Arthur Young to exceed that of
all the rest of the community.

IV. The Eighteenth Century.

During the first half of the eighteenth century industrial
development started and proceeded at a rate, slow indeed when
compared with that of the succeeding period, but still absolutely
fast. Toynbee estimated that between 1700 and 1750 the
population of Lancashire increased 78 per cent., that of the
West Riding of Yorkshire 52 per cent., of Warwickshire and
Durham over 40 per cent., and of Staffordshire nearly 40 per
cent. In other words, the geographical distribution of the people
was rapidly altering and was already tending towards the form
which it has since maintained. Nevertheless by the middle of
the century Lancashire was showing but little sign of her particular industrial future, for we read that " at the coronation of
George III., in 1761, representatives of the principal trades of
Manchester walked in procession through the streets ; tailors
marched in the pageant, worsted weavers, woolcombers, shoemakers, dyers, joiners, silk weavers, and hatters ; but there
were no cotton weavers or manufacturers " (24). On the other
hand, the West Riding of Yorkshire was already a seat of coarse
woollen manufacture, the Midland pottery and hardware industries were becoming important, and the serious development
of the North-Eastern coal-fields had commenced. During this
period the technique of the industries was essentially different
from what we now see, and is well characterised by the oft
quoted remarks of Defoe, contained in an account of a tour
through Great Britain made in 1724-6. " The land (he is
speaking of the country round Halifax) was divided into small
enclosures, from two acres to six or seven each, seldom more,
every three or four pieces of land having a house belonging to
them ; hardly a house standing out of speaking distance from
another. We could see at every house a tenter, and on almost
every tenter a piece of cloth or kersie or shalloon. At every
considerable house there was a manufactory. Every clothier
keeps one horse at least to carry his manufactures to the market ;
and everyone generally keeps a cow or two or more for his
family. By this means the small pieces of enclosed land about
each house are occupied, for they scarce sow corn enough to feed
their poultry. The houses are full of lusty fellows, some at the
dye vat, some at the looms, others dressing the cloths ; the
women and children carding or spinning ; being all employed
from the youngest to the oldest."

Another picture of the system of production has been given us by Ure (25) : " The workshop of the weaver was a rural cottage, from which when he was tired of sedentary labour he could sally forth into his little garden, and with the spade or the hoe tend its culinary productions. The cotton wool which was to form his weft was picked clean by the fingers of his younger children, and was carded and spun by the older girls assisted by his wife, and the yarn was woven by himself assisted by his sons. When he could not procure within his family a supply of yarn adequate to the demands of his loom, he had recourse to the spinsters of his neighbourhood. One good weaver could keep three active women at work upon the wheel, spinning weft." James also tells (26) how at Bradford " on fine days the women and children might be found in the streets and lanes fully employed with the labour of spinning upon the one-thread wheel, in which they greatly excelled." Cunningham (4) and (5) notes that at Pudset, near Leeds, the woollen weavers practised agriculture as a bye employment as late as the beginning of the nineteenth century, and were able to add considerably to their personal comfort and pay high rents for pasture land, although their agricultural methods were backward.

It has been customary to speak and write of the first half of the eighteenth century as a golden age in which the material advantages of industry were happily combined with the health-giving attributes of country life. Those who have so expressed themselves wrote under the shadow of events which we have yet to mention, and no one can deny that there is something to be said in favour of their belief. It is not the less true that seeds of evil had already been sown which were to bring forth a bitter fruit. Creighton has remarked that the vital statistics of England, more particularly perhaps of the great towns from 1700—50, do not support the theory of a golden age. The bills of mortality of London showed on the average no saving of life after the disappearance of plague ; * and in several years the general mortality from fevers reached heights which may properly be termed epidemic. It is also plain that the industrial employment of little children was well established as early as 1671, when Chamberlayne stated that : " In the City of Norwich it hath of late years been computed and found, that

* Reference should be had to the essay by Corbyn Morris, contained in the *Collection of the Yearly Bills of Mortality* (8) (made by Heberden), which was published in 1759. To this work is appended a life table computed by J[ames] P[ostlethwayt]. Doubtless this table is very inaccurate, especially at early ages ; but if we consider the survivors after age twelve, it appears that half were dead before completing the age of forty-seven, while by the London table for 1911—12 this reduction has not been effected until age sixty-four (males) or sixty-nine (females).

yearly, children from six to ten years of age have gained twelve thousand pounds more than what they spend and that chiefly by knitting fine Jersey stockings."*

In the exceeding unhealthiness of towns, and a toleration, indeed an approbation, of the industrial employment of children, we have the clouds of the bigness of a man's hand which were soon to overshadow the whole sky.

Our province is not to tell how the introduction of power to drive machinery—first water power for Arkwright's water frames, and then steam power supplanting it—determined the concentration of industries in those districts where water and coal were plentiful, nor to detail the series of inventions which in the thirty or forty years following 1770 completely transformed first the textile and subsequently nearly all the manufacturing arts of this country. From our point of view, the outcome was (1) to aggregate the hand-working populations in the northern industrial towns ; and, in those towns, to transform the semi-domestic workplaces into factories, and the semi-independent manual labourers into machine-tending operatives ; and (2) to put a premium upon the labour of children, who, owing to the introduction of machinery, were able to perform tasks which had formerly required the physical strength of an adult.

It is certainly not the business of medical writers to sit in judgment upon the general tendencies of an epoch of history. We are aware that, as Lecky puts it, " Human progress rarely means more than a surplus of advantages over evils " ; and we are not concerned to deny that the immense increase of production consequent upon the industrial revolution was an important factor in enabling the nation to emerge unruined (commercially) from a struggle only second in magnitude to that which has now drawn to a close. But no medical man can doubt that Lecky was also justified in the following statement : " The sanitary neglect, the demoralisation, the sordid poverty, the acute and agonising want prevailing among great sections of the population of our manufacturing towns during the fifty or sixty years that followed the inventions of Arkwright and Crompton, can hardly be exaggerated. Human nature has seldom shown itself in a more unlovely form than in those crowded and pestilential alleys, in that dark sulphurous atmosphere. The

---

* See footnote, p. 308, Hull's edition of the *Economic Writings of Sir Wm. Petty*, Cambridge University Press, 1899. Petty incorrectly cites the age limits as six to sixteen. For other comments on the industrial employment of children prior to the factory period, see Hutchins and Harrison, *A History of Factory Legislation* (6), 2nd edition, London, 1910, pp. 1—5. On the public health, see Creighton's *History of Epidemics in Britain* (7), Vol. II., Cambridge, 1894.

transition from one form of industry to another, the violent fluctuations of wages and of work, the sudden disruption of old ties and habits and associations, the transfer of thousands of female spinners from their country homes to the crowded factory, the vast masses of ignorance and pauperism that were attracted to the towns by vague prospects of employment, have all led to a misery and demoralisation of an extreme character. The transitions of industry are always painful, but very few transitions have been so much so, as that in the closing years of the eighteenth century " (9).

These words of Lecky have to-day a special application as we look back upon the transition of industry from peace time activities to those of war, and the even more turbulent transition back again. Industrial turbulence is an expression of industrial psychology which in its turn is largely dependent on what Hannah More at the opening of the nineteenth century styled : " those strange and unpleasant imaginations which are known by persons conversant with the diseases of the poor, to be no unusual consequence of bad food, and great bodily fatigue, joined with excessive grief."

Increased productivity, due to the introduction of power-driven machinery, saved the nation, even though at the cost of an altogether unnecessary strain put upon the vitality of the working classes, from financial ruin after the Continental wars which ended at Waterloo. Again, to-day, there is immediate necessity for increased productivity ; and the means to effect this are to our hand, viz. : the improvement of the health of the working population, which will give the needed impulse to the wheels of industry. The nineteenth century discovered the value to industry of the inanimate machine ; already we can see the twentieth century is discovering the value of the living and intelligent human being.

V. Industry and Epidemic Disease.

From the standpoint of preventive medicine we must distinguish the immediate evils associated with overcrowding and underfeeding from the remoter consequences of industrialisation.

As we have remarked, long before the industrial age towns were very destructive of human life. A frequent history of epidemic disease is, that, upon its introduction or reintroduction (which may be effected through a seaport town as happened at the commencement of the present plague epoch in India, or in the Black Death of 1348-9), it ravages the whole countryside, villages and towns alike. When the first fury of the onset has subsided, independent village pestilences become rare, while towns are still intermittently or even regularly attacked.

An example of this is the history of plague in Great Britain, where the whole country was ravaged in 1348–9, small villages being, if anything, more depopulated than towns ; village outbreaks still continued during the remainder of the fourteenth and fifteenth centuries, but grew rare and, after the beginning of the sixteenth century, plague was essentially a town disease, villages only being affected by direct extension. In the towns it maintained itself for another 150 years ; the final outbreak of 1665—6 being the greatest since the fourteenth century. The history of typhus, probably the next greatest cause of mortality, is much less easily traced, but of its association with towns during the late eighteenth and early nineteenth century, no illustrations need be given. The epidemiological history of typhus indeed affords an exquisite illustration of the general hygienic factors which regulate the course of epidemic disease. We invariably find that the precursors of epidemic typhus are (1) want ; and (2) overcrowding. As an example from the period antecedent to the industrial revolution, we may take the case of Tiverton, which, in the first half of the eighteenth century, was a town of some 8,000 inhabitants mainly occupied in weaving. The condition of the south-western weaving towns seems not to have been unprosperous until we come to the years following 1720, when trade began to be slack ; affairs became worse after a fire in 1735, when much of the town was burned, and finally the hard winter of 1739—40 reduced the inhabitants to acute distress. In 1741 " spotted fever " was epidemic, and one in twelve of the inhabitants died ; even twenty years later the population was 2,000 below its earlier average, and at the end of the century Tiverton was less populous than at the beginning. In Tiverton in 1741 we had upon a small scale what the Irish typhus of the mid-nineteenth century and the Serbian typhus of 1915 displayed upon a large stage.

The outbreaks in the northern industrial towns after the industrial revolution are simply illustrations of the general principle, but one or two special concomitants deserve notice. The fatality of typhus was higher at the later epoch owing to the fact that large numbers of country girls had flocked into the towns and, in accordance with the general rule of epidemic disease, persons not habituated to conditions of misery or normally exposed to the specific contagion suffer more severely from the disease if acquired. This principle has often been exemplified in the case of typhus (as, for instance, the fatal spread of typhus through the judges and spectators at trials of

prisoners, or the enormous mortality of doctors and attendants
on the sick in the Irish epidemics and in Serbia). The other
special point is the partial remission of typhus during the years
1804—16. Creighton has argued that the remission was due to
war wages having risen proportionally more than the price of
food. From the researches of Bowley and Wood it appears that
in most industries the rise of wages during the war was indeed
considerable. In the building trades wages between 1800—10
were 40 per cent. higher than in 1795—1800. In the worsted
and woollen trades the increase was nearly the same, and
amounted to about 25 per cent. amongst agricultural labourers
and in the engineering and shipbuilding trades. If we take the
wheat prices (omitting the years 1810 and 1812 for which the
prices were respectively 182 per cent. and 235 per cent. of that of
1802) the average increase during the war was a little more than
30 per cent. Hence, so far as the trades mentioned are concerned, it would appear that the rise in wages *did* compensate
the increased cost of living, while the volume of employment
relatively to the employable population was almost certainly
much greater than before or since. But it seems that the
Lancashire operative spinners (see Cunningham, *op. cit.*, p. 470)
were very badly off at this time, so that unless we suppose (a
not impossible supposition) that the impetus given to the
employment of children in the mills was so great that a temporary reduction of typhus mortality (children being relatively
immune from *fatal* typhus) was effected at the cost of other evils,
we must not be too confident in our acceptance of the theory of
Creighton.

Upon the whole, however, we feel justified in attributing the
heavy mortality from fevers at the beginning of the nineteenth
century to the combination of want and overcrowding which
had produced the same effects before the rise of modern industry,
and, in the special economic circumstances prevailing at the
beginning of the nineteenth century, were greatly intensified.
So far as this side of industrial hygiene is concerned, it may be
asked whether anything of the kind may be expected again.
The answer is that, given a recurrence of want and overcrowding,
we should inevitably have a recurrence of epidemic disease.
What specific form such disease might take depends upon factors
which are incapable of prediction, since the evolutionary development of diseases, their rise, decline and fall, which Sydenham
in the seventeenth century deemed beyond the compass of man's
intellect, has not even now been reduced to systematic history.
The Serbian experience proves that the epidemic constitution of
genuine typhus has still to be reckoned with in some places;

but, so far as we can judge from the still incomplete data available, want and overcrowding under the less primitive conditions prevailing in central Europe during the war, influenced the public health rather by increasing the death-rate from tuberculosis than by promoting any epidemic manifestation of the zymotics or continued fevers.   How far the recent heavy mortality from influenza and its complications is dependent upon want and overcrowding, is a question we are unable to answer ; we should be apt to suspect that the deleterious influences of industrial life in this connection have been more subtle and come properly under the second group of causes to which we now turn.

As we have said, the consequences of overcrowding and want are not peculiar to modern industrial towns ; they had been observed long before a factory (in modern parlance) existed anywhere, and may be seen in our own time in non-industrial populations.   But factories brought with them ways of life entirely peculiar to modern industry and also aggravated some bad customs which they found in existence.   Of habits quite peculiar to factory life, we note the making man or woman subservient to machinery, the machine setting the pace which the human attendant is bound to maintain.   Of factors not new but intensified, we mention the long hours of labour imposed upon both sexes and all ages, and the preferential employment of young children.   So far as the specific new factor is concerned, we shall not anticipate here the remarks falling to be made under the heading of industrial fatigue and accidents.

VI. Effect of Employment of Children.

With respect to the latter, or at least to that sub-section which relates to the employment of children, something must be said, because the industrial employment of children is no longer tolerated.

All humane persons have shuddered at the horrors of child life in the factories by which, as Gibbins (5) observed, " even the methodical and dry language of official documents is startled into life." The Hammonds have, it is true, pointed out (23) that " child labour was not a discovery of the industrial revolution, but the new industry provided infinite scope for the labour of children, and drove the workmen to rely on them." When labour was scarce, children were imported, and a Yorkshire manufacturer under such circumstances said he was " driven to the expedient of procuring from the workhouses in London 500 poor children to be employed in his workshops " (27).

Hunt has described the practice at the end of the eighteenth and commencement of the nineteenth century : " The greater number of them (the children) were pauper apprentices bound by parochial authorities to mill-owners, others the children of very poor or callous parents. From little more than infancy, sometimes under seven years old, children were condemned to labour for long hours, thirteen or more in a day, at tasks requiring unremitting attention, and in rooms badly ventilated and otherwise injurious to health ; they were half-starved and cruelly punished when their wearied little arms failed to keep up with the demands of the machinery. The smaller mills were the worst in this respect, and as the supply of water power was not constant, the children in mills worked by water were often forced to labour far beyond their strength to make up for lost time. Such of them as survived the prolonged misery and torture of their early years, grew up more or less stunted and deformed men and women, physically unfit for parentage, morally debased, ignorant, and brutalised by ill-treatment " (17). Nor does this unveil the whole scene, for we read (23) : " These cotton mills, crowded with overworked children, were hotbeds of what was called putrid fever, and it was an epidemic at Radcliffe in 1784 that first drew public attention to the condition of the apprentices."

But it is not generally realised that the evils of those times may still be bearing fruit. Quite apart from dramatic outbursts of disease affecting the death-rate suddenly, we notice in all industrial towns down to (and in many beyond) the middle of the nineteenth century, high rates of mortality and natality. We shall illustrate this by a consideration of the vital and industrial statistics of the city of Sheffield in the early Victorian period displayed in Holland's treatise (10). The crude birth and death-rates of Sheffield from 1837—42 were 40·2 and 27·9, or a natural increase of 12·3 (much the same natural increase as in 1913, when the birth-rate had fallen to 28·2, but the death-rate to 15·8). In the chief industries, the extent to which women and children were employed is indicated by the following figures :—Silver and plated manufacture : 9 boys and sixteen women and girls to 56 men. Saw manufacture : 130 boys to 208 journeymen, 1 woman to 8 men. Saw-handle makers : about 100 boys to 120 men, no women. Saw-grinders : 90 boys to 120 men, no women. Edge tool trade : 50 boys to 200 foremen and 200 strikers. Spring knife manufacture (among the worst paid in the city) : about 600 apprentices (" boys nine or ten years of age may be made useful in this branch, but are seldom entrusted to make even inferior articles before the age of 13 or 14 ") to 2,250 men. File trade : 700 boys, 100 women, 1,420 men.* Fork grinders : 97 men to 100 boys, 39 of the latter between the ages of 10 and 15.

For comparative purposes, Holland used the mean age at death, not a very satisfactory statistical constant owing to the effect upon it of disparities in the age constitutions of the populations compared, but yet of some value. He found the mean age at death during the period of which he was writing to be 33·01 years for the county of Devonshire, 29·11 for England and Wales, 24·12 for Sheffield, 24·24 for Birmingham and 21·24 for Leeds. It will thus be seen that, even in Sheffield, the industries of which were less adapated to the employment of juvenile labour than those of the textiles, large numbers of children were employed. As late as 1856, 6·6 per cent. of all employees in the textile industries were children under thirteen, and 57 per cent. were women over thirteen (6). In 1843, the print works of Lancashire, Cheshire and Derbyshire employed 5,646 children to 9,104 adults ((6), p. 124).

We find then in this period widespread industrial employment of children and high birth and death-rates, the instance of Sheffield being easily paralleled in other industrial centres, as appears in Greenhow's survey, published in 1858. In the sentence quoted from Holland as to the employment of children, we have mentioned an important reason for this kind of labour. Notwithstanding the successive extension of factory acts to different industries, the exploitation of children continued throughout the first sixty years of the nineteenth century ; the chief difference between the later and earlier epochs being that the direct exploiters ceased to be the factory owners, whose place was taken by the ill-paid parents. Pearson (28) has called attention to the fact that a decline in the birth rate followed or was hastened by each legislative measure which restricted the industrial employment of children, that in fact the high birth-rate was an instance of demand creating a supply. What happened was that large numbers of children were produced ; these children, winnowed by a heavy infant mortality and similarly high mortality rates at older ages, formed the surviving industrial population of the late seventies, the parents of the existing generation.

Some writers have seen in the co-existence of high birth and death rates a favourable field for the evolution of a virile race,

* " Another important difference between this and the silver-plated branch is the much earlier age at which boys can be employed in the former. The dissipation, idleness, or necessity of parents, causes them to put their children to work, years before they ought to leave school, so that the addition made to the branch, is not from the educated of the rising generation, but from a class which have scarcely received any instruction at all " (10), p. 189.

by the operation of " the survival of the fittest." This type of reasoning, which finds its crudest expression in the pseudo-scientific " Darwinism " of German militarists, rests upon an illegitimate identification of the terms " fittest " and " best." It is a mere truism to say that those who survive the rigours of such an environment as existed in working class dwellings and factories throughout the early and middle years of the nineteenth century are the fittest to survive ; it is a mere dogma to say that such survivors are the best type of citizens. " The survival of the fittest may be the survival of the analogue to ' Frankenstein's Demon,' " says Thorold Rogers (3). " It is possible that the struggle for existence, unless controlled and elevated, may be the degradation of all. It nearly came to be so during the first thirty years of the present (nineteenth) century." The characters of the surviving product obviously depend upon the test applied. Were we to use as a test exposure to infection by typhus, the *habitués* of the eighteenth century jails were much " fitter " than judges, barristers and magistrates. How far, if at all, desirable civic qualities are correlated with powers of resistance to the germs of diseases is a subject of which we know little or nothing. It is in fact quite arguable that the present unsatisfactory state of the national physique (supposing it to be unsatisfactory) is mainly due to the survival of the fittest under the conditions of the early days of factories. The practical importance of this lies in the reflection that, if it be true, improvement of home and factory environment will only lead to a general amelioration of the national physique gradually, by changing the standard of survival values. In making these remarks, we desire to guard ourselves from the assumption of responsibility for the statement that the general physique of this nation *has* in fact deteriorated. No complete or satisfactory national stocktaking has ever been made ; for comparisons between now and fifty years ago we must resort to death rates, and, for the reasons above given, these do not provide us with the necessary information. The one certain conclusion which emerges from the historical data we have attempted to summarise is that the sanitary conditions of the hand-labouring population were changed for the worse by the industrial revolution, and continued to be disgraceful to civilisation for more than fifty years. Certain of these conditions were accidentally associated with industry, being ultimately manifestations of poverty ; others were directly caused by the methods of industrial work. The amelioration of the former belongs to the domain of general sanitary science ; that of the latter falls more particularly into the field attempted to be covered by this book, and what further

historical treatment is required to elucidate the problems will
be found in the chapters devoted to the special topics.

VII. Bibliography.

1. Collis, E. L. *Industrial Pneumonoconioses.* Milroy Lectures,
1915. *Public Health.* 1915.

2. H. T. Buckle. *History of Civilisation.*

3. Thorold Rogers. *Six Centuries of Work and Wages*, p. 557.
Fisher Unwin. 1917.

4. Cunningham. *Growth of English Industry and Commerce in
Modern Times*, p. 480. Cambridge. 1892.

5. Gibbins, H. de B. *Industry in England*, pp. 326 *et seq.* 1896.

6. Hutchins, B. L., and Harrison, A. *A History of Factory Legislation.* 2nd Edition. London. 1911.

7. Creighton. *History of Epidemics in Britain.* Cambridge. 1894.

8. *Collection of the Yearly Bills of Mortality from 1657 to 1758.*
London. 1759.

9. Lecky, W. E. H. *History of England in* 18*th Century.* Chap. XXI.

10. Holland, G. C. *The Vital Statistics of Sheffield.* London. 1843.

11. Thackrah, C. T. *The Effects of Arts, Trades, etc., on Health.*
London. 1832.

12. *Economic Writings of Sir William Petty.* Hull's Edition.
Cambridge. 1899.

13. Bowley and Wood. " Papers on the Statistics of Wages."
Journ. Roy. Stat. Soc. 1898—1906. (14 parts.)

14. Greenhow, E. H. *The Results of an Inquiry into the Different
Proportions of Death Produced by Certain Diseases in Different Districts of England.* General Board of Health. London. 1858.

15. Ramazzini, B. *Treatise on the Diseases of Tradesmen.*
Translated by Dr. James. London. 1746.

16. Greenhow, E. H. *Reports of the Medical Officer to the Privy
Council*, 1860. 1861–2.

17. Hunt, W. *The Political History of England.* Vol. X., p. 278.
Longmans, Green & Co. 1905.

18. Lipson, E. *Economic History of England*, pp. 124–9. A. and C.
Black, Ltd. 1915.

19. Abram, A. *English Life and Manners in the Later Middle
Ages*, p. 87. G. Routledge & Sons. 1913.

20. Cooke Taylor, R. W. *History of the Factory System.* Richard
Bentley & Son. 1886.

21. Jevons, W. Stanley. *The State in Relation to Labour.* English
Citizen Series. Macmillan & Co. 1882.

22. Cooke-Taylor, R. W. *The Factory System.* 2nd Edition.
Methuen & Co., Ltd. 1912.

23. Hammond, J. L., and Hammond, B. *The Town Labourer.*
Longmans, Green & Co. 1917.

24. Hammond, J. L., and Hammond, B. *The Skilled Labourer.*
Longmans, Green & Co. 1919.

25. Ure, A. *Cotton Manufacture of Great Britain.* 1836.

26. James. *History of the Worsted Manufacture.*

27. *Annals of Agriculture.* Vol. XVI.

28. Pearson, K. *The Problem of Practical Eugenics.* Dulan. 1909.

29. Daniels, G. W. *The Early English Cotton Industry.* Longmans, Green & Co. 1920. (This valuable study, which reached us
too late for notice in the text, throws further light upon the 18th
century organisation of this industry.)

CHAPTER II

REVIEW OF INDUSTRIAL LEGISLATION

I. Introduction.

THE summary which has been given in the previous chapter
of the development of industry up to the end of the eighteenth
century, and of the direct and indirect ways in which industry
has throughout the centuries had an influence upon the health
and well-being of the community as a whole, and upon its
votaries in particular, brings us in historical sequence to the
moment when the first efforts at factory legislation were made.
While, however, the first Acts definitely directed to supervising
the conditions of industrial life date from the commencement of
the nineteenth century, regard must be had to the existence
before then of certain statutes upon which this legislation may
be said to have been built.

No attempt at improving the lot of labourers is to be expected
in society so long as it is based on a system of slavery or serfdom.
The utmost that can be expected is ordinances protecting the
lives of slaves together with other property from wilful damage ;
certainly in Rome and Egypt, where labour was carried out by
slaves, there were strict laws for their protection (10, p. 31),
and perhaps some sense of moral obligation towards them.*
When slavery disappears each worker becomes his own master,
and free (in theory) to dispose of his labour as he thinks fit. An
interval, therefore, exists between laws protecting slave labour
and those protecting free labour. During this interval so-called
free labour may be reduced, as it was in England at the end of
the eighteenth century and in the beginning of the nineteenth

---

* Thus Cicero writes (*De Officiis*, I., 13) : " Meminerimus autem etiam
adversus infimos justitiam esse servandam. Est autem infima conditio
et fortuna servorum : quibus, non male præcipiunt, qui ita jubent uti,
ut mercenariis ; operam exigendam, justa præbenda." See also Gibbon
(*Decline and Fall of the Roman Empire*, Chapter II.), who points out that
by the edicts of Hadrian and the Antonines, " upon a just complaint of
intolerable treatment, the injured slave obtained either his deliverance or
a less cruel master."

century, to a condition as bad as, if not worse than, recognised slavery.

Relegation of manual labour to slaves has inevitably led to its being looked down upon and despised, and so has hampered industrial development and progress. Aristotle taught the Greeks that " in the best-governed states, where the citizens are really men of intrinsic and not relative goodness, none of them should be permitted to exercise any mechanic employment or follow merchandise, as being ignoble and destructive to virtue."*

Seneca has left for us a passage which indicates how the Romans, who employed slaves, despised industry :—" In my own time there have been inventions of this sort, transparent windows, tubes for diffusing warmth equally through all parts of a building, short-hand which has been carried to such a perfection that a writer can keep pace with the most rapid speaker. But the inventing of such things is a drudgery for the lowest slaves ; philosophy lies deeper. It is not her office to teach men how to use their hands. The object of her lesson is to form the mind. She is not, I maintain, the mere inventor of tools for everyday use. . . . We shall next be told that the first shoemaker was a philosopher."† While the Emperor Augustus actually pronounced the sentence of death against the Senator Ovinius for having stooped to direct a manufactory (10, p. 4).

It is significant that the great physician, Galen, in his treatise *De sanitate tuenda,* has nothing to say of the hygiene of factories, although he makes some very sensible remarks as to the habits of life of business men. Slave labour had by then become intensified ; Roman industries had languished ; and the proposition is tenable that, later, this outlook on industry contributed to, if it did not actually determine, the decline of Rome. Bryce points out (19) that in mediæval Rome " there was a want not only of fixed authority, but of the elements of social stability which the other cities of Italy possessed. In the greater republics of Lombardy and Tuscany the bulk of the population were artizans, hard-working orderly people ; while above them stood a prosperous middle class, engaged mostly in commerce, and having in their trade-guilds an organization both firm and flexible. . . . Rome possessed neither of these sources of wealth. She was ill-placed for trade ; having no market, she produced no goods to be disposed of. . . . As there was no industry, so there

---

* *The Politics,* Book VII., Chapter IX.
+ Seneca, *Epist.,* 90. We cannot refrain from adding Macaulay's comment : " For our own part, if we are forced to make our choice between the first shoemaker and the author of the three books on Anger, we pronounce for the shoemaker. It may be worse to be angry than to be wet. But shoes have kept millions from being wet ; and we doubt whether Seneca ever kept anybody from being angry."

was nothing that deserved to be called a citizen class. The people were a mere rabble, prompt to follow the demagogue who flattered their vanity, prompter still to desert him in the hour of danger."

II. Ordinance of Labourers.

1349.—The point of view here portrayed remained unaltered through the ages and existed in England until long after the Norman Conquest. As soon, however, as serfdom disappeared, we find the first statutes dealing with labour. The circumstances which led to them were associated with the Black Death, which, by carrying away nearly half the population of the kingdom, caused a great scarcity of labour ; and in 1349 the famous Ordinance of Labourers, which was supplemented by the Statute of Labourers in 1351, was passed. The preamble to the first ran : " Because a great part of the people, and especially of workmen and servants, late died of the pestilence, many seeing the necessity of masters, and great scarcity of servants, will not serve unless they may receive excessive wages. . . . Be it therefore enacted . . . that every man or woman, of whatsoever condition, free or bond, able in body and within the age of three-score years, . . . shall be bound to serve the employer who shall require him to do so, and shall take only the wages which were accustomed to be taken in the neighbourhood where he is bound to serve . . . in the twentieth year of the king, and in five or six common years next before." In the second statute, an elaborate scale of wages was set forth and rendered obligatory under heavy penalty, and the principle of confining labourers to their native districts firmly established. These enactments, which probably had but little influence upon the course of events, are of interest as showing that even then the State attempted to control labour (4).

III. Statute of Apprentices.

The next enactment is that of the Statute of Apprentices, passed in the early years of Elizabeth's reign. Jevons (5) writes of this statute :—" The general theory of the Act is that every servant or artificer shall be compelled to work in the trade to which he was brought up. Any workman departing from his city, town or parish, without a testimonial from his previous employer or some officer, was to be imprisoned until he procured a testimonial ; or, if he could not do so within the space of one-and-twenty days, he was to be whipped and used as a vagabond. The hours of labour were prescribed, not, as in our Factory Acts, by way of limitation, but by imposition. Thus, from the middle of the month of March to the middle of September, all artificers and labourers hired by time were to be and continue at their work at or before five o'clock in the morning, and continue at work and not depart until betwixt seven and eight of the clock at night*—two and a half hours in the course of the day being allowed for meals and drinking, thus the legal day's work was to be about twelve hours at the least." The interesting points in this Act then, are, that compulsion was exerted to prevent a workman from changing his trade or leaving his district and that hours of employment extended from 5 a.m. until after 7 p.m. The provisions of this statute may possibly throw light upon Shakespeare's words in *Julius Cæsar* :—

> " *Flavius.* Hence ! Home, you idle creatures, get you home ;
> Is this a holiday ? What ! know you not,
> Being mechanical, you ought not to walk
> Upon a labouring day without the sign
> Of your profession ? Speak, what trade art thou ?
> *First Commoner.* Why, sir, a carpenter.
> *Marcellus.* Where is thy leather apron and thy rule ?
> What dost thou with thy best apparel on ?
> You, sir, what trade are you ?
> *First Commoner.* Truly, sir, in respect of a fine workman,
> I am but, as you would say, a cobbler."

Even as late as 1746 labour legislation continued to strengthen the authority of the employer. In an Act of that year " power was retained for the justices, on complaint of the masters of misdemeanour or ill-behaviour on the part of the servant, to discharge the latter from service or to send him to a house of correction, ' there to be corrected,' that is, to be held to hard labour for a term not exceeding a month or to be corrected by whipping " (20).

1601. *Poor Law.*—The next Act of interest is the Poor Law of 1601, which provided that substantial householders, acting as overseers of the poor, should in every parish raise money by taxation, in order, among other things, to set to work and apprentice to some trade destitute children and orphans ; and we find that during the seventeenth and eighteenth centuries charitable institutions were started for providing these children with instruction in spinning and weaving (2, p. 2). Possibly this law was the germ from which sprang the widespread employment of children previously referred to, which formed so black a spot in the industrial development of the latter half of the eighteenth and the first half of the nineteenth century. Certainly this question of the employment of children moved the nation to embark upon industrial legislation.

* In winter months work-time was from 5 a.m. until dark.

IV. Truck Acts.

The first definite legislative effort which appears to have been made in favour of labour dealt with the principle of *Truck*, *i.e.*, payment of wages, not by coin of the realm, but by commodities. As early as 4 Edward IV. reference is made to payment to workers in " pins, girdles and unprofitable wares " ; and payment is ordained in true and lawful money (20). An Act dealing with Truck was passed in the first year of Anne's reign ; it referred to woollen, linen, cotton, and iron manufactures. It was re-enacted in 1726, in the reign of George I., and has remained the principle of payment of wages ever since. Although the principle of paying wages by coin of the realm, instead of by kind, was thus early accepted by Parliament, the Act was for long a dead letter, as is clear from the evidence called to support the passing of Acts in 1817 extending the powers to the coal and steel industries, and for further stiffening the law in 1820 (11). Nevertheless, the principle was accepted thus early, and is the basis of the Truck Act, 1831, which was amended in 1887 and in 1896. These Acts in relation to factories or workshops are administered by inspectors of factories, and in relation to mines by inspectors of mines ; they refer to workers of all ages and both sexes, and the more recent Acts have been extended beyond the original principle to control deductions from wages by means of fines.

V. Chimney Sweeps.

The first instance of legislation to protect children was the Chimney Sweeps Act, 1788 ; but " it was very modest on paper, and absolutely ineffective in practice " (11).

The condition of these children sweeps is revealed in the agitation which after years of effort terminated in the Act of 1834, which forbade the binding as a sweep of any boy under ten, and the employment of children under fourteen unless apprenticed or on trial. In 1840 an Act was passed forbidding any one under twenty-one to climb chimneys, and the apprenticing of children under sixteen years of age; this Act was further amended in 1864. Previous to these Acts we learn (14) that the children, who had to be small to negotiate flues only seven inches in diameter, were stolen for the purpose, or were sold by their parents for a few pounds ; were driven up the chimneys and possibly made to climb by a straw fire lighted beneath them; that many, submerged in soot in narrow or horizontal flues, were suffocated ; and that they usually slept in cellars with a bag of soot for a bed and another for a coverlet (11).   The words put by Blake into the mouth of the chimney sweeper are in no way false.

> " When my mother died I was very young,
> And my father sold me while yet my tongue
> Could scarcely cry, ' Weep, weep, weep, weep, ' *
> So your chimneys I sweep, and in soot I sleep."

VI. Health and Morals of Apprentices Act.

1802.—We now come to the Act passed in 1802, which has generally been accepted to be the commencement of factory legislation ; but " it was in reality not a Factory Act properly speaking, but merely an extension of the Elizabethan Poor Law relating to parish apprentices. The Government, having taken upon itself the responsibility of bringing up and placing out these children, found itself compelled, when need was shown, to attempt to regulate their conditions of work " (2, p. 16) ; this appears in the name : " The Health and Morals of Apprentices Act." The Act applied to cotton and woollen factories ; and its provisions, which are of considerable interest, are briefly stated by Cooke-Taylor (10) as follows :—

" 1st : The first section enjoins the ' master or mistress ' of the factory to observe the law. 2nd : All rooms in a factory are to be lime-washed twice a year and duly ventilated (sec. ii.). 3rd : Every apprentice is to be supplied with two complete suits of clothing—one new suit every year—with suitable linen, stockings, hats and shoes (sec. iii.). 4th : The hours of work of apprentices are not to exceed twelve a day, nor commence before six in the morning, nor conclude after nine at night (sec. iv.). 5th : They are to be instructed every working day during the first four years of apprenticeship in reading, writing and arithmetic ' by some discreet and proper person,' the time so occupied to be counted out of their hours of work (sec. vi.). 6th : Male and female apprentices are to be provided with separate sleeping apartments, and not more than two to sleep in one bed (sec. vii.). 7th : On Sunday they are to be instructed in the principles of the Christian religion ; they are to comply with various religious ordinances during their apprenticeship, and to go to church once a month at least (sec. iii.). 8th : Two visitors are to be appointed by the adjacent Justices of the Peace, one of whom must himself be a Justice, and the other a member either of the Church of England or of the Church of Scotland, to enforce the provisions of the Act (sec. ix.). 9th : In case of infectious disorders prevailing,

* Part of the (sweep) apprentices' duty was to advertise their masters by " crying the streets " (11).

these visitors may require the employer to call in medical assistance (sec. x.). 10th : Copies of the regulations of the Act are to be affixed in conspicuous places (sec. xii.). 11th : A list of the factories situated in his district is to be kept by every Clerk of the Peace (sec. xiv.). Penalties are enacted for breaches of the law (secs. xi. to xiii.), and the method of recovering them (secs. xv., xvi.) is provided for."

VII. Controversy.

The history of how, during the nineteenth century, especially during the first half of that century, factory legislation developed from this, its first beginning, is one of great interest. The work is associated with the names of Robert Owen, Lord Ashley, Oastler, Sadler, and Cobbett ; but the acrimonious discussions which took place and the fights have no particular place in this book. The interest for us lies rather in the way in which the employers on the one side resisted legal action, declaring that it would ruin industry, even though each step taken was found in action to be advantageous to industry, and in which the protagonists of factory legislation relied upon the appeal to humanitarian sentiment. Indeed, throughout the long controversy which centred on the Factory Acts, neither side ever appealed to direct experiment to justify their contentions.

The recommendations, for instance, based on careful scientific observations made by Dr. Edward Smith (18), in 1861, do not appear to have in any way affected legislation ; yet he plainly stated the need for many reforms which are only now being adopted. He opposed work before breakfast, writing as follows : " The present arrangements cannot be otherwise than injurious to the working classes themselves, and they are by no means to the advantage of the employers, for it is notorious how apt is the result to be inadequate to the hours occupied and the money paid for it. It is a perpetual struggle between the two classes—the one trying to evade a condition which is unnatural, and the other seeking to obtain the labour which is universally conceded in the morning and actually denied in the evening. In our opinion, no laborious occupation should be followed in this climate before 7 a.m., and it ought in all instances to be preceded by the breakfast. If this plan were adopted, it would do much to save the health of our weakened population, to prevent the distrust between employer and employed, and to obtain a fairer amount of labour from a given day's work. The period of the day in which the human system is the most vigorous and fitted for labour in our climate is from about 8 or 9 a.m. until about 4 or 5 p.m., but it is sufficiently vigorous for a longer period." Again we find Smith before his time in the statement :—" Rest is a necessary alternative to labour, and as small meals are conducive to muscular exertion, it is worthy of consideration if those who are engaged in manual labour for many hours would not perform it with more ease if there were more frequent, but shorter, intervals for rest and for meals, instead of the three meals a day at long intervals, with the single long interval of rest between 8 p.m. and 6 a.m. It is very probable that more work would be done, and at a less cost to the workman."

There is no record of any careful investigation as to the effect of shortening hours until we come to 1893, when Messrs. Mather and Platt, at their Salford Works, shortened the hours and published the result of the first twelve months' working. There were those like Lord Macaulay, who in 1846 spoke (3) as follows : " I do not mean to say that a man will not produce more in a week by working seven days than by working six days. But I very much doubt whether, at the end of a year, he will generally have produced more by working seven days a week than by working six days a week ; and I firmly believe that at the end of twenty years he will have produced much less by working seven days a week than by working six days a week. In the same manner I do not deny that a factory child will produce more in a single day by working twelve hours than by working ten, and by working fifteen hours than by working twelve. But I do deny that a great society in which children work fifteen or even twelve hours a day will, in the lifetime of a generation, produce as much as if those children had worked less. . . . Your over-worked boys will become a feeble and ignoble race of men, the parents of a more feeble progeny ; nor will it be long before the deterioration of the labourer will injuriously affect those very interests to which his physical and moral energies have been sacrificed." In the light of investigations which have been carried out recently (see Chapter V.),—and with the exception of the Mather and Platt experiment already quoted, few investigations worthy of the name were carried out until, during the war, the Health of Munition Workers Committee promoted many,— we can now see that the whole controversy might have been amicably settled to the satisfaction of both parties had they only been content to appeal to facts instead of quarrelling over unsubstantiated statements.

VIII.   1819—31.

The Act of 1802 was followed during the nineteenth century by much further legislation ; but the reader must have in mind that each legislative advance recorded was only gained in the teeth of opposition ; that at each stage commissions were appointed, ostensibly to institute inquiries, but often only as an expedient to defer action ; and that legislation, even when passed, was (at least before the appointment of inspectors) either not enforced, or only put in action in a few flagrant cases (1, 10, 11). This warning having been given, the outstanding features may be summarised as follows :—

1819.—In 1819 the age of children employed was limited to nine years, and it was laid down that any one under sixteen years of age should not be employed for more than twelve hours a day. Since the hours fixed were exclusive of meal-time— one hour and a half per day—the period of work per week was seventy-two hours. Night work was prohibited. This Act only applied to cotton-mills.

1825.—In 1825 it was laid down that one hour and a half should be set aside for meal-times, exclusive of the twelve hours' employment, that is to say, attendance at the factory was for thirteen and a half hours. In this year it was further laid down for the first time that on Saturday only nine hours should be worked. The age of those to whom these provisions applied remained the same, namely, under sixteen years of age.

1831.—The administration of these Acts had been placed in the hands of justices of the peace. This plan was found in practice to be unsatisfactory because the justices in any district were so closely associated with the industry of the district. Some effort to remedy this was made in 1831, when the law laid down that mill-owners and their relations (parents, brothers and sons) were excluded from hearing cases brought under the Acts. In this year the abstract of the Act, which had under the Act of 1819 to be displayed in a conspicuous position, was omitted and a register of hours of employment substituted instead. Hours of labour were in this year limited to twelve hours per day and nine on Saturdays, i.e., sixty-nine hours per week, for those under eighteen years of age ; and night work for those under twenty-one years of age was prohibited. But still, legislation only had reference to cotton mills.

IX. A Sidelight.

Lest the reader lose sight during this exposition of detail of the evils at which legislation was aimed, just one extract may be given from evidence heard by a committee, presided over by Mr. M. T. Sadler, whose deliberations preceded the next Act. An overseer from Dundee said :—

" There were a great many children in proportion to the

number of adults; most of them were orphans. There were some of the orphan children from Edinburgh who had been in the mill, I believe, from four to five years. The children were incapable of performing their day's labour well towards the termination of the day; their fate was to be awoke by being beaten, and to be kept awake by the same method. They were guarded up to their bothies to take their meals, and were locked up in the bothies at night, and the master took the key away with him to his bedroom; they were guarded to their work, and they were guarded back again; and they were guarded while they were taking their meat, and then they were locked up for rest. They were not allowed to go to a place of worship on the Sunday. There were twenty-five or twenty-six of us together. There was one bothy for the boys, but that did not hold them all, and there were some of them put into the other bothy along with the girls. The ages of the boys that were put into the girls' bothy might be, I should suppose, from ten to fourteen, the ages of the girls, perhaps, from twelve to eighteen. The children and young persons were sometimes successful in their attempts to escape from labour and confinement. I have gone after them on horseback and brought them back myself. Those brought back were taken into the mill, and got a severe beating with a strap; sometimes the master kicked them on the floor, and struck them with both his hands and his feet. Those who had made engagements for any length of time, when they ran away, the master, if he could not find them before they got home to their relations, if they had any, he sent after them and put them in gaol. I knew a woman put in gaol, and brought back after a twelve-month, and worked for her meat; and she had to pay the expenses that were incurred."

At this very time Great Britain was by Orders in Council (November, 1831) restricting the hours of work of adult slaves to nine hours a day, and of child slaves under fourteen years of age to six hours a day. " You have limited," said Sadler, " the labour of the robust negro to nine hours; but when I propose that the labour of the young white slave shall not exceed ten, the proposition is deemed extravagant " (12).

X. 1833—53.

1833.—The dispensation of justice, notwithstanding the provision of the Act of 1831, remained unsatisfactory. There-fore, in 1833 legislation was passed under which factory inspectors paid by the State were appointed. In the same year the labour of children under thirteen years of age was limited to forty-eight hours in any week and to nine hours a day, and it was laid down that no one under eighteen years of age, now called " a young person," should be employed on nightwork, *i.e.*, between 8.30 p.m. and 5.30 a.m., or for more than sixty-nine hours per week. Certificates of age were no longer to be given by the parents of the children, but by a physician or surgeon, who had to declare the individual to be of " the ordinary strength and appearance " of a child of not less than nine years of age. The Act of this year extended legislation to cotton, woollen, worsted, hemp, flax, tow, linen, and silk factories.

1842. *Coal Mines.* — Meanwhile the condition of those employed in coal mines was attracting attention. Miners at the end of the sixteenth century in Scotland (and in England their lot was somewhat similar) were the property of their landlords, appurtenances to the estates, and transferable with them to any purchasers (13). The men gradually improved their position, but not always by gentle means, and during the latter half of the eighteenth century, in 1747, 1769, and 1800, measures were passed to protect mining property from damage. As the industry developed with improving transport, by canal and rail, and as deeper seams were worked after the introduction of safety-lamps, the occupation became increasingly dangerous, and disastrous explosions occurred. At this time women and young children were employed underground. Inquiries were set on foot, and, following upon the report of a Commission appointed at the instance of Lord Ashley, a Mines and Collieries Act was passed in 1842. The main provisions of this Act indicate the evils at which it was aimed ; they were :—

(1) Prohibition of employment underground of females. This provision foreshadowed the inclusion of women in the next Factory Act.

(2) Prohibition of employment underground of males under ten years of age (a year older than the requirements of the Factory Act ; but no medical certificate of fitness was or ever has been required for mines).

(3) Prohibition of payment of wages in public-houses. This provision was but ill observed.

(4) No steam or other engine could thereafter be under the care of any person under fifteen years of age where there were vertical or other shafts.

(5) Inspectors were appointed to visit and report to the Secretary of State. The powers given, including right of entry

underground, sec. iii., were similar to, but not as extensive as, those given to factory inspectors.

1844.—The newly appointed factory inspectors found diffi- culty in ascertaining the ages of children ; there was no birth certification before 1837, and the certificates often produced were of doubtful value, signed by cow-doctors, dentists and other totally unqualified persons (2, p. 73). They therefore appointed definite surgeons to certify that the children were of such physique as to justify the probability of their being at least nine years of age. In 1844 this action of the inspectors was accepted by law and the appointment of certifying surgeons was definitely legalised. The fees of these surgeons, sixpence per certificate signed, had to be paid by the children ; not until 1878 was the employer called upon to pay half, and, finally, in 1891 the whole fee. In the Act of this year provision was first made for the fencing of mill-gearing and shafting, and we also find here for the first time women included with the young persons in the limitation of hours. Another innovation was the introduction of the half-time system, which permitted children to be employed for half the day only or on alternate days. Such children had to be at least eight years old, and a register of them had to be kept. Under the Act of 1833 the inspectors had been endowed with the powers of justices of the peace. These powers they found to be unsatisfactory, and, at their own request, they were now removed.

1845.—A further Act was passed in 1845, known as the Print Works Act, which regulated the labour of children, young persons, and women in calico print works. No child under eight was to be employed ; no children under thirteen or women were to be employed between 10 o'clock in the evening and 6 o'clock in the morning, and children under thirteen were to attend school thirty days in each half-year during the last six months preceding admission to the factory, and during the first six months of employment.

1847. *Ten Hours Act.*—What is known as the Ten Hours Act was passed in 1847. It was the outcome of a long period of controversy concerning hours of labour. This Act only applied to protected persons, that is to say, to young persons and to women ; it laid down that no one under the age of eighteen years should be employed in those factories to which the Act applied for more than ten hours in any one day, or more than fifty-eight hours in any one week, and these restric- tions were extended to females above the age of eighteen years. This Act permitted work to be carried on between 5.30 a.m. and 8.30 p.m.—a period which is curiously reminiscent of the

Statute of Apprentices in Elizabeth's reign. During the debates which took place, the position was made clear that the men considered their hours would be similarly limited, because, since their work depended on that of protected persons, they would have to be employed for the same periods ; in fact, this Act is considered a case where the men advanced behind the petticoats of the women.

1850.—The drafting of previous Acts relating to hours of employment allowed the employer to introduce the relay system, that is to say, he claimed to be employing certain protected persons the first half of the day and others in the last half, while the men were employed continuously while the machinery was in action. Inspectors found administration difficult owing to the practical impossibility of ascertaining whether in fact any protected person whom they found employed in the latter half of the day had not been employed in the earlier part ; this difficulty was not rendered any easier by the fact that the workers themselves were ready to collude with the employers, and give false evidence. In order to meet this difficulty the hours of work in 1850 were fixed to be on five days in the week either from 6 a.m. to 6 p.m., or 7 a.m. to 7 p.m., with an hour and a half for meal-time within these twelve hours, and on Saturdays not after 2 p.m. ; and so a normal working week of sixty hours was fixed. Cobbett strongly advocated at this time that the hours of males should be controlled as well as those of protected persons, but no action was taken, nor indeed has action ever been taken from that day to this to control the hours of male labour in factories (except in a few dangerous processes).

1850. *Mines Act.*—Inspectors of mines were given further powers by an Act passed in 1850, which also called upon colliery owners to give notice of fatal accidents, and to keep accurate plans of their mines.

1853.—A short Act was passed in 1853 to regulate the employment of children in factories, which restricted their period of employment so that it fell within the twelve hours per day fixed by the previous Act for women and young persons.

XI. 1855—78.

1855.—A further Coal Mines Act became law in 1855, which, in addition to certain safety provisions, required adequate ventilation of the workings by mechanical means sufficient to render noxious gases harmless. Ventilation so called for was to obviate the danger of explosions ; but following upon this provision, miners' asthma, which was then ubiquitous on the coal fields, has gradually disappeared. This Act also required special rules, approved of by the Secretary of State (in practice the district inspector), to be made for each mine ; this method of procedure was shortly after incorporated in the Factory Act of 1864.

1856.—In 1856 a Factory Act was passed which extended the meaning of the word " machinery " of the 1844 Act, and declared that it should include mill-gearing, which from this time forward had to be fenced.

1860.—A comprehensive and consolidating Coal Mines Act was passed in 1860. This Act also applied to ironstone mines of the coal measures. It raised the age at which boys might be employed to twelve, and at which persons might be entrusted with the care of steam engines to eighteen ; at the same time the scope of special rules was enlarged, and the system of check weighing was introduced.

The application of the provisions of the Factory Acts was extended in 1860 to bleach and dye works, which were declared to be factories within the meaning of the Acts.

1862.—An Act to amend the law relating to coal mines was passed in 1862, which prohibited the working of coal and ironstone with a single shaft.

1862—63.—In 1862 night work, *i.e.*, between 8 p.m. and 6 a.m., in bleach and dye works was prohibited for protected persons, and in 1863 the Bleachworks Act of 1860 was applied to the use of mechanical power in the processes of calendering, dressing and finishing.

1863. *Bakehouses.*—Bakehouses were controlled by an Act of 1863, under which the employment was prohibited of young persons at night, *i.e.*, between 9 p.m. and 5 a.m., and which made certain regulations with regard to sanitation and cleanliness. This Act was administered by local sanitary authorities, and bakehouses were not included in factory legislation until 1878 (10).

1864.—Extension of the Factory Acts was made in 1864, when the following trades were included : manufacture of earthenware, of lucifer matches, of percussion caps and cartridges, paper staining and fustian cutting. Power was also given to masters to make special rules for dangerous trades, subject to the approval of the Secretary of State. The taking of meals in certain rooms where noxious materials were handled was also prohibited.

1867. *Factory Act.*—The powers of the Acts were strengthened and further extended by the Act of 1867, the provisions of which are distinctly complicated. The following industries were brought within its scope : all metal trades, including blast furnaces and smelting of metals, foundries, engineering shops, manufacture of paper and gutta percha, of paper and of glass, the tobacco industry and the printing trade ; in addition, there was a clause stating that places where more than fifty persons were employed on industrial processes should be considered factories. Powers for the fencing of machinery as well as of shafting were taken, and to demand the removal by mechanical means of dust evolved during a manufacturing process, which might be inhaled to an injurious extent. The way in which provisions aimed at protecting health stole into the Acts from time to time must always be one of interest to the industrial hygienist, and we are probably safe in concluding from the coincidence of dates that this last power was introduced in consequence of the work done by Greenhow. Greenhow had been employed by Simon to investigate the occurrence of disease in industries, and his investigations had been published in 1861 and 1862 in the Third and Fourth Reports of the Medical Officer of the Privy Council. There can be little reasonable doubt that this provision for the removal of dust was the outcome of the publication of this work. Here we have something rather unusual, namely, that investigation carried out on scientific lines was embodied in an Act of Parliament. In contrast to work on such lines, the code of factory legislation up to the end of the nineteenth century may not unfairly be said to represent rather an outraged national conscience than to have been based upon scientific inquiry.

In this year also the first Workshops Act was passed which applied to establishments where less than fifty people were employed in any manufacturing process. No children under eight were, under this Act, to be employed in any handicraft, and children from eight to thirteen could only be employed under the half-time system. Young persons and women might only be employed for twelve hours, less half an hour for meals, and no protected person might be employed after 2 p.m. on Saturdays. The duty of enforcing this Act lay with local authorities until 1871, when it was transferred to factory inspectors.

1870—71.—A minor Act relating to danger from spontaneous combustion in bleach and dyeworks was passed in 1870. Two other short Acts followed in 1871. The first allowed young persons and females of Jewish religion to work on Sundays. The second prohibited the employment of children and female young persons in the manufacture of bricks and tiles.

1872.—A further Mines Act was passed in 1872. The Act applied to mines of coal, stratified ironstone, shale and fireclay ;

it strengthened the provisions as regards ventilation, safety-lamps and timbering, and placed check-weighing on a sounder basis, but contained no new principle in relation to health questions. Mines Acts, so far, differ from Factory Acts in containing no provisions relating to hours of employment.

In the same year a Metalliferous Mines Regulation Act was passed, which, in addition to providing for inspection and safety, called for an adequate amount of ventilation and the provision of accommodation for enabling the persons employed in the mine to dry conveniently and change their dresses. This last provision anticipates by nearly half a century similar legislation in other fields of industry. This Act was made applicable to all metalliferous mines, and was based on the report issued in 1864 of an important Royal Commission. This Commission paid particular attention to the extraordinary prevalence of miners' phthisis in tin and lead mines, and collected valuable information justifying the work of Greenhow, which had not long been published. Fifty years later the subject was again inquired into and reported upon in 1902 (16). The prevalence of miners' phthisis had not only not diminished in the interval, it had become more pronounced. Yet again it was the subject of careful and thorough investigation by a Royal Commission, which reported in 1914 (15). Amendments of minor importance were made to this Act in 1875, 1882, and 1891.

1874.—In 1874 a further Factory Act was passed, the main provisions of which were to raise the age for the employment of children from nine years to ten years, and of young persons from thirteen to fourteen ; to prevent the continuous employment of protected persons for more than four and a half hours without half an hour interval, and to provide for attendance of children at recognised schools. The certifying surgeon's certificate was changed from one of age to one of fitness.

1878.—A consolidating Act was passed in 1878, and we obtain here the definition of a factory which holds good still, namely : Premises wherein articles are made, secured, repaired, ornamented, finished or adapted for sale by means of manual labour, for gain, if mechanical power is used on the premises. This Act amalgamated the provisions of the previous Factory, Workshops and Bakehouses Acts, and we get now for the first time the distinction between textile factories and non-textile factories ; apart from this distinction the Act was made to apply not to this or that industry or trade as heretofore, but to all industries and trades as defined above. The employment of children under ten years of age was now prohibited, and children were forbidden to clean machinery in motion. No new principle was introduced.

XII. 1883—1901.

1883.—A short Act, aimed at the prevention of lead poisoning, was passed in 1883, which required every occupier of white lead factories to draw up special rules to be transmitted for official approval.

1886.—A Shop Hours Act became law in 1886, limiting the weekly period of employment of young persons under the age of eighteen years to seventy-four hours, including meal-times. Women were not included.

1886—87.—A temporary measure applicable to mines, passed in 1886, was followed by the Coal Mines Regulation Act, 1887. The principles adopted in previous mining legislation were consolidated and extended in this Act ; but no new ground was broken, notwithstanding the careful recommendations of a Royal Commission in reference to the use of high explosives, testing of safety lamps, the use of electric light in mines, and the introduction of ambulance provision and rescue stations. These matters were all reconsidered and reported on in 1909 by a later Royal Commission.

1889—1897.—Factory Acts were passed in 1889 and 1897 regulating the humidity and ventilation of cotton cloth factories.

1891.—A Factory Act passed in 1891 introduced other new provisions. A register had to be kept of out-workers, and particulars of wages had to be given to workers in textile factories. Men's workshops were brought under the provision for sanitary requirements. A further point was that the employment of any woman within four weeks after childbirth was prohibited. The age of employable children was raised to eleven years. The provision of " fire-escapes " was demanded. Power was taken to prohibit the carrying on of processes and handicrafts dangerous to health, life or limb, until they were made safe, and also to prohibit or restrict employment in trades certified by the Secretary of State to be " dangerous." Laundries were for the first time named in the Act, but only with regard to sanitary provisions.

1892.—A Shop Hours Act, re-enacting the Act of 1886, was passed in 1892, which prohibited the employment of any young person for a longer period than seventy-four hours, including meal-times, in any one week. Enforcement of this Act was entrusted to county and borough councils acting through inspectors appointed for the purpose. Slight amendments were made to this Act in 1893 and 1895.

1894.—Quarries, which had until 1894 been regulated as non-textile factories or workshops by the Factory Act in force, were, if over twenty feet in depth, brought under the jurisdiction of the inspectors of mines. The Quarries Act of this year called for notification of accidents, and the framing of special rules.

1895.—Local authorities were made responsible for the sanitation of factories in 1895 ; in the Act of this year power was taken to extend the particulars of wages clause to other than textile industries by order of the Secretary of State. The maintenance of a reasonable temperature in workrooms was called for. Medical practitioners were called upon to notify cases in their practice, suffering from anthrax, lead, phosphorus, mercury, or arsenical poisoning of industrial origin, and in 1897 the first medical inspector of factories was appointed to deal with these notifications. A weekly limit of hours for laundries was fixed at thirty for children, and sixty for young persons and women ; but permitted children to work ten hours, young persons twelve, and women fourteen.

1896 *and later Mining Acts.*—Acts were passed, in 1896 aimed at the prevention of explosions of gas or dust in coal mines ; in 1900, forbidding in all class of mines the employment below ground of boys under thirteen years of age ; in 1903, regulating coal-mining managers' certificates ; and in 1906, an Act which, for all types of mines, quarries, factories and workshops, extended and made more stringent the obligation to notify the occurrence of accidents.

1899.—An Act concerned with seats for shop assistants was passed in 1899, which called for one seat for every three female assistants employed in each room. The principle of insisting on the provision of seats, here accepted, was not made applicable to factories until 1916.

1901.—Finally we arrive at the Consolidating Factory and Workshops Act of 1901, which is the principal Act now in force. It brings into one code the Acts of 1878, 1883, 1891, 1895, and the two Cotton Cloth Factory Acts. Further powers are also introduced : A standard of sufficient ventilation can be demanded by order, floors must be properly drained, and boilers must be examined and reported upon periodically. This Act raised the age of children to twelve years ; but for the most part it contains little new in principle, and its provisions are those already approved of in previous Acts, but now more exactly defined. The procedure for making special rules for dangerous industries was amended. Previously these rules, which applied to each individual factory and could be modified to suit the requirements of each establishment, were difficult to administer. Under the Act of 1901 the procedure was simplified and improved ; codes of regulations are ~~now~~ *were* made which apply to every factory included under the Application Clause of the Code.

XIII. 1903 and later.

1907 *and later Factory Acts.*—Since the Act of 1901 there have been passed one or two additional Acts ; 1907 saw the passing of a Laundries Act which recognised laundries as non-textile factories, modified the hours permitted and provided for some regulation of charitable institution laundries. In 1908 the use of yellow phosphorus for the manufacture of matches was prohibited ; in 1912 a Cotton Cloth Act was passed which laid down certain provisions in relation to the use of humidity in weaving.

1908.—An Agricultural Children Act was passed in 1873, which stated that no child under eight years of age was to be employed in agriculture, and no child under ten unless school attendance was satisfactory ; but as there was no provision for enforcing the statute it has been a dead letter. A Protection of Children Act under the administration of factory inspectors had become law in 1894, regulating the employment of children between the ages of eight and ten in public entertainments. In 1903 an Employment of Children Act had prohibited their employment : (i.) in any occupation likely to be injurious to their physical health and condition or their education ; (ii.) between 9 p.m. and 6 a.m. ; and (iii.) in street trading under the age of eleven. In 1908 these and other provisions were amalgamated in one Act, which also made illegal the employment of half-timers in any other occupation.

1908. *Mines Eight Hours Act.*—Limitation of hours of labour for miners was first embodied in legislation in 1908 in the Coal Mines Regulations Act which came into force in 1909. When compared with factory legislation, this limitation appears at first sight long delayed ; but in fact it is the first limitation of hours placed upon adult male labour. Female labour in mines required no protection as it was abolished in 1842. Juvenile male labour was protected, not by limitation of hours, but by keeping the minimum age of employment higher than that permitted under the Factory Acts.

1910.—A Mines Accidents (Rescue and Aid) Act was passed in 1910, under which provision at coal mines and metalliferous mines may be required by order with regard to :—

(*a*) The supply and maintenance of appliances for use in rescue work and the formation and training of rescue brigades ;

(*b*) The supply and maintenance of ambulance appliances and the training of men in ambulance work.

Here the mining industry advances ahead of factory legislation, which did not provide for first-aid provision until 1916.

1911.—The Coal Mines Act at present in force was passed. This Act, while maintaining the provisions of previous Acts relating to employment underground, regulates the employment of women and young persons as follows :—No boy between thirteen and sixteen, and no girl or woman may be employed—

(*a*) On Sunday ;

(*b*) On week days, except during the period of employment shown in the prescribed form of notice posted up at the mine. The period must not begin before 5 a.m. or end after 9 p.m. (or on Sunday after 2 p.m.) ;- it must not exceed ten hours in any day excluding the meal intervals, and the total for the whole of the week must not exceed fifty-four hours ; twelve hours must be allowed between the end of the period of employment on one day and the commencement of the next period of employment ;

(*c*) Continuously for more than five hours without an interval of at least half an hour, or for more than eight hours in the day without intervals of at least one hour and a half. The intervals must be specified in the notice posted up at the mine. A different period and different intervals may be fixed for different persons and different days, but they must not be changed oftener than once a quarter ;

(*d*) In moving railway waggons, or in lifting, carrying or moving anything so heavy as to be likely to cause him or her injury.

This Act also contains the following important health clauses :—

Sect. 77 provides for accommodation and facilities for taking baths and drying clothes where the majority of the workmen employed in a mine desire such. Here again one of the provisions of factory legislation, 1916, is anticipated.

Sect. 78 lays down that a drill worked by mechanical power shall not be used for drilling in ganister, hard sandstone, or other highly silicious rock, the dust from which is liable to give rise to fibroid phthisis, unless a water jet or spray or other means equally efficient is used to prevent the escape of dust into the air.

Sect. 79 provides for the notification of disease occurring in a mine or occasioned by the nature of the employment.

1916.—Consecutive to the issue of reports by the Health of

Munition Workers' Committee, important powers were incorporated in the Police, Factories, etc. (Miscellaneous Provisions) Act, 1916. Under these powers special provision may be required by order for securing the welfare of factory workers. The matters to which an Order may apply are :—" Arrangements for preparing or heating and taking meals ; the supply of drinking water ; the supply of protective clothing ; ambulance and first-aid arrangements ; the supply and use of seats in workrooms ; facilities for washing ; accommodation for clothing ; arrangement for supervision of workers." Several valuable orders have already been made under these powers (see Appendix) which are likely to consolidate the advance in conditions of labour made in national factories during the war. By special order addition may be made to the matters of welfare enumerated in the Act, and such an order has been made to include rest rooms.

Workmen's Compensation.—Acts of importance, though not strictly Occupational Acts, relating to the Workmen's Compensation, were passed in 1897, 1900, 1906 and 1918. The Acts of 1906 and 1918 are of special interest ; the former gave compensation to a workman suffering from any occupational disease included by order in a Schedule to the Act (see Appendix) ; the latter provides in a special way for compensation in cases of silicosis due to the inhalation of silica dust, and resulted from the report of the Royal Commission on Metalliferous Mines and Quarries published in 1914 (15). A committee has just reported upon the possible consolidation of the Compensation Acts.

XIV. A Retrospect.

This long series of legislative Acts cannot be properly comprehended unless the social alterations which were taking place in the nation with unexampled rapidity are kept in mind ; not only was industrialism spreading at an extraordinary rate, but new industries were springing into existence ; the population was rapidly multiplying and statutes which concerned only a few thousands in the early part of the century affected millions at the close ; wealth was mounting up and also the cost of living ; facilities for communication and for transport at home and abroad were out-distancing all expectations ; power was centring more and more in the hands of capital. These new conditions called urgently for new laws, for time would not permit leaving the progress of affairs to the slow establishment of reasonable custom. Legislation was needed to decide upon and to preserve some " rule of the road," and so avoid chaos.

One fact, however, stands out as remarkable, viz.: the protection extended to woman and what woman stands for—the rising generation. The individualistic male has for the most part been left to fare for himself. There seems here to be legislative recognition of the supreme importance for racial continuance of protecting women and children; of what Maeterlinck would claim (17) as " the spirit of the hive."

Had this code of laws been enacted by a parliament of women, Schopenhauer (no admirer of women) would have claimed it to justify his contention (8) that woman is the creature to whom the race is more than the individual, the being to whom the future is greater than the present. On the other hand Benjamin Kidd (9), who holds that " *It is not in the fighting male of the race :* it is in *woman* that we have the future centre *of power in civilisation* " ; and that for the future of civilisation the central problem is the relation of women to the needs of society, might claim the progress of industrial legislation as an unguided national effort to attain to his ideal of social power by refusing to allow industry to develop on lines inimical to women, unsuited to their capacity, and uninfluenced by their racial foresight.

Looked at from another point of view, the student of the human machine, and of its requirements to maintain health and efficiency, is astonished first to note how the reasonable recommendations of important committees and Royal Commissions are passed by unheeded, while attention is paid to subjects pressed to the front by the uneducated voice of labour, or required in the interests of production. Thus the workman, fearing the competition of more lowly paid female and juvenile labour, presses for and obtains restrictions regarding their hours of employment, while the mine owner, to enable him to work deeper seams of coal and protect his property from explosions, accepts the safety-lamp and necessary ventilation. Next, legislation is observed seldom, if ever, to lead reform, but to follow in the wake of progress, adopting the procedure of the more advanced employers of the time. Frequently these employers are found seeking for legislative protection, under the impression that their humanitarian customs are a handicap which should be adopted by the rest of the trade, instead of being (as they actually were) a more profitable proposition than any so-called trade secret.

Finally, legislation is discovered, notwithstanding eddies and backwaters, to be gathering volume and flowing steadily onward, as though sure of its own object ; the student will be inclined to postulate an unconscious motive not to be defined in terms of everyday discussion, and to hold, as did Lucretius, that first-beginnings do not station themselves each in its right place by keen-sighted intelligence, but :—

"Propterea fit uti magnum volgata per aevom
Omne genus coetus et motus experiundo
Tandem conveniant ea quae convecta repente
Magnarum rerum fiunt exordia semper." *

XV. Bibliography.

1. Lipson, E. *Economic History of England*, pp. 96 *et seq.* A. and C. Black, Ltd. 1915.
2. Hutchins, B. L., and Harrison, A. *History of Factory Legislation.* P. S. King & Son. 1911.
3. Macaulay, Lord. Works of, Vol. VIII., p. 360.
4. Cooke-Taylor, R. W. *History of the Factory System.* Richard Bentley & Son. 1886.
5. Jevons, Stanley W. *The State in Relation to Labour.* English Citizen Series. Macmillan & Co. 1882.
6. Austin, Evans. *The Law Relating to Factories and Workshops.* 2nd Edition. Knight & Co. 1901.
7. Ernest, Edler Von Plener. *The English Factory Legislation.* Translated by F. L. Weinmann. Chapman and Hall. 1873.
8. Schopenhauer. *Essay on Women.* Belfort Bax's Volume of Selections.
9. Kidd, Benjamin. *The Science of Power.* Methuen & Co., Ltd. 1918.
10. Cooke-Taylor, R. W. *The Factory System.* 2nd Edition. Methuen & Co., Ltd. 1912.
11. Hammond, J. L., and Hammond, B. *The Town Labourer.* Longmans, Green & Co. 1917.
12. Hammond, J. L., and Hammond, B. *The Skilled Labourer.* Longmans, Green & Co. 1919.
13. *Second Report of Royal Commission on Mines.* (Cd. 4820.) 1909.
14. *Life of Lord Shaftesbury.* Vol. I.
15. *Second Report of Royal Commission on Metalliferous Mines and Quarries.* (Cd. 7476.) 1914.
16. *Report on the Health of Cornish Miners.* (Cd. 2091.) 1904.
17. Maeterlinck, M. *The Life of the Bee.* George Allen. 1901.
18. Smith, E. *Health and Disease.* Walton and Maberly. 1861.
19. Bryce, J. *The Holy Roman Empire.* Ch. XVI. Macmillan & Co.
20. Anderson, Adelaide M. *Labour Legislation.* Encyclopædia Britannica.

XVI. Appendix.

In order to facilitate reference, the various Orders, Codes of Special Rules and Regulations now in force under the Factory Acts, a list of diseases scheduled under the Compensation Acts, and the

* *Lucretius, V.,* 428 : " Therefore it is that, after being scattered through æons of time by attempting all sorts of meetings and commotions, they at length come together with unexpected concurrence, and become the lasting warp for mighty history."

Orders and Regulations referring to safety and health under the Mines Acts, are stated below :—

CODES OF SPECIAL RULES ESTABLISHED UNDER THE FACTORY AND WORKSHOP ACTS, 1891 AND 1895.

Manufacture of white lead.
Handling of dry and dry-salted hides and skins from China and the West Coast of India.
Vulcanising of india-rubber by means of bisulphide of carbon.
Chemical works. ·   Bottling of aerated waters.

FACTORY AND WORKSHOP ACT, 1901.

Orders relating to : (*a*) Health ; (*b*) notification of diseases ; and (*c*) dangerous and unhealthy industries (other than those under Section 79).

Health :—
Limewashing or washing—exemption of certain factories (s. 1 (4)).
Cubic space in : (*a*) Workshops used as sleeping places (s. 3 (3)) ; (*b*) bakehouses (s. 3 (2)).
Ventilation in humid textile factories other than cotton cloth factories (s. 7).
Sanitary accommodation, fixing standard of (s. 9).

Notification of Diseases :—
Toxic jaundice (s. 73 (4)).
Epitheliomatous ulceration and chrome ulceration (s. 73 (4)).

DANGEROUS AND UNHEALTHY INDUSTRIES (other than those under s. 79).

Prohibition of taking Meals in Certain Places (s. 78).

DANGEROUS AND UNHEALTHY INDUSTRIES.

Regulations under Section 79.

Benzene, manufacture of nitro and amido derivatives of, and of explosives with dinitrobenzol or dinitrotoluol.
Brass, etc., casting of.   Bronzing.
Chromate and bichromate of potassium or sodium, manufacture of.
Docks, wharves, and quays, loading or unloading, etc., at.
Electric accumulators, manufacture of.
Electricity, generation, transformation, distribution or use of.
Enamelling, vitreous, of metal or glass.
Felt hats, manufacture of (with aid of inflammable solvent).
File-cutting by hand.
Flax and tow, spinning and weaving of, etc.
Grinding of metals and racing of grindstones.
Hemp, jute, and hemp or jute tow, spinning and weaving of, etc.
Horsehair from China, Siberia or Russia, use of.
Lead, smelting of materials containing, manufacture of red or orange lead and of flaked litharge.
Locomotives and waggons, use of on lines and sidings.
Mules, self-acting, spinning by means of.
Paints and colours, manufacture of.
Pottery, manufacture and decoration of, making of lithographic transfers, frits or glazes.

Refractory materials, crushing, grinding, etc., and the manufacture of silica bricks.

Ships in shipbuilding yards, construction and repair of.

Tinning of metal hollow ware, iron drums, and harness furniture.

Wool, East Indian, use of.

Wool, goat hair and camel hair, sorting, willeying, washing, combing and carding.

Yarn, heading of, dyed by means of a lead compound.

ORDERS, MADE UNDER SECTION 7 OF THE POLICE, FACTORIES, ETC. (MISCELLANEOUS PROVISIONS) ACT, 1916, FOR SECURING THE WELFARE OF WORKERS IN FACTORIES AND WORKSHOPS.*

Ambulance and first aid at blast furnaces, copper mills, iron mills, foundries and metal works.

Ambulance and first aid at saw-mills and wood working factories.

Drinking water. Dyeing, use of bichromate of potassium or sodium in.

Fruit preserving. Glass bottles and pressed glass articles, manufacture.

Oil cake mills.   Seats in shell factories.

Tanning, use of bichromate of potassium or sodium in.

Tin or terne plates, manufacture of.

Laundries.

All textile factories, printworks, bleaching and dyeing works, and rope spinning works with reference to providing protective clothing, cloakrooms, mess rooms, washing facilities, seats, first aid and ambulance.

WORKMEN'S COMPENSATION ACT, 1906.
Schedule of Diseases.

Anthrax.   Mercury poisoning or its sequelæ.

Phosphorus poisoning or its sequelæ. Arsenic poisoning or its sequelæ.

Lead poisoning or its sequelæ.

Poisoning by benzene and its homologues, or its sequelæ.

Poisoning by nitro and amido derivatives of benzene and its homologues (trinitrotoluene, aniline, and others), or the sequelæ.

Poisoning by dinitrophenol or its sequelæ.

Poisoning by nitrous fumes or its sequelæ.

Dope poisoning ; that is, poisoning by any substance used as or in conjunction with a solvent for acetate of cellulose, or its sequelæ.

Poisoning by tetrachlorethane or its sequelæ.

Poisoning by carbon bisulphide or its sequelæ.

Poisoning by nickel carbonyl or its sequelæ.

Poisoning by *Gonioma kamassi* (African boxwood) or its sequelæ.

Dermatitis produced by dust or liquids.

Ulceration of the skin produced by dust or liquids.

Ulceration of the mucous membrane of the nose or mouth produced by dust.   Chrome ulceration or its sequelæ.

Epitheliomatous cancer or ulceration of the skin due to tar, pitch, bitumen, mineral oil or paraffin, or any compound, product or residue of any of these substances.

Ulceration of the corneal surface of the eye, due to tar, pitch, bitumen, mineral oil or paraffin, or any compound, product or residue of any of these substances.

* Further Orders are in draft relating to :—
  Gut scraping.
  Manufacture of hollow-ware and process of galvanising.
  Gutting, salting and packing of herring.

Scrotol epithelioma (chimney sweep's cancer).
Compressed air illness or its sequelæ.
Cataract in glassworkers.
The disease known as miner's nystagmus, whether occurring in
    miners or others, and whether the symptom of oscillation of the
    eyeballs be present or not.
Subcutaneous cellulitis of the hand (beat hand).
Subcutaneous cellulitis over the patella (miner's beat knee).
Acute bursitis over the elbow (miner's beat elbow).
Inflammation of the synovial lining of the wrist joint and tendon
    sheaths.
Ankylostomiasis.
Glanders.
Telegraphist's cramp.
Writer's cramp.

WORKMEN'S COMPENSATION (SILICOSIS) ACT, 1918.
Refractories Industry (Silicosis) Scheme.

METALLIFEROUS MINES REGULATION ACT, 1872 AND 1875.
Special Rules for Ore Mines in North Wales.
Special Rules for Installation and Use of Electricity.
Special Rules—Model Code.
                West Scotland Code.
                Newcastle Code.

COAL MINES ACT, 1911.
General Regulations of July 10th, 1913.
    Amending Regulations of May 19th, 1914 (Special Provisions
        for Mines served by a Central Rescue Corps : Definition of
        " Breathing Apparatus ").
    Regulations as to Washing and Drying Accommodation, etc.,
        1913.
    Regulations as to Hours of Winding Enginemen, 1913.
    Regulations as to Ganister, 1920.

Explosives in Coal Mines Order of September 1st, 1913.
    Amending Orders :—
        Storage and Use of Detonators, Clause 1 (e), March 30th,
            1915.
        Non-detonating Explosives—Extension of Period during
            which they may be Used—par. 11, September 18th,
            1918.
        Revised and Consolidated List of Permitted Explosives,
            November 14th, 1919.

Safety Lamps Orders :—
    One was issued in 1913, five in 1914, four in 1915, three in 1916,
        one in 1917, three in 1918, and two in 1919.

Regulations governing :—
    Form of certificate as to eyesight and hearing of firemen, 1917.
    Use below ground of apparatus for the relighting electrically of
        safety lamps, 1912.
    Search of persons employed for prohibited articles, 1912.
    Manner of testing horses for glanders, 1912.

CHAPTER III

THE UTILISATION OF STATISTICAL METHODS IN INDUSTRIAL PREVENTIVE MEDICINE

I. Introduction.

As we have remarked in an earlier chapter, a considerable impetus was given to the study of industrial conditions affecting health by the various commissions and inquiries promoted by the Government after the passing of the first Reform Act of 1832. This epoch saw the foundation of the General Register Office soon followed by medical developments which, passing through such stages as the Poor Law Board, the Medical Department of the Privy Council, the Medical Department of the Local Government Board and the National Health Insurance Commission, have now culminated in the institution of a Ministry of Health.

Two public servants in the early Victorian period contributed more than any others to the advancement of preventive medicine, William Farr and John Simon; they made great use of statistics and statistical methods. Farr was one of the most accomplished and original statisticians who ever lived, while Simon, if less familiar with the theoretical developments of the subject, had a clear appreciation and competent grasp of the principles of quantitative reasoning. To Simon we owe many valuable statistical arguments, to Farr belongs the credit of initiating a periodic evaluation of the general effects of occupation upon longevity and mortality, which has been continued by his successors at the General Register Office, and, despite inevitable imperfections, is still the most useful record we have.

In order that the reader may be able to utilise official statistics, and in his own work employ profitably statistical methods, he needs some acquaintance with the principles of statistical science. It is not possible to incorporate in this treatise an elementary text-book of statistical methods (1), or even to absolve the student of official tables from the necessity of reading the introductory and explanatory matter there to be found; but it may help him if we make a few observations upon the aspects of statistical science which are peculiarly relevant to the art of industrial preventive medicine.

II. Longevity.

Stated broadly, the problem it is desired to solve is to measure the influence of any occupation upon the health of those engaged therein, it being tacitly understood that the influence in question is measurable in quantitative terms. The measure which at once suggests itself is longevity ; and one asks whether on the average persons of the same age entering two different industries, let us say coal mining and shoe making, live the same or a different number of years.

It must be remarked at once that the solution of this problem would not suffice to measure the unique influence of the occupation upon health.   It would only do so if the physical and social class from which coal miners and shoe makers were recruited was uniform, and if neither occupation specially attracted particular types, particular individuals, from that class ; if, further, the industries were carried on under a common extra-industrial environment, *i.e.*, if geographical situation and home environment were identical for coal miners and shoe makers ; and, lastly, if transfers from one industry to another during the period of observation could be accurately enumerated.

These provisoes and limitations are of importance, and we shall have to discuss them later on ; at the moment we confine ourselves to the problem as above stated.

The average longevity of a group of persons is in practice by no means easy to ascertain, although in theory simple enough. Were we able to secure a number of persons born on the same day, to enter particulars respecting them upon cards, and to keep these cards up-to-date by noting the time of death, holding the records open until the last survivor had perished, our task *would* be an extremely simple one ; sorting the cards, we should find that of the original n persons, aged each m years, n_1 died in the first year of observation, n_2 in the second year of observation, and so forth.   The average after-lifetime of the sample would be merely the sum of the number of years actually lived by them divided by the original number, n, of persons. A person who died three months after the cards were commenced would contribute a quarter of a year to the grand total of time lived, a person who lived ten years and six months would contribute ten and a half years to the total, and so on. A proper comprehension of so simple (and altogether impracticable) a scheme as this will save the reader from statistical blunders, which will continue to be made by some medical men and journalists for a long time to come, and which we now proceed to illustrate.

TABLE 1.—*After History of 1,000 Persons observed from Age Thirty to Death.*

(1) Age (x).	(2) No. of persons attaining this age, x (1_x).	(3) No. of persons dying before attaining the age, $x + 1$ (d_x).	(1) Age (x).	(2) No. of persons attaining this age, x (1_x).	(3) No. of persons dying before attaining the age, $x + 1$ (d_x).
30	1,000	8	63	595	22
31	992	8	64	573	23
32	984	7	65	550	24
33	977	8	66	526	25
34	969	9	67	501	25
35	960	8	68	476	26
36	952	8	69	450	27
37	944	9	70	423	27
38	935	9	71	396	27
39	926	9	72	369	28
40	917	9	73	341	28
41	908	9	74	313	28
42	899	10	75	285	27
43	889	10	76	258	27
44	879	10	77	231	26
45	869	11	78	205	25
46	858	11	79	180	24
47	847	11	80	156	23
48	836	12	81	138	20
49	824	12	82	113	20
50	812	13	83	93	17
51	799	13	84	76	15
52	786	14	85	61	13
53	772	15	86	48	11
54	757	15	87	37	9
55	742	16	88	28	8
56	726	16	89	20	6
57	710	17	90	14	4
58	693	18	91	10	4
59	675	19	92	6	2
60	656	19	93	4	1
61	637	21	94	3	2
62	616	21	95	1	1

For purposes of exposition we can simplify the scheme still further by supposing our table relates to persons thirty years old at the commencement; that on the average every one who dies between the anniversaries of his birthday is alive for precisely six months between these termini; and that the table relates to 1,000 persons who died out as shown (see Table 1).

The sum of the column headed (3) is **1,000**, so that all the **1,000** persons died before the ninety-sixth birthday (the example is modified from a real life table).   Now suppose we ascertain how many years on the average these **1,000** people lived after the thirtieth birthday ;   then conformably to our hypothesis, the 8 people who died before the age of 31 lived 6 months each or 4 years in all, the 8 who died before the next birthday $8 \times 1\frac{1}{2}$ years, and so on.   The table gives us in this way an aggregate of **34,721** years of life or **34·7** years per head of the original **1,000**, *i.e.*, the expectation of life is **34·7** years.   As all these people were 30 years old at the commencement, the average age at death must be 30 plus **34·7** years or **64·7** years.   Let us now confine our attention to those who lived to the age of 40 ;   we find by applying the same method that at age 40 the expectation of life is **27·4** years, and therefore the average age at death **67·4** years.   Hence if we found that of two occupations, the average age at death was greater in the one than the other, we could not infer anything to the prejudice of one without information as to the average age at entrance.

The fallacy of comparing average ages at death becomes still grosser when the death records do not refer to a stationary population.   A life table—our table illustrates its main feature— only corresponds in its distribution of persons into age-groups to a real population if the numbers dropping out of the latter are continuously replaced by exactly the same number of persons, so that year by year there are living exactly the same number of persons.   This would only happen in an industrial group if the numbers of entrants just balanced the losses and all losses were by death.   When we have the deaths at ages in an industry, or a country, over a period within which the number of youths entering the industry is much larger than the number of old members dying, the average age at death is sure to be lower, and may be much lower than the expectation of life added to the age at entrance.   Thus, to take an example from general vital statistics the expectation of life at birth in England and Wales seventy years ago was forty-one years, but the average age at death during the period to which the data relate was as low as twenty-nine.   This fallacy has been so happily characterised by Farr that we cannot do better than quote (8) his remarks :—

> " The numbers following different professions fluctuate more than the general population ;   the relative proportion of young and aged persons varies from year to year ;   certain professions, stations and ranks are only attained by persons advanced in years ;   and some occupations are only followed

in youth ; hence it requires no great amount of sagacity to perceive that ' the mean age at death,' or the age at which the greatest number of deaths occurs, cannot be depended upon in investigating the influence of occupation, rank and profession upon health and longevity. If it were found, upon an inquiry into the health of the officers in the army on full pay, that ' the mean age at death ' of cornets, ensigns and second lieutenants was twenty-two years, of lieutenants twenty-nine years, of captains thirty-seven years, of majors forty-four years, of lieutenant-colonels forty-eight years, of general officers ages still further advanced, and that the ages of curates, rectors and bishops, of barristers of seven years' standing, leading counsel and venerable judges, differed to an equal or greater extent, a strong case may no doubt be made out on behalf of those young but early-dying cornets, curates and juvenile barristers, whose ' mean age at death ' was under thirty. It would be almost necessary to make them generals, bishops and judges—for the sake of their health. The assurance societies are happily so considerate and liberal that they do not attach the slightest importance to the mean age at death, but assure the lives of young men of all the professions at the age of twenty-four upon the assumption that they will live thirty-eight or at the least thirty-one years, and pay thirty-eight or thirty-one annual premiums on an average before they die ; while they make the bishops, judges and generals who go to insure their lives at sixty pay as if they would live but thirteen or fourteen years.

" It has somewhere been stated that the ' mean age at death ' of dressmakers is exceedingly low, and this has been adduced as a proof of the destructive effects of their employment. If the inquiries had been extended to boarding schools, or to the boys at Christ's Hospital, the ' mean age at death ' would have been found still lower. Mr. Grainger states, in his interesting report, that the majority of dressmakers are between the ages of sixteen and twenty-six ; and it is understood that if they die after they marry, they are not often designated by that title in the register. This source of error and the increase of population will be found to affect the estimate of the influence of other occupations. That the lives of dressmakers are very much shortened by the severe hardships and ignorant mistreatment to which they are exposed cannot be doubted ; but false arguments injure instead of aiding their cause."

Since the conditions enabling us to deduce the average longevity from the average age at death are hardly ever fulfilled, it

is necessary in order to determine the former average that we
should construct a life table.

III.   Life Tables.

The actual technic of constructing a life table is easy enough
to understand, although its application involves a great deal of
troublesome arithmetic.   We shall merely expound the general
principles, because in the report by Mr. George King which is
included (2) in the list of references at the end of the chapter
the student will find sufficient arithmetical illustrations to
enable him, if he chooses, to construct a life table for himself
without any more knowledge of mathematics than all moderately
well-educated persons have (see also (3)).

Let us suppose to be known the numbers living in different
age groups at the beginning and end of a period, and the numbers
of deaths also occurring in these age groups at the middle of
that period, for instance the number of inhabitants of England
and Wales (males) in age groups from ten years upwards at the
middle of 1910 and again at the middle of 1912, and also the
number of deaths in these age groups in 1911 ; then the ratio
of deaths to the populations (*i.e.*, the death-rate) in age groups
can be calculated.   Owing to misstatements of age (for instance,
the preference for round numbers which leads to an exaggeration
of the numbers said to be aged equal multiples of 5 and 10, so
that too many people are recorded as aged twenty and too few
as nineteen or twenty-one), it is impracticable to base the calculation upon the records at single years' intervals, and pivotal values
for single years of age are obtained by forming sums of grouped
ages and using an interpolation formula ; the same method is
used for deaths, and we thus obtain mean annual death rates
for ages twelve, seventeen, etc.   Now, if we know the death rate
at age x it is easy to find the probability that a person x years
old will not live to be x plus one year old.   In fact, this probability is equal to twice the death rate divided by 2 plus the
death rate (it is a little unfortunate that while the former constant, the death rate of popular language,* is termed by actuaries
the central death rate, the second, less familiar constant, the
probability of death within the next twelve months, is named
" rate of mortality " ; to avoid any confusion we can always
denote it by the letter q).   Having thus obtained a series of
values of q for different years of life, the values of q—or any
function of it—for intervening years are obtained by interpola-

---

* Or rather $\frac{1}{1000}$ of the popular " death rate," since we usually refer to
deaths per 1,000, not per unit.

tion.   A variety of methods are available; that used in preparing the most recent English life tables, due to Sprague, is known as osculatory interpolation and tolerably easy to handle.   In this way a complete sequence of q's can be constructed for persons aged say fifteen years and upwards.   The methods of preparing the data at earlier ages would take long to describe and are of less interest for industrial purposes.   When q has been determined we can compute the numbers dying in each year of life from an arbitrary number of entrants, the expectation of life, etc.   We give below, in Table 2, extracts from certain life tables which are of interest.   The Lancashire Life table was graduated by a different method from that used for the others, but the difference is of little moment from the point of view of comparative results.

TABLE 2.—*Value of the Expectation of Life shown by various recent Life Tables.*

Age.	English Life Table No. 8 (1910-12).		English Life Table No. 7 (1901-10).		County of London (1911-12).		Lancashire (Nathan, "Transactions Manchester Statistical Soc., Session 1917-18," pp. 81-106).		North-Eastern States of U.S.A. (1908-12) (Henderson).
	Males.	Females.	Males.	Females.	Males.	Females.	Males.	Females.	Males.
15	48·57	51·44	47·31	50·08	46·74	51·13	45·42	48·46	47·58
20	44·21	47·10	43·01	45·77	42·35	46·71	41·13	44·23	43·36
25	40·00	42·80	38·86	41·54	38·06	42·29	36·93	39·99	39·38
30	35·81	38·54	34·76	37·36	33·87	37·94	32·83	35·78	35·49
35	31·71	34·37	30·79	33·31	29·84	33·71	28·85	31·63	31·68
40	27·74	30·30	26·96	29·37	26·03	29·67	25·02	27·62	27·96
45	23·92	26·34	23·27	25·53	22·45	25·82	21·36	23·80	24·31
50	20·29	22·51	19·76	21·81	19·09	22·17	17·93	20·17	20·76
55	16·89	18·87	16·48	18·27	15·95	18·66	14·77	16·71	17·38
60	13·78	15·48	13·49	15·01	13·09	15·39	11·92	13·47	14·29
65	10·99	12·36	10·80	11·99	10·51	12·34	9·43	10·57	11·54
70	8·53	9·58	8·39	9·35	8·17	9·57	7·32	8·11	9·08

If all that is required is an abbreviated table showing the probability of dying within five years and the expectations of life at five-yearly intervals, much labour can be saved in the second stage of the above-described process; for practical details Mr. King's report should be consulted.

The essential data for making a life table are (1) a knowledge of the average age distribution of the population; (2) the distribution of deaths by ages.   It is indeed possible upon certain assumptions to compute a life table from a knowledge of deaths at ages alone.   This is of course quite easy if we know that the population is stationary ; it *can* be done, even when this is not so, upon certain assumptions (4), but to do so involves a great deal of labour, and the validity of the assumptions involved needs confirmation.

IV.   Mortality.

Owing to the difficulty of obtaining data fulfilling the requirements of the last paragraph, longevity has seldom been taken as a standard of comparison between industrial groups ; use has been made of mortality or morbidity rates ; each of these is subject to the same criticisms, and since mortality rates have been far more widely employed, we confine our remarks to them.

A death rate in current practice means the per cent. or per mille ratio of deaths occurring in a population over an assigned period (most frequently one year) to the estimated population at the middle of the year. The simplest comparison is of this form, no regard being paid to the age constitution of the population, and such a rate is called a crude or unstandardised rate.

The objections to a comparison of crude mortality rates when it is a matter of industrial groups are obvious ; owing to differences of age constitution, the comparison of crude rates may be very misleading. A stock case (9) is that in the Swiss experience 1879—90 ; the crude rate of mortality for farmers, etc. (*Landwirtschaft*), was 21·2 per mille, for watchmakers 18·2, 'and for employed males 20·9. The excessive crude mortality of the farmers was due, not to the unhealthiness of their occupation, but to the larger proportion of occupied males at later ages, when more deaths naturally occur (in Switzerland the proportion of farmers over fifty was nearly 32 per cent., of watchmakers only 15·7 per cent.) ; after allowance had been made for this the relative mortality of watchmakers proved to be much greater than that of farmers.

V.   Methods of Standardisation.

The difficulty was realised in the treatment of general vital statistics many years ago, and a method of standardising or correcting the crude rate devised to surmount it. There are two such methods, one of which requires a knowledge of both ages at death and the average age distribution of the two or more groups it is desired to standardise ; the second method depends upon a knowledge of the average age distributions of the populations compared, but supposes that the ages at death are not known.

In the former method the death rates at each age group of each occupation, or other aggregate, are computed. A standard population is then chosen (for instance, the population of England and Wales in 1901), and the death rates computed for the occupational age group are applied to each corresponding age group in the standard population. The sum of the deaths derived in this way divided by the standard population gives the standardised or corrected death rate of the occupation.

The second method of correction—the counterpart of that just described—is to choose a standard population as before, and also to take certain death rates at each age group as standards. These standard death rates are then applied to the population in the age groups of the occupation; the sum of deaths thus reckoned divided by the occupational population gives a potential death rate which would have been realised in the occupation if its rates of mortality at ages had been the same as in the standard. The ratio of the standard death rate (all ages) to this potential rate is known as the " standardising factor." The actually observed crude rate of mortality in the occupational group is then multiplied by this factor, that is, multiplied by the crude standard mortality, and divided by the potential crude death rate in the occupation, and the result is taken to be the standardised mortality rate.

TABLE 3.—*Occupied Males in Industrial Districts* (1900–2).

Age group.	Years of life.*	Deaths.	Death rate per 1,000.
15—20	1,187,061	3,151	2·65
20—25	1,189,341	5,379	4·52
25—35	2,014,302	13,024	6·47
35—45	1,511,544	18,526	12·26
45—55	1,051,485	23,263	22·12
55—65	575,952	22,565	39·18
65—	218,604	21,435	98·05
Total	7,748,289	107,343	13·85

The second method of correction can in general lead to the same result as the first only if the ratio of the death rates in the occupational group and in the standard population is the same

* Deaths are taken over three years : 1900, 1901, and 1902 ; and so this is three times the mean population of 1901, the census year.

at all ages, which is seldom true. In practice the former method is the more important in industrial comparisons, although it may happen that the second plan is to be preferred when the total number of deaths in the occupation is small.

TABLE 4.—*Occupied Males in Agricultural Districts.*

Age group.	Years of life.	Deaths.	Death rate per 1,000.
15—20	661,260	1,290	1·95
20—25	525,798	2,213	4·21
25—35	893,781	4,614	5·16
35—45	784,014	5,619	7·17
45—55	610,221	7,158	11·73
55—65	447,492	10,083	22·53
65—	313,359	26,661	85·08
Total	4,235,925	57,638	13·61

TABLE 5.—*All Males.*

Age group.	Years of life.	Deaths.	Death rate per 1,000.
15—20	4,822,566	16,833	3·49
20—25	4,417,932	21,084	4·77
25—35	7,457,862	47,608	6·38
35—45	5,795,829	63,406	10·94
45—55	4,188,627	78,196	18·67
55—65	2,723,835	94,799	34·80
65—	1,983,216	187,641	94·61
Total	31,389,867	509,567	16·23

Some writers have asserted or implied that it is a matter of indifference what standard population is chosen, just as it is a matter of indifference whether a foot-rule is made of one wood or another; this is not true. When we compare the mortalities of two occupations, the ratio of their standardised mortalities is, say, A/B if a standard population, X, say, is used; when another standard, Y, is used, the ratio becomes A′/B′, which need not be equal to A/B. We shall not discuss the algebraical theory of the matter, but proceed to give a few illustrations.

TABLE 6.—*Deaths at Ages which would have occurred in the Population of Table 5 had the Death Rates of Tables 3 and 4 applied.*

Age groups.	Deaths at industrial rate.	Deaths at agricultural rates.
15—20	12,779·8 ·	9,404·0
20—25	19,969·1	18,599·5
25—35	48,252·4	38,482·6
35—45	71,056·9	41,556·1
45—55	92,652·4	49,132·6
55—65	106,719·9	61,368·0
65—	194,454·3	168,732·0
Totals	545,884·8	387,274·8

Standardised rates per 1,000
$$\frac{1,000 \times 545,884\cdot8}{31,389,867} = 17\cdot39 ; \quad \frac{1,000 \times 387,274\cdot8}{31,389,867} = 12\cdot34$$

TABLE 7.—*Deaths at Ages which would have occurred in the Populations of Tables 3 and 4 had the Death Rates of Table 5 applied to them.*

Age groups.	Industrial districts.	Agricultural districts.
15—20	4,142·8	2,307·8
20—25	5,673·2	2,508·1
25—35	12,851·2	5,702·3
35—45	16,536·3	8,577·1
45—55	19,631·2	11,392·8
55—65	20,043·1	15,572·7
65—	20,682·1	29,646·9
Totals	99,559·9	75,707·7

Computed crude potential rates per 1,000
$$\frac{1,000 \times 99,559\cdot9}{7,748,289} = 12\cdot85 ; \quad \frac{1,000 \times 75,707\cdot7}{4,235,925} = 17\cdot87$$

Correction or standardising factors
$$\frac{16\cdot23}{12\cdot85} = 1\cdot263 ; \quad \frac{16\cdot23}{17\cdot87} = \cdot908$$

Standardised mortality (death) rate
$$13\cdot85 \times 1\cdot263 = 17\cdot49 ; \quad 13\ 61 \times \cdot908 = 12\cdot36$$

We will standardise the mortality of males in industrial and males in agricultural districts as recorded by the Registrar-General. The data are set out in Tables 3 and 4. Let us first take as the standard the age distribution of all males, which was as shown in Table 5. Applying the industrial and agricultural death rates at ages to the age groups of the standard, we have the following Table 6, which gives the standard mortality by this method. Passing to the second method, we apply the death rates at different ages in the standard population (tables) to the ages of the two groupings, and we reach the results contained in Table 7. The standardised rates obtained by the second method are not identical with those of the first ; the explanation is that the death rates at ages in the two populations compared do not bear the same proportion to the corresponding rate in the standard population at all ages.

In order to see the effect of adopting a different standard population we will employ an age distribution which would occur if the male population were stationary, the birth equal to the death rate, the latter approximately that of 1911. Table 8 shows the resulting age distribution. Using this as the standard, we obtain the results shown in Table 9.

TABLE 8.—*Age Distribution of a Life Table Population.*

Age group.	Years of life.
15—20	4,002,561
20—25	3,938,451
25—35	7,634,512
35—45	7,184,870
45—55	6,460,430
55—65	5,259,578
65—	5,000,003
Total	39,480,405

TABLE 9.—*Results of Methods of Standardisation when the Standard Age Distribution is that of Table 8.*

	Industrial districts.	Agricultural districts.
Standardised rates by method of Table 6	25·46	18·62
Standardising factors.	$*\frac{23·77}{12·85}=1·85$	$\frac{23·77}{17·87}=1·33$
Standardised rates by second method	25·62	18·10

Although the age distribution of the second standard differs very much from that of the first, as exemplified by the vast

* This is obtained by applying the death rates at ages of Table 5 to the populations at ages of Table 8 and dividing by the whole population of Table 8.

differences between the standardised rates in the two workings, yet the ratios of the two standardised rates are not seriously divergent. Using all males as the standard, the industrial district mortality is 140·9 of the agricultural district rate, an excess of 41 per cent. ; when the life table population is used the excess is reduced to 37 per cent., not a very important change (see Table 10). The reason is that, although the weights assigned to different age groups are considerably changed, the weight of no one group is very small (12).

TABLE 10.—*Percentage Ratios of the Standardised Death Rates using different Standards.*

Percentage ratio of industrial to agricultural district rates.

Standard—All males .	{ Method 1 ..	140·9
	{ Method 2 ..	141·5
Standard—Life table .	{ Method 1 ..	136·7
	{ Method 2 ..	141·5

VI. Probable Error.

A difficulty of another kind arises when the numbers of deaths and lives at risk in the various age groups of the occupation studied are small. This difficulty is of course not peculiar to the use of mortality rates, but common to all statistical averages, and merely expresses the fact that the smaller the experience the less reliable the conclusions deducible from it.

The practice of statisticians is to attach to averages computed from samples a quantity termed the probable error, it being suggested that variations within the limits of two or three times the probable error do not need any special explanation, but may be attributed to " chance " or to " errors of random sampling." The method of calculating these criteria of reliability of course depends upon the form of the average it is desired to test ; to give technical details would involve the incorporation of matter which properly belongs to a text-book of statistical method.

A test which is usually sufficient is to calculate :—

$$S\left\{\frac{d'_s}{a'_s} - \frac{d_s}{a_s}\right\} \frac{A_s}{A} \qquad . \qquad . \qquad . \qquad . \qquad (1)$$

and

$$S\left\{p_s\, q_s\left(\frac{1}{a_s} + \frac{1}{a'_s}\right)\frac{A^2_s}{A^2}\right\} \qquad . \qquad . \qquad . \qquad (2)$$

Here A_s is the population aged s in the standard, A,
p_s the standard death rate (not per 1,000, but per unit) at
age s $(q_s = 1 - p_s)$,
$\left. \begin{array}{l} a_s \text{ and } d_s \\ a'_s \text{ and } d'_s \end{array} \right\}$ = numbers living and dying,
at age s in the contrasted groups.

If (1) is more than three or four times as large as the square root of (2), it is unlikely that the divergence of the two series is due to errors of sampling.

Tables 11 and 12 illustrate the method upon a couple of tables in the Registrar-General's abstract of industrial mortality statistics.

The test we have employed is the simplest available method, and is an imperfect one, because any attempt to summarise the meaning of a complex table in a single arithmetical average must fail; to pursue the matter further would involve a discussion of technicalities out of place in a book such as this, and the reader is advised to consult the paper by Pearson and Tocher cited at the end of the chapter (6).

VII. Reliability of Data.

No statistical tests of the kind we are now discussing can in any way guarantee the material accuracy of the data. It is quite true that any arithmetical differences which do not satisfy the tests cannot be used as a basis for reasoning; but it is not true that to survive the arithmetical *peine forte et dure* is all that is needful before inferences are safe. The application of an arithmetical test presupposes that the aggregates tested are *in pari materia*, that, for example, the material accuracy of the statements of age, of the occupational descriptions, and of the separation into employed and retired, is the same in Lancashire on the one hand and in Northumberland and Durham upon the other. Before elaborate arithmetical calculations are made, the student is advised to test such points as these. The caution is especially needed when a comparison is made between the death rates in occupations for different years and particular diseases. The death rate of some disease may be found to have varied in a manner which is arithmetically significant; that is to say, the difference is so great that, taking into consideration the numbers recorded, it could not plausibly be supposed to have arisen by chance. But the inference that the disease has increased (or diminished) may be wide of the mark. The explanation may be either that a change of classification has been made or that the fashion of diagnosis has varied.

TABLE 11.

(From Supplement to Sixty-fifth Annual Report of the Registrar-General.)

(a)

Age group.	Years of life.		Deaths.	
	Durham and Northumberland coal miners.	Lancashire coal miners.	Durham and Northumberland coal Miners.	Lancashire coal miners.
15—20 . .	64,560	39,447	203	144
20—25 . .	59,373	42,561	290	207
25—35 . .	101,934	70,590	463	424
35—45 . .	72,477	50,298	490	454
45—55 . .	49,314	32,970	680	575
55—65 . .	26,496	13,440	838	570
65— . .	7,014	2,745	1,090	375

(b)

DEATH RATES PER 1,000.

Ages.	15—20.	20—25.	25—35.	35—45.	45—55.	55—65.	65—
All coal miners . .	3·20	4·47	4·93	7·65	14·67	35·98	139·82
Durham and Northumberland coal miners.	3·14	4·88	4·54	6·76	13·79	31·63	155·40
Lancashire coal miners	3·65	4·86	6·01	9·03	17·44	42·41	136·61

TABLE 12.—*Comparison of Mortality Rates in Two Groups of Coal Miners.*

Age group.	$\dfrac{d_s}{a_s} - \dfrac{d'_s}{a'_s}$	$\dfrac{A_s}{A}$	$p_s q_s$	$\left(\dfrac{d_s}{a_s} - \dfrac{d'_s}{a'_s}\right)\dfrac{A_s}{A}$	$\left(\dfrac{A_s}{A}\right)^2$	$\dfrac{1}{a_s} + \dfrac{1}{a'_s}$	$p_s q_s \left(\dfrac{1}{a^s} + \dfrac{1}{a'_s}\right)\left(\dfrac{A_s}{A}\right)^2$
15—20	− ·00051	·16835	·003190	− ·00008586	·0283417	·0000408	·0000000037
20—25	+ ·00002	·16492	·004450	+ ·00000330	·0271986	·0000403	·0000000049
25—35	− ·00147	·27944	·004906	− ·00041078	·0780867	·0000240	·0000000092
35—45	− ·00227	·18922	·007591	− ·00042953	·0358042	·0000337	·0000000092
45—55	− ·00365	·12287	·014455	− ·00044848	·0150970	·0000506	·0000000110
55—65	− ·01078	·05878	·034685	− ·00063365	·0034551	·0001121	·0000000134 ·
65—	+ ·01879	·01641	·120270	+ ·00030834	·0002693	·0005069	·0000000164
Totals	—	—	—	− ·00169666	—	—	·0000000678

Explanation.—The second column gives the differences between corresponding entries in the second and third lines of Table 11 (b) divided by 1,000. The third column gives the proportion living in each age group of all occupied coal miners (used as the " standard " population). The fourth column contains the products of each entry in the first line of Table 11 (b), divided by 1,000, and unity less this quantity; e.g., at age fifteen to twenty we have ·00320 × ·99680 = ·0031898. The fifth and sixth columns are self-explanatory. The seventh column gives the sums of the reciprocals of corresponding entries in the second and third columns of Table 11 (a). The square root of the sum of entries in column 8 is ·0002604, and the sum of entries in column 5 is − ·0016966. The ratio of the latter to the former is − 6·52 ; hence it is very unlikely that the system of differences has arisen by chance, or, in other words, that the mortality of Durham and Northumberland coal miners is really identical with that of coal miners in Lancashire. This case has only been chosen to illustrate the arithmetic.

Many statisticians explained in this way the rapid increase of the recorded mortality from cancer in England and Wales, and although, in this particular instance, it is now certain that nothing like the whole of the increase can be so explained, the principle involved is an important one, especially so to the student of industrial hygiene.

VIII.   Proportionate Mortality.

Lastly, we have to consider what information can be derived from statistics of deaths at ages when the number and ages of the living are unknown. The question is, Given a knowledge of the total deaths occurring between certain age limits and the number of such deaths attributed to a single disease for each of a series of groups, how far do fluctuations of the ratio of deaths due to the specified disease to all deaths at that age, or, if we prefer it, the ratio of deaths from the specified disease to all other deaths at that age, measure fluctuations of incidence of the disease in question ? Such measure is known as the proportionate mortality, and is usually expressed as a percentage.

The importance of this question arises from the fact that it is much easier to obtain a record of a reasonably large number of deaths amongst persons known to have followed a specified occupation than to secure in addition a census at ages of the persons among whom these deaths have occurred. For example, the records of 500 deaths of stone masons in Manchester might be collected over a period of twenty to thirty years ; but not even an approximate estimate could be made of the number and ages of stone masons employed, some perhaps only for a few months, in Manchester during that period.

The proportionate mortality rate of a disease (*i.e.*, the ratio of deaths from that disease to all deaths at the age) cannot of course give us as reliable information as the actual death toll, since we have one less datum. It might happen, for instance, that the proportionate mortalities from a given disease in two industries were identical although the incidence of the disease was much heavier upon one of the occupations than upon the other ; thus, if the death rates from the disease and also the death rates from all other diseases were in the ratio of two to one, the proportionate mortality rates would be equal. But the essence of statistical reasoning is to determine whether a theoretical objection unequivocally sound does really specify practically important difficulties. In this instance we have to learn whether in practice the inference from a high proportionate mortality rate that the real incidence rate of the disease is high is justified.

The point has been tested in two ways. One of us found (10) that in a series of the Registrar-General's occupational groups the proportionate mortality from bronchitis varied with the actual mortality rate ; when one exceeded the average the other did too.

Tebb and one of us (11) investigated the problem in a slightly different way. To make this intelligible a further explanation of statistical terms is necessary. When we have two variable quantities their tendency to vary together is measured by calculating an average called the coefficient of correlation, which takes the value 0 when the two variables are independent one of another, and the value ± 1 when they are inseparably connected ; when the correlation is + 1, the two increase absolutely *pari passu ;* when it is − 1, the increase of one is inseparably connected with the decrease of the other. Any intermediate value of the correlation implies an intermediate degree of association ; when the correlation is ascertained, the probable value of one variable for a given value of the other can be predicted with an accuracy increasing with the size of the coefficient of correlation.

Using this method, it was found that the correlation at ages thirty-five to forty-five between the proportionate mortality from phthisis and the death rate from phthisis in the Registrar-General's occupational groups (mortality experience of 1900–2) (7) was as much as ·754 ± ·04. Applying the method to the mortality experience of 168 large registration districts (populations of each more than 50,000), the correlation proved to be ·629 ± ·03 (deaths at ages thirty-five to forty-five from phthisis in 1890—1900) ; applying the resulting equation connecting the proportionate mortality with the death rate to the prediction of death rate from proportionate mortality, it appeared that, from a knowledge of the proportionate mortality within a group of districts, the *average* true mortality could be inferred with fair accuracy, although individual predictions might be much in excess or defect of the truth.

Proportionate mortality rates may of course be corrected or standardised. In Table 13 we give for a series of occupations the proportionate mortality from phthisis, *i.e.*, the percentage of deaths from all causes due to phthisis. To admit of comparison without disturbance due to age differences, we may proceed as follows. In Table 14 are shown the deaths from all causes at certain ages in the whole population of occupied and retired males ; we apply to these the percentages of Table 13, and thus obtain the appropriate entries in Table 15, which are the numbers of deaths from phthisis which would have been observed in the whole population of occupied and retired males had the percentages of the Table 13 held.   If we now express the entries of Table 15 as percentages of the first entry in that table we reach the figures given in the last column of Table 16.   The column in that table headed " True " is deduced from the Registrar-General's comparative mortality figures (we have expressed the others as a percentage of the figure for all occupied and retired males, which, in the Registrar-General's notation, is not 100 but 187).

TABLE 13.—*Proportionate Mortality from Phthisis in Certain Occupations. (From the Registrar-General's Statistics, 1900–2.)*

Age group.	Butchers.	Cotton manufacturers.	Tailors.	Shoemakers.
25—35 . .	33·1	36·5	45·6	49·4
35—45 . .	24.3	30·0	38·3	42·5
45—55 . .	13·8	17·7	21·1	24·0
55—65 . .	5·4	6·5	9·1	9·4

TABLE 14.—*Deaths from all Causes at certain Ages of all Occupied and Retired Males.*

Age group.	Deaths.
25—35	46,293
35—45	62,116
45—55	76,841
55—65	93,217
Total deaths .	278,467

TABLE 15.—*Deaths from Phthisis at Age Groups 25—65.*

A.   52,077 . Actually recorded for all occupied and retired males.
B.   46,055 . " Expected " from butchers' proportionate mortality.
C.   55,192 . " Expected " from cotton manufacturers' proportionate mortality.
D.   69,596 . " Expected " from tailors' proportionate mortality.
E.   76,472 . " Expected " from shoemakers' proportionate mortality.

TABLE 16.—*Comparative Mortality Figures for Phthisis.*

	True.	From pro-portion.
All occupied and retired . . .	100	100
Butchers	97	88
Cotton manufacturers . . .	105	106
Tailors	132	134
Shoemakers	145	147

The index number based upon proportionate mortality in three cases agrees closely with that deduced from a knowledge of both deaths and exposed to risk ; in the fourth case the discrepancy is considerable. The reason is that the death rate from all causes among butchers is higher than that of all occupied and retired males, but the death rate from phthisis is lower and the fallacy mentioned above is involved. Even in this case—a very unfavourable one, because the comparative general mortality figure of butchers is larger than that of any of the groups here compared and the comparative phthisis mortality figure lower— the inference suggested by the proportionate mortality index is not very misleading.

We could also proceed by taking all occupied and retired males as the standard population as regards age distribution of deaths, and stating the proportionate mortality of this population from phthisis for age groups twenty-five to sixty-five to be $\dfrac{52,077 \times 100}{278,467}$ = 18·7 ; the standardised proportionate mortality for butchers would then be $\dfrac{46,055 \times 100}{278,467}$ = 16·5 ; for cotton manufacturers 19·8 ; for tailors 24·9 ; and for shoemakers 27·1..

The practical inference is that although, as we should have expected, a proportionate mortality index is not just as good, not nearly as good, as a true death rate, yet if we infer from a high proportionate mortality the existence of a high absolute death rate we shall usually be correct, almost always correct if the proportionate mortality rate is much in excess of its average value.

The test of proportionate mortality we have here employed is, however, an unduly severe one ; it tacitly assumes that the material accuracies of both proportionate mortality and actual death rate data are on a par. But, as the estimates of population at ages exposed to risk are necessarily less accurate than the enumeration of deaths at ages, on account of migration from occupation to occupation or from district to district, the real correlation between the two variables may be appreciably higher than these tests show; this could only be determined if we had entirely unimpeachable records of deaths and populations; the nearest approximation to such records would be provided by the data of life offices, and it is to be hoped that they will be scrutinised one day from that point of view.

We must add that a comparison of proportionate mortalities— or, indeed, of death rates—in occupations may be quite fallacious if the nosological attributions vary. If, for instance, current medical opinion inclines to regard particular occupations as involving special risk of specific diseases, doubtful illnesses occurring in those who follow the particular occupations may be assigned to the favourite disease (just as when some epidemic prevails other diseases are certified to be the reigning malady).

Our experience leads us to think that this source of error may be important when the analysis of small collections of data is in question, or when the returns come from an area mainly occupied by workers in a particular industry, but that it is not a serious cause of embarrassment when the returns are derived from the certificates of a large number of practitioners scattered over such a country as England and Wales.

IX. Morbidity.

In the foregoing remarks we have spoken exclusively of mortality rates, but it will be obvious that the same principles apply to the utilisation of morbidity rates, absolute or proportionate, crude or age-standardised (of course the method of age standardisation can be extended to sex standardisation); the utilisable data are not, however, numerous enough to merit extended discussion in this chapter. The whole of the data have recently been collected and discussed by Mr. E. A. Rusher, F.I.A., of the Industrial Fatigue Research Board, in a report which should be carefully studied by all readers of this book. Mr. Rusher shows that differences of method and great changes in the nature of the " population exposed to risk " make it very difficult to compare the morbidity experiences of working class populations now and seventy years ago. We shall return to this point in the next chapter.

In conclusion, we would impress upon the reader the importance of acquiring a sound knowledge of elementary statistical methods. Some branches of statistical analysis involve an acquaintance with mathematical technic which cannot readily be acquired by those engaged in administrative or clinical work, the fate of most to whom this book is likely to appeal ; but a grasp of general principles and, indeed, of much technical detail is no harder to acquire than the knowledge of special branches of medicine which is an obligatory possession of candidates for all the more important posts in the preventive medical service. We do not know any book we would rather see in the hands of the student of industrial hygiene than an elementary work upon statistical methods, and we regret that more emphasis is not put upon the subject in the curriculum of medical students.

X. Bibliography.

1. Yule, G. Udny. *An Introduction to the Theory of Statistics.* 5th Edition. London. 1919. (By far the best text-book in existence.)

2. *Supplement to Seventy-fifth Annual Report of the Registrar-General.* (Cd. 7512.) 1914. (This is Mr. King's report on the English life tables, and contains full details of the method used.)

3. Elderton and Fippard. *Construction of Mortality and Sickness Tables.* London. 1914.

4. Fisher, Arne. " Note on the Construction of Mortality Tables." *Proc. Casualty Actuarial and Stat. Soc. of America.* IV. Part I. 1917.

5. Henderson, R. *Mortality Laws and Statistics.* London and New York. 1915.

6. Pearson, K., and Tocher, J. F. " On Criteria for the Existence of Differential Death Rates." *Biometrika,* XI., p. 159. 1916. (This paper discusses the methods of measuring errors of sampling in the case of death rates.)

7. The most important English collections of data are contained in the decennial supplements of the annual reports issued by the Registrar-General ; the last published appeared in 1908. (Cd. 2619.)

8. *The Collected Writings of Dr. William Farr,* p. 458. Edited by Noel Humphreys. London. 1885.

9. Prinzing, F. *Handbuch der Medizinischen Statistik.* Jena. 1906. (Contains a useful collection of material.)

10. Collis, E. L. *Industrial Pneumonoconioses.* Milroy Lectures, 1915. H.M. Stationery Office. 1919.

11. Greenwood, M., and Tebb, A. E. " An Inquiry into the Prevalence and Ætiology of Tuberculosis among Industrial Workers." *Medical Research Committee. Special Report Series, No.* 22. 1919.

12. *Report of Registrar-General for England and Wales for* 1917, p. lxix.

13. Rusher, E. A. " Historical Memorandum on Standard Sickness Tables in the United Kingdom." *Reports of the Industrial Fatigue Research Board.* Stationery Office. 1920.

CHAPTER IV

THE EFFECTS OF INDUSTRIAL EMPLOYMENT UPON HEALTH AS INDICATED BY VITAL STATISTICS

I. Pioneer Work. II. Returns of Friendly Societies. III. Manchester Unity Investigation. IV. Index of Trade Mortality. V. Difficulties of estimating Effect of Occupation on Mortality. VI. Result of using Brownlee's Method. VII. Relation between Industrial Mortality and Social Unrest. VIII. Morbidity. IX. Bibliography.

I. Pioneer Work.

THE classical work upon industrial hygiene, that of Ramazzini (1), contains no statistics, while the numerical data at the disposal of our English pioneer, Thackrah (2), were very scanty, but in the early years of Victoria's reign the establishment of the General Register Office and the activities of the Statistical Society (founded in 1834) led to the production of a long series of official reports and private researches which throw light upon the subject of this chapter. In those times much greater stress was put upon the evils of defective sanitation in the popular sense than upon special factors of industrial life in causing the heavy mortality which characterised then and, *mutatis mutandis*, still characterises industrial cities. The late Edwin Chadwick* contributed much to influence the public in this direction (3); and although his choice of statistical methods was sometimes unfortunate (13), the general value of his researches was incontestable.

II. Returns of Friendly Societies.

The first statistical writer to challenge the doctrine that sanitation was the paramount factor in determining rates of mortality and morbidity was Neison, who contributed an important paper to the *Journal of the Statistical Society* in 1845, subsequently expanded into a volume, which reached a third edition in 1857 (4). Neison's principal data were derived from the sickness and mortality returns of the British friendly societies for the quinquennium 1836—40. He found that the expectation of life of males who were members of friendly societies was greatest in the rural districts, less in the small towns, and least in the great cities, a result which Chadwick

---

* Another influential writer was Guy (15), who, like Thackrah, had had the advantage of medical training and was also an enthusiastic statistician.

would naturally have attributed to the sanitary conditions of the cities.   But Neison discovered that the difference between the expectations of life of different trades was much larger than that between the averages of all residents in different geographical areas.   For instance, at age twenty the expectation of life of males in rural districts was 45·36 years, in towns 42·27 years, and in cities 40·01 years, falling to as little as 37·96 years in Liverpool.   But clerks in all districts had an expectation of life at twenty of only 31·83 years, plumbers and painters 36·9 years, bakers 40·03 years, miners 40·67 years.   Neison also found that labourers in rural districts enjoyed an expectation of life at age twenty of 47·91 years, other male inhabitants of rural districts of 43·83 years, and the members of sixteen not very nearly related trades in rural districts 43·89 years.   In effect, leaving out of account Liverpool, the difference between the labourers and the otherwise occupied persons in rural districts was as great as between rural and city districts as wholes.   But since the cities for economic reasons necessarily employed a larger percentage of their males in the unhealthy trades than did the rural districts, Neison concluded that the comparison over-rated the importance of geographical factors and reached the following general conclusion :—

" It is evident from all that has been said that the peculiar sanitary condition of large towns has not the remarkable effect which many have supposed in shortening the duration of life ; still it has some effect, and the nature and extent of that influence it is important to understand.   But a rude estimate only can be made until the value of life in every important employment, occupation or trade has been investigated, for the various localities or districts, on some such plan as that given in the present paper ; and then, grouping or classifying a given number of those common to different localities, the result arrived at would show the precise amount of influence which a particular district, city or town has on the duration of life.   A partial or limited comparison of a few trades would not be adequate to answer definitely this question.   But an accurate combination of a sufficiently large number of trades would be necessary to guard against the effect of fluctuation."

Finlaison's analysis (5) of friendly society experience over a period precisely ten years later than that of Neison's research was not so complete.   Expectations of life were not published, and only for members of the friendly societies who were resident in the metropolitan province are the data so presented that expectations can be readily computed.   In that instance the expectation of life at age twenty is found not to differ sensibly from the result reached by Neison from the aggregate experience of city members (Neison's figure was 40·01 years; we deduce from Finlaison's table 39·7 years).

III. Manchester Unity Investigation.

No attempt to carry out the large scale comparison recommended by Neison seems to have been made until Mr. (now Sir) Alfred Watson investigated the sickness and mortality experience of the I.O.O.F., Manchester Unity, over the quinquennium 1893—97. The results of Watson's analysis (6) led him to express a conclusion which reverses the order of importance assigned by Neison sixty years earlier to the several factors of mortality. Neison found that both geographical situation and occupation influenced mortality, the latter more than the former; Watson was led to put more emphasis upon the geographical

TABLE 1.

Area.	Ages.	Percentage of actual to expected deaths.	
		Group A.	Group H.
1 . .	16—44	49	61
	45—64	63	81
	65—	81	94
2 . .	16—44	61	71
	45—64	74	107
	65—	103	124
3 . .	16—44	47	65
	45—64	75	86
	65—	100	107

TABLE 2.

Ages.	Percentage of actual to expected deaths.			
	Group A.H.J.	Group B.C.D.	Group E.F.	Group G.
16—44 .	64	73	72	70
45—64 .	88	95	95	108
65— .	104	106	123	134

TABLE 3.

Ages.	Percentage of actual to expected deaths.			
	Area 1.	Area 2.	Area 3.	Whole society.
16—44 .	61	68	75	66
45—64 .	79	92	112	90
65— .	91	109	128	105

than upon the occupational factor. The experience was tabulated into three areas. No. 1 covered mainly non-manufacturing districts, No. 2 textile districts, No. 3 other manufacturing, coal and metal-working, metropolitan districts.

The occupational groups were :—A. Agriculture. B. Outdoor building trades, including masons, stoneworkers, dock labourers, canal banksmen, bargemen and unskilled labourers employed out of doors. C. Covered the railway services. D. Seafaring, fishing, etc. E. Quarry workers. F. Iron and steel workers. G. Mining occupations, chiefly underground, but including some on the pit brow. Groups H. (rural) and J. (urban) comprised the general body of the society's experience exclusive of the special groups just described. The results are shown in Tables 1—3. The conclusion drawn was that " on a broad view of the facts, therefore, it appears that as between the two elements of geographical situation and occupation the former should chiefly be considered in the formation of monetary tables depending on mortality, and for the construction of the life tables the geographical distribution of the data has been adopted accordingly."

In Table 4 we quote the expectation of life at age twenty, as shown by Watson's analysis into geographical units. It will be seen that the greatest expectation is shown for the combined rural and urban experience of the non-manufacturing districts, the least by the urban experience of the textile districts, a difference of more than four years. The *primâ facie* inference from these researches is that the improvements introduced into the manufacturing arts and the sanitary measures enforced by the Legislature have had a relatively greater effect upon the hygiene of industry in the workplace than the improvements in housing and town planning within industrial areas have had in reducing the difference between the best and worst environmental home conditions. While we do not think the reader

TABLE 4.

		Expectations of life at age twenty (males) (Manchester Unity).
Area 1.	Rural	45·654
Area 1.	Urban	44·398
Area 1.	Urban and rural . .	45·324
Area 2.	Rural	42·734
Area 2.	Urban	41·138
Area 2.	Urban and rural . .	41·648
Area 3.	Rural	44·349
Area 3.	Urban	42·889
Area 3.	Urban and rural . .	43·507

(The expectation at this age by English Life Table for 1901 — 10 is 43·01 years; for 1838—54, 39·45; 1871—80, 39·40; 1881—90, 40·2; 1891—1900, 41·02.)

need accept the *primâ facie* inference as definitely established, there is no doubt that the workroom conditions described in evidence before the Commission of 1842 are rare exceptions in any industries and non-existent in inspected industries of our own generation. On the other hand, the evidence furnished by such inquiries as those of Booth (7) and Rowntree (8), or given in papers such as Wanklyn's (9), demonstrates that a not inconsiderable percentage of the working classes is still housed in conditions of squalor which, if an improvement, are not a very great improvement upon the generality of the dwellings described fifty years ago. It is necessary to remember that we are now concerned with relative mortality, not morbidity. There is hardly any doubt that in all trades and districts the absolute mortality has declined in the last sixty years.

TABLE 5.—*Expectations of Life (Males) at Age Twenty, Eighty Years ago.*

Source of dates.		Expectation.
All England, 1838—41		40·69
Friendly societies, 1836—40.	Rural .	45·36
,, ,, ,,	Towns .	42·27
,, ,, ,,	Cities .	40·01
,, ,, ,,	Liverpool .	37·96

It is true that the expectations of life at age twenty which we have just quoted from Watson's report do not differ much from the figures of Neison (see Table 5), but it is probable, indeed certain, that the friendly society members at the end of the nineteenth century were more nearly a random sample of the working classes at that epoch than were the members of seventy years ago, when the money earnings of hand labourers were almost at their nadir, and the possibility of maintaining weekly contributions (and therefore coming within the actuarial " experience ") restricted. Death rates have declined of recent years in friendly society experience, and at the foot of Table 4 we give figures indicating some increase in the expectation of life for all inhabitants of the kingdom.

IV. Index of Trade Mortality.

A fair measure or index of the hygienic status of a trade or district is, we think, the relation its death rate bears to the best standard of the country. (A still better measure would, as we pointed out in the previous chapter, be afforded by occupational or local life tables, but this is not applicable yet.) Thus the three last decennial valuations of the mortality rates prevailing in various occupations (1890–2, 1900–2, 1910—12) show that the standardised mortality rates of coal miners were 1,068, 846, 727 ; of bricklayers, 1,157, 862, 662 ; of shoemakers, 1,064, 901, 820. In each case the decline is very large. But if we express each mortality index as a percentage of the mortality experienced by the clergy in the corresponding decennium, we find that relatively to clergy the coal miners did not improve at all between 1900–2 and 1912, the percentage being in each period 164 ; bricklayers, etc., improved through the series from 188 to 167 and then to 149 ; shoemakers relatively deteriorated from 173 to 175 and then to 185 in the most recent data. Without desiring to emphasise these figures too much— we shall shortly point out the serious criticisms to which they are subject—we cannot doubt that the satisfaction afforded by the absolute fall in mortality of all three occupations should be tempered by the thought that one of them bears a less favourable relation to the best attained standard of its contemporaries and one a not more favourable relation than obtained ten years earlier. We have above given prominence to the information regarding occupational mortality derived from actuarial researches, and we regret that more is not available, because inferences from death rates, however standardised, are less secure than those sanctioned by the fuller view of the facts afforded by a life table.

V. Difficulties of estimating Effect of Occupation on Mortality.

The official statistics of occupational mortality are, however, presented in the form of death rates, the method adopted being briefly as follows : The age constitution of a series of occupational groups is obtained from the decennial census, and the registered deaths for the three years centring in the census year are then tabulated by ages, rates of mortality being formed for age groups.   To admit of comparison a standardised mortality figure is computed by the method explained in the previous chapter.   The standard population used in the last three decennial analyses, viz., those of 1890–2, 1900–2, 1910—12, was so constituted that had the death rates for all males, 1900–2, been applied to it, 1,000 deaths would have resulted.   This standard has certain advantages, inasmuch as one sees at a glance whether the mortality index of a group is greater or less than that experienced by all males twenty years ago ; it is subject to all the criticisms applicable to standardised rates in general.   A special difficulty of interpreting occupational rates is that the exposed to risk in different age groups are not necessarily or even probably *in pari materia*.   This objection is of course applicable to other tables of death rates at ages.   Thus in a city, the living and exposed to risk at ages twenty to twenty-five will contain a considerable proportion of youths who emigrated from the country in search of employment ; in the rural districts, males at ages over sixty will contain a proportion of those who have left the cities ; all the corrected death rate tells us is the force of mortality (weighted by the choice of standard) upon contemporaneously existing lives ; how far this measures the effect of the immediate environment, how much credit should be assigned to the effect of upbringing elsewhere, we do not know.   This difficulty is still more serious when the grouping is not by geographical, but by occupational, units, since the weeding out of the unfit, the current application of the phrase " too old at forty," must affect certain occupations very much, and all to some extent.   No method is available for circumventing this difficulty ; it could only be completely overcome if the life histories of all citizens were recorded and changes in their occupations returned to the General Register Office with the same completeness as obtains respecting the notifications of their entry to and exit from the stage of life.

TABLE 6.—*Registrar-General's Returns* (14), *Comparative Mortality Figures.*

	1890–2.	1900–2.	1910—12.
Clergy	615 (100)	515 (100)	443 (100)
(a) Agricultural labourers .	731 (119)	572 (111)	470 (106)
(b) Commercial clerks . .	1,056 (172)	837 (163)	802 (181)
(c) Coal miners . . .	1,068 (174)	846 (164)	727 (164)
(d) Bricklayers, etc. . .	1,157 (188)	862 (167)	662 (149)
(e) Saddlers and harness-makers	1,069 (174)	889 (173)	736 (166)
(f) Cotton manufacturers .	1,318 (214)	1,037 (201)	811 (183)
Wool and worsted . .	1,146 (186)	927 (180)	802 (151)
Silk	1,064 (173)	892 (173)	717 (162)
Hosiery	808 (131)	853 (166)	736 (166)
Lace	819 (133)	831 (161)	771 (174)
Carpets	1,010 (164)	942 (183)	643 (145)
(g) Tinplate goods . .	1,148 (187)	974 (189)	673 (152)
Chemical . . .	1,609 (262)	1,031 (200)	653 (147)
Paper	1,043 (170)	654 (133)	679 (153)
(h) Shoemakers . . .	1,064 (173)	901 (175)	820 (188)
Tailors	1,144 (186)	953 (188)	799 (180)
Cabinet-makers . .	1,131 (184)	888 (172)	793 (179)
(i) Printers . . .	1,267 (206)	935 (182)	773 (174)
Bookbinders . . .	1,225 (199)	889 (173)	791 (179)

In Table 6 we reproduce the comparative mortality figures of a series of representative groups of the male population; the figures in brackets are the percentage ratios that each index bears to the standardised mortality of the clergy. The selection has been made upon the principle of choosing industries employing considerable numbers of men and not greatly subject to the specific risks associated with particular occupations—such, for example, as the pneumonoconioses or lead poisoning—which do not fall within the scope of a text-book of general industrial hygiene. The reader will notice how great the range of variation is within a group of allied occupations; even in the most recent experience the worst occupation in group (f) is 38 per cent. of the standard worse than the best, nearly as great an interval as separates the best from the highest practically attainable standard of the time. The difference between the mortality of agricultural labourers, hardly inferior to the standard, and that of the employees in trades the real remunerations of which greatly exceed those of agricultural labourers, is immense.

VI. Result of using Brownlee's Method.

Although it is not possible to construct from the occupational statistics a complete life table, one of the life table constants can be deduced with fair accuracy. Brownlee has shown (10) that the reciprocal of the expectation of life at any age is connected with the standardised death rate at that and higher ages by a linear relation. Brownlee's formulæ reproduce the expectations of life with considerable success. Thus we applied his method to determine the expectation of life at age twenty from the crude data used for the computation of English Life Table No. 7 and obtained 43·1 years, the correct value being 43·01 years; even at age fifty-five years the difference between the approximate and true values (16·8 years approximate, 16·48 true) was of little moment. Unfortunately the Registrar-General does not subdivide the deaths in occupations for ages beyond sixty-five, which prevents the immediate application of Brownlee's formula; we have therefore assumed that for ages older than sixty-five occupied males in 1900–2 died at the same rate as all males in England and Wales. With this assumption, the expectations of life at twenty for a number of occupations have been calculated and are shown in Table 7.

TABLE 7.—*Expectations of Life at Age Twenty* (*approximate*) *based on Mortality of* 1900–2.

Clergy.	47·1
Agricultural labourers . .	46·2
Clerks	43·3
Coal miners	43·2
Cotton manufacturers . .	41·4
Carpet „ . .	42·2
Shoemakers. . . .	42·6
Tailors	42·3
Printers	42·1

This table underestimates the difference between the best and worst groups because it is probable that the death rate continues to be differential after age sixty-five, although the rates must tend to converge at the older ages. Hence the difference of nearly five years between the farm labourers and the cotton operatives in no way overstates the advantage of the former class.

VII. Relation between Industrial Mortality and Social Unrest.

Mortality statistics are not merely interesting figures. They represent the end product of prodromal ill-health. Ill-health in itself is an important factor conducing to irritability and discontent. Social unrest should then be related to mortality; nor is the possibility of this relation a mere surmise, as may be gathered from the following instance :—A coal-miners' ballot was taken in August, 1920, to ascertain whether a general strike should not be declared if (i.) the price of house coal were not lowered by 14s. 6d. per ton, and (ii.) 2s. extra wages per shift were not paid. The voting on seven of the coalfields was as follows :—

TABLE 8.—*Result of Coal Miners' Ballot.*

| | | In favour of strike. | |
Coalfield.	Total vote.	Number.	Per-centage.
Yorkshire	*114,509*	*58,530*	*51·1*
Nottinghamshire . . .	30,897	17,010	55·0
Durham and Northumberland .	146,070	101,924	69·1
Derbyshire and South Derbyshire	45,793	32,921	71·9
South Wales	181,768	141,721	77·9
(Midlands)	(58,735)	(48,044)	(81·8)
Lancashire	83,379	74,832	89·7

The position, in the order stated, of the Yorkshire field is one of special interest. A strike, affecting this coalfield alone, took place in August, 1919; and the effect of the rest then taken is generally thought to have influenced the voting. The figures in the above table refer, as nearly as the data published permit, to those seven coalfields for which the Registrar-General issues separate mortality data. The next table contains these mortality data (the most recent available) arranged in order of comparative mortality. The coalfields are found approximately in the same order as the ballot placed them. Yorkshire only is notably out of place, and reason has already been given for anticipating such a displacement. The data for the Midlands in the first table, it should be noted, refer to a larger area than those for Staffordshire in the other.

TABLE 9.—*Comparative Mortality of Coal Miners from Certain Causes*, 1910–12.

Coalfield.	All causes.	Comparative mortality due to			
		Respiratory diseases.			Accidents.
		Phthisis.	Bron-chitis.	Pneu monia.	
Nottingham . . .	570 (1)	53 (1)	25 (1)	40 (2)	66 (1)
Derbyshire . . .	591 (2)	70 (2)	39 (3)	34 (1)	73 (2)
Durham and Northumber-land	635 (3)	70 (2)	33 (2)	54 (3)	83 (3)
Staffordshire . . .	(717)	(74)	(61)	(70)	(109)
Yorkshire . . .	*758*	*81*	*45*	*69*	*117*
Monmouthshire and South Wales . . .	777 (4)	70 (4)	66 (4)	69 (4)	131 (4)
Lancashire . . .	941 (5)	107 (5)	88 (5)	100 (5)	183 (5)
Occupied and retired males	790	142	38	67	—

The mortality experienced from accidents, the unusual height of which is a feature of all mining mortality statistics, is of particular interest. Any community subjected to an unduly high accident rate may be expected to suffer unduly from psycho-neuroses, just as do soldiers in war time. Practitioners in colliery districts are aware that miners suffer unduly in this way. Signs of social unrest as indicated by the ballot are correlated with the accident mortality.

Data are also given of the mortality from respiratory diseases as instances to indicate that the question does not entirely depend upon the prevalence of accidents but that general ill-health plays its part.

Probably the conditions of life on the different coalfields were but little altered between 1920 and 1910-12. A concerted effort to lower the mortality, especially from accidents, upon the fields most affected, to the level of Nottinghamshire, might be expected to do much to remove unrest.

The above instance is here given in order to stimulate interest, not only in mortality data but also in morbidity, as indicated, for instance, by lost time, a direct measure of prevailing ill-health (see Chapter V.); to support the view that the reasons given for trade disputes are incomplete; to point out that, if such data are regarded, ample time intervenes for remedying adverse conditions before a disruption occurs; and to maintain the position that industry, with such information at its disposal, cannot, in its own interests, afford to disregard it.

VIII. Morbidity.

It may surprise the reader that we have not in the course of this chapter made any mention of morbidity statistics, although the actuaries, Neison and Watson, whose writings we have extensively drawn upon, devoted a major part of their studies to this question. Sickness precedes death, and should therefore logically be discussed first. There are sufficient reasons for the plan we have adopted. Both Neison, seventy years ago, and Watson, in our own time, found that in friendly society experience little positive correlation existed between sickness and mortality rates ; in fact, the two indices might be negatively correlated. For instance, while Watson noted that geographical variations of mortality were greater than occupational variations, the reverse held for sickness. Prinzing has pointed out (11) that the same occurs in the experience of Continental State health insurance departments. From this we are not to infer that an occupation or place of residence which increases the longevity of its population also increases their days of illness. The true explanation was suggested long ago by Farr in a review of Neison's work (16, p. 505), and has been substantially repeated by Prinzing, who writes : " The causes of this inverse relation " (i.e., high sickness and low mortality in certain occupations) "are partly occupational, partly social and economic. Many trades (e.g., those of a tailor or shoemaker) can still be exercised by those slightly ill ; in others (e.g., railway service, lock and black smiths' work) it is impossible. The rate of sick-pay is also important. If it is not much less than his ordinary wages, the worker is more likely to keep the house with a slight illness. Again, the dispensability of workpeople varies much ; the factory hand can be spared most easily, while the absence of employees in small workshops, servants, waiters, business assistants, shopgirls, etc., leads to an appreciable disturbance of the business ; hence such persons even when not really fit for work are stimulated to carry on to the best of their ability " (11, p. 126). The recent investigations of Rusher support, we think, the opinions here expressed.

We have no doubt that statistical sickness, in the sense of the friendly society actuary, is an incomplete measure of the real morbidity of occupations ; and the investigation of Loveday (12) into the causes of lost time in munitions factories, the evidence he adduced that a large proportion of what figures in the records as time culpably or negligently lost was really due to sickness, confirms the opinion we express.*

* It must be noted that Loveday was not able to take account of age distribution, and that the incidence of sickness is, other things being

We believe that by improvements in the form of certificate a better statistical appreciation of the morbidity in factories can be obtained; indeed, something has been done since the war in this matter, and more remains to be accomplished. No such arrangements, however, can obliterate the distinctions between occupations; it will always be true that a degree of physical disability which incapacitates a coal miner would not be a sufficient barrier against the continuance of his work by a shoemaker. Stone-dead, says the proverb, has no fellow; to mortality statistics we shall continue to appeal in order to form accurate statistical pictures of the sanitary status of a trade or profession.

IX. Bibliography.

1. Ramazzini, B. *Treatise on Diseases of Tradesmen.* English translations. 1702 and 1746.

2. Thackrah, C. Turner. *Effects of Arts, Trades and Professions on Health and Longevity.* 2nd Edition. London. 1832.

3. Chadwick, E. *General Reports on Sanitary Condition of the Labouring Population.* London. 1842.

4. Neison. F. G. P. *Contributions to Vital Statistics.* 3rd Edition. London. 1857.

5. Finlaison, A. G. *Return on Sickness and Mortality of Friendly Societies.* London. 1853 and 1854.

6. Watson, A. W. *An Account of an Investigation of the Sickness and Mortality Experience of I.O.O.F., Manchester Unity.* Manchester. 1903.

7. Booth, C. *Life and Labour of the People.*

8. Rowntree, W. S. *Poverty : A Study of Town Life.* London. 1902.

9. Wanklyn, W. McC. " Working-class Home Conditions in London." *Proc. Epidem. Sect. Royal Soc. Med.* October, 1913.

10. Brownlee, J. " The Relationship between Corrected Death Rates and Life Table Death Rates." *Journ. Hygiene,* XIII., p. 178. 1913.

11. Prinzing, F. *Handbuch der Medizinischen Statistik.* Jena. 1906.

12. Loveday, T. " The Causes and Conditions of Lost Time." *Health of Munition Workers Committee. Interim Report.* (Cd. 8511.) 1917.

13. Chadwick, E. " On the Best Modes of representing accurately by Statistical Returns the Duration of Life, etc." *Journ. Stat. Soc.,* VII., p. 1. 1844.

14. *Registrar-General, Supplement to Sixty-fifth Annual Report of.* Part II. (Cd. 2619.)

15. Guy, W. A. " Contributions to a Knowledge of the Influence of Employment upon Health." *Journ. Stat. Soc.,* VI., p. 197, 1843 ; *ibid.,* p. 283 ; VII., p. 232, 1844.

16. Farr, W. *Collected Writings on Vital Statistics,* p. 505. Edited by Humphreys. London. 1885.

equal, a function of age. This must always be remembered in comparing occupations. Between forty-five and fifty-five as much sickness per head is experienced as in the preceding twenty years, twenty-five to forty-five.

PART II

CHAPTER V

INDUSTRIAL ACTIVITY AND FATIGUE

I. Introduction.

Activity is the cause of fatigue ; activity may be mental or physical, may be excessive or moderate ; moderate activity is followed by healthy fatigue, *i.e.*, by fatigue which entirely disappears during rest—cessation of activity ; but activity systematically pursued despite feelings of tiredness carries fatigue past the limits of perfect recovery into the regions of disordered metabolism. Sir James Paget's saying that." fatigue has a larger share in the promotion or permission of disease than any other single causal condition you can name " is probably truer for industrial employment than for any other walk of life. In industry the call for physical activity is great, and in industry is to be found a large proportion of those whose daily bread depends upon each week's earnings ; here opportunity for physical strain is, or may be, associated with mental anxiety for the immediate future. No matter in the whole field of industrial hygiene is of more fundamental importance than the occurrence of fatigue ; further, research is clearly demonstrating that in the field of industrial economics its importance is equally great. Researches into activity, into the way in which the human machine works, are showing that optimum output is obtained by not allowing fatigue to exceed physiological limits ; that the goal of the economist—output—can be best attained through the same agencies as allow the medical man to obtain his objective—health. Wider recognition of this simple but startling fact must transform a civilisation which has been so rudely shaken in the last 150 years by the development of industrialism. Had it only been recognised in the first half of last century, there would have been no fight over the Factory Acts. Its application to the industrial problems of the present needs no exposition. Industrial fatigue is a drag on the wheels of industry impeding the course of progress ; we should surely reply to-day in the affirmative to Berkeley's query " whether we should not cast about, by all manner of means, to expedite industry and to remove whatever hinders it, and whether every one should not lend a helping hand ? " But, if the medical profession is to play the part it should in expediting the desired transformation by removing the drag of fatigue, there must be some clear understanding of what is meant by fatigue, of its manifestations, and of the way in which it can be measured and prevented.

II. Definition.

Fatigue has been defined (1) as " the sum of the results of activity which show themselves in a diminished capacity for work." Activity must then precede fatigue, and a diminished capacity for doing work is its measure. This definition lays down that fatigue is essentially a negative quantity, namely, a diminished capacity for doing work ; and capacity for doing work must first be estimated before any diminution in it can be established. Bodily sensations are often appealed to as an indication of the presence of fatigue, but are uncertain guides. Fatigue may be progressively advancing without any appreciation by the worker that his activity is decreasing ; the steady maintenance of the quality and quantity of his output is the only sure indication that his activity is being maintained. Since the activities productive of fatigue in industrial workers are mainly concerned with the performance of external work, other activities, such as mental work, also productive of fatigue, will receive only passing consideration here.

III. The Animal Body considered as a Machine.

The animal body considered as an agent for performing external work consists of three parts : first, the brain and spinal cord, where impulses originate or are transformed ; second, the nerves, which convey these impulses through end-organs to the muscles ; and third, the muscles themselves, which contract on receipt of these impulses and so may do external work. As a mechanism the body may be likened to a motor car, in which an electric charge, originated in the magneto, is conveyed by wires to the sparking plug in the cylinder, where on discharge of an electric spark combustion takes place, driving down the piston to do external work.

Fatigue is not merely due to the using up of the combustible material in the muscles, or to loss of the power of the nerves and end-organs to convey impulses, or to weakening of the capacity of the brain and spinal cord to originate impulses; it is not merely the running down of the car for want of petrol; it is not the cessation of a chemical reaction because the latter is complete. It is rather interference with the mechanism due to accumulation within of the chemical products of activity, i.e., of katabolism; somewhat as the products of combustion by fouling a sparking plug may slow down or stop a motor which still contains a plentiful supply of petrol, or somewhat as some chemical reactions are interfered with by one of the products formed: thus water reacts with ethyl acetate with the formation of ethyl alcohol and acetic acid; but the reaction, rapid at first, slows down as the acetic acid accumulates, and long before the total possible reaction is complete the process tends to reverse with the re-formation of water and ethyl acetate, so that the following formula may be read from left to right, or from right to left, according as to whether the solution of acetic acid is weak or strong; finally a state of equilibrium is reached in which the action and reaction are equal and opposite, and the strength of acetic acid in the solution remains the same:—

$$C_2 H_5 COO CH_3 + H_2O = C_2 H_5 OH + CH_3 COOH$$

Ethyl acetate   Water   Ethyl alcohol   Acetic acid

Katabolic products of activity act like a governor on an engine to prevent undue expenditure of energy; fatigue, which is the sign of their presence, may be considered as nature's check to prevent exhaustion.

The analogy of a machine with an animal body must, however, not be pushed far, even though, as Hele-Shaw has pointed out, curves representing fatigue or endurance of metals (26) agree remarkably in shape with those for human endurance (27). Curves for human endurance for this purpose were constructed by plotting as vertical ordinates the pace (in miles per hour) of record velocities when cycling, skating, running, walking, and swimming, while the abscissæ represent the distances over which the respective speeds were maintained. The conclusion is drawn that muscular fatigue corresponds in a certain way to the results of endurance tests of metals.

The method of inquiry adopted by Hele-Shaw, so far as living beings is concerned, was anticipated in a careful statistical investigation by Kennely (30), who investigated the records for trotting, pacing, and running horses, and those for running, walking, rowing, skating, and swimming men. Kennely, after analysis of these records, obtained curves similar in shape in each case to those shown in Fig. 1 ; and put forward certain approximate laws for fatigue caused by athletic effort :—(a) doubling the distance means increasing the time by 118 per cent. ; (b) doubling the speed cuts down the racing time 512 times ; (c) doubling the time of the race allows of increasing the course length by 85 per cent. ; (d) doubling the speed cuts down the distance that can be covered 256 times ; (e) doubling the distance brings down the speed about 9·3 per cent. ; (f) the

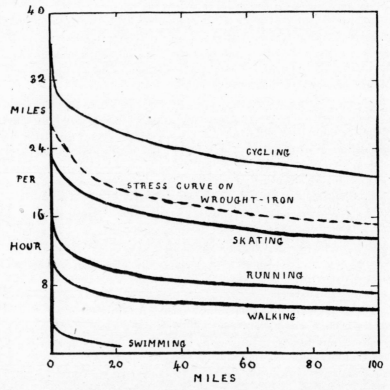

FIG. 1.—Comparison of Alternating Stress Curve on Wrought-Iron with limit of Muscular Fatigue.   Reproduced from (26).

speed over the course varies approximately as the inverse ninth root of the racing time ; (g) the law of fatigue in racing is the same, or very nearly the same, with horses as with men, in air or in water, as indicated by the records analysed. This inquiry is suggestive ; possibly the pace of industrial work when not controlled by machinery may similarly be found, particularly in relation to hours of labour, to obey definite laws.

The three parts of the body now under consideration form only a portion of the whole live organism, they react one on another, and on the whole organism, and are in their turn reacted upon by it. Thus the katabolic products of activity generated in the muscles may affect the central nervous system, just as the presence of an excess of carbon dioxide or of oxygen in the blood flowing through the medulla stimulates or inhibits the respiratory centre. These products are being constantly removed from the tissues either directly or indirectly by the blood ; if the rapidity of removal were always equal to that of formation no accumulation would occur, but normally during work this is not so, and accumulation occurs ; consequently if external activity—the capacity for doing work—is to be maintained, a pause or rest must be interposed during which (a) the waste products may be removed, and (b) anabolic processes—the replacement of the transformed energy—may take place. Rest then is really an active state, a period of internal activity ; and the occurrence of fatigue, whether it is stayed at the stage of healthy physiological fatigue or passes over to that of pathology, depends on the time relations between external activity—work—and internal activity—cleaning and repair. If work is continued too long or is too quickly repeated, the cleaning and repair processes cannot be completed ; then katabolic products accumulate and hamper further action, even to the stage of preventing any action at all. Macaulay, when condemning Sunday labour in the House of Commons, expressed the position eloquently : " While industry is suspended, while the plough lies in the furrow, while the Exchange is silent, while no smoke ascends from the factory, a process is going on quite as important to the wealth of nations as any process which is performed on more busy days. Man, the machine of machines, the machine compared with which all the contrivances of the Watts and Arkwrights are worthless, is repairing and winding up, so that he returns to his labours on the Monday with a clearer intellect, with livelier spirits, with renewed corporal vigour."

IV. The Site of Fatigue.

The three parts of the animal mechanism, the muscles, the nerves and the central nervous system, differ in structure and in chemical composition, and also in their reactions to activity.

Neuro-muscular Mechanism.—A muscle can be made to contract until no response follows by stimulation of its motor nerve ; at this stage direct stimulation of the muscular tissue can still provoke contraction. Hence the conclusion follows that the nervous control of the muscle is fatigued before the muscle.

The nervous control is carried out by two parts, the nerve

and its end-organ in the muscle ; these two parts differ in their reaction to fatigue. If the passage of impulses to a muscle on, say, the right side be inhibited by passing an ascending current along the distal portion of the right motor nerve, and if both right and left motor nerves be stimulated near their origin from the spinal cord ; then the left muscle can be made to contract until it finally responds no longer, while the right muscle remains impassive. At this stage removal of the inhibiting ascending current is immediately followed by contraction of the right muscle (see Fig. 2). Hence the conclusion follows that the final lack of response of the left muscle was due to fatigue of the nerve end-organ, since the proximal portion of the right nerve

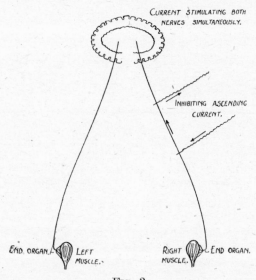

FIG. 2.

remained unfatigued by the stimulation to which it was subjected throughout ; indeed, except by asphyxiation due to entire deprivation of oxygen, fatigue of a nerve trunk cannot be shown to occur.

The central nervous system from which motor impulses normally originate still remains for consideration. Sherrington has found that if a reflex act, say the scratch reflex in a " spinal animal," be started by irritating one spot of the skin and maintained until no response follows, the reflex can be obtained as vigorous as ever by irritating a neighbouring spot of the skin. Here the same motor mechanism of muscles, end-organs and nerves is concerned in both cases ; but the central connection between the arriving afferent impulses and this mechanism has been changed, and also the sensory site from which these impulses start. Sherrington gives reasons for considering that the sensory site is not fatigued, and hence concludes that the central mechanism, the synapse between the afferent and efferent nerves, feels fatigue before the motor mechanism.

We must then suppose that the central nervous system feels the effect first, the nerve end-organs second, and the muscles themselves last ; while the effect of activity upon the nerves is so slight that it may for practical purposes be neglected. The muscles, that part of the mechanism which performs external work, are thus protected against complete exhaustion, by fatigue interfering first with the transmission of impulses, and secondly with their acceptance. Voluntary effort cannot therefore entirely exhaust the muscles, and fatigue is not, as bodily sensations suggest, really located in the muscles themselves, but in the delicate and complicated structure of the central nervous system and possibly of the end-organs.

An impulse of greater extent is required to obtain a stronger contraction from a muscle ; that is to say, the activity of the central nervous system, as well as of the muscle, is increased with the work done. But a minimal impulse is required to make a muscle contract at all ; and the sum of a number of minimal or medium impulses which result in but a small foot-poundage of work may be more fatiguing to the central nervous system than a few impulses followed by a larger output of energy. The conclusions follow that (1) the number of impulses originated as well as their size determines the onset of fatigue : that is to say, rapidity of movement is important as well as the amount of work done ; and (2) industrial fatigue is essentially a problem of the central nervous system.

Central Nervous System.—Impulses reach an efferent or motor nerve through the synapse in the cord from two sources : (1) from the afferent nerve of the part controlled by the efferent nerve and (2) from the higher nervous centres ; these impulses may agree or interfere. The scratch reflex in an experimental frog is an instance of afferent impulses *stimulating* muscular action. Afferent impulses also exert *inhibitory* influences on muscular action ; thus when muscular contraction can no longer be obtained by voluntary effort (as in an ergograph experiment), if a local anæsthetic be applied, further voluntary muscular contraction can be obtained ; in this case afferent impulses must have been causing the primary cessation of muscular action by inhibiting the voluntary messages. This experiment also suggests that voluntary effort—the capacity of the higher brain centres for originating impulses—may remain active even when the muscle has ceased to respond; *i.e.*, fatigue does not primarily originate where the impulses originate. The continued existence of activity in the higher centres may also be shown by replacing the weight which was being lifted by a slightly smaller one, when a fresh set of excellent contractions can voluntarily be obtained.

Evidence points to fatigue being first manifested in that part of the nervous system whence the impulses, whether voluntary or involuntary, are finally transmitted to the efferent motor nerves. Fatigue is the manifestation of inhibitory processes affecting this part of the nervous system, the synapse in the spinal cord ; and is protective against over-exertion of the muscles. The mechanism may be likened to interference with messages in a telephone exchange while both conversing subscribers are as ready as ever to continue their conversation.

Mental Fatigue.—A grasp of the position in relation to muscular fatigue will render easier understanding of the mental fatigue which enters into many industrial processes. Myers writes (23) :—" In monotonous *mental* work a similar protective function can be seen. When we are engaged on any one piece of mental work other mental processes are inhibited which are incompatible with it ; but the effects of fatigue are safeguarded by the gradual failure of these processes of inhibition. The inhibited mental processes sooner or later refuse to be suppressed. Other mental activities accordingly intrude, and by their inhibitory action make the continuance of the monotonous mental work impossible. The continued effort to repress these intruding activities is accompanied first by a feeling of ' boredom ' as interest—*i.e.*, the pleasure or incentive in the work— wanes, and later by a feeling of ' weariness ' as the effort is invoked with greater difficulty. . . . Higher control is actually fatigued and cannot be immediately employed for concentration in another direction, for the synapses concerned in the effort of the self at inhibition are most sensitive to fatigue, and this fatigue enters into and affects other subsequent self-effort.

" We conclude, then, that monotonous application for long hours at relatively light work induces an incapacity as serious as employment for shorter hours at more strenuous work. Indeed, the incapacity may be more serious—*e.g.*, when the lighter work is mainly of a mental character, watching and controlling a small piece of machinery that does everlastingly the same job—and when the heavier work is mainly of a mechanical character—*e.g.*, lifting huge weights of iron. In the latter case the main source of fatigue arises, as we have seen, from the accumulation of waste products in the muscles, and especially from the nervous inhibitory processes arising from unchanging muscular exercise. But such nervous inhibition has its seat in far lower and less important nerve centres than in the former case. The volitional efforts made to overcome such muscular incapacity are much less effective and less baneful than those made to overcome the boredom and weariness arising from mental work. Hence the pathological expression of continued fatigue—i.e., over-strain—is far less prevalent in muscular than in mental exertion."

Practice Effect.—Stimulation of a muscle is followed at first by increase in the strength of the response ; that is to say, the same strength of stimulus produces a greater and greater result. The phenomenon is called the staircase, treppe, or practice effect ; its existence with regard to muscular action is well recognised.

Psychological experiments (in which muscular effort needed for indicating the results of mental work has been as far as possible eliminated) point to a similar practice effect in mental activity, to the existence of a site or sites—nerve exchanges or synapses—probably distinct from the seat of mental activity, where fatigue originates and inhibits over-action.

Industrial muscular work calls both muscular practice and mental practice into play, since it is the result of voluntary impulses calling forth muscular action. Such voluntary muscular work may increase, due either to practice affecting the muscles or to practice affecting the origination of impulses. How far these two forms of practice advance together at equal pace has not been determined, nor whether they are interfered with simultaneously and equally by the inhibitory influence of fatigue. The suggestion may, however, be put forward that there are two forms of practice effect and of fatigue inhibition, and that the irregularity found in certain curves of output is possibly an expression of the two forms not acting synchronously.

Practice effect is a matter of great importance in judging of the presence or onset of industrial fatigue, since the conclusion seems a safe one that, so long as it is being manifested and the inhibitory effect of fatigue is a subsidiary influence, work is being carried on within the limits of healthy metabolism.

V. Chemistry of Activity.

The law of conservation of energy applies to muscular activity as definitely as if the living body were an inanimate machine. The energy of muscular work is derived from internal combustion, as a result of which oxygen is abstracted from the blood and carbon dioxide and water are formed, just as oxygen is abstracted from the air in the case of the combustion of petrol in a motor car.

Muscle consists of 75 per cent. of water and 25 per cent. of solids ; of the 25 per cent. twenty parts are protein, and the remaining five parts extractives and inorganic salts. The extractives consist of nitrogenous and non-nitrogenous substances. The protein and nitrogenous extractives of muscle may for present purposes be neglected, because nitrogenous output is not increased by work. The most important of the non-nitrogenous substances and the one which most readily provides the energy of muscular work is glycogen, or animal starch, n ($C_6 H_{10} O_5$), which forms from 0·1 to 2·5 per cent. of resting muscle. Its storehouse is the liver, whence it appears to be carried by the blood stream to the muscles ; certainly during activity it disappears first from the liver and only after prolonged activity from the muscles. Energy for muscular contraction is mainly obtained by oxygenation of this intra-muscular starch. The oxygenation passes through various stages represented by sugars—dextrin, maltose and glucose—and finally by lactic or sarco-lactic acid, CH_3 (CH.OH) COOH, before the last products of combustion, water and carbon dioxide, are reached ; all the energy possible to be obtained has then been yielded.

Fletcher and Hopkins consider (2) the phenomenon of muscular contraction to be a physico-chemical one. They point out that a catgut fibre in water will contract if its temperature be raised, or if acid be brought to it, relaxing again on removal of the acid ; and that the artificial application of lactic acid to muscle causes contraction, reversible by removal of the acid. They suggest that normal contraction may be caused by a development of lactic acid, with free H- ions, in the neighbourhood of colloidal fibrils, when work will be done according to the opposition given during the contraction. Exactly how the formation of lactic acid from some carbohydrate forerunner takes place when an impulse reaches the muscle from the central nervous system is not clear ; but once formed, contraction would be maintained if the acid were not removed. This removal is effected by oxygenation, which takes place rapidly, if oxygen is present, with the formation of carbon dioxide and water. Relaxation then occurs, and the original state of tension in the fibrils is restored.

When muscular work is being done some of the intermediary products, due to incomplete oxygenation, may gain access to the blood stream ; indeed, Ryffel has found that even after moderate exercise lactic acid can be detected in the urine and sweat. The claim has been made that during activity a toxin is formed which causes fatigue, that if blood, or serum, containing this toxin is injected into animals they exhibit signs of fatigue, and that this toxin is not lactic acid. But which of the products of muscular work acting on the central nervous system inhibits the transmission of impulses, or, indeed, whether the inhibition or fatigue of the central nervous system is so caused rather than by some unknown product of nervous activity, has not been determined.

VI. Metabolism and Rhythm.

An essential of living matter is that it is always building up and breaking down, anabolism and katabolism going on simultaneously ; but at any moment one or other process is normally in excess. The period when anabolism is in excess is the " resting " period (really a period of internal activity), and the period when katabolism is in excess is the period of external activity.* Just as accumulation of the products of katabolism limits activity and compels rest, so do the products of anabolism limit further rest and urge on activity. This is a fundamental law of life : rest must be earned by work, and work must be followed by rest. Throughout life the two alternate in a steady rhythm. Like the swing of the pendulum, the higher swings the bob on the one side the more insistently does gravitation tend to reverse its movement ; to and fro it swings, the external activity of work changing place with the internal activity of rest, until the onward urge of the spring of life is exhausted. In the varied actions of the human mechanism rhythmic alternation of work and rest is in some instances involuntary, in others subject to voluntary limitations. The action of the heart, which is involuntary, is made up of contraction and relaxation, systole and diastole, work and rest, as follows :—

	Systole.	Diastole.
Auricle .	0·1′	0·7′
Ventricle.	0·3′	0·5′

Breathing, which may be modified voluntarily, is compounded of the acts of expansion and contraction of the chest, and under ordinary circumstances each takes up a nearly equal time—about two seconds. Sleeping and waking, even more under the control of the will, also alternate normally every twenty-four hours.

Other examples of rhythm are to be found connected with anatomical structure. The length, for instance, of the leg

* A beautiful analogy is afforded by the phenomenon of successive contrast in vision, and one of the classical theories of colour vision (that proposed by Goethe and expanded by Hering) explains the facts on the above lines.

influences the periodicity of the pendulum-like swing of the foot in walking ; repeated arm movements, in a similar way, tend to take on a natural periodicity dependent on the length of the bones and their muscular attachments. The shorter is the pendulum the quicker is the periodicity of the natural swing.

This question of rhythm is important in industrial work which goes on day by day and week by week. Action, like the wielding of a heavy hammer, repeated in a rhythm which permits the movements of respiration to coincide with the rise and fall of the arms, may be continued longer and more effectively than irregular blows. An oarsman breathes in as he reaches forward, and exhales as he gets on to his work and pulls the stroke through ; and every rowing coach knows how a crew becomes ragged and slovenly when the stroke set is too slow to permit of sufficiently rapid breathing ; while a rapidity of stroke over forty per minute cannot long be maintained, even by a practised crew, because respiration becomes too shallow to be effective. The exercise of dancing to music is another excellent example of the effect of rhythm : the musician sets the rhythm, while the dancers choose their own pace. Here delicate girls (often without the companionship of the opposite sex) will indulge in active exercise for hour after hour, although many of them might with difficulty be induced to walk far fewer miles than they cover in an evening while dancing. The value of rest-pauses is also well exemplified in the arrangement of a dance programme. In industry the pace of the worker is frequently determined by the pace of the machine he tends, but the pace of the machine should be set in relation to his natural rhythm. The optimum pace will vary somewhat for different workers ; moreover, by practice an increase of individual pace can be attained, for the same sequence of impulses often repeated seems, like increase of traffic over a byeway, to open up the paths of communication, while at the same time the rhythms of the heart and lungs adjust themselves to new requirements. Weeks and months are required before a worker at a fresh process comes to his best level of output, and even then every morning he takes some time " warming up to his work." Rhythm in industrial work is being carefully investigated in America ; and a preliminary note (28) suggests that a high level of output maintained throughout the day is found associated with processes, such as lathe work, which lend themselves to rhythm ; and that an experienced operative, the rhythm of whose work is more steadily maintained throughout the day, gives a higher output, and an output which is more consistently maintained, than one whose work is less rhythmical. The teaching of physiology is that there should be rhythm in work,* action keeping time with reaction; and Burton expressed this idea in his *Anatomy of Melancholy*: "Labouring men that sing to their work can tell us much." Regard must be had to such physiological factors as pulse rate and breathing and to anatomical structure if maximum effort is to be obtained with a minimum of fatigue. Here is work calling for the human element of scientific management, which is as important as determining the optimum length of work by the day, by the week, and by the spell, and the right moment for interposing rest periods and their length. However, before action can be taken on these lines the indications of fatigue and the ways in which they can be measured must be understood.

VII. Indications of Fatigue.

The ways in which fatigue may be measured and the influences which contribute to it may be set forth as follows :—

Contributory influences.		Subject for investigation.	Means of measurement.
Outside the period of employment.	(i.) Housing. (ii.) Transit. (iii.) Recreation and personal habits.	Industrial activity and fatigue.	Direct : Personal tests.
During the period of employment.	(iv.) Hours of work. (v.) Conditions of labour. (vi.) Methods of work.		Indirect : (a) Output. (b) Lost time. (c) Wastage of workers. (d) Accidents.

The study of activity and fatigue consists in estimating the effect of alterations in the "contributory influences" upon the "means of measurement"; this may be done (1) by altering outside conditions, as by improving transit facilities or providing opportunities for healthy recreation, or (2) by shortening or rearranging hours, altering conditions, or modifying methods, and then ascertaining the effect (i.) upon output, lost time or other means of measurement, or (ii.) upon some personal reaction.

Means of Measurement.

" The results of activity which show themselves in a diminished capacity for doing work " are, according to our accepted defini-

* The comparative ease with which poetry can be memorised provides an instructive analogy.

tion, the indications that fatigue is present. The problem before -us is how to establish the existence of a " diminished capacity," and for this purpose some direct or indirect means of measurement must be employed. By direct means are meant tests applied directly to individual workers to ascertain whether at any given moment their capacity for doing work is in any way diminished. By indirect means are meant, not tests applied directly to individual workers, but applied so as to deduce their capacity for work from their actions, e.g., from their output, from the amount of time they lose, or from their tendency to change their place of employment, i.e., labour turnover.

Direct Tests.—Direct tests capable of indicating at any moment the presence in any worker of a diminished capacity for doing work would clearly give the desired information ; but such tests are difficult to devise and are tedious to apply ; further, if the worker can in any way control his reaction to the test, that is to say, if the test is not purely objective, the sensations of the worker (already pointed out to be fallacious) may cause him to modify or attempt to modify his reaction according to his feelings. A direct test should, therefore, be purely objective, a difficult thing to ensure.

Many efforts have been, and are still being, made to establish a satisfactory direct test, and for the moment the best prospect is offered by physiological tests. Thus Ryan places reliance upon a vascular skin reaction : " This test consists in making a light stroke with a blunt instrument on the skin of the forearm and measuring by stop-watch the time from the moment of stimulation to the beginning of the fading of the white streak that presently appears. The time required for this vascular skin reaction, designated fading time, was uniformly found to be decreased by work and increased by rest " (28) ; shortened fading time in the evening as compared with the morning is held to be an indication of fatigue resulting from the day's work.

Martin again has applied a muscular strength test, originally developed by him and Lovett (31), to industrial workers. " The test consists of overcoming the maximum resistance of the muscle-group under examination by means of traction applied through a self-indicating spring balance " (32). Various groups of muscles, as indicators of total strength, are tested under varying conditions of work. " A lower strength record at the end of the working period than at the beginning is looked upon as indicating fatigue. . . . Where a single worker regularly shows a falling-off of strength at the end of the day, or where a group of workers all show such a strength-loss on a particular day, fatigue may justly be assumed."

Another test now under observation which promises to be of value depends upon the reaction of pulse-rate to respiratory effort ; the rate is stated to quicken after effort when the subject is fresh, but to slow when he is tired.

. No test yet devised has commanded general acceptance. Discussion of the difficulties associated with this problem and of failures to solve it would be unprofitable ; suffice it to say that the use of ergometers and subjective reaction-time tests has now been rejected.

Indirect Tests.—The results of activity may affect either industrial efficiency, causing a falling off in the quality and quantity of work done, or the health and vigour of the workers, causing an increased frequency of accidents and more lost time and sickness, or the psychology of the workers, causing an undue labour turnover, *i.e.*, change in *personnel.* Each of these results, if properly recorded, provides for investigation data which the workers are not likely to influence, since they might be quite unaware that any investigation is contemplated. Fortunately for investigation purposes, at most industrial establishments records are kept for business purposes—(1) of output, (2) of lost time and sickness, and (3) (although not so generally) of labour turnover.

Output.—Records of output, which are direct tests of industrial efficiency, are the most valuable data available. Through them the results of activity can be directly measured. Care must, however, be exercised before making deductions from output records ; the work done throughout the period under investigation must not have altered ; the supply of materials and of tools and the pace of machines must have remained the same ; there must have been the same incentive to work with no alteration in methods of payment ; if possible, the output should refer to the same group of workers, and these workers should have been employed at the work sufficiently long to have passed through the stage during which practice increases their output ; conditions of temperature and humidity and of artificial and natural lighting should be similar. These conditions are difficult to satisfy ; when, however, they are satisfied, how do the records throw light on the presence or absence of industrial fatigue ?

Examination of diagrams A to D (Fig. 3), which show graphically the hourly output of workers engaged at different processes, discloses entirely different relations between the rates of hourly output. Diagram A shows a maximum output obtained in the first hour and then falling rapidly away ; B also shows a maximum in the first hour with a less rapid falling away ; C, which is saddle-back in shape, shows an initial rise fairly maintained, but falling away later; D shows a steady rise and a maintenance

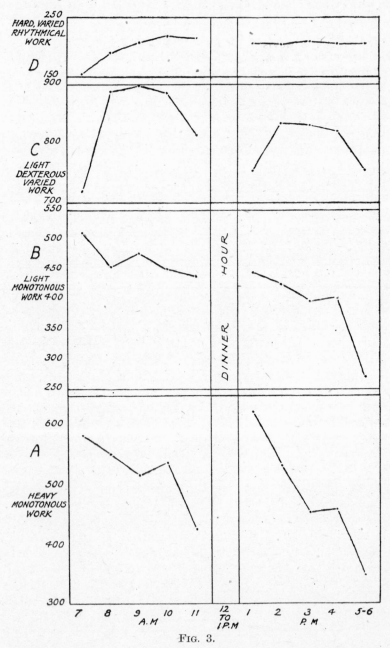

FIG. 3.

throughout the period of work of the height reached. A theoretical maximum of output would be represented by a chart with a vertical rise on commencement and a horizontal line thereafter, and D tends to approximate to this theoretical maximum. Now examine the work done, of which these charts represent the hourly output. In the case of A the work was unrelieved, unremitting monotony of physical effort at which the workers plainly could not maintain the pace ; in the case of B no strenuous work was involved, but the process was one of constant repetition and unrelieved monotony ; the operation concerned with C required both efficiency and dexterity, but no physical effort ; in the case of D the work was hard, but with movement and variety lending itself to balanced rhythm.

Study of these hourly output records indicates that fatigue, contributed to by influences under control, is present most distinctly in A, less in B, and still less in C, and that it is not manifested in D, where these influences are well arranged for the work in progress.

Note also that although the presence of fatigue is more distinct in A, which represents heavy physical work, than in B, where no physical exertion was called for, yet the indications of fatigue become progressively less, not as the severity of physical exertion becomes less, but as repetition of the same monotonous series of nerve impulses becomes less, and that D, where fatigue is not manifest, represents hard physical work second only to that of A, but characterised by a varied series of movements which lends itself to rhythmic repetition.

Acceptance of the suggestion already put forward that there are two forms of fatigue and of practice, one nervous and the other muscular, may possibly throw further light upon the meaning of these diagrams. In A fatigue is, by hypothesis, since the work was heavy manual work, mainly muscular ; but both in the morning and afternoon a less tired nervous system introduces an interference into the regular fall of output. In the case of B the fatigue is by hypothesis mainly nervous, and here a less tired muscular system interferes with the fall ; in this case, as nervous fatigue is less quickly recovered from than muscular, the afternoon output commences low instead of as in A. In C, arguing from the low start in the afternoon, the only fatigue present may be held to be nervous. In D neither form of fatigue can definitely be said to be present. Interpretation of output curves on these lines, however, while interesting to attempt, cannot yet be accepted as legitimate.

The way in which the influences at work affecting the output represented in these diagrams should be modified to lessen fatigue and increase output is fairly indicated. In such processes as that with which A is concerned short rest pauses

should be introduced before the rate of hourly output commences to fall; the effect which may be expected to follow was
demonstrated at a munitions factory, where the "men engaged
in the heavy work of moulding were required by the management to rest fifteen minutes in every hour of work. The manager
was satisfied that this was an arrangement good for the men
and for the output. But the men objected to this long spell of
rest in each hour because the work was piece work, and they
thought the production would be lessened by it. The manager
accordingly found it necessary to set a foreman to watch and
to make the hourly rest compulsory. When this was done the
output per hour was found to be actually increased " (1). In
the case of B again rest pauses are indicated, as the following
instance shows: "At another munitions factory the committee learnt that the manager had given a break of fifteen
minutes daily at 11 a.m. to girls engaged in sedentary work of
a monotonous, repetitive kind. During the break the girls had
recreation in the open air. In spite of this deduction from their
working hours of the time so spent, the output per day was
increased " (1). In the case of C the length of spell—five
hours—seems mainly at fault, and probably at least the last
half-hour of each spell could with advantage have been omitted.
The case of D presents an interesting position in relation to
industrial efficiency. The chart does not exhibit indications of
fatigue, but the further problem is not solved as to whether
under other conditions the vertical rise might not have been
higher with the horizontal line of hourly output maintained
at a higher level. An instance bearing upon such a possibility
has come under notice of a highly organised engineering factory
employed on repetition work. The chart of the hourly output
of this factory in 1918 was of D type. On January 1st, 1919,
the hours of work were reduced from forty-eight per week to
forty; no other alteration was made except that the wages,
which were paid on time basis (not on piece rates), were raised
so that each worker received rather over 15 per cent. more
for the forty-hour week than he did previously for the forty-
eight-hour week. Soon after the reduction in hours the previous
output was by so much overtaken and passed (the curve of
hourly output maintaining the D type) that the costs of production were reduced.

Examine now in the same way the daily output records shown
graphically in Fig. 4, in which the output of Saturdays,
for reasons unnecessary to enumerate, is neglected and not
shown. In chart 1 the output rises fairly steeply from Monday
to Wednesday and then falls off; in chart 2 it rises less steeply

and attains its maximum on Thursday and then falls off; in chart 3 it rises less steeply still, attains a maximum on Thursday, and falls off less on Friday; in chart 4 the rise is slight and very gradual up to Friday : in fact, the line approximates to the horizontal line in chart D. The hours of labour and the character of the work, of which the diagram represents the daily output, threw (having regard to the workers being women or men) relatively more strain on the 140 women employed at cartridge case (rifle) operations than on the 1,000 women at lathe operations, and on the latter group more than on the 1,000 men and 300 women of chart 2 ; while the lightest

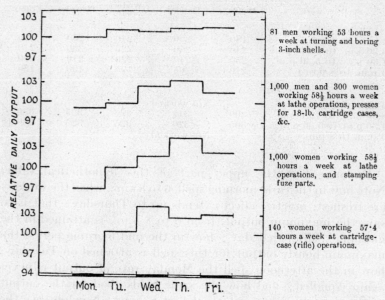

Fig. 4.—Diurnal Variation of Day-shift Output. Reproduced from (3).

task fell to the eighty-one men employed fifty-three hours turning and boring three-inch shells. The conclusion to be drawn is that in charts 1, 2, and 3 the week-end rest did not permit fatigue to be recovered from, and that some was carried over to the next week. Practice effect, however, comes into play and increases the daily output until overcome by further fatigue effects ; and this occurs earlier in the week, as the strain of the previous week has been greater. The less the strain the later in the week does the practice effect extend until in chart 4 it reaches Friday, and the workers start again on Monday but little below their full capacity.

Further evidence of the effect of fatigue, not recovered from at the week-end, being carried over into the next week, and sooner or later neutralising practice effect, is suggested by data published by Kent (4). As, however, the output records published only concern small groups of workers (three in number), and consequently the actual values are subject to large errors of sampling, the following table (which does not give real output figures) has been constructed merely to show the method of investigation. The workers are considered to have been employed for the hours stated for several months :—

Scheme of Probable Hourly Output where Long Hours are practised and then shortened.

Spell of work.	Monday.	Tuesday.	Wednesday.	Thursday.	Friday.
6 a.m. to 8 a.m. .	180	200	240	250	220
8.30 a.m. to 12.30 p.m.	240	250	225	230	210
1.30 p.m. to 5.30 p.m..	250	240	220	210	200
6 p.m. to 8 p.m. .	210	205	195	190	180
6 a.m. to 8 a.m. .	—	Not worked	—	325	330
8.30 a.m. to 12 noon .	300	315	320	325	330
1.30 p.m. to 5.30 p.m. .	305	320	325	325	330
6 p.m. to 8 p.m. .	—	Not worked	—		

Examine first the upper part of this hypothetical table. Note how in the early morning spell, 6 to 8 a.m., when the workers are freshest, practice effect extends up to Thursday : that is to say, the maximum output, from 6 to 8 a.m., is attained in the morning spell of that day ; how in the mid-morning period the maximum hourly output for this spell is attained on Tuesday ; how in the afternoon spell the Monday rate of output is never again equalled ; and how the same holds good for the output of the overtime hours, which at best is poor. Now observe the output during each day ; on Monday it rises to the afternoon spell, on Tuesday it only rises to the morning spell, while on Wednesday, Thursday and Friday the hourly output before breakfast is greatest. Look now at the lower part of the table, which is supposed to represent the output when overtime and before-breakfast work have been discontinued for some weeks ; the rate of hourly output now climbs both in the morning and in the afternoon up to Friday, and the daily rate of hourly output is increased or maintained throughout each day.

The instances given above refer to groups of workers, and, although when large groups are under investigation valuable deductions can be drawn, they are open to the grave objection that individual workers are lost sight of in the averages calculated. Thus theoretically a group of twenty workers might be made up of ten exceptionally good workers and ten exceptionally bad workers, and the average output of the group would not be representative of either component. Where the output of individual workers can be obtained, especially if paid piece rates which ensure the maintenance of an incentive, more valuable information can be obtained by intensive investigation of the output of each worker. An instance which recently came under notice will illustrate this point : Investigation of the group output for several small sets of workers suggested that alteration in hours or conditions was needed for the processes concerned ; intensive study, however, brought out that in each set the output of two or three workers rose steadily throughout the week, and further that the output of these workers was uniformly considerably above that of the others : *i.e.*, although their output was much greater, they were in no way subject to over-fatigue. The conclusions which emerged were that the processes were suited to the best workers, to the round pegs in round holes, and that the poorer workers, whose output data indicated the presence of over-fatigue, were square pegs attempting unsuccessfully to accommodate themselves to round holes ; the hours of work and conditions of labour were not so much at fault as the selection of workers for the particular processes (25).

Charts should be kept for each worker showing the rise and fall of earnings. Normally the line should rise steadily from day to day, and from week to week, as the worker becomes more and more expert, or at least keep on a level. If, on the other hand, the line is falling, inquiry should be made by the welfare superintendent into the health and well-being of the worker concerned. Other instances might be quoted of the use of output records to detect the presence of industrial fatigue, but enough has been said to indicate their value and to point the way for their extended use.

Lost Time and Sickness.—The axiom being accepted that fatigue has a large share in the promotion of disease, the occurrence of sickness among the *personnel* of a factory (apart from seasonal variations and epidemics like those of influenza) must be discussed when the presence of fatigue is under consideration. The amount of sickness experienced is, however, for various reasons (discussed by Loveday in his able monograph (5)), often not disclosed by medical certification, and lies concealed in records of total time lost ; further, a worker may not be definitely on the sick-list, but will miss work before breakfast or even for half a day on account of fatigue. Total lost time includes not only time lost due to industrial fatigue, whether in the stage of tiredness, which may appear as indifference, slackness, laziness, or discontent, or in the stage of definite sickness, but also time lost for other reasons, for example, a breakdown of transit facilities, wintry weather, domestic duties of women or alcoholic habits. Generally speaking, time lost for these other reasons will remain steady or only fluctuate with non-industrial conditions, such as weather and the season of the year. The way general sickness varies with the seasons is well shown in the following diagram, which is based on the statistics of sick benefit of a large and important trade union. On the other hand, time lost due to industrial fatigue will be related to industrial phenomena, and examination of lost time records should be made to see whether such a relation exists.

The method of calculating lost time must first be determined. Different methods are employed in different places, and the

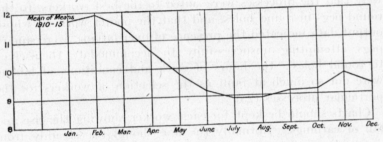

FIG. 5.—Seasonal Variations in Sickness. Reproduced from (5).

method in use must be carefully ascertained. The simplest method is a statement of the total hours possible to have been worked and of the total number of hours lost. Thus, in a factory working a fifty-hour week and employing 200 workers the total possible hours would be 10,000 ; if each worker lost on an average two hours a week, there would be 400 hours lost altogether, that is 4 per cent. of lost time. The crude figure so obtained is a useful one when investigating industrial fatigue. Managers, however, in the interests of industrial efficiency, dislike unexpected absences, and often classify lost time as " unavoidable " due to certified sickness or by leave obtained, and as " avoidable " when no certificate is sent in and no leave has been obtained ; and in some establishments a bonus is given to those who have no " avoidable " lost time debited against them at the end of the week. Since, however, " nearly all records under-state, and most records under-state greatly, the proportion of lost time due to sickness and other unavoidable causes," this distinction must not be pressed too far when considering lost time records as indications of fatigue; still valuable information can be obtained by subjecting lost time records to close analysis, which may be done in a variety of ways. For example, the number of workers losing time may be grouped according to the length of periods lost, whether less than a day, a whole day, or longer. Investigation on these lines has established that an undue number of periods of less than a day are lost when the hours of work are so distributed that work commences before breakfast. The following table shows the result of an investigation conducted on these lines :—

Factory.	System.	Percentage of men losing avoidably				Hours lost.					
		Under five hours a week.	Five hours but under ten.	Ten hours or more.	Any time at all.	Avoidably.		Through sickness or. leave.		Total.	
						Per employee (hours).	Per cent. of possible normal hours.	Per employee (hours).	Per cent. of possible normal hours.	Per employee (hours).	Per cent. of possible normal hours.
(1)	(2)	(3)	(4)	(5)	(6)	(7)	(8)	(9)	(10)	(11)	(12)
No. 1	1-break	—	—	—	—	0·470	—	1·200	—	1·670	3·1
	2-break	23·9	5·5	6·6	36·1	1·692		1·237		2·929	
No. 2	2-break	22·3	2·8	5·7	30·9	1·458	3·2	1·197	2·3	2·655	5·5
No. 3	1-break	0·4	0·5	0·06	1·0	0·060	2·7	1·197	2·2	1·257	5·0
							0·1		2·2		2·38

Three factories are concerned, working the same number of hours—fifty-three per week. These hours were, however, distributed differently. For No. 3 and No. 1 under the one-break system the hours were :—

Monday to Thursday .   8—1, 2—7.
Friday   .   .   .   8—1, 2—6.
Saturday .   .   .   8—12.

For No. 2 and No. 1 under the two-break system the hours were :—

Monday to Thursday .   6.45—8.30, 9—1, 2—6.
Friday   .   .   .   6.45—8.30, 9—1, 2—5.30.
Saturday .   .   .   6.45—8.30, 9—12.

Information, except for the figures given in columns 11 and 12, is lacking for No. 1 under the one-break system ; and the figure in column 7 is obtained by subtracting the average of column 9, i.e., 1·2, from the figure 1·67 of column 11. The data for No. 3 may be taken to represent the normal distribution of lost time under the one-break system, and the data of No. 1 while under this system are seen to have a similar distribution ; the data for No. 2 may be taken to represent the normal distribution under the two-break system, and again the data of No. 1 are

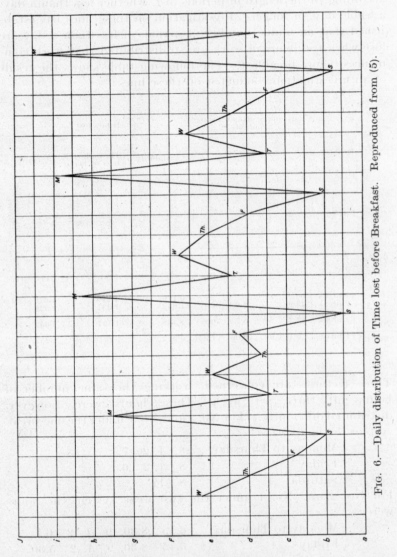

Fig. 6.—Daily distribution of Time lost before Breakfast.   Reproduced from (5).

seen to conform.   Examination of lost time records can then, as in these instances, indicate that the hours of work are badly arranged.   Loveday has investigated carefully on these lines, and from the body of evidence collected concludes that of the disadvantages arising from working before breakfast the most serious perhaps—though all are serious—is the inferiority of hungry work, its bad effect upon health, and the temptation to lose time owing to the shortness of the early spell, a conclusion of great import to the well-being of industrial workers.

Another way of investigating records of lost time is to examine the distribution according to the days of the week. An irregular distribution day by day when repeated week by week, as shown in diagram 6, suggests that employment and not home conditions is the real influence. This diagram shows the distribution for each day of the week of " quarters " * lost by men employed long hours at heavy engineering work ; and the curve has had this form for years. Pay in this factory is accounted to Tuesday, which may explain the drop on that day ; otherwise the tendency is for improvement to occur throughout the week. This tendency is so contrary to what might have been expected as a result of fatigue accumulating day after day during the week that it calls for comment. The real explanation seems to be that the week-end break is not long enough to enable recuperation to be completed ; the swing of the pendulum of internal activity, i.e., rest, is still ascending on Monday morning, and it can with difficulty be reversed. There is each Monday the drag of the flesh against beginning the same old grind again instead of the urge to activity which should follow rest. Accepting this explanation, a distribution of lost time which is highest at the beginning of the week, and falls off through the week, may be held to indicate that the week-end rest in relation to the hours worked is too short. Either of two remedies can be applied : the week-end can be lengthened, or the number of hours worked can be shortened.

Extra-factorial influences, such as domestic duties of women, transit facilities, personal habits and hobbies, have been found to affect lost time ; in one instance a firm on investigation found that the group of best time-keepers included a large proportion of allotment gardeners, whereupon several hundred pounds annually were devoted to encouraging gardening among the workers, with excellent results in diminishing lost time.

Important investigations could be made into the relation between occupation and sickness of different kinds if the medical certification of time lost due to sickness were accurate and the kind of sickness suffered from were stated. Unfortunately in this country no data exist for such investigations, a matter which has been dealt with in an earlier chapter. The importance of such investigations in throwing light upon the causation of common ailments, often the forerunners of serious illness, can

---

* A " quarter " is a term used to denote the before-breakfast spell of work.

hardly be over-estimated. The environment of industrial employment exposes workers to a variety of influences not to be found elsewhere, and the science of medicine would be greatly advanced if the effect of these influences could be ascertained.

Labour Turnover.—The subject of labour turnover, or wastage of workers, is discussed later, and the method of measuring it described. Attention is there drawn to the way in which the rate of wastage is usually greatest immediately after engagement and becomes steadier as the length of employment becomes longer. If industrial fatigue is a function of industrial activity, wastage of workers would seem at first sight to be in no way connected with fatigue. In fact, the reverse is the case. The fresh worker on engagement has forthwith to keep the pace of the factory ; there is no period of breaking in ; boys and girls who were yesterday attending school in familiar surroundings are expected to-day for eight, nine or even ten hours to face the noise and toil of modern industrial life surrounded by strange faces and stranger tasks. Even if they have been employed before and are accustomed to the hours of work, still they find themselves strangers amid unfamiliar surroundings. No wonder then that the strain is greatest and the effects of fatigue are obvious in the first few days and weeks of employment ! Those least able to withstand it leave, and only the fittest survive. The importance of this question has only recently been expounded, and sufficient data have not yet been gathered to establish accurately the possible relations between the amount of wastage, hours of labour, and severity of work. Evidence has, however, been gathered by one of us (6) to show that organised welfare work is of great value in lessening wastage by tempering the wind to the shorn lamb, and to justify the recommendation that where more than 20 per cent. of entrants are lost within three months a special inquiry should be made. If a high rate of wastage depends upon strain and fatigue, then the " survivors " must also be exposed to the same influences ; and, although they have withstood them better, in the long run they should also be affected. Agnew has investigated (7) this point in relation to hours of labour by subjecting a large number of " survivors " (*i.e.*, workers found at work) to medical examination. He found that among men employed for less than seventy hours a week he was unable to place 22·1 per cent. in the physical class A, but that 31·4 per cent. of those working seventy hours or more failed to reach this standard ; and of the boys 6·7 per cent. of those working less than sixty hours were below class A, as contrasted with 10·6 per cent. of those working sixty hours or more, a serious difference. He considers it permissible to draw the conclusion that long hours exercise a prejudicial effect upon average general health.

Wastage of workers may then be considered a useful but indirect way of determining that the strain of employment is producing among the workers a diminished capacity for doing work.

Looked at from another point of view, wastage of workers, especially in the early months of employment, indicates a lack of efficiency. Vernon has shown (3) that even for simple repetition processes workers may require from three to four months of practice in order to attain a level of efficiency. A high rate of wastage therefore during these months must mean that an undue proportion of the workers never acquire a reasonable proficiency, and that the *personnel* of the establishment as a whole is maintained with a diminished capacity for doing work.

Industrial Accidents.—The claim has been made that an accident is frequently the result of inattention and clumsiness resulting from fatigue, and that the frequency of accidents may be taken as a measure of fatigue. The insistence with which this claim has been advanced entitles it to consideration, but before it can be accepted it requires carefully sifting. An industrial accident is the result of industrial activity ; *ceteris paribus* the greater the exposure to accidents—that is, the greater the activity—the greater is the chance of accidents occurring. And that is what occurs, as has been shown by Vernon, who, after an intensive inquiry (8), concludes that speed of production is the *essential* factor in accident causation which can never be neglected. After pursuing his inquiries into the frequency of accidents by the hour, by the day, and by the month, and comparing it with variations in output for similar periods, he states as regards :—

(*a*) *Day Shift Variations :* That varying speed of production is the factor largely responsible for variations of accidents in men and not fatigue. Even in women fatigue is of only moderate importance as a rule.

(*b*) *Diurnal Variations :* That they generally correspond with the output variations, as both rose to a maximum in the middle of the week and declined at the end of it.

(*c*) *Monthly Variations :* That they correspond with output variations, for the accidents increased gradually about 40 per cent., whilst the hourly output at the same time increased 50 per cent.

Vernon stresses the point that the speeding up of 10 per cent. in output may induce a larger increase of accidents, even up to 50 or 100 per cent. Every process carries its own liability to accident ; increase of output, while increasing this liability, will increase it to an extent which cannot be determined except by experiment. Increase of accidents is then primarily an indication of an increase rather than a decrease in working capacity, of activity rather than of fatigue.

TABLE A.—*Cuts per 10,000 Lathe Workers per Week.*

Hour.	Men.		Women.	
	75-hour week.	54½-hour week.	75-hour week.	54½-hour week.
7.30 to 8.30 .	24	34	17	15
8.30 to 9.30 .	33	55	26	33
9.30 to 10.30 .	64	65	72	47
10.30 to 11.30 .	54	75	90	50
1.30 to 2.30 .	50	55	80	42
2.30 to 3.30 .	46	61	72	42
3.30 to 4.30 .	48	58	80	37
4.30 to 5.30 .	44	72	63	35

Nevertheless Vernon has been able to show that fatigue does affect the frequency of accidents. Compare the figures of Table A, in which the average number of cuts sustained per hour during the day per 10,000 workers are given for the same hours of the day for both men and women under two periods of employment, the one very long, seventy-five hours a week, and the other shorter, fifty-four and a half hours per week (alternating every fortnight with sixty-two and a half hours on night shift). The data for the first and last half-hours of each spell of work are omitted from the table. The workers were employed using lathes, drills and other machines with cutting tools. From these and other data Vernon concludes that as a rule for men employed at such work fatigue has but little influence in the causation of accidents ; but that fatigue due to overlong hours, such as seventy-five per week, does increase the accident rate among women, and does this by raising the accident rate throughout the spell rather than by causing an excess of accidents at the end of the day, when fatigue should be most present. This point is clearly established by comparing the accident rates for women during the afternoon spell of the two periods.

Dr. Vernon's interesting study of the effect the length of working hours exerts upon the occurrence of accidents brought out further the difference between the reactions of men and women, as shown in the following table :—

TABLE B.—*Relationship between Accidents in Fatigue Period and in Subsequent Period.*

| Type of accident. | Ratio of accident frequency in fatigue period to that in subsequent fourteen months. | | Ratio of afternoon accidents to morning accidents. | | | |
| | | | In fatigue period. | | In subsequent fourteen months. | |
	Men.	Women.	Men.	Women.	Men.	Women.
Cuts . . .	1·14	2·73	1·07	1·45	1·08	1·17
Foreign bodies in eye .	0·65	2·09	0·90	1·51	0·98	1·67
Burns . . .	1·16	3·50	1·31	1·29	0·76	1·12
Sprains . . .	1·27	2·95	0·92	0·72	0·63	0·80
Previous injuries .	1·43	3·01	(0·46)	(0·82)	(0·59)	(0·53)
Weighed mean .	1·20	2·87	1·06	1·29	1·00	1·11

The women suffered 2·87 times as many accidents in the seventy-five hour week as subsequently, but the men only 1·20 times, an increase practically identical with the extra number of hours worked. Translated into figures in relation to cuts (far the most frequent of the accidents included), from November 2nd, 1915, to January 31st, 1916 (during which time a twelve-hour day was worked), the weekly rate per 10,000 men was 491, and from February 1st to May 1st, 1916 (when a ten-hour day was worked), the rate was 426 ; while for women the rates were 678 and 257 respectively.

A further detailed investigation has been conducted in America (28) into the effect upon the occurrence of accidents in the first place of work and in the second of diminishing neuro-muscular co-ordination of which the occurrence of accidents may be taken as an indication. The evidence as given exhibits the influence which speed of production, owing to increased exposure to risk, exerts upon the prevalence of accidents, and the way in which accidents increase out of proportion to production when fatigue is present due either to long hours or to heavy work. Emphasis is also laid on the way in which the accident rate varies inversely with the experience of the workers ; and information embodied in the following table shows how 48·5 per cent. of the accidents occurred among 34·2 per cent. of the workers in their first six months of employment, while only 51·5 per cent. occurred among the 65·8 per cent. of the workers with longer periods of employment. This distribution of accidents must invalidate any conclusion drawn from a comparison between the hourly incidence of accidents and the hourly output of workers unless both accidents and output refer to workers with similar periods of employment. Such a comparison would be further invalidated owing to output (taken to represent increased exposure to risk) varying directly with the experience of the workers, so that the 65·8 per cent. of workers with more than six months' experience would be responsible for considerably more than 65·8 per cent. of the output.

TABLE C.—*Distribution of Accidents and of Workers at a Ten-hour Plant according to Period of Employment.*

Percentage of	Period of employment.				
	First three months.	Three to six months.	Six to nine months.	Nine to twelve months.	Twelve months and over.
Workers	28·0	6·2	6·6	6·2	53·0
	34·2			65·8	
Accidents	34·7	13·8	5·1	2·5	43·9
	48·5			51·5	

The conclusions to be drawn are that :—

(1) Accident rates vary hour by hour with the rate of output, but the variations bear no definite relation to the rise and fall of this rate.

(2) Pronounced fatigue increases the frequency of accidents, but the rate of accident occurrence hour by hour or spell by spell does not provide any definite measure of the presence of fatigue.

The utmost that can be suggested is that if the accident rate of the afternoon exceeds by much that of the morning, then a case is made for further investigation into fatigue by other methods.

VIII. Influences contributing to Industrial Fatigue.

Industrial fatigue is the sum of the results of industrial activity ; it depends primarily on expenditure of physical energy in doing work which varies as the work is medium or light, quick or slow, intermittent or continuous ; but other influences affect the amount of energy available and the way in which it is expended. These influences can be placed in two groups. The first comprises influences not generally considered to be under the control of employers, which concern time spent outside hours of labour. They include housing conditions, facilities for transit to and from work, and means for healthy recreation. The second includes the number of hours of labour and their distribution, the conditions of employment and methods of work.

The first group is of undoubted importance, and, during the stress entailed in producing munitions for the war, was thrust forward to the public notice. Overcrowding of houses resulted in single beds being used for three workers at once, and being used for night workers by day and day workers by night; inadequate train, tram, and omnibus services rendered the capture of even standing room a daily struggle in which only the fittest survived; the absence in crowded munition centres of places wherein to spend a quiet hour or to vary the monotony of toil with healthy recreation left the worker only the streets with their undesirable associations. These influences, accentuated in war time, but normally present, materially affect the amount of energy available for working hours. They call for close attention from employers of labour; but opportunities seldom arise of demonstrating accurately their influence upon the production of industrial fatigue, and up to the present no comprehensive study has been made setting out statistically the importance of this group of influences.

The second group of influences which are more intimately under control has been the subject of much inquiry and research. It includes the length and distribution of hours of labour, the varying conditions of factory life under which work is carried on, and methods of employment practised. Modification of either of these influences may have a great effect upon the occurrence of fatigue.

Hours of Labour.

The importance of fixing the right number of hours of labour is coming more and more to be recognised. The idea that if a worker can make 100 articles in an hour he ought to make 1,000 in ten hours, 1,200 in twelve hours or even 1,400 in fourteen hours, is seen to be as foolish as to expect a runner, who can sprint 100 yards in ten seconds, to cover a mile in 176 seconds; and the dictum of the Manchester School of Industrial Economists in the middle of last century that " it is in the last hour of work that profits are made " (without any regard to the number of hours previously worked *) is now countered by the

* Even then controverted by the experience of Owen (9)

truth that "overtime does not pay." In many cases the shortening of hours has resulted in an increase in total output, because there is a longer interval for the removal from the tissues of fatigue products and for the building up of fresh energy. The classic instance of the shortening of hours took place March 1st, 1893, to February 28th, 1894, when the engineering works of Messrs. Mather and Platt at Salford changed from a fifty-three-hour week to a forty-eight-hour week by abolishing all work before breakfast and re-arranging hours to 7.45 a.m. to 12 noon, and 1 p.m. to 5.30 p.m. The results showed : (a) that there was an increase of 0·4 per cent. in the ratio of the wages cost to the turnover ; (b) that there was a saving in gas, electricity, fuel, wear and tear, etc., amounting, by coincidence, to 0·4 per cent. ; (c) that there was a fall in the amount of lost time from 2·46 per cent. in the fifty-three hour period to 0·46 per cent. in the forty-eight-hour period ; (d) that though pieceworkers lost 1·76 at the beginning of the trial year, this fell to 0·78 per cent. at the end ; and (e) that there was " increased cheerfulness and brightness " on the part of the workpeople. " We seem," wrote Sir William Mather in 1894, " to have been working in harmony with natural law, instead of against it, as in the unnatural conditions of men beginning the work of the day without provision required by nature for the proper exercise of their mental faculties and physical powers . . . Of this I am assured, that the most economical production is obtained by employing men only so long as they are at their best— when this stage is passed there is no true economy in their continued work."

TABLE D.—*Fifty-six Men sizing Fuse Bodies.*

Week ending	Actual hours of work per week.	Relative output per working hour.	Hours of work × relative output.
Nov. 14 to Dec. 19 . .	58·2	100	5,820 (= 100)
Feb. 27 to April 16 . .	50·5	122	6,161 (= 106)
May 28 to July 16 . .	52·1	119	6,200 (= 107)
July 22 to Aug. 5 . .	46·3	123	—
Sept. 2 to Sept. 23 . .	47·6	135	6,426 (= 110)
Oct. 7 to Nov. 4 . .	51·3	137	7,028 (= 121)
Nov. 11 to Dec. 16 . .	51·2	139	7,117 (= 122)

Another demonstration is furnished from the work done by Dr. Vernon during war-time (3). The following tables summarise his study of output of workers employed for varying hours upon different operations. Table D refers to men employed in sizing fuse bodies—a heavy, strenuous task, comparable to that with which Chart A on p. 94 is concerned ; the rate of work was entirely determinable by the operatives, not by the pace of machines. The hours were reduced 12 per cent. and the output rose 22 per cent.

The next table (Table E) shows how, when the hours of women employed on moderately heavy work, turning aluminium fuse bodies—a process in which speeding-up was possible to a limited extent—were reduced 31 per cent. the output rose 9 per cent.

TABLE E.—*Ninety-five or Eighty Women turning Aluminium Fuse Bodies.*

Week ending	Actual hours of work per week.	Rela- tive output per work- ing hour.	Hours of work × relative output.	Remarks concerning output.
Nov. 14 to Dec. 19 .	66·2	100	6,620 (=100)	
Feb. 27 to April 16 .	53·4	123	6,568 (= 99)	Total output only 1 per cent. less than in pre-Christmas period, though weekly hours of work are 12·8 less.
May 14 to July 2 .	54·8	134	7,343 (=111)	Total output reaches a maxi- mum—11 per cent. greater than that of pre-Christmas period, though weekly hours of work are 11·4 less.
July 9 to July 23 .	50·0	132	—	Workers went on to night shift for three weeks.
July 30 to Aug. 19 .	47·0	124	—	Fall of output may be due to slackness resultant on depriva- tion of usual holiday. No more Sunday labour after August 6th.
August 26 . .	—	—	—	Holiday for a week (to compen- sate for loss of Whitsuntide and August holidays).
Sept. 2 to Sept. 23 .	49·9	135	6,737 (=102)	Hourly output rises again to that of the May-June period, but abolition of Sunday labour has not yet had any obvious effect.
Sept. 30 . .	—	—	—	Further four days' holiday (general holiday, by Govern- ment order).
Oct. 7 to Nov. 4 .	48·3	144	6,955 (=105)	Further rise of hourly output due to holiday and to abolition of Sunday labour.
Nov. 11 to Dec. 16 .	45·6	158	7,205 (=109)	Influence of shorter hours and of abolition of Sunday labour now well established. Total out- put 9 per cent. greater than it was a year ago, though weekly hours of work are 20·6 less.

The third table (Table F) records the output of women employed on light work, milling screw threads—a process at which for four-fifths of her time the operative stood idly watching her machine, and could only quicken her working speed in the remaining one-fifth. Here a reduction in hours of 25·9 per cent. only reduced the output 1 per cent

TABLE F.—*Forty Women milling a Screw Thread.*

Week ending	Actual hours of work per week.	Relative output per working hour.	Hours of work × relative output.	Remarks concerning output.
Nov. 21 to Dec. 19 .	64·9	100	6,490 (=100)	
Feb. 27 to April 16 .	55·4	—	6,039 (= 93)	
May 28 to July 9 .	54·6	114	6,224 (= 96)	
July 16 to Aug. 6 .	54·8	121	6,631 (=102)	Total output reaches its maximum—2 per cent. more than in November–December period, though weekly hours of work are 10·1 less.
Aug. 12 . . .	29·5	123	—	Reduction of hours owing to temporary shortage of material.
Aug. 19 . . .	38·1	122	—	
Aug. 26 . . :	—	—	—	Holiday for a week.
Sept. 2 to Sept. 23 .	45·5	121	5,506 (= 85)	No immediate response to abolition of Sunday labour, so total output falls considerably.
Oct. 14 to Nov. 18 .	48·1	133	6,397 (= 99)	Total output only 1 per cent. less than in November–December period, though weekly hours of work are 16·8 less.

The fourth table (Table G) is of interest because, although the process—boring top caps—was light work, it gave hardly any opportunity for acceleration. The hours were reduced 24·8 per cent., and output fell by 3 per cent.

TABLE G.—*Fifteen Youths boring Top Caps.*

Statistical period.	Actual hours of work per week.	Relative output per working hour.	Hours of work × relative output.
Nov. 15 to Dec. 19 . .	72·5	100	7,250 (= 100)
Jan. 3 to Feb. 13 . .	69·1	106	7,325 (= 101)
Feb. 21 to April 16 . .	54·8	108	
May 1 to May 28 . .	54·7	117	6,400 (= 88)
May 29 to July 2 . .	47·4	124	
July 3 to Sept. 23 (day shift).	52·8 ⎫	129 ⎫	
	⎬ 54·5	⎬ 129	7,030 (= 97)
July 2 to Sept. 23 (night shift).	56·2 ⎭	128 ⎭	

Emphasis must be laid upon this first-rate piece of statistical investigation. We find that to immure women within the factory walls twenty hours longer than a particular time actually results in obtaining fewer manufacturerd articles ; this cannot, therefore, be defended on any grounds. By application of the statistical method of plotting gross outputs as ordinates against working hours as abscissæ (see Fig. 7) Vernon, using the data of the tables, suggests the possibility of estimating the probable hourly output to be anticipated if the hours are further reduced ; this is shown by the dotted continuations of the curves in the chart. Thus, had the hours of the " men sizing " been further reduced to 47½ per week, the probable relative output per hour would have risen from 139 to about 158 ; but with the " youths boring " a reduction of hours to fifty could only be expected to raise the hourly output from 126 to about 133. This method provides a means of determining for any task the critical point beyond which lengthening the working day becomes crudely bad business. Humanity, and perhaps policy, as Burke said, might justify us in interfering at a level well below the critical point ; certainly no policy would justify non-interference at that point. This research has placed at the disposal of the State, the *entrepreneur*, or the trade union, a new and valuable instru-

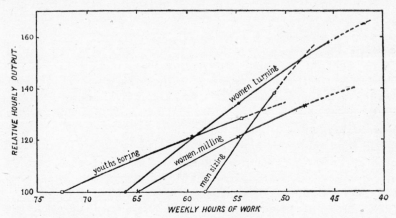

FIG. 7.—Relation of Output to Hours of Work. Reproduced from (3).

ment of regulation ; it seems to give a new significance to part of the negative confession which, according to the *Book of the Dead*, the Egyptians held a dead man was called upon to declare to be true when he came for judgment—" I have not made to be the first consideration of each day that excessive labour should be performed for me."

Hours of labour may be modified in other ways than by lengthening or shortening the hours worked. The hours may, instead, be redistributed ; thus a fifty-hour week may be distributed in either of the following ways :—

A.			B.		
6.30—8.30	⌉		7.30—12	.	.	$4\frac{1}{2} \times 5 = 22\frac{1}{2}$
9—12	⌋	(2+3) 6=30	1—5.30	.	.	$4\frac{1}{2} + 5 = 22\frac{1}{2}$
1—5	.	4×5 =20				
						45
		50	7.30—12 (Saturday)			5
						50

Experience shows that in Scheme A the first two hours worked before breakfast are not so productive as work done after food has been taken, and that this scheme is also associated (5) with much lost time owing to workers not coming to work until after breakfast, a practice which interferes with the work of those who do come (see p. 101).

Hours may also be modified by the interposition of rest pauses and the classical instance here is that given by Frederick Taylor (18), the originator of scientific management. Taylor accepted as a principle *that rest must adequately balance exertion ;* and after much research (details of which have not been published) into the periods that a man should be under load and entirely free from load concluded that, " For example when pig iron is being handled (each pig weighing 92 pounds), a first-class workman can only be under load 43 per cent. of the day. He must be entirely free from load during 57 per cent. of the day. And as the load becomes lighter, the percentage of the day under which the man can remain under load increases. So that, if the workman is handling half-pig, weighing 46 lbs., he can then be under load 58 per cent. of the day, and only has to rest during 42 per cent."

He then examined the output of men employed loading pig iron into railway cars, and found that a gang of about seventy-five men, considered to be good average pig-iron handlers, were loading on an average about twelve and a half long tons per day. This amount he considered fell below his estimate of what could be done, which indeed suggested the figure of forty-seven long tons. A man was found who submitted himself to work exactly as he was instructed, and Taylor describes as follows his first day's work : " Schmidt started to work, and all day long and at regular intervals, was told by the man who stood over him with a watch, ' now pick up a pig and walk. Now sit down and rest. Now walk, now rest,' etc. He worked when he was told to work, and rested when he was told to rest, and at half-past five in the afternoon had his forty-seven and a half tons loaded on the car. And he practically never failed to work at this pace and do the task that was set him during the three years that the writer was at Bethlehem." This man was not an exceptional person, for other members of the gang were subsequently taught how to work in this way, and they attained a similar figure.

Another instance (1) is that of two officers at the front, who for a friendly wager competed in making equal lengths of a certain trench, each with an equal squad of men. One let his men work as they pleased, but as hard as possible. The other divided his men into three sets, to work in rotation, each set digging their hardest for five minutes and then resting for ten, till their spell of labour came again. The latter team won easily. Organisation of heavy industrial work paid by time rate on such lines would probably provoke hirers of labour to say they were paying men for two-thirds of their time for doing nothing ! While if paid by piece rate, labour is found to object that opportunity is withheld for earning more wages !

Workers will often arrange their work to obtain pauses, and one of the authors found " a group of workers, men and women, paid on a time wage, employed from 6 a.m. to 6 p.m. with two half-hour meal intervals at the process of emptying and filling a series of presses. Each press, after being filled, has to be left under hydraulic pressure for thirty-five minutes, during which time other presses in the series are emptied and filled. The management calculated the number of presses to each series, which would allow the work to be done in thirty-five minutes at a reasonable pace ; but the workers on their own initiative have adopted a different method. They work with a rapidity so organised that the series of presses is emptied and filled in less than twenty-five minutes, after which they rest for ten or twelve minutes until the time comes to begin again. The work entails the expenditure of a fair amount of physical energy ; and it was interesting to watch these operatives swing into their labour in order to obtain their rest pause " (10).

The employers at another factory fix the day's work of juveniles employed on packing, and allow them to leave when the work is done. This plan was adopted because wages, which were simply handed over to parents each week, were found to provide no sufficient incentive to quick and accurate work ; but the incentive offered of earning an hour or more of freedom each day by working quickly has proved an entire success ; and the pride felt by a young girl in finishing at 3 p.m. is reflected in her gait as she smilingly leaves the factory.

A further instance of the value of rest-pauses, in this case as long as twenty minutes in every hour, is reported from the boot and shoe trade by J. Loveday (25). A total increase of output on six power presses of over 44 per cent. was obtained. The output of the comparatively unskilled and less robust workers, who would naturally be more liable to fatigue, was found to be increased to a greater extent than that of the more skilled workers.

Additional evidence bearing upon the value of rest pauses is to be found in the American publication already referred to (28). In the majority of processes submitted to the experiment of introducing in five-hour spells of work a ten-minute break mid-morning and mid-afternoon a distinct increase of output resulted, amounting in one instance to 25·9 per cent. ; less satisfactory results followed a similar experiment in the case of four-hour spells.   Generally the tendency of the ten-minute break to increase output both in the five-hour spells and in the four-hour spells was greatest among those workers whose original output was lowest, that is to say, among those whose efforts were expended with the least result ; these workers who might be expected to tire more quickly benefited more than rapid workers.

The effect of hours of labour upon output has been discussed at some length because the subject is one of immediate practical value, and there is sufficient evidence available to demonstrate methods of investigation ; the effect upon other indications of fatigue—of lost time, labour turnover, and the occurrence of accidents—require similar close study, but references other than those which are given elsewhere are here unnecessary.

Conditions of Employment.

The conditions under which work is done are intimately concerned with the occurrence of fatigue ; a close and overheated room will produce a condition of lethargy and a diminished capacity for doing work ; too cold a workplace on the other hand will slow down fine movements of the fingers and increase the liability to accident ; dim light renders work difficult ; lights badly placed throw troublesome shadows or cause headache ; seats, tables and machines not adjusted to the height of the workers do not allow of maximum efficiency ; excessive noise acting through the organ of hearing tires the whole system ; absence of adequate canteen provision often, especially in the case of women, leads to the consumption of food insufficient in energy value, or lacking in food accessory factors.

Ventilation.—The subject of ventilation of factories and workshops has been dealt with elsewhere in this volume. The effect of bad ventilation in diminishing the capacity for work and in lessening output is certain ; but there is still a lack of statistical evidence in support. No study of output data under varying conditions of ventilation has been made. Similarly, the effect of ventilation upon lost time and sickness has not been carefully demonstrated, although (22) contains some suggestive evidence ; there is only the fact that in summer, when more fresh air is admitted, the general sickness rate is lower (*vide* p. 100). Nor is there evidence exhibiting the influence ventilation has on labour turnover, or on the occurrence of accidents.

Temperature.—As will be explained later (p. 288) the question of temperature cannot be separated from that of humidity, and when a high temperature, over 72° F., is combined with a high humidity the effect in producing fatigue is

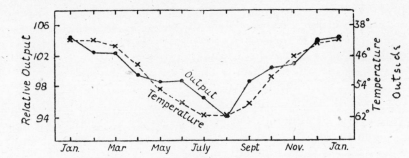

FIG. 8.—Seasonal Variation of Output and of Temperature. Reproduced from (11).

pronounced. Such conditions occur in humid cotton weaving-sheds, and also in the flax industry; but exact data as to the effect upon human activity are difficult to obtain, since alterations in temperature and humidity in these industries affect the condition of the threads. There are then two factors

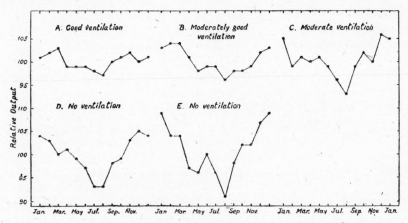

FIG. 9.—Seasonal Variation of Output at Individual Factories. Reproduced from (11).

concerned, the human body and the thread, both of which react to altered conditions; and so far the two have not been disentangled.

Where the material used is unaffected by temperature, the effect upon output has been studied by Dr. H. M. Vernon (11); thus the appended diagram (Fig. 8) shows how output in the

tinplate trade varies with seasonal variations in temperature.
At factories where special provision was made by mechanical
ventilation to reduce the temperature in summer the seasonal
effect upon output was less pronounced than in those factories
where no such provision was made (see Fig. 9). The same
investigator has also shown (12) that in the iron and steel
industry output varying round a mean of 100 may reach as
high as 107·7 in January, February and March, and fall as low
as 96·2 in June, July, August and September.

An indication of the effect of temperature upon bodily activity
may be gathered from a study of accident frequency. This
question also has been investigated among munition workers by
Vernon (19), who found that accidents were at a minimum at a
temperature of 65° to 69° F. ; that as the temperature fell, the incidence of accidents, especially among women, increased steadily ;
and that when it rose above 70° the incidence rose rapidly.

Observations made in the silk industry by P. M. Elton (24)
show that within a range of temperature of 58° F. to 65° F.
output tends to increase with temperature.

Human activity, whether measured by output or liability to
accident, appears to be at an optimum at about 65° F. (see
also (33)).

Lighting.—The effect of light upon activity and health is
discussed in Chapter XIV.

The only direct observations with which we are acquainted
demonstrating the effect of lighting upon output have reference
to the silk industry (24). Here, even with a good system of
electric lighting, production was found to be less than during
daylight hours. " The magnitude of this fall is of the order of
10 per cent. of the daylight value of the rate of output. Every
unnecessary hour under artificial light means a direct loss of
production and makes the task of the worker more difficult
than it need be."

Methods of Work.

There is a wrong way and a right way of doing everything,
and the right way is often only to be acquired by conscious effort.
In the athletic world this is well understood, and those who wish
to excel at any sport place themselves under teachers. The
boxer is taught how to poise his body and use his arms, the
cricketer is coached at the nets, the golfer is instructed how to
use his clubs, the oarsman undergoes a course of strenuous
teaching. Indeed, professional teachers and trainers belong to
every form of exercise, and their duty is to expound how the
maximum result can be attained with least expenditure of

energy. Up to the present, however, the matter of instructing manual workers how to use their muscles so as to earn their living with the least possible fatigue has not received enough attention. Their employers are content to explain what the task to be performed is, and then to leave them to carry it out as best they can. Any one accustomed to the *régime* of athletics is appalled by these haphazard methods of industry. Industry, indeed, has much to learn from athletics. Instances have already been given to show that, left to themselves, workers do not know how to get their best output by the interposition of rest-pauses ; where their movements and actions are concerned, the remark is even more apposite.

An important move, however, in the right direction was made some years ago in America by Frederick Taylor, who introduced motion study as a part of his system of scientific management. Under this system the necessary movements in any manual process are carefully analysed and timed, and the worker taught how to carry them out. Wonderful results have been obtained, but, unfortunately, the system has earned unpopularity with the workers. One reason for this is that piece-rate prices have been based on these studies, and the workers claim that the system has degenerated into a new form of slave driving, in which they are compelled to work much faster to obtain the same wages. In some instances again (13), the "scientific" experts have been . venal quacks, mere tools of unscrupulous employers. This is not the place to enter into the economic rights of the case, which have been fully discussed by Hoxie ; but we may point out that the greater is the output obtained from any plant, the more can the employer afford to pay in wages, because the overhead charges are spread over a larger bulk of product ; from this it follows that, within limits, as a worker's output increases he should receive a steadily increasing piece rate (10). Once this principle is grasped by employers, workers are found ready to adopt the system of motion study and to submit to being taught how to work.

Motion study and improved methods of work are only of professional interest to the physician when they eliminate or lessen fatigue ; if they only effect a greater production by an equal expenditure of energy with a similar degree of fatigue, the result medically is no advance (unless better wages enable better food to be taken). The physician is interested in the human machine being in order, the efficiency engineer in the output of that machine. Improved methods have, however, lessened fatigue in many cases, and so they have a medical interest, but in the main they belong rather to the province of the engineer than to that of the physician.

Arrangements for adjusting work to the physique of the workers are especially of medical interest. Chairs and tables all of the same height do not provide optimum conditions for all operatives, some of whom—perhaps 5 feet 10 inches in height —have to sprawl over the table to find room for their arms, while others—only 5 feet 2 inches—have to sit with their feet dangling off the floor ; yet neglect in this simple matter is the rule, not the exception, in modern factories. Machines such as lathes and looms are all constructed on a uniform pattern for tall and short alike ; sometimes foot-boards are provided to help the short, but the tall are left to bend all day at their tasks. We are unaware of any study determining the relation which should exist between the height of a worker and the height of, say, a lathe chuck. Gilbreth (14) has made an interesting study of chairs, and points out the value of high chairs provided with well-sloped backs and foot-rests for doing work which may always have been considered standing work, and of chairs with springs or other shock absorbers to eliminate vibration from floors carrying much high-speed machinery. This study of chairs is but an example of the many and varied devices required to avoid faulty and tiring postures, concerning which medical advice is often invaluable.

Apart from such necessary adjustments, study of the average capacity of workers has led to the suggestion of some useful rules. Amar states (15) a few simple results obtained : A spade when loaded should weigh $20\frac{1}{2}$ lbs. This means that a spade to be used for shovelling heavy iron ore should have a small blade which, when loaded, will carry this burden, and that a spade for shovelling light coke should have a blade large in proportion. With spades thus graduated to the material to be shovelled, a far greater bulk of material can be moved in a given time.

He states that a wheel-barrow should carry a load of 220 lbs., and that the pressure on the handles should be 44 lbs. And he fixes the most economical rate of walking along a flat surface at 2·8 miles per hour, at which pace, with two minutes' rest every mile and a half, twenty-eight to thirty miles can conveniently be covered. If a burden of about 45 lbs. is being carried, the pace should be slowed down to 2·6 miles per hour. " But to realise the maximum daily performance, the weight of the load should be 99 lbs., and the rate of progress three miles an hour, while the day's work should consist of seven and a half hours, with two minutes' rest every 650 yards. An adult of twenty-five to forty years can carry this load of 99 lbs. for an average distance of sixteen miles a day. But if the pace is increased to 3·4 miles an hour, the distance will be reduced by almost one half, no matter how the intervals of rest may be arranged."

Interest here attaches to some similar conclusions arrived at in a different way by the Research Committee on mine rescue apparatus. The committee, after remarking (29) that "like a steamer or an airship, a man has a most economical speed at which he goes furthest per litre of oxygen or per pound of food," gives for four subjects tested with a load of 43 lbs. three miles per hour as the most economical speed and four miles for two other subjects.

Amar has investigated the process of filing brass with a "half-rough" file about $13\frac{3}{4}$ inches long. "The body of the worker should be vertical, but without rigidity, at a distance of about 8 inches from the vice, the latter being at the level of the navel; the position of the feet should be as follows : the angle of divergence, 68°; the distance between the heels, 10 inches; the left arm should be completely extended, and should press upon the tool rather more heavily than the right arm, their respective efforts being $18\frac{3}{4}$ and $17\frac{1}{2}$ lbs. The return stroke of the file should consist of a simple sliding movement. without pressure. Finally, the rhythm of the movement is seventy per minute. All these conditions being fulfilled, five minutes' work will be followed by one minute's complete rest, the arms falling to the sides. The respirations and the heart beats then undergo an average increase of not more than 25 and 20 per cent. respectively, in comparison with the figures obtained during repose. The local fatigue of the right forearm is endurable, while the general fatigue is hardly perceptible. The maximum output is at least double the ordinary output of the great majority of workers. In this particular case 1·32 lbs. of filings were removed per diem, the day consisting of seven hours' effective work." Whether Amar's observations were extended over a sufficient number of individuals to authorise general conclusions is open to doubt.

Motion study is based on investigations like the above ; but often highly technical analysis is required in order to simplify movements and reduce them to a minimum. The objects aimed at from the fatigue point of view are stated by Gilbreth as follows (14) :—

" (1) To determine what fatigue* is unnecessary.

* We consider that greater accuracy would be obtained by reading "expenditure of energy" in each case for the word "fatigue."

" (2) To determine what fatigue* is necessary.

" (3) To eliminate all unnecessary fatigue* possible.

" (4) To distribute the necessary fatigue* properly, and to provide the best possible means for speedy and complete recovery."

Some examples may be of interest to indicate results obtained by this new art, which, however, if it is not to be unduly and harmfully exploited, requires to be watched closely by the medical profession. Far more attention to the provision of adequate statistical controls is also needed. Some published work on " scientific management " is very crude.

The method of bricklaying was studied by Gilbreth, who eliminated unnecessary movements and re-arranged the way in which the supply of bricks was placed to hand. A bricklayer who had previously been accustomed to lay 120 bricks per hour was by this means enabled to lay 350 per hour and, notwithstanding, was much less tired.

The use of shovels graduated, as mentioned above, doubles or trebles the performance of the shoveller. Many other instances are to be found in the literature on the subject; for example, of production increased from 400 to 1,800 per cent. in machine shop work, and of output increased 100 per cent. in the manufacture of cotton goods. Gilbreth also gives (16) the following instances :—

" In folding cotton cloth, twenty to thirty motions were reduced to ten or twelve, with the result that instead of one hundred and fifty dozen pieces of cloth, four hundred dozen were folded, with no added fatigue. The motions of a girl putting paper on boxes of shoe polish were studied. Her methods were changed only slightly, and where she had been doing twenty-four boxes in forty seconds, she did twenty-four in twenty seconds, with less effort."

One particular instance which has been reported upon by the Industrial Fatigue Research Board (17) may be referred to. During war time the plant of a certain foundry, the buildings of which were then somewhat dilapidated and out-of-date, was estimated by the Government to be capable of an output of 3,000 articles per week. The accuracy of the estimate may be accepted, since another firm with a larger plant found difficulty in maintaining an output of 5,000 articles. The manager, however, directed his attention to increasing this estimated output by improved methods of work : this he did by :—

" (a) Analysing the various jobs into their elemental units,

* We consider that greater accuracy would be obtained by reading " expenditure of energy " in each case for the word " fatigue."

studying each individual element with the assistance of a stop watch in order to arrive at the best method of performing it when all superfluous movements had been eliminated.

" (b) Arranging the tools and materials employed in such a standard manner as to avoid unproductive movements.

" (c) Establishing a standard set of movements for each process, together with a standard time for the performance of each.

" (d) Combining such movements as could be performed simultaneously.

" When the movements had been finally standardised, a card of typewritten instructions was prepared for each job. This card contained a list of the standard movements necessary for each process, together with the times they should take to perform, and it gave such details as whether the right or left hand should be used, or both. The elemental times, when added up at the foot, gave the total time in which the whole job should be completed. This card was placed before each operator during the period of training." At the same time the hours of work were reduced from fifty-four to forty-eight, and an improved system of wage payment was introduced. These alterations, undoubtedly, co-operated with the improved methods in contributing to the result, which was that 20,000 articles were produced per week. The increase, however, is so great, even if considerable allowances be made for the effect of shorter hours, and of better food arising from higher wages, that a substantial margin remains to be attributed to economy of effort due to systematic training, and to organisation and improved efficiency of material. The workers themselves stated they found their work less monotonous and more interesting, and that they experienced less or no more fatigue, although their output was nearly seven times as great.

IX. Bibliography.

1. "Industrial Fatigue and its Causes." *Health of Munition Workers Committee.* Memo. No. 7. (Cd. 8213.) 1916.

2. Fletcher, W. M., and Hopkins, F. G. " The Respiratory Process in Muscle and the Nature of Muscular Construction." Croonian Lecture. *Proceedings of Royal Society*, B, Vol. LXXXIX. 1917.

3. Vernon, H. M. " Further Statistical Information concerning Output in relation to Hours of Work." *Health of Munition Workers Committee.* Memo. No. 18. (Cd. 8628.) 1917.

4. Kent, A. F. Stanley. *Report on an Investigation of Industrial Fatigue by Physiological Methods.* (Cd. 8056.) 1915. *Second Report on an Investigation of Industrial Fatigue.* (Cd. 8335.) 1916.

5. Loveday, T.   " The Causes and Conditions of Lost Time."
Health of Munition Workers Committee. Interim Report.   (Cd. 8511.)
1917.

6. Greenwood, M.   " A Report on the Causes of Wastage of
Labour in Munition Factories." *Medical Research Committee.
Special Report Series, No. 16.*   1918.

7. Agnew, T. H.   " Report on the Health and Physical Condition
of Male Munition Workers." *Health of Munition Workers Committee.
Interim Report.*   (Cd. 8511.)   1917.

8. Vernon, H. M.   " An Investigation of the Factors Concerned
in the Causation of Industrial Accidents." *Health of Munition
Workers Committee. Memo. No. 21.*   (Cd. 9046.)   1918.

9. Cunningham.   *Growth of English Industry and Commerce in
Modern Times.*   Cambridge.   1892.

10. " Incentives to Work."   *Health of Munition Workers Committee. Interim Report.*   (Cd. 8511.)   1917.

11. Vernon, H. M.   " The Influence of Hours of Work and of
Ventilation on Output in Tinplate Manufacture." *Industrial Fatigue
Research Board. Report No. 1.*   1919.

12. Vernon, H. M.   " Fatigue and Efficiency in the Iron and Steel
Industry." *Industrial Fatigue Research Board. Report No. 5.*
1920.

13. Hoxie, R. F.   *Scientific Management and Labour.*   D. Appleton
& Co.   New York.   1915.

14. Gilbreth, F. B.   *Fatigue Study.*   G. Routledge & Sons.   1916.

15. Amar, Jules.   *The Physiology of Industrial Organisation.*
Translated by M. Miall.   Library Press, Ltd.   1918.

16. Gilbreth, F. B.   " Motion Study as an Increase of National
Wealth." *Annals of American Academy of Political and Social
Science.*   Publication No. 871.   Philadelphia.   May, 1915.

17. Myers, C. S.   " A Study of Improved Methods in an Iron
Foundry." *Industrial Fatigue Research Board. Report No. 3.*
1919.

18. Taylor, F. W.   *Principles of Scientific Management.*   Harper
and Brothers.   New York.   1911.

19. Goldmark, Josephine.   *Fatigue and Efficiency.*   Charities
Publication Committee.   New York.   1912.

20. Lee, F. S.   *The Human Machine.*   Longmans, Green & Co.
1918.

21. Spaeth, R. A.   " The Problem of Fatigue." *Journal of
Industrial Hygiene.*   May, 1919.

22. Huntingdon, E.   *World Power and Evolution.*   (Chapter V.)
Oxford University Press.   1919.

23. Myers, C. S.   " Industrial Overstrain and Unrest." *Lectures
on Industrial Administration.*   Sir Isaac Pitman & Sons, Ltd.   1920.

24. Elton, P. M.   " A Study of Output in Silk Weaving during
the Winter." *Industrial Fatigue Research Board. Report No. 9.
(Textile Series, No. 3.)*   1920.

25. Loveday, J.   " Preliminary Notes on the Boot and Shoe
Trade." *Industrial Fatigue Research Board. Boot and Shoe Series,
No. 1.*   1920.

26. Hele-Shaw, H. S.   " Endurance of Metals." *Proc. Instit.
Mechan. Engineers,* p. 895.   October, 1911.

27. Hele-Shaw, H. S.   " Travelling at High Speeds." *Nature.*
May 4th, 1911.

28. " Comparison of an Eight-hour Plant and a Ten-hour Plant."

Public Health Bulletin, No. 106. Government Printing Office, Washington. 1920.

29. " Second Report of the Mine Rescue Apparatus Research Committee." *Department of Scientific and Industrial Research.* H.M. Stationery Office. 1920.

30. Kennely, A. E. " An Approximate Law of Fatigue in the Speeds of Racing Animals." *Proc. of Amer. Acad. Arts and Sciences,* Vol. XLII., No. 15. December, 1906.

31. Lovett and Martin. " The Spring Balance Muscle Test." *Amer. Journ. Orthop. Surg.,* 14, p. 415. 1916.

32. Martin, E. G. " Strength Tests in Industry." *Public Health Reports,* Vol. 35, No. 33. Government Printing Office, Washington. 1920.

33. Huntington, E. *Civilisation and Climate.* Yale University Press. 1915.

CHAPTER VI

TUBERCULOSIS AND INDUSTRY

I. Epidemiology.

TUBERCULOSIS, or at least its pulmonary form, is a disease which has been familiar in all ages and to all civilised peoples ; records of it exist which were made in the time of the Assyrian Empire ; all the Græco-Roman authors speak of it and hardly a mediæval or modern physician whose works have survived failed to give a clinical account of pulmonary consumption.

Predisposition and Infection.—Although the possibility that consumption was an infectious disease had been discussed in more or less detail by such men as Aristotle, Galen,* Avicenna, Lommius, Morton and Morgagni, and fully examined by Thomas Young 100 years ago, the general trend of opinion before the days of Villemin, William Budd and Koch was to the effect that an inherited disposition, predisposition or diathesis (these terms as one of us has pointed out (1), are *not* synonymous) played the chief *rôles* in the production of phthisis. After the unequivocal demonstration of the infective element by Villemin and Koch, opinion veered round completely, and in our own generation the hygienic problem of tuberculosis has been largely regarded as one of diminishing the opportunities for transferring the tubercle bacillus from man to man or from domestic animals to man. Although the practical measures inspired by the two theories were not necessarily or usually different, some change of emphasis has resulted. It was as fully accepted fifty years ago as it is now that tuberculosis was a *pestis pauperum.* But in pre-bacterial days the explanation was that the unfavourable environment of the poor, acting upon a population containing a relatively high percentage of physically inferior stocks, led to the manifestation of the innate physical vices of the con-

* The doctrine of contagion in ancient medicine was, however, essentially different from that entertained in modern times after the days of Fracastorius.

stitution, and gave the predisposition its chance. It was thought that the only policy to pursue was to improve the general social and sanitary conditions of the working classes, thereby to improve their general powers of resistance. In our time more attention has been devoted to attacking in detail particular evils associated with poverty, as, for instance, the purification of urban milk supplies or the segregation of " open " (i.e., actively infective) cases of phthisis in sanatoria, or again by the disinfection of the consumptive's discharges.

To crystallise tendencies into epigrams is always to overstate the antithesis, but we shall perhaps help the reader to grasp the distinction if we say our grandfathers believed that in the case of consumption what was the matter with the poor was poverty, and that consumption would not be eliminated without the eradication of poverty ; since they did not believe that poverty could be eradicated, they did not expect to " stamp out " consumption. The latter-day view is less pessimistic (or, if we look at it from another point of view, more pessimistic) and suggests that consumption might be eliminated without any obliteration of the distinction between class and class.

From the point of view of the present work we have to try to ascertain which tendency of thought is in the true direction, and the problem we formulate for discussion in this chapter is whether the conditions of industry have any special effect in increasing or diminishing the toll taken by tuberculosis of human life. An attempt to answer this question will, however, involve a general examination of the epidemiological problems presented by the group of diseases due to the tubercle bacillus.

Effect of Poverty.—We said above that tuberculosis was always held to be a *pestis pauperum ;* this statement must now be justified.

Two criteria may be appealed to : type of domicile, and occupational status.

The size of the house may be taken as a fair estimate of the poverty or affluence of the occupants ; but, in instituting a comparison between the mortality from tuberculosis among the occupants, we are aware that poverty in this case may be held to stand for imperfect hygiene, general and personal, and also for overcrowding. The figures here quoted (10) clearly show on this test that a close relation exists between poverty and the disease ; and they may also be claimed in support of the view (to which we shall refer again later) that the home exerts a powerful influence in its dissemination.

Type of dwelling.	Death rate per 100,000 from tuberculosis.		
	Greenock (1913).	Glasgow (1913).	Edinburgh (1910—12).
Four or more rooms	87	70	56
Three rooms. .	106	120	111
Two rooms . .	179	180	146
One room . .	222	240	225

Occupational status provides further evidence.   If we contrast the experience of the clergy on the one hand with that of general labourers (1900–2) we find that, although from nearly all causes of death, the latter died at a greater rate than the former, the contrast reaches an extreme in the matter of phthisis.   The mortality of general labourers from cancer was 231 per cent. that of the clergy ; from all causes other than cancer and phthisis it was 344 per cent. ; but from phthisis no less than 849 per cent. In London metropolitan boroughs, while the death rate from phthisis varies with differentiæ of poverty (such as the proportion of general labourers, or the proportion of pawnbrokers), the correlation between the (corrected) cancer rate and measures of poverty is not pronounced.   Although the work of Maynard (2) and of Brown and Lal (3) suggests that there is a correlation between the incidence of cancer and lack of social well being, it is not very large ; but the comparison for phthisis mortality between clergy and general labourers which we have made is representative of the general statistical relations observed in most kinds of data, e.g., the death rate from phthisis (1909—12) was 1·86 in the poor district of Shoreditch, and 0·57 in more prosperous Hampstead.   Hence the close relation between a high death rate from tuberculosis and poverty may be deemed to be established.

Decline of Tuberculosis.—We shall now consider the course of tuberculosis mortality in England and Wales as a whole.   In the past fifty years the rate of mortality in all areas has declined ; taking the age standardised death rate of males 1851—60 for pulmonary tuberculosis—phthisis—as 100, we have the results shown in Table 1.   The decline has been substantial in both sexes, but greater for women than for men ; in 1851—60 the female death rate from pulmonary tuberculosis was 106 per cent. of the male rate ; in 1901—10 it was 70 per cent. of the corresponding male rate.   In the next table we give the death rates per million living at certain age groups of males and

TABLE 1.—*Comparative Phthisis Mortality of England and Wales since* 1851.

	Males.	Females.
1851—60 . .	100	106
1861—70 . .	97	96
1871—80 . .	88	79
1881—90 . .	73	62
1891—1900 .	61	46
1901—10 . .	50	35

TABLE 2.—*Death Rates per Million. Phthisis.*

Group.	Age periods.						
	15–20.	20–25.	25–35.	35–45.	45–55.	55–65.	65 and over.
Males { Urban, 1891—1900 .	1,010	1,815	2,448	3,581	3,798	3,150	1,907
Rural, 1891—1900 .	1,039	2,195	2,269	2,248	2,116	1,995	1,349
Urban, 1901—1910 .	764	1,433	1,959	2,751	3,330	2,915	1,895
Rural, 1901—1910 .	755	1,796	2,049	1,907	1,839	1,656	1,174
Females { Urban, 1891—1900 .	1,233	1,500	1,925	2,331	1,799	1,313	852
Rural, 1891—1900 .	1,557	1,967	2,108	1,849	1,409	1,155	826
Urban, 1901—1910 .	948	1,161	1,448	1,666	1,465	1,148	799
Rural, 1901—1910 .	1,182	1,585	1,681	1,383	1,078	964	754

TABLE 3.—*Urban Mortality as Percentage of Rural Mortality. Phthisis.*

Group.	Age periods.						
	15–20.	20–25.	25–35.	35–45.	45–55.	55–65.	65 & over.
Males { 1891—1900 .	97	83	108	159	179	158	141
1901—1910 .	101	80	96	144	181	176	161
Females { 1891—1900 .	79	76	91	126	128	114	103
1901—1910 .	80	73	86	121	136	119	106

females in successive decennia recorded by the Registrar-General, contrasting groups of urban and rural counties. In Table 3 these are expressed as ratios. A noteworthy point is the greater death rate of women in the rural counties at the earlier ages. This has usually been explained by supposing that the migration to towns of healthy young women and the departure from the cities of phthisics have favoured the urban death rates. The decennial abstracts do not transfer deaths of non-residents from

one registration area to another ; but this has been done in the
Registrar-General's annual reports since 1911. After this
correction we find that although the rural death rate at fifteen
to twenty (females) is less than the urban rate, in the three
following quinquennial age groups the urban rate remains lower
than the rural rate (Table 4). This transfer of deaths from the

TABLE 4.—*Phthisis Death Rates per Million*, 1911. *Females.*

Age.	Rural districts.	All urban districts.
15—20	972	1,031
20—25	1,273	1,227
25—30	1,480	1,316
30—35	1,463	1,344

area in which they were registered to that of the home of the
deceased possibly corrects one of the assumed errors ; but the
other, the migration to towns of healthy young women in search
of employment, remains. This could only be effectively corrected by an elaborate process for which data are not available ;
but by the following considerations we may perhaps reach some
approximate measure of its importance. In the enumerated
population of England and Wales (1911) the ratio of women
aged twenty to twenty-five to females under five was 0·872 ;
of women aged twenty-five to thirty, 0·846 ; and of women
aged thirty to thirty-five, 0·783. If we multiply the number of
female children under five enumerated in the rural districts by
these fractions we shall obtain the numbers of women in each
age group who would be living in the rural districts if the ratio
observed in the general female population were maintained.
The numbers actually enumerated fell short by 47,783, 40,101
and 30,299 respectively of the computed numbers. If we suppose that these deficits represent the numbers of women who
had passed from the rural to the town districts, and further
suppose that their death rate from phthisis was negligibly
small—all being by hypothesis selected lives—the deaths
recorded in the urban districts (including London and the
county boroughs) divided not by the enumerated population,
but by the enumerated population less the conjectured number
of migrants, will give the true urban death rate ; while the
sum of deaths in rural districts divided by the enumerated
population plus the migrants will give the true rural death rate.
This calculation gives for ages twenty to twenty-five, 1,275 per

million for urban, and 1,106 for rural districts ; for ages twenty-five to thirty, the figures are 1,361 and 1,311 ; and for ages thirty to thirty-five, 1,383 and 1,327 respectively. The result tends to support the doctrine that the favourable rates at early ages in towns are really due to migration ; but the method is very rough, and the point deserves a more detailed examination.

No such simple explanation will account for the more rapid decline of female phthisis mortality in the whole country in comparison with that of males. It is conceivable that the decline in birth rate has been a factor, in view of the unfavourable effect of childbirth upon the prognosis of phthisis ; but female mortality was already declining faster than that of males in the decennium prior to that in which the decline of the birth rate began to be of serious import.

Male and Female Mortality.—Returning to Table 2, it will be noticed that from age thirty-five onwards, although the female mortality in the urban counties is considerably higher than in rural counties, the discrepancy between the urban and rural

TABLE 5.—*Phthisis Mortality, 1911. Ages Thirty-five and Over.*

Age.	Males.			Females.		
	Rural districts.	All urban districts.	Ratio.	Rural districts.	All urban districts.	Ratio.
35—40	1,361	2,256	166	1,201	1,490	124
40—45	1,328	2,469	186	975	1,423	146
45—50	1,300	2,498	192	832	1,310	157
50—55	1,163	2,787	240	817	1,070	131
55—60	1,293	2,539	196	706	1,029	146
60—65	1,144	2,440	213	862	988	115

Sex Ratios for Urban and Rural Districts.

Age.	Rural districts.	Urban districts.
35—40	113	151
40—45	136	174
45—50	156	191
50—55	142	260
55—60	183	247
60—65	133	247

male rates is much greater, amounting to no less than 80 per cent. excess in the age group forty-five to fifty-five. The same result is brought out in Table 5, which embodies the shorter series of more exact figures relating to the year 1911.

In these later age groups the factor of migration is of much less moment than at earlier ages, and to explain the facts we are led to choose between the following hypotheses :—

(a) The heavier incidence upon males is a direct consequence of urban industrial employment ; (b) home environment reacts more unfavourably upon males than upon females ; (c) the physical selection of urban females is more stringent than that of males.

With respect to the third hypothesis, we have only to remark that there is no evidence at all that the struggle for existence is less keen or the physical criteria of survival less exacting among men than among women ; young male adults are not subject to a lower death rate from all causes than are females.

Passing now to the other two direct environmental factors, (a) and (b), we have to examine the evidence that tuberculosis does affect with especial severity those engaged in occupations associated characteristically with urban life.

Assuming that this were the true explanation, the Great War led to a control experiment upon a large scale, because a vastly greater proportion of the female population than usual was suddenly plunged into factory life ; if, then, industrialisation were a serious epidemiological factor we should expect, since the war, women in this country would die of tuberculosis at a higher rate than immediately before it. This actually happened and was noted by Dr. Stevenson in his official review of the statistics of 1916 ; he pointed out that the increase (of the order of 5 per cent.) did not affect the women over forty-five, and might, therefore, be connected with munition factory work. In this country we have no statistical data of the incidence of tuberculosis upon women employed in industry ; but such rates are available for the women of Leipzig, and, since it has been found by one of us (4) that the Leipzig rates for males corresponded very closely with those of similarly employed English males, the probability is that the rates for females correspond equally closely. Now the distributions of women in industries just before the war and at the end of 1916 were known with some exactness. For instance, in July, 1914, about 170,000 women were engaged in the metal industries ; in January, 1917, the number was 443,000 ; the numbers employed in chemical industries doubled in the same period ; those employed in commerce increased 50 per cent.; and so forth. Hence, to form a statistical appreciation of the magnitude of the industrial factor, we could proceed as follows : Apply to the industrial groupings in 1914 and 1916 the Leipzig occupational death rates from tuberculosis and see how far the calculated numbers agree with the observations. The female tuberculosis death rate of Leipzig was 4·04 per 1,000 per annum in the metal industries, 3·13 in chemical industries, and 2·80 in textiles, as contrasted with 0·97 for domestic servants, etc. (mainly women fifteen to thirty-five) ; so that substantial transfers would increase the mortality. In the result we reached the conclusion that there should by calculation be 22,446 deaths in 1914, and 23,986 in 1916, an increase of 1,540 ; the recorded numbers were 22,214 and 24,131, an increase of 1,917 ; the agreement is reasonably good, although the actual increase was larger than predicted. A further confirmation was afforded by a study of the proportion deaths due to pulmonary tuberculosis bore to all deaths in the great industrial centres since the war. It was found that this proportion had increased from under 35 per cent. to over 42 per cent. between 1913 and 1916 in the group of large towns (Birmingham, Coventry, Manchester, Newcastle and Sheffield) much affected by war influx of workers ; it had increased less characteristically in towns less affected by war industries, such as Ipswich, Norwich, Stoke-on-Trent, York and Worcester ; but it had not increased at all or even fallen in non-industrial towns like Bournemouth, Brighton, Oxford, and Great Yarmouth. This result is, of course, not decisive, because an increase in the proportion of deaths from a disease might be found although the absolute number of deaths declined, but this is unusual. Like all Nature's economic experiments, this of wartime was not planned on precisely the lines we desired, yet it does generally support the inference that industrial employment is a factor in the production of tuberculosis. During the period considered no other relevant new factors were introduced ; the country was well fed, and there was not among women any withdrawal of the healthy persons from the ambit of our civilian statistical records (which occurred in men, and, of course, rendered the wartime male rates of death from tuberculosis quite useless for any general epidemiological purpose). The one great factor which might have played a part was industrial employment itself inseparably connected with aggregation in urban districts.

The conclusion here suggested, that increased industrialisation has been the main factor determining the increased prevalence of phthisis among women which occurred during the war period, receives some confirmation from the data for the year 1919.

TABLE 5A.—*Comparative Mortality from Phthisis among Women.*

Year.	Age period.			
	15—20.	20—25.	25—35.	35—45.
1913 .	100	100	100	100
1917 .	150	131	113	114
1919 .	130	120	103	94

The phthisis mortality experienced among women in the United Kingdom at different age periods in 1913 is, for comparative purposes, stated above as 100. The data for 1917 illustrate how the phthisis rate rose ; while the data for 1919 show how a swing back took place as women came out from industry. This swing has actually carried the mortality below the 1913 standard for the older women, who naturally were the first to resume normal life, while the swing is less at younger ages, where the proportion of women still remaining in factories was considerable, and there are still probably more women in industrial employment than before the war.

Occupation and Male Mortality.—We shall now consider the occupational incidence of tuberculosis upon males, the problem being to learn whether there are any industries particularly associated with urban life which are unduly subject to tuberculosis.

This question has been investigated upon the following lines. We used the occupational mortality records compiled decennially by the Registrar-General and a similar set of data prepared in Holland, eliminating occupations to which a direct occupational risk attaches, viz., those forms of mining, quarry and metal work in which injury inflicted upon the pulmonary tissues by silica particles is known to enhance the tuberculosis death rate. The residue of occupations was then analysed and the death rate from tuberculosis correlated with that from all other causes. The equation connecting the death rate from other causes with that from tuberculosis was then computed, and those occupations noted which experienced a death rate from tuberculosis or from pulmonary tuberculosis at least 25 per cent. greater than predicted from a knowledge of the death rate due to other causes. The reason for this proceeding was that we wished to find trades specially liable *in se*, not trades the followers of which were generally unhealthy, perhaps owing to some negative selection (such as might happen if bad wages bring together only the failures of other occupations, a factor which, no doubt, explains the high mortality of "general labourers "). In this way, bookbinders, printers, tailors and cabinetmakers emerged as on the black list of all the data (three English decennial returns and one Dutch record) used (see Table 6). Hosiery makers and shoemakers also in the

TABLE 6.—*Comparative Mortality Figures, 1890-2 and 1900-2 ; Phthisis, 1910—12. All Forms of Tuberculosis.*

Occupation.	1890–2.	1900–2.	1910—12.
Clergy	100	100	100
Agricultural labourers . .	175	155	156
Coal miners	147	160	163
Bricklayers, etc. . . .	338	355	273
Saddlers, etc.	358	402	323
Commercial clerks . . .	327	360	356
Cotton manufacturers. . .	303	362	256
Wool and worsted manufacturers.	287	296	262
Silk manufacturers . . .	294	375	273
Hosiery manufacturers . .	286	398	377
Lace manufacturers . . .	242	345	325
Carpet manufacturers. . .	342	315	246
Tinplate goods manufacturers .	327	394	263
Paper manufacturers . . .	217	262	210
Cabinetmakers	373	409	412
Shoemakers	386	483	456
Tailors	408	445	383
Printers	491	547	421
Bookbinders	490	515	427

English, but not the Dutch, experience, were unduly subject to tuberculosis. But these occupations are pre-eminently associated with the great urban aggregations of mankind, so that qualitatively the result reached is in good agreement with our geographical findings. We now come to a subtle point in the epidemiology. Assuming it to be proved that the higher incidence of male tuberculosis amongst town dwellers is due to industrial employment, is the effect a direct or an indirect one ? It being certain that men employed in a printing works, say, suffer from tuberculosis at a higher rate than, say, agricultural labourers, is this because they are more likely to be infected in the indoor association enforced by their employment, and if so, do they infect their families ? Or is it that the circumstances of the work make them more readily susceptible to deleterious influences in the home environment ?

To test the point so far as it could be tested, Miss C. M. Thompson, working with one of us, has made a careful study of the inter-relations of the death rate from tuberculosis, the death rate from all other causes, the percentage of the population housed more than two to a room, and the proportions in age groups employed in factory industries in the twenty-eight metropolitan boroughs. If we accept the proportion more than two to a room as a fairly good measure of home conditions—which it probably is in the London boroughs—the proportion industrially employed as a criterion of the amount of factory work (the occupations taken out were those in which little home employment exists), and if we regard the death rate from other causes as some measure of general physique, the net, or in technical language, partial correlations of highest order, between the variables should tell us something about the respective importance of the different variables in the two sexes.

TABLE 7.—*Co-efficients of Partial Correlation for each Pair of the Four Variables shown, the Remaining Two being made Constant. Data Twenty-eight London Boroughs, Years 1911—13.*

Variables.	Ages.					
	15—25.		25—45.		45—65.	
	Males.	Females.	Males.	Females.	Males.	Females.
Tuberculosis and overcrowding	− ·48 ± ·10	− ·38 ± ·11	+ ·71 ± ·06	+ ·05 ± ·13	+ ·46 ± ·10	+ ·60 ± ·08
Tuberculosis and other diseases	+ ·21 ± ·12	+ ·31 ± ·12	+ ·15 ± ·12	+ ·74 ± ·06	+ ·19 ± ·12	+ ·50 ± ·10
Tuberculosis and factory employment	+ ·56 ± ·09	+ ·48 ± ·10	+ ·25 ± ·12	+ ·19 ± ·12	+ ·19 ± ·12	− ·40 ± ·11

Taking first the overcrowding index. At ages fifteen to twenty-five this is negatively correlated with the tuberculosis death rate for both sexes, and is not significantly different in the two sexes. At ages twenty-five to forty-five the correlation becomes large and positive for males, but it is insignificant for women. At ages forty-five to sixty-five the correlation for males is still large, although smaller than for the previous group, and is also large for women. The deduction follows that at ages between twenty-five and forty-five the home environment factor is *more* important for males than for females.

The industrial factor is positively correlated with the death rate from tuberculosis at all ages, save that of women forty-five to sixty-five, and continuously decreases with age, being largest for the young adults and adolescents. The correlation with deaths from other diseases is positive at all ages, but much larger for women than for men in the age group twenty-five to forty-five, and also at forty-five to sixty-five. The apparent meaning of these coefficients is of so much epidemiological importance that they will need most careful testing upon larger collections of data, and our inferences are plainly subject to modification when knowledge is less fragmentary. That in the earliest age group there is actually an inverse relation between tuberculosis and overcrowding, which latter is a measure of bad home conditions, may reflect the circumstance that in the casual trades the most prosperous period is that of early man-hood prior to marriage ; at that age the blind alley trades often provide a better wage than is earned by apprentices to skilled trades. Of the relation between tuberculosis and underfeeding, the recently published statistics of Prussia, showing an increase of deaths from 56,861 in 1913 to 86,217 in 1917, are an impressive example. Again, the death rate from phthisis in the Registrar-General's occupational group of messengers and porters is below the average at the earliest age tabulated, although above the average subsequently. This group covers much " blind alley " work.

In adult life twenty-five to forty-five, the greater effect of overcrowding upon the male than upon the female suggests that the influence of factory life is an indirect one. In London, the proportion of males employed in factories is much greater than that of women. In London, percentages in factories are :—

	Men.	Women.
15—25	18	16·1
25—45	18	7·1
45—65	18	10·1

The suggestion is that the conditions of factory life render the male especially susceptible to unfavourable home conditions. The women, exposed nearly the whole time to the home condi-tions, do not respond so delicately to it ; the chief cause of variation amongst them is their natural physique, hence the high correlation between the death rate from other causes and that from tuberculosis for women. This statistical surmise is borne out by the field-investigation of Tebb in Birmingham (4). He found that no specific source of tubercular infection could be traced in any munition factories, good or bad ; but the employees in the unhygienic factories did suffer much more from tuberculosis than those employed at good modern factories. The inference is that the factories act as sensitisers, making the operative particularly susceptible to home conditions ; the epidemiological importance of the factory is indirect, that of the home direct. This finding is in agreement with the view expressed by Thomson (10), who, drawing his conclusion from different data, is emphatic that tuberculosis " is the morbid expression of unhealthy home conditions."

We provisionally answer the epidemiological question posed as to the relation between industrial employment and deaths from tuberculosis in the following terms : *The rôle of the factory is, by confinement in monotonously ventilated rooms and by causing general fatigue, to reduce the resistance of the operative to those sources of infection to which he is exposed in the natural course of life, to make him react more sharply to home influences than does his wife or sister.* The physiological basis of this lowered resistance has been explored by Dr. Leonard Hill in his recent investigations (5). Dr. Hill has shown that there is a considerable correlation between variations, not only of the sense of well-being, but of actual prevalence of sickness, and of the degree of stagnation of the air, and that stagnation of the air is revealed badly, if at all, by the time-honoured thermometer and hygrometer, but made patent by Hill's instrument, the katathermometer, which measures the rate of cooling of the air. Much is to be expected, not only from improvement of the dwellings of the working classes, but also from rational attention to the ventilation of workplaces ; the fetish of a low CO_2 content must be replaced by the sound doctrine—long enough known instinctively to the people—that moving air, not a draught but a breeze, is health-giving.

Types of Phthisis.—So far we have discussed the epidemiology of tuberculosis as if it were necessarily one and the same disease everywhere. Naturally, one should distinguish between pulmonary tuberculosis and other clinical forms, and we have done so in some collections of data, but not always, because at the adult ages of life pulmonary tuberculosis is the predominating form ; of the deaths assigned to tuberculosis in the decennium 1901—10 in persons between twenty and sixty-five, 90·9 per cent. were due to pulmonary tuberculosis and (undefined) phthisis. But it is a pure assumption to say that all these clinically similar causes of death are epidemiologically identical. We are dealing with death records, and there are numerous instances of diseases, *e.g.*, the typhoid group and the malaria group, which are clinically similar, and may even have a common bacteriological origin, but which none the less are epidemiologically different. Plague is a case in point. Persons dead of pneumonic plague may belong to two different epidemiological categories. In an epidemic of bubonic plague—the epidemiological features of which are non-transmission from human being to human being and maximum prevalence in moderately warm weather—deaths from a secondary pneumonia occur, and the exudate teems with plague bacilli. But another epidemiological type, that of primary pneumonic plague, is known ; here the disease prevails in cold weather and is probably, or certainly, transmitted from person to person. This is a rarer form, of which, however, the great Manchurian epidemic a few years ago provides a recent example. If we were furnished with statistics of plague deaths in a country subject to both epidemiological forms we might draw very erroneous conclusions from an analysis of the combined data. The question is, whether a form of this error has to be reckoned with in discussing pulmonary tuberculosis from the epidemiological side. Subdivisions of the clinical types of pulmonary tuberculosis were effected years ago, and we most of us learn about them in our hospital courses—the galloping or florid consumption, the ordinary chronic phthisis, and the long-drawn-out fibroid phthisis. But, so far as we know, Dr. John Brownlee was the first epidemiologist to attempt statistical analysis of phthisis into different forms (6). Brownlee's starting point was the great difference in shape of the curves of death rates at different ages in different parts of the country. For instance, in the Shetland Islands the death rate is at a maximum (5·85 per 1,000 living per annum) at the age twenty to twenty-five ; in London the maximum, 5·47, is at the age group forty-five to fifty-five. Brownlee did not think that such great differences in the form of the death rate curves were due to migration, occupation or natural selection, and he attempted to explain them upon the hypothesis that pulmonary phthisis *sans phrase* is a mixture of three epidemiological types :—

(1) A type of phthisis which chiefly affects young adults, the commonest age of death being between twenty and twenty-five.

(2) A type of phthisis which chiefly affects persons of middle age, the commonest age of death being between forty-five and fifty-five.

(3) A type of phthisis which chiefly attacks persons in old age and most frequently causes death between fifty-five and sixty-five years.

Brownlee's first test of his hypothesis was an attempt to graduate the death rate curves for various parts of England upon the assumption that they were compounded of three elementary types, the death rate at any age being $aY + bA + cO$, where Y, A and O are the death rates at that age of the three pure types, and the small letters are constants to be determined. As it could not be expected that any one of these types existed pure anywhere, it was necessary to proceed by a method of approximation. Starting with the phthisis death rates of Ireland, of London and of coal miners as predominatingly appertaining to the three hypothetical types, Brownlee was ultimately able to approximate to the hypothetical types, and to graduate with success the composite death rate curves of different parts of England and Wales.

Phthisis and Environment.—We now come to an extremely important point. Brownlee correlated the death rate from phthisis with the death rate from other causes, and it proved to be ·178 at twenty to twenty-five (males), ·390 at thirty-five to forty-five, ·272 at fifty-five to sixty-five (averages of ten districts or periods), while the value of the co-efficients varied with the proportion of the total di tribution attributable to middle-age phthisis, being large when that was large, and *vice versâ*. If then the death rate from other causes is taken as a measure of general unhealthiness, or, again, the general standardised death rate (which gave similar correlations), the middle-age type is more susceptible to environment than the others, and the fact that this is the predominant type in London, Lancashire and the great industrial districts explains why in these the phthisis rate becomes excessive in the later adult ages ; in these districts that type most responsive to environment prevails.* There is a vicious circle. We need hardly remark that Brownlee's conception is of great importance and, if true, would explain more than one difficulty. For instance, take the variety of opinions held as to the clinical value of tuberculin. Nobody is surprised that a typhoid vaccine does not protect against para-typhoid, and it would on Brownlee's hypothesis be equally unreasonable to expect a tuberculin derived from the middle-age type to protect against the young adult form of pulmonary tuberculosis. In Glasgow, for instance, the middle-age type is unusual. In London it is common and predominant ; if vaccines are usually made from the latter type they would give less satisfactory results in Glasgow than in London.

It must, however, be admitted that the evidence so far published by Brownlee, while consistent with the truth of his hypothesis, does not suffice to establish it. The test of effective

---

* It may also explain why the method of p. 136 applied to a heterogeneous collection of county boroughs leads to discrepant results.

graduation, although necessary, is not sufficient. It is a common enough experience in statistical practice to find that a set of data can be effectively graduated by mathematical formulæ the bases of which are altogether disparate.

Before a hypothetical law can be accepted as the correct description of statistical phenomena we must *first* show that the law will adequately graduate the observations which were the starting point of the inquiry, but we cannot rest there. It is necessary to proceed inductively and to show upon a wide collection of examples that the graduation by the proposed law is definitely more effective than graduation by other formulæ. It is no reproach to Brownlee that this condition has not yet been fulfilled by him; he has, at least, used all the data at present available.

The deductions from the co-efficients of correlation are also open to criticism.* It is perhaps doubtful whether either the standardised death rate or the death rate from causes other than tuberculosis at the same age is a really effective measure of environment; it might with at least equal plausibility, perhaps with greater plausibility, be asserted that the residual death rate is a measure of individual resisting power, of natural physique. In any event the various measures used, crude death rate, death rate from causes other than tuberculosis, standardised death rate, are not independent one of another, so that the series of co-efficients does not really represent a like number of independent measurements of the phenomenon under study. Brownlee has perhaps rather slighted the probable effect of industrial employment. While recognising that the parallelism of the death rate curves of both sexes makes in favour of his contention, we still have to reckon with the much greater incidence upon urban males in contrast with the urban females (see Table 5); it is difficult to avoid the conclusion that this is really a function of industrial employment, whether direct or, as suggested by the investigation detailed above, implicit.

Summary.—We may now sum up the results of our epidemiological inquiry, not because these results are clear cut and decisive, but to help the reader to distinguish between the partly solved and the wholly unsolved problems.

Looking at the country as a whole and the changes which have taken place during the last fifty years, a period in which steadily increasing industrialisation and its associated effect of aggregation within urban areas has been accompanied with

---

* It is proper to add that our own use of co-efficients of correlation is open to criticism, inasmuch as only three years' data were available, too short an experience for final deductions.

improvements of general sanitation, we find that the death toll
of tuberculosis has diminished in both sexes, but has diminished
faster among women than amongst men. When we make
synchronous comparisons of urban and rural districts—whether
the mass comparison of counties mainly urban with counties
mainly rural without correction for deaths of non-residents, or
the more detailed comparison possible after 1911—we find that
with advancing age the disadvantage of the town dwellers
increases, and that the apparent advantage of young female city
inhabitants can be accounted for more or less completely by
immigration from the country of healthy females. At ages over
thirty-five in both sexes the town dwellers die from phthisis at
a much greater rate than the denizens of rural districts, but the
excess is far greater amongst males than amongst females. This
excess is most at the age periods of life at which the largest proportion of urban males are industrially employed and the
smallest proportion of urban females—the age of married life.
Hence we surmise that industrial employment is a great factor
in producing the difference. In support of this we find that in
great industries, such as printing and shoemaking, necessarily
associated with urbanisation, the death rate from phthisis is
extremely high, higher than is to be expected from the death rate
due to other causes sustained by the members of the trade, and
therefore can hardly be attributed to a generally low standard of
physique attained by them (see diagrams, p. 178). Whether the
deleterious influence of industry is direct and a result of factory-
produced infection, or indirect, has been investigated by comparing the correlation between tuberculosis rates and indices of
employment and of home environment in the two sexes for the
metropolis. The result has been to show that during the period
of life when male industrial employment is at or near a
maximum and female industrial employment at an absolute
minimum, the period in which the greatest proportion of living
persons are married, the index of bad home conditions varies
closely with the male death rate from tuberculosis. From this
the inference is drawn that the deleterious influence of factory
life acts through the home environment. The males, whose
vitality is lowered by factory conditions, become more susceptible to evils associated with the home itself; amongst women
the factor of varying home conditions is less directly associated
with variation of the tuberculosis death rate, which in them
seems most closely correlated with the death rate from other
causes than tuberculosis. Lastly, there is reason to believe
that a full epidemiological analysis may involve the separation of the clinical entity phthisis into three types characterised

by differences of age susceptibility, and, perhaps, differences in responsiveness to good or bad environmental conditions. Both the inferences as to the differential effect of home conditions and the epidemiological subdivision of phthisis are not yet to be accepted as proven; much more statistical work is needed thoroughly to test them.

In the light of what we do know, or more or less shrewdly guess, as to the essential epidemiology of phthisis, what are the practical measures to be taken to mitigate its ravages? Upon balance it appears that the general belief of our fathers and grandfathers is sound, and the policy which ought to have been, and to some extent was, inspired by that belief is a sound policy. What is the matter with the poor is largely poverty. Not through any special intensive measures of campaigning against the tubercle bacillus, not even by the segregation of the actively tuberculous, does there seem any real hope of salvation. We have to improve the homes of the working classes in the first place—it is a sound popular instinct that inspires the popular outcry against urban and even rural housing conditions; in the second place, we have to ensure better factory conditions; here it is not so much sanitation in the popular sense as hygiene in the wider apprehension of the term. We require regulation of the hours and intensity of work, of the physical characters of the atmosphere, and of the quantity and quality of the meals taken, so that the workman returning home shall not reach it in a condition of definitely lowered resistance to an infection which must still be regarded as ubiquitous.

II. Adverse Influences.

Influences of Ventilation.—While each of these factors exerts an important effect upon resistance to infection and to disease generally, one or other may be of more importance in relation to pulmonary tuberculosis. This disease attacks the organs of respiration; and, although the line of thought may be dangerous, it is tempting to consider that atmospheric conditions upon which the functions of these organs depend may exert a paramount influence. Certainly conditions of ventilation in industrial establishments vary most from natural outdoor conditions in industries, such as printing, tailoring, and making boots, where purely physical labour is not very strenuous; and in these industries phthisis is unduly prevalent. Inadequate respiratory activity due to the defective ventilation may possibly be the potent influence. Some support of this view is derived from study of an essentially occupational disease, tubercular

silicosis. This disease has been shown by one of us (7) only to
develop among those exposed to the . prolonged inhalation of
fine silica particles. Pathological changes, with extensive
formation of fibrous tissue in the lungs, follow, until the
amount of normal tissue useful for respiratory purposes is greatly
reduced. Respiratory activity becomes quite inadequate ;
and those so affected with silicosis fall an easy prey to tuberculosis. The statistical distribution of the resulting mortality
among sandstone masons, tin miners, grinders of metal on sandstone wheels, or potters, coincides with Brownlee's middle-age
type. Without claiming that the evidence is conclusive, we
suggest there is a *primâ facie* case for considering phthisis, when
influenced by industry, as being mainly contributed to by
conditions which conduce to shallow breathing and inadequate
respiratory activity. The effect of silicosis in limiting working
capacity and metabolic processes is definite ; Hill has em-
phasised (5) the effect of sedentary occupations in still warm
atmospheres in lowering basal metabolism. " Growth may be
stunted and consumption predisposed to by an actual deficiency
of food. . . . These results may also be caused in the confined
sedentary worker who has enough food to satisfy his appetite,
but whose metabolism is depressed by occupation and conditions
of environment to a very low level. . . . Contrast these," he
writes, " with the wild ass of Sind, whose skin shines with the
wonderful gloss of perfect condition, and whose strength and
fleetness is such that to ride him down a horseman has to take
in relay seven fresh horses. ' The wild asses snuffed up the
wind like dragons.' ' Who hath sent out the wild ass free,' and
men into slavery ? "

Influence of Diet.—There is also another point for consideration, for, as has been written, " the defects involved in civilised
environment and more particularly met with in urban life are
(*a*) dietetic ; (*b*) involving confinement and lack of fresh air " (8).
With (*b*) we have just dealt. The discovery of accessory food
factors (vitamines) has recently shed new light upon the question
of dietetics ; and we must now recognise that the worker
requires not only energy in his food sufficient for his activities,
but also a supply of vitamines sufficient to render the food
supply available. There are indications that adults, carrying
on hard physical exercise, require (just as growing children do)
an additional supply of vitamines ; that without it they lack
vitality and resistance to disease ; and that " bacterial agencies
are often but weeds which flourish in soil made ready for them
by dietetic defects " (9). Foods especially rich in vitamines,
e.g., eggs, butter, animal fats, and fresh vegetables, are expen-

sive; further, "considering in the first place the fat soluble accessory, it is noteworthy that milk, cream, butter, cod liver oil, all rich sources of this factor, form the basis of the treatment of diseases of malnutrition and of tuberculosis, and it must be admitted that such foodstuffs are more than mere sources of fat, otherwise the cheaper fats, such as lard and the vegetable oils, would long ago have been adopted as equally efficient for the purpose " (8). Herein may lie the reason (i.) why phthisis is a *pestis pauperum;* (ii.) why the urban industrial male, doing heavier work and requiring an additional supply of food energy and of vitamines, is more prone to phthisis than the female; and (iii.) why female munition workers, who at first tried to obtain energy from buns and tea, succumbed to the disease. Industrial dietetics are dealt with in another chapter; here it is sufficient to point out the influence that food may exert upon the incidence of phthisis among industrial workers.

Eugenic Aspect.—These conclusions are essentially supported by the general epidemiological facts and opinions detailed. One further consideration remains, the eugenic aspects of tuberculosis. Little or nothing about them has been said here, because there is little to say; many important facts are not suitable for dissertations. But the contention of Karl Pearson, a contention which clothed in scientific form the ancient belief of an inherited predisposition to take phthisis, has never been seriously weakened by hostile criticism. It remains true, or at least highly probable, that a predisposition is inherited, and inherited with as much intensity as any of the normal variable characters of man. Hence it follows that the marriage of and consequent reproduction by members of tainted stocks will help to perpetuate the disease; the discouragement of parenthood amongst members of such stocks will help to diminish it. The numerical importance of this factor no man can evaluate; but it is to be a bad epidemiologist, and, what is worse, a bad citizen, to pretend that this eugenic aspect of disease is a mere fad made ridiculous by the discoveries of modern pathology. There is no opposition whatever between the sane epidemiology of environmental factors and that of innate factors; the apparent opposition has been due to the tendency we all possess to love wrangling better than truth. After all, " In my Father's house are many mansions."

A suggestive example of the commingling of the several factors we have discussed is provided by Dr. Arthur Reed Perry (15), who has studied the vital statistics of the population of Fall River, one of the great centres of cotton manufacture in America. It appears from his data that in contradistinction to our experience in this country the incidence of tuberculosis is excessive upon the operative population ; at ages fifteen to forty-five, the employed men have 51 per cent. and the employed women 142 per cent. more fatal tuberculosis than the non-operative population of like ages. In one department, that of spinning, the excess is much greater ; the males have a death rate from tuberculosis 104 per cent. above the standard, the women surpass their standard by 207 per cent. The physical labour in this department is not excessive, but " the most striking physical features of the spinning room are the heat and moisture of the atmosphere. The cotton cannot be spun successfully if it is dry and the effort to keep it sufficiently moist for good handling often leads to an excess of humidity." Here we have an atmospheric condition not particularly appropriate for the distribution of the specific germ, but sinning against the canons laid down in our chapter on ventilation.

Turn now to a department where the conditions are ideal for the dissemination of the bacillus ; an atmosphere not over-moist and warm, but hazy with vegetable fibres, dust and " fly." These conditions are furnished in the card room, and in that department the death rate among women is still more excessive, 235 per cent., than amongst the female spinners. But amongst the *men* employed in the two departments there is a contrast, for while the male spinners have 104 per cent. excess, the male carders show only 24 per cent. excess (we are to remember that, the numbers at risk being small, only large differences are significant). Dr. Perry explains this discrepancy ; he says of the male carders : " Since to a large extent they are newly arrived immigrants, they are still in good physical condition, for any definite weakness would have barred them from entering the country, and since they leave the card room for better-paying work as soon as possible they are not so long exposed to the dust, poor light, and bad ventilation as the females are." This study then exemplifies the effects of (*a*) bad general conditions, (*b*) specific hazard, (*c*) physical selection.

III. Prevention, Detection and Treatment in relation to Industry.

Examination of the incidence of tuberculosis from an industrial standpoint has thrown some light upon the influences which contribute to its occurrence. The organisation of industry also provides powerful means if properly used for preventing its occurrence, for detecting its presence, and for providing for its cure.

Prevention.—The conclusion arrived at that tuberculosis among adults is predisposed to by industrial occupation suggested the importance of three influences—pathological fatigue, inadequate ventilation, and insufficient food. Each of these influences is dealt with in other chapters, and we need only remark here that if attention is paid to their elimination, then those industrially employed should be at least equally able to resist the morbid influence of the home as those not so employed, and the result would be to reduce the incidence of tuberculosis among males to that among females, while, in so far as females also come under the influence of industrial conditions, the incidence among them would also be lowered.

Detection.—The establishment of an adequate factory medical service through which all applicants for work would be examined and the health of those at work would be supervised, would bring under medical review adults—among whom pulmonary tuberculosis is especially prevalent—in the same way as school children—among whom the disease is far less prevalent—are reviewed to-day. No one can gainsay the value of medical review of school children. The general importance of factory medical service is discussed later ; but attention may here be drawn to its special value in relation to tuberculosis. Dr. Mock, an industrial surgeon of great experience, in America, employed by a large engineering concern where the *personnel* of the workers increased rapidly between 1909 and 1913, tells (11) how, when he commenced work, he " found forty-five cases of tuberculosis in 1909 working in a plant. Five of these died from the disease because they were discovered in an advanced stage. In 1913, five years later, 101 cases of this disease were found with only two deaths resulting. This reduction in the death rate has been constant ever since the general house cleaning took place eight and nine years ago." He also gives an instance of early detection of the disease which is so important a factor in effecting a cure ; an epidemic of influenza occurred in the winter of 1915–16 ; " in March, 1916, eighteen cases of tuberculosis were found among the employees. All of these had suffered during the winter from the epidemic. Twelve of these cases had been examined during the year previous to the attack, and no signs of tuberculosis had then been discovered."

Industrial treatment.—The importance of industrial occupation in the treatment of phthisis is only coming to be recognised as the influence of each patient's psychological outlook on life is coming to be more appreciated by the profession, as his capacity for physical exertion is rightly understood, and as the *pâté-de-foie-gras* rest-treatment is surrendering its hold. Treatment spread over long periods during which the well-being of the patient is essential to cure has little chance of success if the mind

is not healthily occupied.   Only during an acute exacerbation
need most phthisical patients be entirely precluded from all
forms of physical exertion.   No form of occupation is so interesting to the convalescing patient as that to which he hopes finally
to return.   Phthisical patients take a long period, two or three
years, before they can safely undertake regular heavy work.
These facts indicate that the convalescing phthisical should be
encouraged to undertake, under medical supervision and for
such periods as are found safe, that occupation at which they
are skilled ; and that only a small minority should be directed
to outdoor pursuits which for the most part are too arduous for
them.

The object should be to make the conditions of daily work fit
for the recovering patient, rather than to divert skilled workers
to poorly paid employment for which they have no aptitude and
which possesses no intrinsic advantages over their own handicrafts.   What is required is to provide for " industrial convalescence " by passing the patients into factory sanatoria where
they can work under medical supervision and receive pay for
what they do.   Action on these lines was advocated (12) in
1914 in these words :—" I wish every great industrial centre
would establish a sanatorium factory where the chief industry
of the district could be carried on, and where such cases could
continue their handicraft under the best possible conditions ;
such an institution would become semi-self-supporting and would
remove the objection early cases have to submit themselves to
treatment, while the problem of how to make the premises in
which certain industries are carried on hygienic would be set
forth for all to see.   Then we might go into the highways and
byways and compel the unwilling guests to come in."   In the
following year the scheme was more fully elaborated in a report
published by the Medical Research Committee (13), as follows :—

" The Provision of Employment for Sanatorium Patients.

" The advantages of sanatorium treatment are now generally
recognised, and the State has organised a scheme for providing
it.   In practice, however, it is faced with two chief difficulties.

" 1. The patient frequently comes under treatment too late.
Often this results from the patient being a wage earner with
others dependent on him.   Though consciously failing in health
he may hesitate to seek medical service, or even after he has
ascertained the nature of his malady he may decline to surrender
his livelihood by going into a sanatorium.

" A patient who under sanatorium treatment has so far

recovered as to be discharged may return to work, but before he has settled down to the pace of the factory, working fifty-four hours a week, he may break down again.

" These difficulties have been carefully considered, and in order to meet them we desire to advocate a modified form of sanatorium treatment. Briefly, the scheme is to establish, in connection with the ordinary form of sanatorium, a work place for the manufacture of boots and shoes. Here consumptive operatives in an early stage of the disease, and convalescing patients could carry on their trade under medical supervision for such hours as they are able, and earn wages in proportion. The value of work mentally and physically as an integral part of treatment is certain, and at present in sanatoria physical labour of a character unremunerative compared with the earning power possessed by skilled craftsmen is being invented. Such work often deteriorates the character of the young operative and turns him into a loafer.

" As health is re-established the working hours and earning capacity would be increased, until, finally, normal hours could be safely undertaken in many cases and factory employment resumed.

" . . . It would be among the more important advantages offered by the plan for a factory sanatorium if, as a result of his stay, an operative could be taught how to carry on his handicraft under hygienic conditions. The influence upon his fellow men of his acquired habits after his return to the factory might be considerable."

Steps in this direction are under consideration in this country, especially for reclaiming tuberculous soldiers, but no definite data can be quoted to instance the success of the plan. In America, on the other hand, practical results are being obtained at least at one post-sanatorium factory at Hoboken (11) :—

" Here under the best hygienic conditions, and constantly supervised by a competent doctor, over 200 tuberculous employees have been given graduated work until they were finally able to return to full time employment, when they graduated from the (sanatorium) factory. Tinsmiths, clerks, jewellers, junk men, and many others have learned to be garment makers and are drawing larger salaries now than they made previous to their sickness. This factory has demonstrated that the garment industry, when properly conducted, is not a hazardous occupation predisposing to lung trouble. . . . Over 90 per cent. of the families of the patients at the factory were under the care of relief agencies. Of fifty-eight who received relief from three months to five years, seventeen are partially self-supporting, and forty-one are entirely self-supporting. Patients whose families were granted from 40 dollars to 80 dollars a month by charities and relief agencies are now earning from 60 dollars to 160 dollars a month."

TABLE 8.—*Earnings in a Factory Sanatorium.*

Number of patients.	Earnings in dollars per week.	Period of work permitted.
2	9 or less.	Half a day or less.
2	9 or less.	} Half a day to six hours.
3	9 to 15.	
2	9 or less.	
14	9 to 15.	
24	15 to 25.	} Six hours to full day.
12	25 to 40.	

The table here given shows the earnings of fifty-nine patients at work at one time ; of these seventeen were in the first stage of the disease, forty in the second stage, and two in the third. Fifty-four had previously been through sanatorium treatment, while five had been treated at home.

Dr. Mock says (11): "The establishing, therefore, of industries in certain centres where these ex-sanatoria patients could be sent for graduated employment under proper medical supervision is a duty which should no longer be neglected. Those States which are providing sanatoria for the tuberculous should at once provide these State industries where they can work until such time as it is safe for them to return to private employment. It is a fallacy to recommend outdoor employment, such as farming, for all arrested or apparently cured tuberculous patients. Many of these are not vocationally trained or physically fit for the strenuous outside work, and to others it is abhorrent. Experience in caring for the tuberculous employee has proven that the majority of these can return to their former occupations, providing there are no known hazards connected with it."

The same author states that, " of the total number of employees who have received treatment, approximately 250 have returned to work in the same concern, at their old occupations or in some other position less hazardous. There have been twenty recurrences among those cases kept under observation, and in all but three of these the disease has again been arrested. This is a far lower recurrence rate than is usually found in this disease, thus demonstrating the value of health supervision. The use of short vacations when threatening symptoms developed prevented many of these employees from breaking down." The claim made that the recurrence rate under this form of treatment is low is justified by comparing these results with figures published by Dr. W. H. Dickinson (14). He deals with applicants for sanatorium benefit in Newcastle-upon-Tyne for the period July, 1912, up to December 31st, 1919, and finds that out of 1,163 " completed " cases only eighty-one are now working or fit to work, while over 800 are known to have died.

A factory sanatorium, where, of course, the doctor is the " boss," clearly approaches near to being a self-supporting institution, and can be used for passing on patients from ordinary sanatorium beds upon which the demand to-day is so heavy. Greater economy is, therefore, to be effected by establishing these less expensive institutions than by increasing the amount of sanatorium accommodation, from which the patients are too often passed back to ordinary life, only to break down and return. Much more might be written on this interesting scheme which could be applied *mutatis mutandis* to convalescence from other forms of serious illness among the industrially employed. We are content to outline the scheme, and to point out that to-day unnecessary and misplaced ingenuity is being expended in inventing quite unsuitable and unremunerative forms of physical exercise for the recovering phthisical—typists and needlewomen are set to damage their sensitive finger tips using pickaxes and spades, and skilled mechanics are turned on to the land; the only underlying principle appears to be the shibboleth of " open-air " work; and that lack of after-care treatment, lack of preparation of the arrested case for resumption of civilian life, is to-day the blot upon our treatment of tuberculosis. Industries can and should provide this after-care on the lines here outlined for a disease in the prevalence of which, as we have pointed out, they play so conspicuous a part.

Spittoons.—Prevention of the spread of infection is of undoubted importance. Notices are frequently displayed commanding persons not to spit. The intention of these notices is admirable, but personal observation makes manifest to all that they do not effect their purpose. Even if the rising generation adopt better manners and do not acquire the habit of expectorating (of which we can at present see no obvious signs), the present generation possess the habit, which must be dealt with as an existing custom—an objectionable thing which may be ameliorated before it is abolished. Few persons unacquainted with industry can be aware of the danger to the public as well as to the workers themselves arising from spitting. When, however, we state that expectoration takes place into tea, dough troughs, fish, vegetables and other comestibles, as well as upon materials used for wearing apparel, the necessity for action becomes clearer.

The provision of spittoons or cuspidors is the only practical remedy. Working men are accustomed to their use in inn-parlours, and can be persuaded to use them. Spittoons should be placed in readily accessible positions—not on the floor where they are readily knocked over. They should be made of enamelled metal with long handles for convenience of removal. Every day they should be washed out with hot water and exposed to a jet of steam during five to ten minutes.

The provision of spittoons is of value for the control, not only of tubercular infection, but of the more frequent catarrhal infections. The main objection to dry sweeping of floors rests upon the presence there of dried sputa ; if all spitting was into spittoons, floor dust would become less infectious. While the provision and proper use of spittoons would go far to minimise the danger arising from spitting, a new custom would thereby be introduced. Workers, like others, are naturally conservative and might readily object, and a manager would be well advised to place the matter in the hands of the welfare committee of the works. If this committee decide in favour of spittoons, they will ensure that promiscuous spitting no longer takes place.

IV. Bibliography.

1. Bulloch, W., and Greenwood, M. " The Problem of Pulmonary Tuberculosis considered from the Standpoint of Disposition." *Proc. Roy. Soc. Med., Sect. Epidem.* p. 143. 1911.

2. Maynard, G. D. " A Statistical Study of Cancer Death Rates." *Biomet,* VII. 1909—10.

3. Brown, J. W., and Mohan Lal. " An Inquiry into the Relation between Social Status and Cancer Mortality." *Journal of Hygiene,* XIV., No. 2. 1914.

4. Greenwood, M., and Tebb, A. E. " An Inquiry into the Prevalence and Ætiology of Tuberculosis among Industrial Workers, with special reference to Female Munition Workers." *Medical Research Committee. Special Report Series, No.* 22. 1919.

5. Hill, L. E. " The Science of Ventilation." *Medical Research Committee. Special Report Series, No.* 32. 1919.

6. Brownlee, J. " An Investigation into the Epidemiology of Phthisis in Great Britain and Ireland." *Medical Research Committee. Special Report Series, No.* 18. 1918 ; *Part III., No.* 46. 1920.

7. Collis, E. L. " Industrial Pneumonoconioses." *Milroy Lectures* (1915). H.M. Stationery Office. 1919.

8. " Report on Accessory Food Factors (Vitamines)." *Medical Research Committee.* *Special Report Series, No.* 38. 1919.

9. McCarrison, R. " Effects of Deficient Dietaries on Monkeys." *Brit. Med. Journal.* February 21st, 1920.

10. Thomson, H. Hyslop. *Tuberculosis and Public Health.* Longmans, Green & Co. 1920.

11. Mock, H. E. *Industrial Medicine and Surgery.* W. B. Saunders Co. Philadelphia. 1919.

12. Collis, E. L. " The House in Relation to Tuberculosis, considered with regard to the Conditions of Factory Life." *Trans. Sixth Ann. Conf. Nat. Assoc. Prev. Consump.* Leeds. 1914.

13. " Report of Special Investigation Committee upon the Incidence of Phthisis in relation to Occupations." *Medical Research Committee.* *Special Report Series, No.* 1. 1915.

14. Dickinson, W. H. *A Survey of Sanatorium Benefit.* Newcastle-upon-Tyne. 1920.

CHAPTER VII

CANCER AND INDUSTRY

THE influence exerted by industry upon the prevalence of the tubercular group of diseases has been discussed to show how it affects a disease, the *pestis pauperum*, especially prevalent in industry and among those whose health is impaired by either insufficient food (as in the case of the central nations of Europe in the Great War), by illness, or over-fatigue. There is no sufficient body of evidence relating to the effect exerted by industry upon the prevalence of most of the important causes of death, such as heart disease or rheumatism, to place before our readers ; but something may be said of the group of diseases included under the heading of cancer, not so much on account of the plenitude of the evidence available, but because of the contrast, already referred to on p. 128, which appears to exist between cancer and tuberculosis. The age incidence of the two groups of diseases shows one marked contrast (see Diagrams 1 to 6, Chapter VIII., pp. 178–80) ; tuberculosis occurs when the activities of life, and the metabolic changes they represent, are in full swing, and dies away as those activities diminish ; cancer appears as the vigour of life wanes, and gathers strength as vitality diminishes.

We have pointed out how the influence of modern industrial life, which is exerted predominantly on the male, may have retarded the fall in mortality from tuberculosis, especially at the ages of middle life. The facts are open to the interpretation that modern industry, by increasing wealth, *i.e.*, by increasing the amount of production per head of population and so the surplus of production, has diminished poverty, and so has led to a decrease in tuberculosis. That this is not the whole explanation is shown by the facts that (*a*) the decline has been as great amongst such classes as agricultural labourers whose economic status improved little as amongst skilled operatives whose status has improved greatly, and (*b*) the decline has been more rapid among women than among men.

I. Increase in Cancer Mortality.

The question now for consideration is whether this industrial influence has in any way directly or indirectly affected the mortality from cancer. Certainly there is *primâ facie* a reason for investigation, since the mortality from cancer has been advancing rapidly (while that from tuberculosis has been falling, see p. 129) in those countries in which industrialisation has been advancing. Thus the combined returns (1, p. 28) from the United Kingdom, Norway, Holland, Prussia, Baden, Switzerland, Austria, the cities of Denmark, the Commonwealth of Australia, and the Dominion of New Zealand, show that these countries in 1881 had 44,047 deaths from cancer among an aggregate population of 98,380,000, a mortality rate of 44·8 per 100,000 of population ; in 1891 the rate had risen to 59·6 ; in 1901 to 76·3 ; in 1911 to 90·4 ; and in 1912 to 91·9 (with 125,832 deaths from cancer in an aggregate population of 136,892,000). In England and Wales considered alone the standardised cancer death rate per 100,000 of population in 1906—10 was 88·2 ; in 1911 it was 91·4 ; it rose in 1912 to 93·7 ; and in 1913 to 97·2. Another instance is provided by the State of Massachusetts, U.S.A., for which, as it contains the important medical centre of Boston, death certification should be particularly reliable ; here the cancer death rate in 1871 was 36·9 per 100,000 population ; in 1881 the rate had risen to 52·3 ; in 1891 to 60·9 ; in 1901 to 73·1 ; and in 1911 to 92·6. Instances might be multiplied almost indefinitely ; thus in New South Wales in 1881 the crude rate was 28·2, and in 1913 it was 73·6 ; in England and Wales in 1881 it was 52·0, and in 1913 it was 105·5 ; and in Berlin in 1881 it was 64·6, and in 1912 it was 132·8 ; but sufficient additional evidence is given in Table 1 to justify the conclusion that " the mortality from cancer is increasing at a more or less alarming rate throughout the entire civilised world " (1, p. 218).

II. Cancer and Civilisation.

This conclusion has been attacked on two grounds : (i.) " *Owing to improved medical certification, cases previously not accurately diagnosed are now ascribed to cancer.*" As long as medical knowledge continues to advance, this objection can be raised against the value of any statistics based on medical certificates, the more readily in that it is not open to proof or disproof. Even if a sound objection to a comparison of the statistics of 1871 or 1881 with those of 1911, hardly any one will maintain that medical diagnosis has changed suddenly through

TABLE 1.—*Death Rate from Cancer per 100,000 Population.*

Year.	Uruguay.	Italy.	Holland.	Bavaria.	Switzerland.	Japan.	Tokyo.	Australia.	Sydney.	U.S.A. Registration States. Rural.	U.S.A. Registration States. Urban.	New York City.	Ireland.	England and Wales.	London.	Year.
1900	46·2	52·2	91·7	98·8	129·9	45·6	—	62·6	72·7	61·5	66·1	66·7	60·8	82·9	96·3	1900
1901	53·1	52·7	93·8	102·6	127·8	49·1	—	63·3	74·6	62·0	69·0	69·0	65·1	84·3	93·7	1901
1902	50·8	53·9	95·2	103·3	125·8	53·8	—	64·1	77·7	63·3	68·3	66·2	64·5	84·6	101·0	1902
1903	52·0	54·1	99·3	107·4	129·7	55·2	—	61·5	78·9	66·6	72·3	68·0	69·0	87·4	103·8	1903
1904	54·2	57·1	98·4	110·3	128·6	55·5	76·7	60·1	85·5	68·3	73·9	68·3	69·3	88·2	103·0	1904
1905	59·0	58·3	101·8	108·4	129·5	56·3	73·4	63·5	83·0	71·1	75·4	70·1	74·8	88·9	103·3	1905
1906	66·0	62·0	101·4	110·0	129·0	58·1	72·7	64·2	96·2	60·9	76·2	71·0	79·2	92·2	110·2	1906
1907	67·7	61·7	102·6	106·5	122·5	58·7	70·3	71·3	74·0	63·9	77·6	73·9	76·1	91·5	107·9	1907
1908	63·5	64·5	103·5	107·9	128·0	62·1	74·4	69·6	88·2	64·9	77·2	75·6	75·6	93·3	111·2	1908
1909	65·2	64·2	103·3	109·6	126·7	65·6	75·5	72·8	95·5	67·1	80·1	75·3	79·8	96·1	113·1	1909
1910	67·7	65·6	106·5	113·5	123·5	65·3	71·1	73·3	88·7	70·1	81·4	77·8	83·5	96·7	112·8	1910
1911	63·4	66·8	108·9	112·5	123·6	63·9	—	74·0	93·3	65·9	81·9	79·0	81·7	99·3	107·2	1911
1912	70·3	64·7	109·7	115·1	120·0	—	—	76·1	92·1	68·5	84·9	80·9	85·2	102·2	114·2	1912
1913	73·4	—	109·5	—	—	—	—	75·0	95·6	69·4	87·8	81·7	—	105·5	114·9	1913

Compiled from data published by Hoffman (1).

out the world between 1900 and 1912 to an extent required by the data embodied in Table 1.

This objection is not called in to explain the general fall in mortality from tuberculosis, or the higher rate of tuberculosis in Ireland than in England, but it is claimed to disprove the general rise in mortality from cancer, and the lower mortality from cancer in Ireland than in England.

We are aware of the importance attached by various authorities to this objection, and consider it sufficient to modify the exact amount of cancer increase, but not to refute the evidence that cancer has been steadily increasing.

One of the authors, in collaboration with the late Frances Wood, has dealt (2) with this objection for the specific cases claimed to support it, and has shown that, after full allowance is made, it is hard to believe that the mortality from cancer has not really increased.*

Were this objection valid, the increase of cancer should be mainly due to increase of cancer of inaccessible organs, which is difficult of diagnosis, and only to a slight extent to increase of cancer of accessible organs, which is more obvious ; but, in fact, this is not so.   Thus for England and Wales the male cancer rate of accessible organs increased 27·4 per cent. between 1897—1900 and 1901—10, and that of inaccessible organs 22·2 per cent. between the same periods ; while the female rate of increase for accessible organs was 16·7 per cent., and for inaccessible organs 16·6 per cent. ; and for Bavaria the increase of male rate between 1905—07 and 1905—10 for accessible organs was 25·5 per cent., and for inaccessible organs 5·2 per cent. ; while the female rate of increase was 15·6 per cent. for accessible organs, and 4·3 per cent. for inaccessible organs.

(ii.) " *Increased longevity has permitted a larger proportion of the population to reach the cancer period of life.*"   In order fully to justify this objection the cancer rate, distributed by age periods of life, should have remained unaltered ; and the gross rate should only appear greater than formerly because the distribution of the population in these age periods has altered.   While the gross cancer rate is greatly affected by the age distribution of the population, it is not true that the cancer rate for the different age periods has remained unaltered, as may be seen from Tables 2 and 3, p. 158.

The figures given in Table 1 further show that the cancer rate is not uniform throughout the world, but varies considerably, town from town, and country from country, lower rates usually prevailing in rural districts, and higher rates in large

* For a discussion of the specific case of Irish hospitals see (10, p. 36).

TABLE 2.—*Cancer Rate per* 100,000 *Population for all Males,
England and Wales, at certain Age Periods.*

Period.	Years of Age			
	35-44.	45-54.	55-64.	65 and over.
1890—92	36·6	117·6	276·2	461·7
1900—02	39·9	144·7	362·2	638·3

TABLE 3.—*Cancer Rate per* 100,000 *Population for all Persons,
United States Registration Area, at Age Periods.*

Period.	Years of Age.										
	under 5.	5-9.	10-14.	15-19.	20-24.	25-34.	35-44.	45-54.	55-64.	65-74.	75 and over.
1901	3·4	1·0	0·9	2·1	3·9	13·4	60·2	146·5	268·3	418·8	557·6
1911	3·0	1·2	1·3	2·3	4·8	13·9	61·0	166·3	352·4	566·7	794·7

towns ; thus the rate for Ireland is below that for England and
Wales, and the latter is below that for London ; further, we
find that, when standardised, the urban cancer death rates in
·England and Wales are somewhat higher than the rural rates,
and the same holds good in the United States. Generally,
cancer appears to be more prevalent and to be increasing more
rapidly where industrialisation is more pronounced, and this
conclusion receives support from the world distribution of
cancer according to latitude (see Table 4). The density of

TABLE 4.—*Mortality from Cancer in Cities according to
Latitude,* 1908—1912.

No. of cities.	Degrees of latitude.	Mean annual temperature.	Rainfall.	Rate per 100,000 population.
35	60 N.—50 N.	48·0°	29·1 ins.	105·7
48	50 N.—40 N.	50·3°	34·0 ,,	92·4
24	40 N.—30 N.	58·5°	37·9 ,,	78·1
7	30 N.—10 N.	72·5?	57·1 ,,	42·3
4	10 N.—10 S.	74·6°	83·3 ,,	40·9
7	10 S.—30 S.	65·9°	40·3 ,,	37·7
5	30 S.—40 S.	62·7°	36·7 ,,	89·8

Compiled from data published by Hoffman (1, pp. 142-3).

population is not here the ruling factor, since in great cities, like Bombay and London, it is not so pronouncedly different as between urban and rural areas in any country, but the extent to which modern industry is carried on in great cities varies with their distance from the equator. The objection may reasonably be raised that cities nearer the equator are inhabited by more primitive races who subsist on a pronouncedly vegetarian diet and are exposed to greater temperature and rainfall.

Maynard has investigated (7) for the cities of the United States the possibility of meteorological conditions influencing the incidence of cancer, but after considering sunshine in hours, mean temperature and rainfall, he was unable to discover the existence of any connection. The North American Indians and the Esquimo population of Labrador and Alaska provide further evidence in reply to this objection ; among these primitive peoples cancer is remarkably rare,* although they live to an unusual extent upon a meat diet, while the Indians are exposed to the same geographical and climatic conditions, and possess an age distribution as favourable to cancer as that of their white neighbours. The one distinguishing feature is their lack of civilisation. Still, the proposition may be advanced that a low cancer rate is innate in primitive races ; certainly " all the available evidence is to the effect that the recorded cancer death rate of primitive races is materially below the average for civilised countries " (1, p. 15). As against this we find that when a primitive race, the negroes of America, became an intimate part of a civilised country, their cancer death rate rose. " Evidence is available to substantiate the conclusion that cancer was relatively of rare occurrence among our negro population during a condition of slavery, but that the frequency has rapidly increased during the last thirty years " (1, p. 147). Matas, as well, considers " the negro constitution has probably undergone some change under American civilisation, since it cannot be doubted that cancer is comparatively rare in the native African, rare also in the original slave population in this country (U.S.A.), and has only become a common disease in the American negro of the last few generations. It is also probable that the conditions that are causing an increase in the prevalence of cancer among the whites are also acting with the same effect upon the negroes " (8). We find (1, p. 128) that while in the Southern cities of America the cancer death rate among the white population was 52·7 in the period 1891—95,

* " Among some 63,000 Indians of all tribes, living under a variety of social, economic and climatic conditions, there occurred only two deaths from cancer as medically observed in the year 1914 " (1, p. 151).

and 96·6 in 1913, that of the negro population was 39·1 and 73·5 in the two periods, *i.e.*, the negro mortality rate from cancer in 1913 was well above that experienced by whites in 1891—95. There would not, therefore, on the evidence, appear to be any innate resisting power in primitive races against cancer. The conclusion which may legitimately be drawn seems to be that *the sudden change which has taken place in the conditions of life consequent upon the development of modern industry, has been associated with a rapid rise in cancer mortality, and this rise is greatest where modern industry is most developed.*

III.   Effect of Modern Civilisation on the Life of the People.

Any given generation can with difficulty grasp the enormous changes which civilisation has brought about, or measure the influence of these changes upon the habits and life of the people, upon their activities and nutrition, and so upon their power to resist or succumb to disease. Reference has been made in the first chapter to the way in which these changes affected the working class population in England ; but the effect of change of environment upon a race cannot be expected to become fully manifest in one or two generations ; it is cumulative and pro- gressive. And when considering the present prevalence or increase of a disease so general as that represented by the cancer group we must look back and compare the conditions of life to-day with those of the past. Compare, for instance, the present inhabitants of Scotland with those of the fourteenth and fifteenth century, of whom Buckle writes, " Their minds must have been immersed in a darkness which we can now barely conceive. No trades, or arts, being practised which required skill, or dexterity, there was nothing to exercise their intellects. They consequently remained so stupid and brutal, that an intelligent observer who visited Scotland in 1360, likens them to savages, so much was he struck by their bar- barism and their unsocial manners. Another writer, early in the fifteenth century, uses the same expression and classing them with the animals they tended, he declares that Scotland is fuller of savages than of cattle." The state in the sixteenth and seventeenth century is quoted by the same author : " The hovels of the common people were slight erections of turf or twigs, which, as they were often laid waste by war, were merely built for temporary accommodation. Their towns consisted chiefly of wooden cottages. Even as late as 1600 the houses of Edinburgh were chiefly built of wood." Another account, written in 1670, says : " The houses of the commonalty are very mean, mud wall and thatch, the best, but the poorer sort live in such miserable huts as eye never beheld. In some parts where turf is plentiful, they build up little cabins thereof, with arched roofs of turf, without a stick of timber in it ; when the house is dry enough to burn it serves them for fuel, and they remove to another." Industries in Scotland were, in the eighteenth century, of small account, as Buckle quotes : " Our manufactures were carried on by the meanest of people, who had small stocks, and were of no reputation. These were, for the most part, workmen for home-consumption, such as masons, house carpenters, armourers, blacksmiths, tailors, shoemakers, and the like. Our weavers were few in number and in the greatest contempt, as their employments were more sedentary, and themselves reckoned less fit for war."

Knowledge relating to health was at a minimum before the nineteenth century, and Public Health Acts did not appear until the middle of that century. Previously the conditions of life were primitive ; there is no record, for instance, previous to 1812 of even the streets of Edinburgh being scavenged or watered, and J. A. Young says (9) : " The old days when the cry of ' gardey-loo ' was the warning that the street was being used as the common sewer were days when the streets were in a condition of filthiness difficult to imagine in the present day." The same author sets forth the rapid strides which have been taken since.

This comparison is enough to convince any one that to-day civilised races are subjected to an environment vastly different from that to which through long ages they had been accustomed, and to which natural selection had more or less accommodated them. Reason would suggest looking for a clue to the increasing prevalence of cancer where the alterations in environment have been most pronounced, and the diverse conditions of industrial life undoubtedly present the greatest alteration, even though the changes may not always have been favourable. Social history, then, is not opposed to the conclusion suggested by statistical inquiry, and further justifies close research into the way in which cancer prevails in various occupations, always mindful that " general mischiefs depend upon general causes."

IV. Cancer and Social Status.

The alterations in conditions of life which have taken place are the results of industrialisation, which has brought about greater social differences affecting health than probably ever existed before, and the so-called upper classes have been farther

11

separated from the poor as regards personal cleanliness, housing, food supply, fresh air, clothing and other hygienic conditions than were the nobility from the proletariat in any period of the world's history of which we have knowledge. There has been improvement in every class, but far greater in the higher grades of society than in the lower. The industrial classes include all the lower grades and permeate upwards. Interest, therefore, attaches when considering the relation of cancer to industry to any relation which may exist between social status and cancer mortality. This question has been dealt with by Maynard (7) in America, and also by Brown and Mohan Lal in this country (3). Maynard arranged occupations according to social status, and found the lowest cancer death rates among occupations of the highest social status. Brown and Mohan Lal followed a somewhat similar plan, arranging the occupations in the following order : (i.) professional men, (ii.) clerks and commercial men, (iii.) shopkeepers and assistants, (iv.) skilled workers, (v.) domestic servants, and (vi.) unskilled workers. They found that the cancer death rate tended to diminish with increasing social status and concluded, " there appears to be some slight association between a high cancer death rate and low occupational status." These investigators also examined for the city of Hamburg the relation between the average income of the inhabitants of different divisions of that city and the cancer mortalities experienced, and found evidence in support of the conclusion that cancer is not more but less fatal among well-to-do citizens.

V. Cancer and Industrialisation.

The next matter for consideration is whether industrialisation *per se* has been a determining influence in civilisation which has led to the increase in cancer mortality, or whether the increase has been due to some concomitant influence. When discussing tuberculosis, valuable evidence was obtained by contrasting its prevalence among males, as representative of industrial employment, with that among females, who, as a sex, are far less so employed. When cancer is under consideration, this method of comparison is not simple ; the total cancer mortality is composed of cancer of the various organs and parts of the body, some of which are not common to the two sexes, and, in order to obtain an estimate of the effect of any given influence upon the cancer mortality of the two sexes, the cancer mortality for some neutral organ or part must be considered alone. Mortality from cancer, when stated for organs and parts is now generally given for

(1) buccal cavity ; (2) stomach and liver ; (3) peritoneum, intestines and rectum ; (4) female generative organs ; (5) female breast ; (6) skin ; and (7) other and unspecified. Of these for present purposes the buccal cavity must be rejected, because there is a positive correlation between a high cancer rate for this part and masculinity, due perhaps to the male habit of smoking ; the group peritoneum, intestines and rectum must be rejected on account of the proximity of these parts to the generative organs, and the possibility in the female, particularly in the case of the peritoneum, of cancer originating, say, in the ovaries, being erroneously ascribed to this group ; the skin group is so small that errors from age-distribution are likely to creep in ; the group other and unspecified is obviously un-satisfactory. There remains only the stomach and liver group, which includes cancer of the liver, gall bladder, pharynx, œso-phagus and stomach ; this group may be considered fairly neutral to the two sexes, and the inaccessibility of the organs may be disregarded, as the standard of diagnosis in any given period and locality will be the same for the two sexes. Cancer of the liver group is not as a rule primary, and many cases so certified are secondary to primary growth elsewhere ; but this factor is likely to increase the female, rather than the male, cases on account of the frequency of cancer of the female organs. Cancer of the pharynx, on the other hand, is rather more prevalent among males, possibly being associated, like the buccal cavity, with the male habit of smoking ; but the total number of cases is small. Another uncertain element in the comparison arises from the age-distribution of the two sexes, for which no allowance is made in most published data ; since, however, women live rather longer than men, the tendency should be for the cancer rate at all ages for the stomach and liver group to be rather higher for women. For the comparison to be a fair one, the age-distribution of cancer for this group should be similar for the two sexes ; and we find (see Table 5) in the United States, where in 1908—12 the mortality rates for this group in the two sexes are not far apart—28·8 for males and 30·5 for females per 100,000 population—that the rates at various age periods approximate in the two sexes for the periods 1903—07 and 1908—12 ; this evidence receives support from the distri-bution of cases in Norway, 1896—1910, and in Amsterdam, 1897—1902 (see Tables 6 and 7). In so far as the evidence from Norway and Amsterdam shows inequality of the age-distribution, the tendency is for more cases to occur among females from about sixty years of age onwards, i.e., that period of life when there is normally an excess of women over men ; so here again

Table 5.—*Mortality from Cancer of Stomach and Liver for United States Registration Area per 100,000 Population at certain Age Periods.*

Sex.	Under 10.				Years of age.				Period.
		10-24.	25-34.	35-44.	45-54.	55-64.	65-74.	75 and over.	
Males .	0·3	0·5	3·0	16·2	55·1	129·5	215·6	219·1	1903—
Females .	0·3	0·4	3·9	19·1	59·2	125·9	211·9	229·6	1907
Males .	0·4	0·5	3·1	15·4	57·6	145·0	242·4	278·9	1908—
Females .	0·3	0·4	3·8	19·1	62·4	143·9	242·4	290·0	1912

Table 6.—*Cancer of Stomach and Liver in Norway, 1896—1910. Percentage at certain Age Periods.*

Sex.	Under 30.			Years of age.				All ages.	Total cases.
		30-39.	40-49.	50-59.	60-69.	70-79.	80 and over.		
Males .	0·4	2·3	9·7	24·2	26·1	30·8	6·5	100·0	9,839
Females .	0·5	2·7	9·7	21·0	30·0	28·0	8·1	100·0	8,947

Table 7.—*Cancer of Œsophagus, Stomach and Liver, Amsterdam, 1897—1902. Percentage at certain Age Periods.*

Sex.	Under 34.		Years of age.				All ages.	Total cases.
		35—44.	45—54.	55—64.	65—74.	75 and over.		
Males .	1·0	4·3	17·5	35·1	30·5	11·6	100·0	905
Females .	0·7	5·3	10·6	28·1	33·5	21·8	100·0	737

Table 8.—*Cancer of Œsophagus, Pharynx, Stomach and Liver, Ireland, 1901. Duration of Illness.*

Sex.	Under 6 months.	6 months to 1 year.	1 year to 2 years.	2 years to 3 years.	3 years and over.	Total cases of known duration.
Males . .	230	190	89	8	6	523
Females . .	222	172	88	11	6	499

such error as exists favours the gross rate among women. Further evidence of the similarity of this group of cancer cases in the two sexes is provided by the duration of illness which is stated in Table 8, for cases which occurred in Ireland in 1901.

Another requirement to justify the cancer rate of the stomach and liver group being used to compare the liability of the two sexes to cancer is that the rate for this group should represent a reasonable proportion of the total cancer rate. The rate for the stomach and liver group fulfils this requirement, as in the period 1908—12 it comprises for :—

England and Wales 41·4% { of the total male } 29·2% { of the total female
                          { cancer deaths and }   { cancer deaths.
United   States
  registration area 49·9%   ,,   ,,   32·9%   ,,   ,,
Ireland   .   .   45·9%   ,,   ,,   36·5%   ,,   ,,
Holland   .   .   67·5%   ,,   ,,   51·7%   ,,   ,,
Italy   .   .   51·5%   ,,   ,,   33·3%   ,,   ,,
New York City .   49·1%   ,,   ,,   33·3%   ,,   ,,

The next step is to investigate the cancer rate for the stomach and liver group as it occurs among males and females. This has been done for various parts of the world, and the results are embodied in Table 9, from which it will be seen that, with the single exception of the United States, the male mortality is in excess of the female. Even in America, when New York City alone is considered, the male rate is slightly above the female. On the test applied then, in so far as the two sexes are alike, males appear to be more liable to cancer than females. This conclusion is one of considerable importance, as by hypothesis males are taken to represent the industrial influence of modern

TABLE 9.—*Mortality from Cancer, Stomach and Liver. Rate per* 100,000 *Population by Sex.*

Locality.	Male rate.	Female rate.	Period.
England and Wales . . .	35·7	31·5	1908—12
Ireland	35·3	31·1	,,
United States registration area .	28·8	30·5	,,
New York City. . . .	30·9	30·5	,,
Italy	30·2	23·8	,,
Australia	32·7	21·9	,,
Holland	72·0	54·9	,,
Bavaria	62·7	55·1	1905—10
Switzerland	84·1	57·2	1906—10
Japan	48·4	31·4	1909—10
Uruguay	45·8	26·9	1907—11
London	41·5	27·9	1911—12

civilisation ; if this is accepted it appears that industrialisation
per se may have been a determining influence leading to the
increase in cancer mortality.

Granting the correctness of the deduction, then cancer should
be found to be more prevalent where industrialisation is more
pronounced. Table 1 shows that this holds good as between the
cancer death rates for London and for England and Wales ; for
England and Wales and for Ireland ; for New York City and
United States registration area ; for Tokyo and Japan ; and
for urban and rural districts in America. When standardised
the urban cancer death rates for England and Wales are also
somewhat higher than the rural rates ; and in Ireland in 1901—
10 the cancer rate, 48·8, for rural Connaught was much below
that, 83·8, for more industrial Ulster, while Munster with a rate
of 61·1 stands between. Further, for England and Wales,
1900—02, the standardised cancer death rate among occupied
males in industrial districts was 102·9, as compared with 92·2
among occupied males in agricultural districts (see Table 12).
Thus, evidence is in support of the conclusion already
drawn.

The position, then, seems to be that (i.) the mortality from
cancer has been increasing rapidly ; (ii.) this increase has been
synchronous with the advance of modern civilisation ; (iii.) the
increase has been most in countries where the conditions of
modern civilisation are most pronounced ; (iv.) it is greater in
cities than in the country ; (v.) it is greater in the lower
grades of society than in the upper ; and (vi.) it is greater
(when considered on a neutral basis) among males than among
females.

We hope the reader will fully understand that the remarks
made in previous sections are tentative ; that we are alive to
the extreme complexity of the problem and the imperfection of
the data. We are quite aware that changes in fashion of diagnosis and increased surgical and medical skill have prejudiced
the comparability of the records. Similarly, we do *not* suggest
that a specific for cancer is reversion to the barbaric conditions of
former ages ! We do, however, very strongly feel that the complex of factors acting upon the human microcosm, the tempera-
mental and procatarctic factors of the Greeks, deserve the fullest
attention, and that the solution of the " cancer problem " is not
likely to be found in the discovery of some one specific factor.
Man is a very old animal ; civilisation as we know it is the
creature of a day. The adaptation of the human race to these
novel conditions cannot be complete, and in the process there
must be many painful incidents.

VI. Cancer in Occupations.

The ways in which any disease may become more prevalent must be kept in mind when embarking on an investigation. First, it may become more prevalent owing to the general resistance of the community to that disease being lowered, so that the potency of the disease, previously minimal, becomes relatively more powerful ; increase of tuberculosis during partial famine is an instance in point. Secondly, trauma may permit disease with otherwise subminimal potency to obtain a local foothold ; injuries to joints in childhood, followed by tubercular

TABLE 10.—*Mortality from Cancer in England and Wales. Percentage by Organs and Parts and Sex. 1897—1900 compared with 1901—10.*

Organ or part.	Males.		Females.	
	1897–1900.	1901–10.	1897–1900.	1901–10.
Skin	2·5	2·3	1·0	1·1
Lips	1·6	1·6	0·1	0·1
Mouth	1·3	1·7	0·2	0·2
Tongue	5·3	5·5	0·4	0·5
Jaw	2·7	2·9	0·6	0·7
Lymphatic glands of neck	2·7	2·8	0·6	0·6
Pharynx and throat	2·2	2·3	0·5	0·5
Larynx	1·8	2·0	0·5	0·5
Lungs	1·3	1·3	0·6	0·7
Œsophagus	5·8	6·6	1·4	1·6
Stomach	20·8	21·4	13·4	14·2
Pancreas	1·4	1·9	0·8	1·2
Liver and gall bladder	13·7	12·4	13·9	13·2
Rectum	9·1	10·1	5·2	6·0
Other intestines	6·8	8·3	5·8	7·9
Peritoneum	1·0	0·8	1·7	1·5
Kidney	1·0	1·1	0·7	0·8
Bladder and urethra	2·9	3·1	0·9	0·9
Breast	0·2	0·2	15·7	16·8
Male generative organs	2·5	3·0	—	—
Uterus	—	—	22·9	21·8
Ovary	—	—	1·7	2·0
Other organs	8·8	7·8	6·8	6·3
Not specified	4·6	0·9	4·6	0·9
All organs	100·0	100·0	100·0	100·0
Mortality rate per 100,000 population	65·72	77·31	95·27	102·73

TABLE 11.—*Mortality from Cancer, United States Registration Area. Percentage by Organs and Parts and Sex. 1900 compared with 1913.*

Organs and parts.	Males.		Females.	
	1900.	1913.	1900.	1913.
Buccal cavity . .	5·8	8·1	1·0	1·1
Stomach and liver. .	46·9	48·7	29·0	33·5
Peritoneum, intestines and rectum . .	10·8	14·0	8·0	12·8
Female generative organs	—	—	11·6	15·1
Female breast . .	—	—	22·3	25·8
Skin	5·4	5·6	1·7	2·0
Other or not specified organs . . .	31·7	23·6	26·4	9·7
All organs . . .	100·0	100·0	100·0	100·0
Mortality rate per 100,000 population . .	47·3	61·3	78·6	97·6

arthritis, and prolonged inhalation of silica dust, followed by tubercular silicosis, are instances. Thirdly, increase in disease-potency may break down an unaltered natural resistance, of which infections of massive doses of tubercle bacilli provide experimental evidence.

Increase in the prevalence of a general disease like cancer, if due to a lowering of general resistance to an influence normally present but previously more powerfully resisted, should be found distributed statistically in different communities over the various organs and parts of the body in the same proportion as formerly ; and, in fact, this is what is found to occur, as may be seen from the figures of Table 10, in which the number of cases of cancer in each organ or part are expressed as a percentage of the total number of cases of cancer. There are in this table no notable variations in the percentages, and such small variations as are present may be accounted for by more accurate specification of the part affected. Indeed, far the most notable variation for both sexes has occurred under the heading " not specified." The data embodied in Table 11 show a similar maintenance of the proportion of cases occurring in various parts of the body ; and here again the variations present may be fairly ascribed to more accurate specification.

Increase due to trauma should only increase the incidence of the disease in the organ or part affected, and study of such increase can only be expected primarily to disclose the causation of the trauma ; thus a study of injuries to joints, or of pulmonary silicosis, would not *per se* have disclosed the part played by the tubercle bacillus.

Increase of disease-potency affecting any group should, on the other hand, increase the incidence of the disease in that group without altering the statistical tendency for various parts of the body to be attacked in a definite proportion.

The information available to-day relating to the prevalence of cancer in occupations distributed according to the parts of the body affected is unfortunately quite inadequate for any intensive investigation on the lines indicated above. The only useful data are those published (i.) for mortality from cancer for England and Wales, which are standardised for age-distribution (see Table 12) ; unfortunately they refer to males only, not to females, and no information is given as to the organs and parts affected ; and (ii.) for morbidity from cancer in Germany by organs and parts (see Tables 13 and 14), which are concerned with " only those suffering from the disease who were actively employed or employable, or, in other words, persons in the advanced stage of the disease were apparently excluded " (1, p. 74). These sets of data are in many ways unsatisfactory ; nevertheless interest attaches to considering the two sets of data together. Any deductions, however, from such a method of inquiry must be treated with the greatest reserve.

The textile industry appears in both sets ; in Table 12 the textile workers are shown to have a high and rapidly increasing cancer death rate ; in Table 13 they appear with an undue proportion of cancer of the digestive organs. Considerable attention was given in this country during the later years of last century to studying the conditions of humidity and temperature most favourable for manipulating threads, especially of cotton and flax, and various devices were introduced for warming and artificially humidifying the air of weaving sheds. The workers experienced ill-effects and complained. Thereupon the Government instituted a careful inquiry, and the amount of humidity permitted is now controlled by definite regulations. The inquiry is important, because it established that conditions favourable for weaving altered the metabolism of the workers (see also pp. 289–291), who as a class " appear to be small in stature, spare in build, thin in face, pale in complexion, and have a wearied look. Many of them complain that their appetites are poor and require tempting, and that they suffer from indigestion. These conditions cannot be explained otherwise than by the prolonged exposure to the effects of the warm moist atmosphere in which the weavers work."

These observations point to disorders of digestion being caused by conditions of work in one branch of the textile industry, and suggest the possibility of these conditions being the trauma

TABLE 12.—*Mortality from Cancer in England and Wales in Selected Occupations, 1900—02. Males, Ages Fifteen and over. Standardised Death Rates per 100,000 Population.*

Occupation.	Standardised death rate.	Increase or decrease since 1890—92.
Chimney sweeps	224·9	— 40·6
Seamen	170·5	+ 57·0
Brewers	166·6	+ 45·5
Tailors	112·9	+ 36·4
Textile workers . . .	112·6	+ 37·3
Fishermen	111·9	+ 10·9
Lawyers	111·8	+ 22·1
Innkeepers	108·8	+ 15·7
Gasworks service	107·1	— 6·7
Corn millers	105·3	+ 22·7
Shoemakers	103·2	+ 20·1
Occupied males in industrial districts .	102·9	+ 21·9
Butchers	102·8	+ 5·6
Maltsters	101·6	— 7·5
Physicians	101·1	+ 9·7
Metal workers	101·1	+ 15·8
Hatters	101·0	+ 16·7
Occupied males	101·0	+ 22·5
Glass workers	100·9	+ 4·2
Bakers	99·3	+ 20·4
Carpenters and joiners . . .	97·6	+ 17·3
Tobacconists	95·4	+ 8·4
Farmers and graziers . . .	94·8	+ 21·9
Domestic indoor servants . . .	93·2	+ 11·4
Printers	92·9	+ 15·6
Occupied males in agricultural districts	92·2	+ 16·9
Quarrymen	91·2	— 15·8
Potters	91·0	+ 27·2
School teachers	90·1	+ 18·9
Clergymen	87·3	+ 20·0
Coal merchants	85·7	+ 0·9
Railway engine drivers and stokers .	85·3	+ 12·7
Gardeners and nurserymen . .	85·2	+ 16·0
Coal miners	82·4	+ 21·0
Farm labourers	79·7	+ 13·1
Farmers	78·2	+ 14·2
Grocers	76·5	+ 18·5

TABLE 13.—*Cancer in Germany, by Organs and Parts, according to Occupation. Males.*

Organ or part.	All occupations.	Agriculture.	Textile manufacture.	Common labourers.	Retired.	Metal workers.	Wood-working industry.	Transport.
Bones . . .	25	21	19	21	20	30	41	23
Skin . . .	150	250	99	140	163	90	110	112
Respiratory organs.	20	7	19	16	24	30	21	14
Digestive organs .	703	642	783	718	703	750	685	748
Urinary organs .	15	8	—	10	45	30	13	5
Glands . . .	59	54	53	56	28	35	96	70
Breast . . .	4	1	—	2	4	15	13	9
Generative organs .	24	17	27	37	13	20	21	19
Total . . .	1,000	1,000	1,000	1,000	1,000	1,000	1,000	1,000

TABLE 14.—*Cancer in Germany, by Organs and Parts, according to Occupation. Females.*

Organ or part.	All occupations.	Agriculture.	Textile manufacture.	Common labourers.	Retired.	Restaurant, etc., keepers.	Laundresses.	Domestic service.
Bones . . .	11	18	10	11	10	—	8	20
Skin . . .	73	151	52	95	88	—	116	81
Respiratory organs	3	—	5	4	—	—	—	—
Digestive organs .	306	338	235	374	311	244	349	323
Urinary organs .	6	4	10	4	4	—	—	10
Glands . .	55	73	26	54	38	122	16	61
Breast . . .	243	208	287	154	374	220	240	111
Generative organs .	303	208	375	304	175	414	271	394
Total . .	1,000	1,000	1,000	1,000	1,000	1,000	1,000	1,000

which leads to the digestive organs succumbing to cancer in undue proportion, as indicated in Table 13. The distribution of cancer, given in Table 14, for female textile workers may also be noted ; the outstanding feature is the high proportion of cancer of the breast and generative organs ; too little is known of the effect of the conditions referred to above on the female organs to justify any suggestion of the existence here of cause and effect ; but a case appears to exist for further inquiry. The female textile workers, although exposed to the same atmospheric conditions as males, appear to suffer proportionately much less from cancer of the digestive organs ; but as the total death rate for these workers is unknown it is impossible to say whether even this low proportion of digestive cases may not represent a high actual death rate.

Agriculture, which occurs in Tables 13 and 14, is represented

TABLE 15.—*Mortality from Cancer, Urban and Rural, by Organs and Parts. United States Registration Area, 1908—12.*

Organ or part.	Rate per 100,000 population.		Per mille of cancer of all organs.	
	Urban.	Rural.	Urban.	Rural.
Buccal cavity	2·9	2·8	·36	41
Stomach and liver ‘. . . .	31·3	28·0	38·4	416
Peritoneum, intestines and rectum	11·2	7·9	137	117
Female generative organs . .	13·2	8·7	162	130
Breast	7·6	6·6	94	98
Skin	2·1	3·6	26	54
Other or not specified organs .	13·0	9·7	161	144
All organs.	81·3	67·3	1,000	1,000

in Table 12 by farmers and graziers, gardeners and nurserymen and farm labourers, all of whom stand low down on the list. This class may be taken as representative of rural conditions, for which, as has already been pointed out, the cancer death rate is lower than for towns (see also Table 15). The figures of Tables 13, 14 and 15 indicate an undue proportion of and a high death rate from cancer of the skin. Oliver states that " gardeners who are in the habit of sprinkling soot upon plants to protect them from slugs, occasionally develop cancerous ulceration of the hand," and the German Committee of Cancer Research advance the theory that cancer of the skin among agriculturists is the result of contact with infected earth. Both suggestions are combined in an idea propounded by Green (4), who asks whether a possible cancer parasite might not be akin to the myxomycetes, and points out that the ravages of plasmodiophora in agriculture are associated with the modern use of artificial manures, which have been treated with *sulphuric acid ;* he quotes Stockhardt in evidence that pure carbon soot from burnt benzine has no ill effects on the leaves of plants such as coal soot has, and ascribes to the sulphurous compounds present in soot in the form of ammonium sulphate (which is itself largely used in agriculture) the value of soot to farmers and gardeners, and its injurious action on the skin.

Apart from Green's idea that artificial manures and soot act as stimulants of plasmodial life, there is definite evidence afforded by occupation that exposure to the products of coal distillation and the higher hydrocarbons is associated with skin cancer. Thus chimney sweeps occupy an unenviable position in Table 12, which they have acquired owing to an extraordinary prevalence among them of cancer of the scrotum and skin. The connection between the disease and their occupation is undoubted ; in this country the sweep's method of work with use of the chimney brush brings him into contact with soot to an extent which has become a national bye-word—" as black as a sweep." Abroad, where the English method is not used, chimney sweeps' cancer is rare ; thus, " in the United States sweeps' cancer is unknown ; in Belgium, where coal like the English coal is used, there is almost complete immunity, *but great care is taken to prevent contact with soot ;* in Germany the practice is to wash daily from head to foot " (1, p. 58). Further, the English method is being modified, greater cleanliness is being observed, and the cancer mortality is falling.

Another instance of the effect of coal-distillation products is afforded by the manufacture and handling of pitch. Pitch is the residuum left after distilling off the more volatile parts from coal tar obtained from gasworks. The hot fluid pitch is run off from the stills into beds, where it solidifies on cooling ; it is then broken up and sent to the manufacturers of briquettes and patent fuel. The men who break up the pitch suffer from pitch warts on their hands and arms, and the warts in some cases become epitheliomatous. Patent fuel is made by binding together coal dust with pitch sufficiently warmed to make it plastic ; the mixture is moulded into briquettes, which, on cooling, become hard and are sold as fuel. The workers in this industry suffer in a similar way from pitch warts and epithelioma, but to a greater extent, and their exposure to the pitch is greater (11).

The distillation of shale, which geologically is a form of coal, in order to obtain paraffin, provides another instance. The process is associated with the occurrence of cancer of the skin, known as paraffin cancer, among the shale oil workers in Scotland, where the shale is found.

Cancer has also been ascribed to other coal tar products ; thus, where aniline, naphthylamine and their homologues and benzidine are made, the workers have been found to suffer from papillomatous growths of the bladder.

The greater prevalence among males than among females of cancer of the buccal cavity (see Tables 11 and 12) also falls into line here, since it may be due to the male habit of smoking, which exposes this part of the body to the products of distillation, not of coal, but of other vegetable matter in the form of tobacco.

These instances are sufficient to suggest that the products of vegetable distillation have a traumatic action on the tissues, which determines the incidence of cancer in the organ or part of the body exposed to their influence.

Other instances of cancer definitely recognised as being determined by trauma are Röntgen-ray cancer among X-ray operators, which affects the part exposed to the light rays; cancer of the cheek among the natives of Ceylon, due to their habit of chewing betel nut; and cancer of the skin of the abdomen, Kangri cancer, among natives of Afghanistan, due to burns caused by wearing charcoal stoves for the sake of warmth. But such instances, the full description of which, so far as they occur in industry, belongs rather to a work on diseases of occupation, can hardly be expected to explain the general increase of cancer mortality, which is too wide spread to be attributed in every case to some local trauma. Study of cancer, as it occurs in occupations, has thrown much light on the part played by trauma, and further information as to its distribution by organs and parts in different occupations would probably carry the study forward. More than this, occupational groups would probably be disclosed with divergent mortality rates, due to no obvious local trauma, that is to say, rates distributed over the various organs and parts according to a standard distribution. Close study of the environmental conditions of these groups might be expected to lay bare some of the causes associated with modern civilisation to which the present increase of cancer is due.

The principles of investigation we advocate are of course to be extended beyond the limits of the class of industrially employed workers, and should be so extended because the increase of cancer mortality is not restricted to one section of the community. As we remarked before, the ætiology of disease as studied by the ancient physicians was mainly what we should now call non-specific. The word contagion is indeed to be found in ancient writings, but the idea it represents in our minds is not older than the sixteenth century. This fact, together with a tendency, rightly repugnant to us, to rely upon loose analogy and dialectic, has led to an almost complete neglect of ancient medicine as affording stimuli for modern research. We are now, however, beginning to realise that the emphasis put upon non-specific factors, upon individual resisting power and upon its modification under stress of habits of life and exposure to the common assaults of environment, was not altogether a false emphasis. This remark applies with particular force to the subject of this chapter.

VII. Bibliography.

1. Hoffman, F. L. *The Mortality from Cancer throughout the World.* The Prudential Press. New Jersey, U.S.A. 1915. (Most of the data used in this chapter are compiled from this useful work, and passages in inverted commas, with page references in brackets, are quoted from it.)

2. Greenwood, M., and Wood, F. " On Changes in the Recorded Mortality from Cancer." *Proc. Epidem. Sect. Roy. Soc. Med.* March, 1914.

3. Brown, J. W., and Mohan Lal. " An Inquiry into the Relation between Social Status and Cancer Mortality." *Journal of Hygiene,* XIV., No. 2. 1914.

4. Green, C. E. *The Cancer Problem : A Statistical Study.* Edinburgh. 1911.

5. King, G., and Newsholme, A. "On the Alleged Increase of Cancer." *Proc. Roy. Soc.,* LIV., p. 209. 1893.

6. Payne, J. F. " Address on the Increase of Cancer." *Hunterian Soc. Trans.* 1899.

7. Maynard, G. D. " A Statistical Study of Cancer Death Rates." *Biomet,* VII., pp. 278—304. 1909—10.

8. Matas, R. " The Surgical Peculiarities of the American Negro." *Trans. Amer. Surg. Assn.* 1896.

9. Young, J. A. *Evolution and Development of Public Health Administration in the City of Edinburgh.* Pillans and Wilson. Edinburgh. 1919.

10. Greenwood, M., and Wood, F. " The Relation between the Cancer and Diabetes Death Rates." *Journ. Hygiene,* XIV., pp. 83—118. 1914.

11. O'Donovan, W. J. " Epitheliomatous Ulceration among Tar Workers." *Brit. Journ. Dermatol. and Syph.,* Vol. XXXII. 1920.

CHAPTER VIII

CAUSATION AND PREVENTION OF ACCIDENTS

I. Causation of Accidents :—Industrial Accidents : The Human Factor ; Reaction to Environment Influences—(a) Fatigue, (b) Psychical Influences, (c) Lighting, (d) Temperature ; The Personal Factor ; New Workers ; General Conclusion. II. Prevention of Accidents :— Observation and Research : *A priori* Reasoning ; Administration : How to Minimise Risk, How to Reduce Personal Lack of Interest— Safety Committees, Safety First, Suggestion Box ; A Duty for the Medical Profession. III. Bibliography.

I. Causation of Accidents.

LIFE is always exposed to risk. Sometimes, as in the case of the diseases referred to in the foregoing chapters, the circumstances which determine the risk are more or less obscure, although appearing to obey certain epidemiological laws ; in other cases the circumstances are manifest and appear to be avoidable. Accidents belong to the latter class, and, since records of their occurrence in various industries are available, industrial accidents present a useful field for study. But the general community is liable to accidents ; professional men, clerks and shopkeepers, for instance, experience an accident rate to which for the period they are employed in factories, mines, quarries or railways, manual labourers are not liable. This " normal " accident liability should be subtracted when estimating the special liability of any industrial group to suffer from accidents as a result of their occupation ; it may, however, be disregarded when comparing various occupational groups one with another, as is done in Table 1. In this table and in the diagrams the accident mortality for age groups is compared with that for two diseases, phthisis and cancer. The curves representing each of the three causes of death so far retain the same shape for each occupational group that after examining one diagram we can tell with certainty which is the accident curve, which the phthisis, and which the cancer ; indeed, of the three the phthisis curve shows the greatest variation in shape. The difference between the highest death rate for all ages from phthisis (5·62 for general labourers) and the lowest (1·02 for South Wales coal miners) is 4·6 ; and this suggests that if we could, so far as phthisis is concerned, place general labourers in the position of South Wales miners, we should reduce their mortality per 1,000 by 4·6. The difference between the highest

TABLE 1.—*The Mortality of Males in Several Occupations, 1900—02. Occupied and Retired Males. Rate per 1,000 Years of Life.*

	Years of life.	Cause.	Ages.							
			15.	20.	25.	35.	45.	55.	65 and over.	All ages.
(58) Nail, anchor, chain and other steel and iron manufacturers.	660,372	Accident	·42	·32	·51	·59	·96	1·94	2·74	·73
		Phthisis	·51	1·20	2·04	2·79	3·59	2·41	2·08	2·07
		Cancer.	·01	·03	·07	·44	1·46	3·63	8·32	·87
(53) Engine, machine, boilermakers, fitters, millwrights.	1,054,128	Accident	·34	·38	·33	·63	·69	1·17	1·15	·52
		Phthisis	·60	1·74	1·87	2·36	2·74	2·58	1·61	1·86
		Cancer.	·04	·02	·07	·37	1·30	3·79	6·59	·71
(48) Shoemakers	592,665	Accident	·10	·09	·16	·26	·43	·63	1·33	·36
		Phthisis	1·04	2·95	3·27	4·41	4·40	3·21	2·15	3·18
		Cancer	·03	·09	·11	·39	1·57	3·81	6·80	1·35
(47) Tailors	415,530	Accident	·14	·13	·18	·23	·73	·61	2·08	·42
		Phthisis	·76	2·11	2·64	4·12	4·22	3·43	1·79	2·82
		Cancer	·06	·05	·08	·44	1·55	·445	7·19	1·23
(45) Bakers, confectioners.	305,712	Accident	·15	·18	·30	·44	·40	·51	1·55	·37
		Phthisis	·37	1·54	1·90	2·53	2·80	2·30	1·34	1·80
		Cancer	·02	·04	·11	·47	1·44	4·14	6·57	·89
(43) Butchers	327,162	Accident	·11	·14	·25	·49	·76	1·29	1·74	·42
		Phthisis	·21	·62	2·03	3·04	3·04	2·28	1·19	1·74
		Cancer	·05	—	·07	·33	1·52	4·50	7·90	·83
(40) Printers	280,008	Accident	·25	·15	·14	·14	·45	·82	2·16	·28
		Phthisis	1·03	3·45	3·65	5·13	4·34	3·68	1·87	3·38
		Cancer	—	·02	·13	·31	1·38	3·68	6·19	·58
(95) General labourers.	1,281,000	Accident	·71	·95	1·22	1·62	2·07	2·48	3·64	1·68
		Phthisis	1·11	3·30	5·26	8·06	8·36	6·72	3·78	5·62
		Cancer	·04	·10	·18	·78	2·77	6·56	11·52	2·32
(88) Miners	1,943,046	Accident	1·19	1·18	1·23	1·62	2·08	2·68	3·20	1·54
		Phthisis	·42	1·02	1·04	1·22	1·72	2·36	1·85	1·16
		Cancer	·01	·05	·11	·33	1·04	2·89	5·64	·56
(83f) Coal miners (Mon. and S. Wales).	426,261	Accident	1·62	1·74	1·84	2·25	2·67	3·65	5·19	2·10
		Phthisis	·35	·90	·95	1·20	1·43	2·34	1·44	1·02
		Cancer	—	·05	·08	·24	1·11	2·39	4·90	·40
(83) Coal miners	1,856,196	Accident	1·20	1·19	1·23	1·64	2·13	2·74	3·30	1·55
		Phthisis	·41	1·03	·96	1·09	1·52	2·04	1·47	1·05
		Cancer	·01	·05	·11	·33	1·05	2·85	5·48	·55
(17) Seamen	312,528	Accident	3·79	3·26	3·05	4·15	4·02	3·51	1·99	3·47
		Phthisis	·85	3·10	3·80	3·80	3·98	2·71	1·42	3·22
		Cancer	—	·07	·20	·75	2·39	5·10	9·07	1·65
(18) Dock and wharf labourers	270,594	Accident	·54	·70	1·15	1·27	1·81	2·38	3·64	1·43
		Phthisis	·42	1·67	3·21	4·93	5·68	4·08	3·06	3·83
		Cancer	—	—	·10	·52	1·75	3·81	6·32	1·09
(92) Platelayers, navvy, railway and road labourers	510,099	Accident	1·12	1·11	1·04	1·14	1·47	2·04	2·43	1·37
		Phthisis	·22	1·07	·91	1·36	1·82	1·71	·79	1·23
		Cancer	·04	·03	·09	·33	·91	2·85	5·01	·98
(72) Wool, worsted manufacturers.	238,758	Accident	·13	·20	·12	·23	·54	·88	2·33	·40
		Phthisis	·69	2·38	1·81	2·26	2·89	2·35	1·88	1·98
		Cancer	—	·17	·16	·59	1·13	3·27	9·92	1·18
(28) Stationery manufacturers, stationers, newsagents, publishers.	149,718	Accident	·04	·20	·13	·35	·28	·79	1·26	·31
		Phthisis	·98	2·49	2·84	3·29	3·51	2·04	1·01	2·53
		Cancer	—	0·5	·11	·28	1·23	3·93	5·18	·87

and lowest death rates from accidents is 3·2 ; and from cancer 2·0. The mortality from accidents is, then, as worthy of attention as that from these two important diseases ; it is as definite a statistical entity, and its reduction would have an effect upon the total occupational death rate similar in magnitude to that of reducing the disease death rates.

Industrial Accidents.

The prevalence of accidents in this country has received close attention in two groups of workers, those employed in factories, and those employed in mines and quarries. The official figures

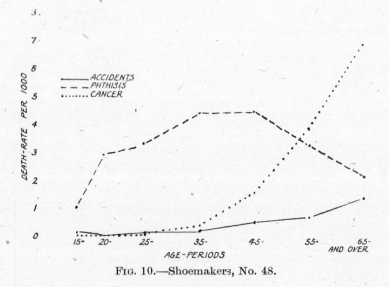

FIG. 10.—Shoemakers, No. 48.

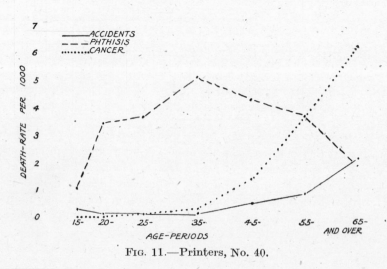

FIG. 11.—Printers, No. 40.

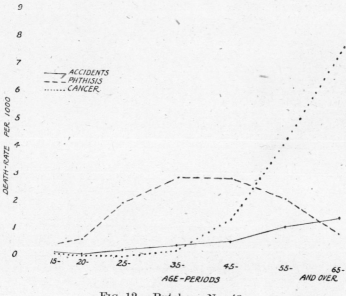

FIG. 12.—Butchers, No. 43.

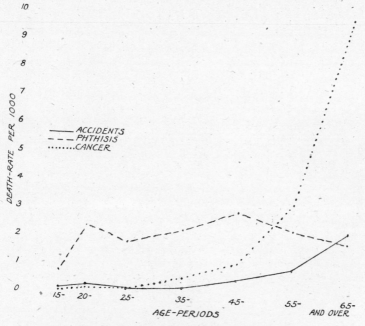

FIG. 13.—Wool, Worsted Manufacturers, No. 72.

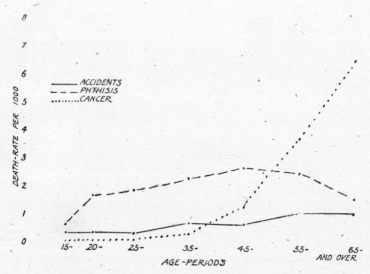

FIG. 14.—Engine, Machine, Boilermakers, Fitters, Millwrights, No. 53

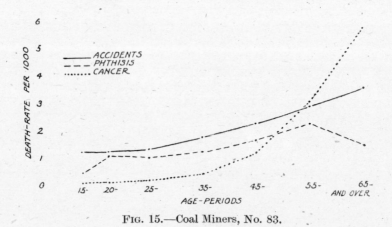

FIG. 15.—Coal Miners, No. 83.

published from year to year show that accidents recur with a frequency as regular as the occurrence of disease ; even when grouped according to the causes which contribute to the gross total, the groups are found maintaining from year to year a definite relation to the total accident rate (see Table 2) ; just as

TABLE 2.—*Accident Death Rates due to Mining in the United Kingdom.*

| Period. | Death rate per 1,000 persons employed. | | | | | | Total accident death rate per million tons of mineral raised. |
| | Underground, caused by | | | | Above ground. All causes. | Under and above ground. | |
	Explosions.	Falls of ground.	Shaft accidents.	Miscellaneous.			
In and about Mines under the Coal Mines Acts.							
1873—1882	0·65	1·12	0·32	0·47	0·92	2·24	7·42
1883—1892	0·32	1·00	0·19	0·50	0·96	1·81	5·65
1893—1902	0·18	0·76	0·13	0·45	0·83	1·39	4·70
1903—1912	0·17	0·74	0·11	0·44	0·78	1·33	4·76
In and about Mines under the Metalliferous Mines Regulation Acts.							
1873—1882	—	0·94	0·72	0·68	0·58	1·62	—
1883—1892	0·02	0·94	0·52	0·67	0·39	1·44	—
1893—1902	—	0·83	0·44	0·69	0·38	1·31	—
1903—1912	—	0·93	0·41	0·53	0·47	1·30	—

Compiled from *Annual Report of Chief Inspector of Mines for* 1913 (Cd. 7,452).

TABLE 3.—*Non-fatal Accidents due to Mining which Disabled for more than Seven Days.*

| Occupation. | Year. | Number. | | Per cent. injured. |
		Employed.	Injured.	
Coal mining . .	1912	1,089,090	150,652	13·8
	1913	1,127,890	177,189	15·6
Metalliferous mining .	1912	28,058	1,650	5·5
	1913	27,412	1,773	6·5

Compiled from *Annual Report of Chief Inspector of Mines for* 1913 (Cd. 7,452).

the mortality from cancer or phthisis for any portion of the community from year to year maintains a definite relation to the total death rate. The number sustaining injuries, like the number accidentally killed in any group, varies from year to year in a similar way, and not according to random chance (see Table 3); and when the tendency of the accident rate experienced in any industry to rise, to fall, or remain constant is known for several years the rate to be anticipated in the future may be expected to belong to the same numerical series. Nor does this regularity apply only to the number of accidents and to their distribution according to causation, it applies also to the liability of various parts of the body to sustain injuries (see Table 4).*

TABLE 4.—*Accidents in Factories and Workshops (reported upon by Certifying Surgeons).*

Degree of injury.	1907.		1913.	
	Number.	Per cent.	Number.	Per cent.
Loss of right hand or arm . .	89	0·2	88	0·2
Loss of left hand or arm . .	62	0·1	73	0·1
Loss of part of right hand. .	1,831	4·2	1,938	3·3
Loss of part of left hand . .	1,658	3·8	1,841	3·2
Loss of part of leg or foot . .	132	0·3	119	0·2
Fracture of limb or of bones of trunk	1,059	2·4	1,018	1·7
Fracture of hand or foot . .	902	2·1	943	2·1
Loss of sight of one or both eyes.	64	0·2	105	0·2
Other injury to eyes. . .	1,902	4·4	2,518	4·3
Injury to head or face . .	3,263	7·5	2,985	5·1
Burn or scald	5,823	13·4	8,832	15·2
Wounds, bruises and other injuries not specified above .	25,514	58·7	36,410	62·6
Fatal . . . . :	1,179	2·7	1,309	2·3
Total	43,478	100·0	58,179	100·0

Compiled from *Annual Reports of Chief Inspector of Factories for* 1907 and 1913.

* While the information embodied in Table 4 refers to operatives employed in factories and workshops, and not like that of Tables 2 and 3 to miners, there can be no reasonable doubt that the distribution of miners' accidents according to the parts affected would be found to be similarly regular ; no information, however, is published on this matter. Similarly no information is published giving the accident rate per 1,000 employed in factories and workshops ; but, while no suggestion can be hazarded with regard to this latter group of accidents as to whether the rate has been increasing or decreasing, here also the probability is that the rate has varied, as it has among miners, in a regular way. The tables contain no data which refer to the war period, because from 1914 onwards the stress of work and the distribution of workers has so varied from what prevailed before that time that for the study of the incidence of accidents, as for the incidence of disease, statistics from 1914 onwards cannot be considered as comparable with those of previous years.

The statistical regularity of accident data, which would appear to be comparable with those referring to the occurrence of disease, raises the question as to whether the causes that lead up to accidents depend merely on random chance, or, in other words, whether the majority of accidents are really accidents in the sense of being—to use a legal phrase—" acts of God."

The Human Factor.—A glance at a table stating the causation of accidents immediately indicates the importance of the human factor. Thus, in Table 5, if the ill-defined group " other causes " be subtracted from the total, there remain 116,209 fatal and non-fatal accidents, of which 58,804 (*i.e.*, over 50 per cent.) were caused by (*a*) machinery not moved by mechanical power, (*b*) falling bodies, (*c*) persons falling, and (*d*) tools in use. This group may be said to be in the main caused directly by human agency and to be under the control of individual workers. Many accidents in the other groups also are the result of direct action by the workers who expose themselves or their comrades through thoughtlessness or carelessness to contact with moving machinery or hot liquid.

TABLE 5.—*Accidents in Factories and Workshops*, 1913.

Causation.	Number of	
	Injuries.	Fatalities.
Machinery moved by mechanical power .	47,177	421
Molten metal, hot liquid	7,306	26
Explosion	870	33
Escape of gas or steam	1,021	36
Electricity	496	19
Machinery not moved by mechanical power { Cranes . .	736	18
Presses for metal articles	394	—
Other . .	843	2
Struck by falling body	27,497	131
Persons falling.	21,637	445
Struck by tools in use	7,096	5
Other causes	61,779	173
Total.	176,852	1,309

Compiled from *Annual Report of Chief Inspector of Factories for* 1913.

Thus Bellhouse (5), after stating that from factories and workshops during 1918 " notices were received of 1,579 fatal cases, of 53,491 accidents due to machinery, and of 108,663 non-machinery cases," divides accidents under two headings, (1) machinery accidents and those preventable by safeguards, and (2) non-machinery accidents and accidents not due to want of fencing, and he goes on to point out as regards machinery accidents, "that it has been the experience of the inspectors that, even in these cases, not more than 35 per cent. have been due to the absence of a guard, the remainder being attributed largely to such causes as negligence, carelessness, want of thought, and perhaps, more than all, to lack of proper appreciation of the danger." The same authority has also said (22) that " however well machinery is guarded we cannot look for more than 10 per cent. reduction in the accident rate by the provision of safe-guards alone. This is rather a startling fact which is not gener-ally recognised, but it is interesting to note that our experience here corresponds exactly with that in America, and that they too estimate 10 per cent. to be the maximum reduction of accidents obtainable by better safeguarding of machinery."

TABLE 6.—Shaft Accidents in Factories.

Employment.	1908.		1909.	
	Fatal.	Non-fatal.	Fatal.	Non-fatal.
Oiling bearings, pulleys, or clutches	2	34	6	44
Putting belts on pulleys . .	10	36	9	36
Taking belts off pulleys . .	1	4	1	5
Adjusting belts, pulleys, etc.. .	1	24	2	14
Holding belts during repairs . .	5	6	2	8
Examining shafting, pulleys, etc. .	1	4	—	4
Reaching over unfenced shafting .	3	29	6	17
Cleaning shafting in motion . .	1	16	1	15
Cleaning under or near shafting .	1	19	—	15
Other occasional work near shaft-ing :—				
Cleaning windows . . .	1	9	—	3
Electric wiring . . .	1	1	—	3
Erecting piping or machinery.	1	10	3	9
Joinery or building . .	1	1	—	6
Limewashing walls or ceilings.	6	7	2	2
Painting walls or ceilings .	—	4	2	3
Other	11	—	2	4
Stepping under or over shafting .	3	6	—	7
Attending machines . . .	—	21	1	17
Larking	1	9	—	2
Falls of overhead shafting . .	1	9	—	13
Miscellaneous	4	27	4	6
Total	44	287	41	233

From Report on Fencing and Safety Precautions for Transmission Machinery. W. S. Smith. H.M. Stationery Office, 1913.

TABLE 7.—*Shaft Accidents in Factories. Severity of Injuries.*

Nature of injury.	1908.	1909.
Fatal	44	41
Severe :—		
Arm fractured	30	29
Arm amputated	6	8
Foot fractured	1	—
Foot amputated	—	2
Hand amputated . . .	—	1
Leg fractured	6	7
Ribs fractured	8	9
Scalp torn off	8	5
Shoulder fractured . . .	10	3
Skull fractured	4	—
Spine fractured	—	1
Thigh fractured	6	4
Other lacerations and contusions .	47	39
Slight	161	125
Total.	331	274

From *Report on Fencing and Safety Precautions for Transmission Machinery.* W. S. Smith. H.M. Stationery Office, 1913.

One group of accidents provides an instance in point, viz., those occurring from revolving shafting. Here, says Mr. W. Sydney Smith (6), " the same type of accidents recur year after year, due chiefly to workers coming into contact with mill-gearing in motion when oiling bearings, adjusting belts, cleaning shafting, limewashing ceilings, or performing other work in the vicinity of revolving shafts " (see Table 6). Practically all shaft accidents follow upon direct action by the workers, in contrast to injuries of indirect causation due to, say, the sudden breaking of a belt, over which the worker concerned has no control, and the table indicates that " fully 60 per cent. of the accidents were due to work being carried on in the immediate vicinity of mill-gearing *in motion.*" Smith in this connection writes, " The fact is generally overlooked that the worker's clothing is liable to be seized if sufficiently long and loose to allow a portion of the garment to wrap once round the shaft ; the presence of tacky oil on the shaft in the neighbourhood of bearings increases the dangers. Even on a smooth shaft, in such cases, the worker will probably be caught and carried round by the revolving shaft unless the garment gives way and releases him. Loose hair, also, on account of its lightness is extremely liable to become wound on revolving shafting, possibly owing to cyclonic movement of the currents of air set up in the vicinity of the shaft, and, if the hair is caught, a portion or the whole of the scalp is usually torn off. In 1908 and 1909, 56 per cent. and 60 per cent. respectively of the reported shafting accidents were due to contact of either loose clothing, loose hair, or cleaning rags, with revolving parts of mill-gearing." He goes on to say that " over twenty persons injured on high shafting had climbed on tables or work benches, seventeen were standing on machinery and sixteen on planks, boxes, stools or temporary stages within reach of shafting. Insecure footing on beams, walls, window-sills and piping was responsible for nine accidents, while three occurred to persons climbing over goods piled near overhead shafting." The severity of the accidents which resulted is shown in Table 7, from which it will be seen that eighty-five out of 605 were fatal, or 16 per cent., as compared with 0·9 per cent. for all accidents due to machinery in motion (see Table 5). The standard of notification is the same in each class of accidents, and so the percentage of fatalities is strictly comparable. Here is a group of accidents particularly severe in degree, and recurring year after year, although they are entirely under the control of the personal factor.

TABLE 8.—*Eye Injuries among Granite Dressers.*

Character of injury.	Aberdeen Eye Institution, 1st July, 1908, to 30th June, 1909.	Aberdeen Royal Infirmary, 1st Jan. to 31st Dec., 1910.	Total for twelve months.
Foreign bodies in, and abrasions of, the eye	580	142	722
Septic ulcers.	43 (28 cases cauterised)	5	48
Traumatic cataracts	2 (lens extracted)	2	4
Foreign bodies in ciliary region	2 (globes enucleated)	—	2
Dislocated lens	1	3	4
Corneal wounds	17	2	19
Corneal nebulæ	—	4	4
Other injuries	—	6	6
All injuries	645	164	809

From *Report of Royal Commission on Metalliferous Mines and Quarries.* Vol. III. *Minutes of Evidence*, p. 67. (Cd. 7,478.)

Another group of industrial accidents—eye injuries—entirely under the control of the workers, has been investigated, especially by one of us (7) in the stone-cutting industry. Eye injuries account for less than 5 per cent. of all industrial accidents (see Table 4), but in this industry the percentage is much higher; thus, in the Operative Masons' Society of England and Wales in the ten years, 1902—11, a sum of £10,825 was paid in compensation for illness, of which £829, *i.e.*, 7·7 per cent., was on account of injury to eyes. The injuries are caused by particles flying from the tool or the stone as the mason or his neighbour applies mallet and chisel or the pneumatic tool. Inquiry in the granite industry in Aberdeen, where pneumatic tools are largely used, revealed that over 800 granite dressers out of a total of about 1,700 employed, *i.e.*, nearly 50 per cent., are known to have sought medical aid in one year on account of eye injuries more or less severe (see Table 8). The excessive prevalence of this type of injury among these men is further borne testimony to by the payments for compensation of an important insurance company; during three years, 1908—10, the amount paid out in respect of claims for eye injuries was nearly exactly equal to that paid out for all other injuries put together. These injuries (called by the men " fires " in the eye) are practically entirely preventable by the wearing of suitable goggles; the glass of goggles, however, in a few weeks becomes frosted from the frequent impact of particles and requires renewal. The men prefer to run the risk rather than take this small trouble, and men are to be seen at work, who have already lost the sight of one eye, still declining to wear goggles. Parsons, with his wide experience at Moorfields in London, tells (10) the same story of the prevalence of avoidable eye injuries. " If one reckons up the loss of the workmen's time entailed and the consequent loss of money to employers and the State, the total is enormous. In many hospitals it is customary to put a drop of atropine in the eye after removing a foreign body from the cornea. This must in most cases mean several days away from work. Certainly all emery-wheel cases—and they are the vast majority—could be avoided by the simple precaution of using protective goggles. Even when they are provided by the employers the men will not use them."

Apart from natural conservatism, which stands in the way of the adoption of a new habit, and from the fascination—notwithstanding the proverb to the contrary—the burnt child has for fire, there are inconveniences associated with the wearing of protective goggles. These are minimised if the following principles are attended to in design : Eye guards to be effective (i.) should prevent particles from reaching the eyes from in front, from either side, and from below, the eyebrows naturally guard the eye from particles coming from above ; (ii.) should be light and comfortable, and allow free play of air so that moisture does not condense on the transparent medium ; (iii.) should not impede vision, or become obscured by impact of particles ; and (iv.) should be strong and cheap.

The fact that no particles are likely to enter from above is important, because the upper part of the goggle may 'be left open and so allow of ventilation.   A closed screen not only becomes hot and uncomfortable, but the transparent medium, usually glass, may be obscured by condensation of moisture. Where fine work has to be executed there must be clear vision, and for this purpose no medium is better than glass.   The objection has been raised that glass broken by a flying particle may be driven into the eye and cause a worse injury than if it were not present.   Injuries to eyes by glasses or spectacles broken by a foreign body are rare.   Such an accident is quite exceptional ; a considerable-sized foreign body would be neces- sary to inflict it, and the damage to the eye would probably not be less if no spectacles or protecting glass were in use.   An American shop bulletin states that " in no instance was an eye even slightly injured by flying glass where the lens was broken by a flying chip."   The main objection to glass, or indeed to any other transparent medium, is that after a time it becomes pitted and obscured.   For this reason eye-guards should be so made that the glass can be easily removed and cleaned or replaced (13).

Two forms of eye-guard designed to meet the requirements stated above are here illustrated ; the first has the advantage that spectacles needed to correct any error of refraction can be worn behind it (14).

Where there is exposure to bright light, as in the process of acetylene welding, the glass of the goggles should be tinted or specially prepared to obscure the chemically active rays at or beyond the violet end of the spectrum, otherwise troublesome irritation and conjunctivitis result (15).

This simple examination of accident data supports the view that industrial accidents are largely dependent upon the per- sonality of the workers, and represent reaction to environment. Careful examination of a large number of accident reports has led to the estimate that from 60 to 80 per cent. of all industrial accidents are due to mistakes under the control of the workers, rather than to agencies outside their control, such as breakages of machinery, escapes of gas and explosions.   Many even of the latter group of accidents have to be attributed to human carelessness in erecting plant and in keeping it in order. We are thus driven to the conclusions that (i.) the bulk of industrial accidents are not due to random chance, but are representative of the reaction of the workers, and that (ii.) accident

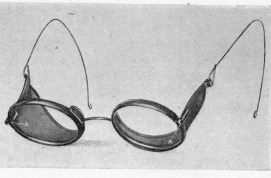

FIG. 16.

Reproduced from *Second Report of Royal Commission on Metalliferous Mines and Quarries* (14).

frequency may possibly be employed for investigating this reaction.

Recognition of the first of these conclusions is to be found in the steps now being taken to interest the workers in their own safety, which are considered later under the heading of Prevention of Accidents.

Reaction to Environmental Influences.—If the second conclusion holds good, then influences, such as hours of work, variations in lighting, temperature and ventilation, which affect the activity and health of workers should influence the incidence of accidents. Accidents of the severity of those already instanced do not, fortunately, occur with sufficient frequency in any industrial establishment to provide material for intensive investigations, but the recent introduction of ambulance stations into factories, where minor cuts and scratches as well as more serious injuries are treated and recorded, has provided the required data. Degree only separates minor from major injuries ; a falling body may fatally injure the head or slightly bruise the foot ; a flying shuttle may destroy an eye or graze an arm ; a circular saw may as quickly abrade the skin as remove half of a hand. Previous to the installation of ambulance rooms no information as to the frequency of minor injuries was available, but now each ambulance room provides a large mass of data for examination.

Vernon (8) has made use of the records of minor injuries thus provided at factories engaged on the production of munitions of war. His inquiries in the first place support the view that the frequency of accidents varies directly with the amount of risk, i.e., the greater the output the higher the accident rate. He found that "the incidence of accidents showed a qualitative resemblance to the output variations, and . . . that varying speed of production is the factor largely responsible for the day shift variations of accidents in men, and not fatigue. Even in women fatigue is only of moderate importance as a rule. . . . The

TABLE 9.—*Relationship between Accidents in Fatigue Period (Seventy-five Hours Week), and in Subsequent Period (Ten Hours Day).*

Type of accident.	Ratio of accident-frequency in fatigue period to that in subsequent period.		Ratio of afternoon accidents to morning accidents.			
			Fatigue period.		Subsequent period.	
	Men.	Women.	Men.	Women.	Men.	Women.
Cuts . . .	1·14	2·73	1·07	1·45	1·08	1·17
Foreign bodies in eye .	0·65	2·09	0·90	1·51	0·98	1·67
Burns . . .	1·16	3·50	1·31	1·29	0·76	1·12
Sprains . .	1·27	2·95	0·92	0·72	0·63	0·80
Previous injuries .	1·43	3·01	0·46	0·82	0·59	0·53
Weighted mean .	1·20	2·87	1·06	1·29	1·00	1·11

From " An Investigation of the Factors concerned in the Causation of Industrial Accidents." H. M. Vernon. *Health of Munition Workers Committee. Memo. No.* 21. 1918. (Cd. 9,046.)

diurnal variations of accidents . . . generally corresponded with the output variations, as both rose to a maximum in the middle of the week and declined at the end of it. The monthly variations of accidents . . . corresponded with output variations, for the accidents increased gradually about 40 per cent., whilst the hourly output at the same time increased 30 per cent." He then traced the secondary effects of other influences :—

TABLE 10.—*Ratio of Night-shift Accidents to Day-shift Accidents.*

Type of accident.	Men.						
	Factory A.		Factory C.		Factory B.	Factory D.	Mean.
	First period.	Second period.	63¼ hours weekly.	54 hours weekly.			
Cuts	0·94	0·85	0·82	0·74	0·81	0·76	0·82
Foreign bodies in eye .	1·46	1·32	0·87	0·91	0·77	1·09	1·07
Burns . . .	1·43	1·43	0·89	0·40	0·59	0·96	0·95
Sprains . . .	0·85	1·19	1·02	1·22	0·89	0·78	0·99
Previous injuries .	0·65	0·87	0·74	1·31	0·71	0·59	0·81
Weighted mean .	0·92	0·94	0·83	0·80	0·78	0·81	0·85
	Women.						
Cuts	0·82	0·76	—	0·74	0·88	—	0·80
Foreign bodies in eye .	1·30	1·58	—	1·09	1·11	—	1·27
Burns . . .	1·09	0·83	—	0·72	0·88	—	0·88
Sprains . . .	0·95	1·00	—	1·17	0·76	—	0·97
Previous injuries .	0·64	0·87	—	0·89	0·57	—	0·74
Weighted mean .	0·88	0·85	—	0·80	0·83	—	0·84

From " An Investigation of the Factors concerned in the Causation of Industrial Accidents." H. M. Vernon. *Health of Munition Workers Committee. Memo. No.* 21. 1918. (Cd. 9,046.)

" Fatigue. The influence of fatigue on accidents to women was strikingly shown . . . when the operatives were working a twelve-hour day, or seventy-five hours week. The women's accidents were two-and-a-half times more numerous than in the subsequent ten-hour day period, but the men's accidents showed no difference (see Table 9). Also the women were treated for faintness nine times more frequently than the men, and were given sal-volatile twenty-three times more frequently, whereas in the subsequent ten-hour day period they were treated for

TABLE 11.—*Women's Night Accidents compared with Morning Accidents.*

Type of accident.	Ratio of night-shift accidents to morning-shift accidents.		
	Factory C.	Factory D.	Mean.
Cuts	0·71	0·80	0·76
Foreign bodies in eye .	1·29	0·98	1·14
Burns	1·18	0·86	1·02
Sprains. . . .	0·92	0·80	0·86
Previous injuries . .	0·94	0·58	0·76
Weighted mean . .	0·83	0·82	0·83

From " An Investigation of the Factors concerned in the Causation of Industrial Accidents." H. M. Vernon. *Health of Munition Workers Committee. Memo. No.* 21. 1918. (Cd. 9,046.)

TABLE 12.—*Accidents per Spell in relation to Outside Temperature.*

External temperature. Degrees Fahrenheit.	Average number of cuts in each spell.			
	Factory B.		Factory C.	
	Women.*	Men.*	Women.*	Men.*
32 or less .	2·84	3·77	1·72	4·16
33—37 . .	2·12	2·88	1·53	3·64
38—42 . .	1·96	2·64	1·38	3·00
43—47 . .	1·55	2·44	1·28	3·33
48 or over .	1·17	1·76	1·16	2·99

From "An Investigation of the Factors concerned in the Causation of Industrial Accidents." H. M. Vernon. *Health of Munition Workers Committee. Memo. No.* 21. 1918. (Cd. 9,046.)

faintness and given sal-volatile only three times more frequently." Vernon gives data, not reproduced here, to justify this statement, and when discussing them points out that " in both sexes the cases rapidly increased during the morning spell, and

* No comparison should be instituted between the relative number of cuts at the two factories, or among women and men, as the processes concerned were different in both instances.

reached a maximum in the last hour or the penultimate hour, just as the accidents did. In the afternoon spell they were relatively much less numerous than in the morning, the ratio between the morning and afternoon cases treated in full working hours being in women as 1 to 0·43 for the fatigue period and as 1 to 0·68 in the subsequent period, whilst in men it was as 1 to 0·75 and 1 to 0·96 in the respective periods. It will be remembered that accidents were almost always more numerous in the afternoon than in the morning, ratios of 1 to 1·29 and 1 to 1·11 being observed in women. There can be little doubt that the smaller proportion of faintness cases observed in the afternoon was chiefly due to the workers getting a good dinner in the 12 to 1 break, in contrast with the inadequate breakfast they often partook of before the morning spell of work.

" In the night-shift the distribution of the faintness cases resembled that of the accident cases, except that the maximum occurred in the second hour of the first spell instead of the first hour. The relative proportions of the cases in the three spells likewise resemble those observed in accidents. This is to be expected, for the night-shift would not suffer from the disability of inadequate food before starting work. However, the night-shift conditions taken as a whole, appear to upset nutrition considerably in comparison with day-shift conditions, as the proportion of faintness cases treated by night was half as great again as those treated by day, both in the men and the women.

" Psychical Influences. At the factories the night-shift workers suffered fewer accidents than the day-shift workers, the average defect being 16 per cent. This was not due to the output being smaller, as . . . it was distinctly bigger by night than by day. It was psychical in origin, and due to the night-shift workers settling down to a calmer mental state than the day-shift workers, and so becoming less careless and inattentive. The psychical factor is one of the most important in accident causation. (See Tables 10 and 11.)

" Lighting. Accidents due to foreign bodies in the eye were 7 to 27 per cent. more numerous in the night-shift than in the day-shift, though all the other accidents were considerably less numerous. This was due to the artificial lighting, as the excess of eye accidents was most marked in the worst lit factory. (See Tables 10 and 11.)

" Temperature. The temperature . . . was recorded continuously for six months by means of a thermograph. Accidents were at a minimum at 65° to 69° F., and increased rapidly at higher temperatures (e.g., by 30 per cent. at temperatures above 75° F.), and slowly at lower temperatures. Continuous records were obtained of the *external* temperature of the town, . . . and it was found that . . . the accidents increased considerably as the weather grew colder, and diminished as it grew warmer. In one factory the women's accidents were nearly two and a half times more numerous when the temperature was at or below freezing point than when it was above 47° F., whilst the men's accidents were twice as numerous." (See Table 12.)

The figures given show that, if the mean frequency of accidents when the temperature *within* the factory was from 65° to 69° F. be taken as 100, then the relative frequency at a temperature of 60° to 64° F. was 103, and at 59° or less it was 108 ; while at 70° to 74° it was 121, and at 75° or over 130. Data showing the number of cuts in relation to the *external* temperature are quoted in Table 12. External temperature, as well as that prevailing, due to means of heating, within the factory, calls for consideration, as a proportion of accidents treated at ambulance stations result from work done in the open air, while others are unconnected with factory work, such as bicycle accidents, cuts sustained at home and during meals at the canteen, and scalds from tea-making ; thus at one factory Vernon found that, out of 235 accidents treated among men and 251 among women, 77 and 80 respectively were not connected with work.

The conclusions drawn, so far, point to accidents occurring with a regularity of frequency similar to that of disease, to the frequency being dependent mainly on the human factor, and to its being affected by environmental conditions in the same way that these conditions affect human activity and sickness.

Vernon's conclusion that, given moderate length of hours and a reasonable arrangement of shifts, speed of production is the chief factor of accident causation has been criticised (21, p. 139 *et seq.*). The investigators provide curves showing the ratio of accidents to production throughout the shift and find that this ratio increases towards the end of the shift ; hence they infer that fatigue is the prime ætiological factor. The data utilised are, in our opinion, inadequate, because no allowance has been made for the fact that a large proportion of the operatives whose accidents and output were averaged were inexperienced. The statement that this circumstance does not affect the argument, " For the factor of inexperience, whether large or small, is always present, and whether large or small, is constant throughout the day, not varying from hour to hour like the other elements in the causation of accidents " (21, p. 130), is *a priori* improbable, and supported by no new evidence. Common observation teaches that both the intensity of and the rate at which fatigue develops are quite different in trained and in untrained athletes.

Probably the curves of output throughout the day of beginners and of experts differ not merely in scale but in form. We do not therefore accept the conclusions, but, at the same time, we do not think that the respective *rôles* of the two factors, fatigue and speed of production, can be assigned by any simple graphical method based upon the variations of output and of accidents throughout a working day. Fatigue, rate of production and accidents are three correlated variables, connected one to another by functional relations which are certainly complex, perhaps so complex that a satisfactory numerical or mathematical formulation of them will prove impossible. In our opinion, the problem must be first simplified. What we need to determine is the influence of each putative factor upon the accident rate when isolated from its co-factors.

It appears least difficult to isolate the speed of production factor. To this end, the measures of output and the record of accidents should be correlated for the *same hour of the shift, i.e.*, a table showing the output per head and the accidents per head measured upon workers of equal experience and extending over a period of many days ought to be prepared. From such material it might be practicable to determine the arithmetical law describing the relation between accidents and rate of production. Armed with this result, we could, perhaps, determine the influence of the other factor, viz., increasing fatigue, in varying the accident incidence throughout the shift. Even so simplified the problem is complex. There is the factor of mere duration, *i.e.*, fatigue is not a function of rate of production alone, it is also a function of mere duration of exposure to factory conditions. However simplified, the problem is extremely complex, and its solution will certainly tax both our mathematical and our observational resources. The point we wish to make here is that any attempt to reach final conclusions from an inspection of graphs deduced from simple averages of the conditions through a working day is likely to lead only to confusion.

The Personal Factor.—There remains still for consideration the question as to whether the occurrence of accidents, like exposure to the infection of disease, picks and chooses its victims as though they possessed some innate tendency or inherited predisposition to succumb. This question has been investigated by one of us (9), who approached the subject by examining the incidence of multiple accidents happening to the same individuals ; the problem was to ascertain which of the following three hypotheses was true :—(1) " that there is *no* differentiation, that industrial accidents are really accidents in the strictest sense, just as it is an accident if one draws the ace of spades from the well-shuffled pack, an accident if a particular pigeon-hole receives a ball at any particular throw, and so on : in that event, the statistics of multiple accidents would conform to the type

TABLE 13.—*Occurrence of Accidents among Thirty-six Women employed on Heavy Lathe Operations, and Twenty-nine employed on Profiling Operation.*

Number of accidents sustained.	Number of workers concerned.	Number of accidents distributed amongst the same workers.	Average number of accidents per worker.
During the second three months.		During the first three months.	
0	19	7	0·4
1	21	21	1·0
2	11	19	1·7
3	9	14	1·6
4	2	5 ⎫	
5	1	4 ⎪	3·8
6	1	3 ⎬	
11	1	7 ⎭	
During the first three months.		During the second three months.	
0	26	16	0·6
1	21	36	1·7
2	6	8	1·3
3	6	13	2·2
4	3	12 ⎫	
5	2	4 ⎬	4·5
7	1	11 ⎭	

Compiled from " The Incidence of Industrial Accidents upon Individuals with Special Reference to Multiple Accidents." M. Greenwood and H. M. Woods. *Industrial Fatigue Research Board. Report No. 4, 1919.*

This table is to be read as follows :—The total numbers of accidents sustained by sixty-five women in two successive periods of three months were recorded. In the second period nineteen women had no accidents, and in the first period seven accidents occurred amongst these nineteen women, or nearly 0·4 per head. Of the twenty-one women who had each one accident in the second period the average accident rate in the first period was also one, etc. The second half of the table records the average accident rate of women who had 0·1, etc., accidents in the first period. Note that the rate tends to increase if we arrange the women in groups according to their experience in the other period.

of a pure chance distribution ; (2) that all the workers did start equal, but that, an accident having happened to any individual, that individual's chance of sustaining a second accident became different from what it was before ; (3) that all the workers did not start equal, but that some were more liable to suffer casualties than others." If the first hypothesis were true, then diminution in the number of accidents " would be effected by a change of scale through administrative reforms inspired by researches into general conditions, but not into the individual physiology or psychology of the worker. Were the second-mentioned hypothesis in better accord with the facts, there would be need for consideration whether the enhanced liability to accident after a first casualty (supposing the bias were in that direction) might not be reduced, perhaps by a compulsory period of rest, possibly by a short interval of different work. If, on the other hand, the third possibility materialised, it would follow that both initial selection of recruits and also rapid elimination of those sustaining accidents should have a great effect in reducing the casualty rate of the factory."

The method of investigation called for somewhat intricate mathematical calculation depending on the laws of chance, for description of which the original paper must be consulted ; certain of the data employed are given in Tables 13 and 14. For our present purpose the conclusion arrived at is sufficient, viz. :—" These results indicate that varying individual susceptibility to ' accident ' is an extremely important factor in determining the distribution, so important that, given the experience of one period, it might be practicable to foretell with reasonable accuracy the average allotment of accidents amongst individuals in a subsequent period (see Table 15). This result is in itself of considerable interest, because it shows that by weeding out susceptibles the accident rate would necessarily decline." This conclusion receives support from the following additional facts : (a) no measurable difference of output was found between the women who had and those who did not have accidents ; (b) those who sustained many accidents were on the average neither more nor less productive than their fellows ; and (c) no certain connection was found between the incidence of multiple accidents and sickness, age, or civil state, but these matters call for further inquiry, and their importance cannot be deemed small. " So far as our present knowledge goes, it seems that the genesis of multiple accidents under uniform conditions is an affair of personality and not determined by any obvious extrinsic factor, such as greater or less speed of work. We cannot say that the victims are less healthy persons than those who escape, or that

TABLE 14.—*Mean Number of Accidents per Month.*

Month.	Period, October, 1917, to March, 1918.	
	Fifty women having no accident in March, 1918.	Fifty women having accidents in March, 1918.
October . .	0·42	0·64
November .	0·24	0·74
December. .	0·34	0·34
January . .	0·60	0·58
February . .	0·34	0·50
March . .	—	1·36
Total . .	0·39	0·69

Month.	Period, October, 1917, to January, 1918.	
	Sixty-one women having no accident in January.	Fifty-five women having accidents in January.
October . .	0·43	0·91
November .	0·16	0·93
December. .	0·12	0·64
January . .	—	1·67
Total . .	0·23	1·03

Month.	Period, February, 1917, to July, 1918.	
	One hundred and thirty-six women having no accident in February.	Sixty-two women having accidents in February.
February . .	—	1·31
March . .	0·06	0·65
April . .	0·30	0·45
May . .	0·10	0·21
June . .	0·26	0·40
July . .	0·01	0·03
Total . .	0·15	0·41

Compiled from "The Incidence of Industrial Accidents upon Individuals with Special Reference to Multiple Accidents." M. Greenwood and H. M. Woods. *Industrial Fatigue Research Board. Report No. 4*, 1919.

TABLE 15. — *Showing how many Accidents occurred to Thirty-six Women on Heavy Lathe Operations during a Period of Three Months in comparison with the Numbers of Accidents calculated from the Average Relation found between Accidents in the Successive Periods.*

Accidents.	Previous three months.	Observed three months.	
		Observed.	Calculated.*
0	14	9	9·4
1	12	10	7·9
2	4	7	6·8
3	1	6	5·1
4	2	2	3·1
5	2	1	1·7
6 and over	1	1	1·9
Total .	. .	36	35·9

they are better workers—so far as our data go there is no reason to think that they are specially productive workers. If this conclusion be confirmed by a wider investigation the practical corollary is obvious. The ' susceptible workers ' should be transferred so far as practicable from processes involving any special risk of accident to occupations not exposing to any such risk." It is further pointed out that " trivial accidents are indicators of unsafe people whom the record of the ambulance room can be employed to discover," and that " from the present point of view a worker who has had three trivial accidents is a more dangerous person than one who has had a single bad wound."

The main conclusions of Greenwood and Woods have been confirmed on ampler data by Miss Newbould and Miss Allan, working for the Fatigue Research Board. The suggestion of our Tables 13—15 that an operative who has more (or fewer) accidents than the average in any one period will occupy approximately the same position in another trial period can be more

---

* Owing to an arithmetical error, the " calculated " values as printed in the original report are incorrect, and should be replaced by those given here.

adequately tested by the method of correlation.   The claim is that individual variations from the means of successive periods are correlated.   Coefficients were found (9) of the order of 0·4 to 0·7 (the maximum possible value is 1·0), but the samples were small.   Newbould and Allan have traced the accident records of 387 women through two periods each of five months, and find a correlation of 0·608 ± 0·022 between the successive records.* The correlation persists when the record is limited to accidents due to flying particles, it holds when the division is made between morning and afternoon shifts, and may be deemed an established result.   This later investigation also shows that, although the absolute value of the correlation between individual accidents and individual output is small, it is usually negative, *i.e.*, persons liable to accident are slightly less productive than others.

These results are much what we should expect.   All will agree that some people are " all thumbs " and others nimble-fingered or sure-footed, but further elucidation is of importance to enable the student of industrial hygiene to diagnose. a liability which may cause disaster and must cause minor inconvenience and ill-health.

The most promising line of investigation is suggested by the researches of Spearman (see 26, 27, 28) and his pupils.   This investigator extended and gave scientific precision to the view that success in a variety of intellectual tests depended upon the concurrence of two " factors," one a general factor, a function of the total intellectual make-up of the subject, the other specific to the particular test.   The statistico-mathematical criteria by which Spearman measured the intensities of the action of the several factors have been criticised (see 24 and 28), but, although certain details may be open to objection, the general lines followed are interesting and logical (see 24).   The importance of the matter is that Spearman's pupil Webb (see 25) brought forward evidence of the existence of a second general factor concerned with efficiency in what we may call (although the word is not technically correct) the emotional sphere.   Now if we conceive that success in a variety of actions depends more or less upon their respective " saturations " with one general factor, it is possible by statistical methods to measure the extent of " saturation " of each test by the general factor.   Thus Webb (see 25, p. 58) concluded that the following characters : (1) Ten-

* As an illustration from more extensive data of the tendency brought out on p. 196, we may note that among 124 women who sustained no accident between Jan. 1st, 1918, and June 1st, 1918, the average in the next six months was 0·97 ; for 97 who each had one accident in the first period, 1·32 ; for 66 who had two each before, 2·0.

dency not to abandon tasks from mere changeability; (2) Tendency not to abandon tasks in face of obstacles ; (3) Kindness on principle ; (4) Trustworthiness ; (5) Conscientiousness ; (6) Readiness to become angry ; (7) Eagerness for admiration ; (8) Bodily activity in pursuit of pleasure, were all more or less saturated with the second general factor. Hence, if one desired to select persons endowed with a large measure of this general character and had not the opportunity to apply all the tests as a routine, one would determine, upon a moderate sample carefully analysed, which particular characteristic capable of being tested was most highly saturated with the general factor, and use *that* characteristic as a routine test. This is not a mere arm-chair suggestion. The report on flying temperament (29) is concerned with a problem cognate with that of selecting industrial workers ; to select a test which will reveal the appropriate psychological make-up of a good air pilot was a very urgent problem in the later days of the war. In the earlier stages of the investigations, one of us derived statistical suggestions of (a) the existence of a general factor and (b) the extent to which particular routine tests were saturated with the general factor and, therefore, practically useful. These particular investigations were neither sufficiently detailed nor based upon a sufficient number of instances to justify their discussion now, but the inferences they suggested have since been confirmed by other methods applied to better data. It seems to us probable that research on these lines will eventually give us an instrument of industrial selection which may help us to reduce industrial accident risks considerably.

New Workers.—Closely associated with personal predisposition to accidents comes the tendency of new workers to sustain accidents, a matter of importance in relation to labour turnover. The occurrence of accidents may in itself be one reason leading to the elimination from dangerous processes of those with an accident susceptibility. Mock states (17) that he found an accident rate of 111·3 per 1,000 workers employed for six months and less, as contrasted with a rate of 42·4 per 1,000 employed for three to five years.

A further investigation (21) into the relation between length of employment and the occurrence of accidents is summarised in the table on p. 202, whence it will be noted that about 34 per cent. of the workers within their first six months of employment accounted for nearly 50 per cent. of all the accidents.

Here again the incidence of accidents resembles the incidence of disease. Legge has pointed out (18) that cases of lead

TABLE 16.—*Distribution by Period of Employment of Accidents, Persons at Work, and Persons Leaving, at a Ten-hour Plant.*

Period of employment in months. (i.)	Percentage of all accidents. (ii.)	Percentage of persons employed. (iii.)	Percentage of persons leaving. (iv.)
Under 1	14·4 ⎫	14·0 ⎫	38·1 ⎫
1—2	10·6 ⎬ 34·7 ⎫	8·9 ⎬ 28·0 ⎫	21·6 ⎬ 68·0 ⎫
2—3	9·6 ⎭ ⎬ 48·5	5·2 ⎭ ⎬ 34·2	8·3 ⎭ ⎬ 76·9
3—6	13·8 ⎭	6·2 ⎭	8·9 ⎭
6—9	5·1 ⎫	6·6 ⎫	6·5 ⎫
9—12	2·5 ⎬ 51·5	6·2 ⎬ 65·8	4·1 ⎬ 23·0
Over 12	43·9 ⎭	53·0 ⎭	12·6 ⎭

Column iv. is included here for reference later in Chapter XVI.

poisoning are most numerous in the first weeks of employment and fall off as the period of exposure lengthens; the workers appear to acquire a degree of immunity. The same fact was noted by one of us in relation to the occurrence among munition workers of T.N.T. poisoning, the incidence of which approached the vanishing point among those employed for six months and over. Length of employment has also been found an important factor in the occurrence of lost time due to all causes. These facts suggest that the human body requires time to adjust itself to a new environment, just as Vernon has shown that increased output does not follow immediately upon altered hours of work, but is only attained after several months (19). The worker who has gained this adjustment is a more useful member of the staff, not merely because he has learnt his work, but because he is less liable to sustain accidents or succumb to illness; and a constantly changing staff of workers may be expected to experience a high rate of sickness whether due to the occurrence of accidents or of illness.

General Conclusion.

The result of this examination of the incidence of accidents appears to us not without value. Here is a group of cases contributing to the general morbidity and mortality, the exact method and moment of the occurrence of which is clearly known; here we have no uncertain intervention of microbic influence, no recourse to hypothetical variations in the potency of epidemic attack. Yet we find an incidence and frequency resembling in every way what we are accustomed to when investigating disease attributed to biological influences. In the physiological and psychological condition of the worker and in his reaction to the conditions of his environment lies the origin of the vast majority of accidents, rather than in any lack of guards and of fencing of machinery.

Is it possible to draw a moral herefrom, namely, that other forms of disease and mortality similarly depend, far more than is at present appreciated, upon the physiological and psychological condition of each individual, and that the most promising way of attacking the incidence of sickness and of premature death is through personal health and resisting power rather than by fencing the public about with protective guards against disease ? What is really the matter with the sick is their tendency to be sick.

The most famous of the Greek physicians taught this doctrine 1,800 years ago. `` In all this discussion we must remember that no cause can be efficient without an aptitude of the body, else all who are exposed to the summer sun, move about more than they should, drink wine, get angry or grieve, would fall into a fever. Or again all would fall sick at the rising of the Dogstar, and all would die in a pestilence. As I have said, the chief factor in the production of disease is the preparation of the body to suffer it. Let us imagine that the air is carrying divers seeds of pestilence, and that of the bodies exposed thereto some are choked with excrementous matters, some not ; some plethoric and with obstructed pores, others not ; some given to luxurious life, to banquetting, to drinking, to sexual excess, and their attendant evils, others moderate in exercise and temperate in diet. All this being supposed, judge which class is likelier to be harmed by inspiring polluted air. . . . This has been said in connection with a particular example of disease, but it is an universal truth.''*

In industrial life we may remove from risk those who show a tendency to accidents ; we cannot remove from risk those with a tendency to sickness, but we can endeavour to interest each person in himself, in his own health, and how to maintain it. Then just as in industry safety committees, by interesting each worker in the causation of accidents, are reducing their frequency by 50 per cent. and more, so may general ill-health be reduced by interesting the community to understand that *non est vivere, sed valere vita* (living's not life's wealth ; 'tis health).

* *Galenos de Differentiis Febrium,* Book I., Chap. VI. (Kühn's edition, Vol VII.).

II. Prevention of Accidents.

The foregoing argument establishes that accident prevention, which may be considered an important branch of preventive surgery, must be approached from two directions, (i.) observation and research and (ii.) administration.

Observation and Research.

No line of action for accident prevention can be thoroughly effective unless based upon sure knowledge, which can only be obtained through research. Records should be made of the occurrence of each accident, stating (a) the name, sex and age of the worker, (b) the process involved, (c) the time of occurrence, (d) the nature of the injury, (e) the exact cause as ascertained at the time, (f) in the case of machinery accidents the exact part of the machinery which caused the accident, and (g) the length of invalidity, if any, which results. These records should be classified as a routine procedure and the results shown by a graphic method, so that the rise and fall of accident-occurrence by the week and the month, by the processes involved, the machinery and the departments concerned, can be rapidly observed and checked. Close observation should at the same time be directed to noting workers possessing an " accident susceptibility " with a view to moving them to some other process.

The effect of modifying environmental conditions which influence vitality, such as temperature, ventilation and lighting, can be noted by watching the graphs, which will show whether modifications introduced are producing any effect and, if so, in which direction. Only through such observation and research carried out on scientific lines can administrative efforts at accident prevention be pursued with any expectation of success.

" A priori " Reasoning.—Particularly would we warn against action based on a priori reasoning. He who is content to direct administration according to what is known as " common sense " will sooner or later find that unexpected and unthought-of influences produce results quite opposed to preconceived ideas. What is said here is applicable throughout the industrial world before administrative action is taken in relation to human beings ; two instances may serve to illustrate the necessity for constant appeal to, and search after facts.

Some years ago a Government Committee gave (16) as one reason against employing boys by night that they slept worse by day, but this conclusion, although based on evidence heard, was an example of *a priori* reasoning. During the war inquiries made by Capt. Agnew (11) to investigate the point elicited that 376 boys working by day slept on an average 7·8 hours, while 1,080 boys, working by day and by night alternate weeks, slept on an average 7·7 hours when on day work but 8·0 hours when on night work. " The boys were found generally to enjoy longer sleep when they slept during the day, one of the chief reasons being that the boy is not on tenterhooks about being up in proper time for reaching his work. When sleeping during the day he generally remains in bed until the last moment, and then is ' called ' by his mother or some other occupant of the house, being allowed sufficient time to partake of a meal comfortably and get to his work. When sleeping during the night it is obvious that the risks of being late through not being called are very much greater."*

The second instance refers to whether a worker should continue on night-shift for many weeks on end, or should change over to day work every week or fortnight—a matter of considerable importance during the war. Some knowledge of previous physiological observations made upon monkeys and among arctic explorers as to the length of time required to reverse the diurnal rhythm of physiological functions, and of the usual practice adopted by hospital nurses of continuing for months on night work, induced one of us to advocate strongly the " continuous " night-shift. An investigation in which the subject was approached by several observers from different aspects was promptly set on foot (12). When a considerable body of reliable information referring to output and to lost time was collected, it was found to agree in establishing the inferiority of the continuous night worker as compared with the " discontinuous " night worker. This was embodied in the Committee's report, that it was " *undesirable to adopt for women continuous night-shifts in any factory not at present so working or not yet open, and that wherever practicable this system should be discontinued.*" The reason for this unexpected result is thus stated : " Women on continuous night work are likely to perform domestic duties, which, when they work alternately in the two shifts, is impracticable, and this extra domestic strain may account for the inferior results of their industrial activities." The inferiority of the male on continuous night work, although clearly established, was not so pronounced. " This result is what might be expected, if the surmise regarding the cause of the inferiority seen among women were correct. Men do not naturally take so much part in domestic work as women, and

* The position was found to be reversed for men.

the temptation to burn the candle at both ends is, from this point of view, smaller. On the other hand, the incitement to devote the time which should be given to sleep to amusement is certainly as intense among men as among women, so that some inferiority might be anticipated."

Here then are instances of conclusions apparently reasonable being arrived at without due allowance being made for interfering social influences, the value and, indeed, the existence of which could not be determined without careful investigation.

" One method of delivery alone remains to us, which is simply this : we must lead men to the particulars themselves, and their series and order, while men on their side must force themselves for a while to lay their notions by and begin to familiarise themselves with facts."*

Administration.

Administrative efforts must be of two kinds, (a) to minimise risk and (b) to reduce personal lack of interest.

How to Minimise Risk.—Efforts in this direction hardly fall within the scope of this book. Engineers, especially H.M. Inspectors of Mines and of Factories, have for many years concentrated their attention on mechanical devices and appliances, on fencing and guarding machinery, on testing hauling gear and the like. Powers to ensure safety are provided for in the Factory Acts, the Mines and Quarries Acts and Explosives Acts. Much inventive genius has been displayed, and a whole literature has been created in reference to safety devices.

For reasons already given, while in no way minimising the value of efforts in this direction, we are of opinion that more immediate results and a great reduction in the incidence of accidents can be obtained by attention to the personal tendency to accidents.

How to reduce Personal Lack of Interest.—Action is required in several directions which in the past have not received sufficient attention. The first and, undoubtedly, the most important step to take is a psychological one, viz., to interest the workers themselves in their own safety ; unless the step is effective, the provision of guards and safety appliances will be to a great extent nullified, while the co-operation needed to render successful the recommendations which are hereafter made will be lacking.

Safety Committees.—Committees of the workpeople (by preference elected by themselves) for each workshop should

* *Novum Organum*, Book I. Aphor. XXXVI

be appointed and entrusted with the task of investigating and reporting upon the causation, and possible means for preventing the recurrence, of each accident immediately it occurs. Such committees in a large establishment may be represented on a central safety committee presided over by a safety inspector—a full time official entrusted with the duty of examining all machinery, advising with the engineering staff as to points of danger, presiding over accident inquiries, and possibly of organising the first-aid ambulance brigade. The *personnel* of the shop committees should be kept changing, each worker only acting for a limited period, say, six months, in order to inculcate the principles of safety first and accident prevention among a large number of workers (23).

Safety committees should form an integral part of the welfare department of any industrial establishment.

Safety First.—Safety committees should be the keystone to the arch upon which administrative measures for accident prevention are built. The arch itself is instruction and education. Accidents represent the psychological as well as physiological reaction of human beings to environment, and, unless the mind is taught what to avoid, rectification of unhealthy surroundings will fail in effect. Good ventilation, for instance, will not enable workers to detect danger in a live electric wire. Safety rules should be posted and notices displayed; notices should be short and pithy if they are to arrest attention. Since some will not read rules or regard notices, recourse should be had to pictorial placards showing how accidents occur through carelessness and the results which follow. Notices and placards* should be changed frequently, as familiarity soon breeds contempt. They should be displayed in well-chosen positions so as to challenge observation; a useful device is to paint on a machine a warning which only becomes visible when a guard is removed.

Each industry has its own particular risks to guard against, and must design its own notices and placards. Many excellent ones have been brought out in America as well as in this country, and there is no need here to do more than to mention their value.

Suggestion Box.—A further useful way to interest workers in safety methods is the provision of a suggestion box. This is simply a box for posting letters containing suggestions by the workers. All proposals should be submitted to the safety com-

---

* Posters for exhibition and pamphlets for distribution can be obtained on application to the British Industrial " Safety First " Association, 31, Westminster Broadway, London, S.W. 1.

mittee for consideration, and the author of any one adopted should be rewarded. Workers often know better than any one else how to prevent accidents occurring, but will not place their views before a foreman. Many valuable devices have originated in this way. The suggestion box need not, of course, be restricted to dealing only with accident prevention ; suggestions of all kinds should be welcomed and considered by those whom they concern.

Susceptibility.—Reference has already been made to the possession by certain persons of a predisposition to suffer from accidents, a predisposition which can be discovered by watching records. Once the fact is established for any given worker, he or she should be transferred to other work. The new process need not of necessity be entirely free from accident risk ; a lad who sustains accidents while feeding a machine, the pace of which is not adjusted to his physiological rhythm, may cease to have accidents when working a lathe or power-press. Careful consideration, however, will be required in fixing the new process, and the worker may feel aggrieved at being moved. Such matters may, with advantage, be referred to the safety committee, whose interest will be stimulated by the line of action adopted. The question of eliminating workers with an accident susceptibility, both in their own interest and that of their fellows, is probably one of the most important in relation to reducing the incidence of industrial accidents.

Attention must also be directed to reduction in labour turnover ; new workers experience more accidents than those of long service. Every influence which tends to maintain the *personnel* of the workers unchanged is of value in reducing the incidence of accidents, and one effective influence is a well-organised welfare department entrusted with the duty of engaging labour and versed in the methods of vocational selection.

Working Clothes.—One further matter calls for note, viz., the suitability of working clothes. The tendency which is growing for overalls to be worn (see p. 345) should go far to prevent the occurrence of the class of accidents due to loose clothing ; the importance of the matter is clear from what has already been said of the causation of shafting accidents.

A Duty for the Medical Profession.

The prevention of industrial accidents has been correctly named a branch of preventive surgery, but it is a field of work which has been left in the main to laymen to develop. A doctor who sees two or three cases of enteric fever straightway informs the local health authorities in order that steps may be taken to prevent the occurrence of more. Yet the causation of accidents is more obvious than the causation of disease, while the part played by the psychology of the victims is clearly more readily appreciated by a medical man than by the laity.

The circumstances which surround the occurrence of an accident are manifold. They concern the external conditions under which work is done, and skilled knowledge as to the way in which human beings react to these conditions is required before improvements can be effected. They concern the temporary or permanent physiological and psychological conditions of the workers themselves, and skilled knowledge is required for the selection of workers for various processes, and for eliminating or temporarily suspending those not fitted for their work. The surgeon, far more than the physician, has in the past been content to concentrate upon the "handicraft" side of his work, and has left undeveloped not only after-care, but also prevention.

Accidents, the cause of much mortality and far greater incapacity and suffering, are more manifestly preventable than disease. A duty to take part in their prevention lies with the profession as a whole, and with factory medical officers in particular.

III. Bibliography.

1. *Supplement to Sixty-fifth Annual Report of the Registrar-General of Births, Deaths and Marriages in England and Wales.* Part (II.). (Cd. 2619.) 1908.

2. *Annual Report of Chief Inspector of Mines for* 1913. (Cd. 7452.)

3. *Annual Report of Chief Inspector of Factories and Workshops for* 1907.

4. *Annual Report of Chief Inspector of Factories and Workshops for* 1913.

5. *Annual Report of Chief Inspector of Factories and Workshops for* 1918.

6. Smith, W. S. *Report on Fencing and Safety Precautions for Transmission Machinery.* H.M. Stationery Office. 1913.

7. Collis, E. L. "Minutes of Evidence." *Report of Royal Commission on Metalliferous Mines and Quarries,* III. (Cd. 7478.)

8. Vernon, H. M. "An Investigation of the Factors Concerned in the Causation of Industrial Accidents." *Health of Munition Workers Committee.* Memo. No. 21. (Cd. 9046.) 1918.

9. Greenwood, M., and Woods, H. M. "The Incidence of Industrial Accidents upon Individuals, with special reference to Multiple Accidents." *Industrial Fatigue Research Board.* Report No. 4. 1919.

10. Parsons, J. H. "Preventive Ophthalmology." *Trans. Ophthalmol. Soc.,* XXXIX. 1919.

11. Agnew, T. H. "Report on the Health and Physical Condition

of Male Munition Workers." *Health of Munition Workers Committee. Interim Report.* (Cd. 8511.) 1917.

12. " The Comparative Efficiencies of Day Work and Night Work in Munition Factories." *Health of Munition Workers Committee. Interim Report.* (Cd. 8511.) 1917.

13. " The Effect of Industrial Conditions upon Eyesight." *Health of Munition Workers Committee. Memo. No.* 15. (Cd. 8409.) 1916.

14. *Royal Commission on Metalliferous Mines and Quarries,* pp. 110—112. Second Report. (Cd. 7476.) 1914.

15. Collis, E. L. " Eye Injuries Caused by Occupation." *The Ophthalmoscope.* October, 1915.

16. *Report of Departmental Committee on Night Employment of Male Young Persons in Factories.* (Cd. 6503.) 1912.

17. Mock, H. E. *Industrial Medicine and Surgery.* W. B. Saunders & Co. Philadelphia. 1919.

18. Legge, T. M., and Goadby, K. *Lead Poisoning and Lead Absorption.* 1912.

19. Vernon, H. M. " The Speed of Adaptation of Output to altered Hours of Work." *Industrial Fatigue Research Board. Report No.* 6. 1920.

20. Greenwood, M., and Yule, G. U. " An Inquiry into the Nature of Frequency Distributions representative of Multiple Happenings." *Journ. Roy. Stat. Soc.,* LXXXIII., p. 256. 1920.

21. " Comparison of an Eight-hour Plant and a Ten-hour Plant." *Public Health Bulletin No.* 106. Government Printing Office, Washington. 1920.

22. Bellhouse, G. *Accident Prevention and " Safety First."* Manchester University Press. 1920.

23. *Appendix to Welfare and Welfare Supervision in Factories and Workshops.* H.M. Stationery Office. 1919.

24. Garnett, J. C. M. " On Certain Independent Factors in Mental Measurements." *Proc. Roy. Soc.,* A., XCVI., p. 91. 1919.

25. Webb, E. " Character and Intelligence." *British Journal of Psychology, Monograph Supplements,* Vol. I. Cambridge. 1915.

26. Hart, B., and Spearman, C. " General Ability." *Journ. of Psychology,* V., p. 51. 1912.

27. Spearman, C. " The Theory of Two Factors." *Psychological Review,* XXI., p. 101. 1914.

28. Spearman, C. " Manifold Sub-theories of the Two Factors." *Psychological Review,* XXVII., p. 159. 1920.

29. " The Medical Problems of Flying." *Medical Research Council, Special Report Series, No.* 53. H.M. Stationery Office.

CHAPTER IX

INDUSTRIAL EMPLOYMENT OF WOMEN

I. Introduction. II. Place of Women in Historic Times. III. Lack of Morbidity and Mortality Data. IV. Physical Capacity :—Strength ; Athletic Capacity ; Lack of Training ; Liability to Hernia ; Liability to Fatigue. V. Physiological Characteristics :—The Blood ; Varicose Veins ; Nutrition ; Menstruation ; Anæmia and Digestive Disturbances ; Respiration ; Shock ; Maternity ; General Resistance to Disease. VI. Psychological Aptitude :—The Brain ; Psychoneuroses ; Industrial Experience ; Effect of Women on Industry. VII. Other Considerations. VIII. Summary. IX. Conclusion. X. Bibliography.

I. Introduction.

THE scarcity of male labour during the war caused a heavy demand for female labour (see Chapter VI., p. 132), and this sudden demand drew public attention to the drift of women towards factory employment which had been steadily going on during the whole of the nineteenth century. Several influences had been at work. The introduction of mechanical power had made possible the employment of women on work previously done by men. Simultaneously there arose a call for unskilled or semi-skilled labour, such as that of women who, with matrimony in view, do not as a class look forward to a life of industrial employment and so do not apprentice themselves to skilled trades. At the same time the factory was steadily absorbing the manufacture of articles which women had formerly made at home; the loom, the spinning frame, the lace machine, the hosiery knitter, the power-driven sewing-machine, the steam laundry, the biscuit factory, the bakehouse, the model dairy and the jam factory were producing finished articles cheaper than the requisite raw materials could be purchased retail ; and " in the United States, in 1840, Harriet Martineau found only seven employments practically open to women as alternatives to marrying for a living, namely, teaching, needlework, keeping boarders, working in cotton mills, book-binding, typesetting, and household service " (1). Thus, while the mother of a rising family remained fully occupied with her household, there came to be an increasing proportion of unmarried women and girls with no home work. These women were ready to supply the demand for semi-skilled labour at a cheap rate ; and as opportunity arose, they followed their work into the factory ; while their better-off sisters devoted their energies and free time to political propaganda and to forcing open to women the door of the learned professions.

This chapter is concerned with the effects of factory work upon the health of female, as contrasted with male, workers ; only indirectly with the social question as to whether women should or should not be so employed. That the lives of women should be fully occupied we hold to be axiomatic for both economic and physiological reasons. For economic reasons, because no nation can afford to leave half its population unproductive ; " no redistribution of wealth can in itself create a sufficiency of commodities, . . . The necessity for increased production at the present time, if a reasonable standard of comfort is to be created and maintained, is generally accepted " (5). For physiological reasons, because activity is necessary for the preservation of health ; as Bhartrihari has expressed it in the *Niti Sataka*, " mankind's great enemy is idleness. There is no friend like energy, and if you cultivate that you will never fail."

But the industrial employment of women raises social questions as to the position of women in modern civilised life which cannot be entirely separated from its medical aspect. We must have some idea of the place occupied by woman in the past, and of her physical, physiological and psychical capacity, before being in a position to discuss the effect of industrial employment upon her health, and, through her, upon that of the next generation. Should history show that woman has never undertaken laborious work, that she has never been a labour-sharing colleague of the male, that she has only functioned as the mother and nurse of children, and that in the evolution of the race she has merely been a sort of queen bee, necessary for the continuation of the race, then the question of her employment to-day, even if no physical or physiological reason to the contrary is apparent, could only be looked upon in the light of a dangerous experiment.

II. Place of Women in Historic Times.

The allocation of particular industries or tasks to primitive woman has no doubt been influenced by religious motives or, to speak more accurately, by a belief in magic. " When a Catholic priest remonstrated with the Indians of the Orinoco on allowing their women to sow the fields in the blazing sun, with infants at their breasts, the men answered, ' Father, you don't understand these things, and that is why they vex you. You know that women are accustomed to bear children, and that we men are not. When the women sow, the stalk of the maize bears two or three ears, the root of the yucca yields two or three basketfuls, and everything multiplies in proportion. Now, why is that ? Simply because the women know how to bring forth, and know how to make the seed which they sow bring forth also. Let them sow, then ; we men don't know as much about it as they do ' " (25). In some tribes amongst which the manufacture of pottery is confined to women (26) a like magical explanation can be sought. In assessing the historical facts of industrial organisation as evidence of sexual aptitudes, we must not forget the potent influence of beliefs, an influence still mighty long after the beliefs themselves and the *Weltanschauung* from which they arose have faded from the memory of man.

The subject has been carefully considered by Thomas (2), who draws his conclusions not merely from what is known of the respective positions of the male and female of other mammalia and of what may be conjectured of prehistoric man, but from primitive races as they exist to-day. He holds, and we think he is justified in holding, that the customs of aborigines represent, in principle at any rate, the stages through which the more civilised races passed a few thousand years ago, and that there is no clear evidence that during the process of civilisation the human race has been profoundly modified. Reviewing the evidence, he finds that in primitive times—

" Man represented the more violent and spasmodic activities, involving motion and skilful co-ordinations, as well as organisation for hunting and fighting, while woman carried on the steady, settled life. She was not able to wander readily from a fixed point, on account of her children ; and, indeed, her physical organisation fitted her for endurance rather than movement. Consequently her attention was turned to industries, since these were compatible with settled and stationary habits. Agriculture, pottery, weaving, tanning, and all the industrial processes involved in working up the by-products of the chase, were developed by her. She domesticated man and assisted him in domesticating the animals. . . . In the course of time, however, an important change took place in environmental conditions. While woman had been doing the general work and had developed the beginnings of many industries, man had become a specialist along another line. His occupation had been almost exclusively the pursuit of animals or conflict with his neighbours, and in this connection he had become the inventor of weapons and traps, and in addition had learned the value of acting in concert with his companions. But a hunting life cannot last for ever; and when large game began to be exhausted, man found himself forced to abandon his destructive and predaceous activities, and adopt the settled occupations of woman. To these he brought all the inventive technique and capacity for organised action which he had developed in his hunting and fighting life, with the result that he became the master of woman in a new sense. Not suddenly, but in the course of time, he usurped her primacy in the industrial pursuits, and through his organisation of industry and the application of invention to the industrial processes became a creator of wealth on a scale before unknown. . . . Among peasants, also, and plain people the proverb recognises that the ' gray mare is the better horse.' The heavy, strong, enduring, patient, often dominant type frequently seen among the lower classes, where alone woman is still economically functional, is probably a good representative of what the women of our race were before they were reduced by man to a condition of parasitism which, in our middle and so-called higher classes, has profoundly affected their physical, mental and moral life " (2, pp. 228—232).

Ellis (22, p. 8), when dealing with the early history of human development, quotes from Otis T. Mason, who claims that primitive woman in her daily work originated industry after industry, an eloquent and suggestive passage which concludes :— " In the early history of art, language, social life, and religion women were the industrial, elaborative, conservative half of society. . . . Along the lines of industrialism she was pioneer, inventor, author, originator."

Another authority, Sir J. G. Frazer, approaching the subject from an entirely different point of view, namely that of evidence drawn from folk-lore and tradition, draws similar deductions. He writes (34) : " We have to bear in mind that at a certain stage of social evolution a wife is valued, not merely as a companion and mother of children, but also as a labourer, who contributes in a large measure to the support of the family."

The Hebrews certainly employed their women on heavy work, as is indicated by such passages as " the maid-servant that is behind the mill " (*Exod.* xi. 5) ; " Every wise woman buildeth her house " (*Prov.* xiv. 1) ; " Two women shall be grinding at the mill " (*Matt.* xxiv. 41) ; while the following quotation, anent the virtuous woman, sets out their ideal of feminine capacity :—

" She seeketh wool and flax, and worketh willingly with her hands. She is like the merchants' ships ; she bringeth her food from afar. She riseth also while it is yet night, and giveth meat to her household, and a portion to her maidens. She considereth a field, and buyeth it : with the fruit of her hands she planteth a vineyard. She girdeth her loins with strength, and strengtheneth her arms. She perceiveth that her merchandise is good : her candle goeth not out by night. She layeth her hands to the spindle, and her hands hold the distaff. She stretcheth out her hand to the poor ; yea, she reacheth forth her hands to the needy. She is not afraid of the snow for her household : for all her household are clothed with scarlet. She maketh herself coverings of tapestry ; her clothing is silk and purple. Her husband is known in the gates, when he sitteth among the elders of the land. She maketh fine linen, selleth it, and delivereth girdles unto the merchant."

Work at flour mills was recognised by the Greeks and Romans as severe drudgery which fell chiefly upon slaves and criminals, yet Homer refers to fifty females in the house of Alcinous being employed on this service ; and the passage already quoted from Antipater in Chapter I. indicates that the Romans employed women to turn millstones. In the time of the Roman occupation of Britain the manufacture of linen and woollen articles was so far carried on by women that an institution for this purpose was known as a gyneceum, of which there was one at Winchester (35).

The work of women has been accepted in England for as long as evidence exists. The records of Leicester (1264) state (12) how the remuneration of weavers and women wool-wrappers was fixed by the guild. Women and girls in the time of Edward II. worked in Derbyshire lead mines, where Arthur Young still found them employed in the eighteenth century, as well as in the plated ware trade of Sheffield, in spinning wool, and in the potteries at Burslem.

Fourteenth-century pictorial records, reproduced by Green (32), show women occupied not only at carding and spinning, but on the land, weeding, reaping, and breaking up stony ground, and also as iron workers, armourers, and at sawing ; the evidence indeed suggests that Eve delved as well as span in the days of John Ball. Certainly the Ordinance of Labourers (1349) laid it down (11) that all able-bodied men and women, free and bond, without definite means of support, were to accept service at the old rates of payment. In 1388 and 1444 we find fixed by statute the wages of a woman labourer, and again in 1444 and 1495 the wages of a woman servant of husbandry.

Thorold Rogers (10) writing of the thirteenth century, says :— " The hoeing of the land was generally undertaken by women. There was full opportunity for this employment until the middle of the fourteenth century, after which the outdoor employment of women almost disappears for a long time. In harvest time, women worked at piece work, as the men did, and generally at

the same rates." Referring to the fifteenth century, he states :—
" The man (*homo*) who is employed as a help to the thatcher or
tiler, and often to the mason, later on to the bricklayer, is paid
at the rate of agricultural labourers in ordinary times, or a little
less. This help was sometimes a woman, as was generally the
case in the earlier period ; and thus it is seen that women's
work, when of what we may call an unskilled kind, was equally
well paid with that of men. In 1467, two girls are hired to work,
and are paid twopence a day. They are also boarded, and this
is put at twopence a day more. In the same year, at Selborne
Priory, in Hampshire, the board of men is put at twopence, of
women at three-halfpence."

Lipson concludes (13) that, although the economic position
of women in the Middle Ages is obscure, they took a considerable
share in industrial life. " They were admitted to the member-
ship of certain craft guilds, especially among the Barber Surgeons
of London* and York ; they were enrolled as apprentices ; and
the brewing industry was largely in their hands. They also
shared in the woollen industry as spinners, weavers and dyers.
One-fourth of the cloth woven in York at the end of the fourteenth
century is said to have been produced by women, and the
ordinances of the Weavers' Guild (1400) provide that no woman
should weave unless she were well taught and approved. In
the time of Edward I., Wallingford contained as many as fifty
women traders. There seems, therefore, no adequate ground
for the view that working women were mainly ' unpaid domestic
workers ' following household occupations, rather than wage-
earners supplying a market. The Act of 1363 restricting craftsmen to a single trade did not apply to women, and incidentally
throws light upon their industrial pursuits. ' But the intent of
the king and of his council is that women, that is to say brewers,
bakers, carders, and spinners, and workers as well of wool as of
linen cloth and of silk, brawdesters and breakers of wool, and
all other that do use and work all handiworks, may freely work
and use as they have done before this time.' . . . Of the various
industries in which craftswomen were engaged, we hear most
about silk-weaving. . . . In 1370 a merchant of Lombardy was
indicted upon a petition presented to the king ' by the poor
women called silk-women ' on the ground that he engrossed all
the silk raw and spun in order to raise the price."

A passage quoted by Unwin (14) shows that in 1585 "wenches"
were employed as feltmakers. Ramazzini writes at the end of

---

* By an ordinance passed in London, 1390, the masters of the craft
were ordered to scrutinise not only men but also " women undertaking
cures or practising the art of surgery " (19).

the seventeenth century in Italy that " the country women in winter time, when not employed in tilling the ground, weave linen or flaxen webs " (33). The extent to which unmarried girls were employed in spinning has passed into the language of the country in the word " spinster " ; and we find that " in 1760 spinning and weaving were domestic industries, carried on, that is, in the homes of the workers. The women and children in farmhouses and cottages spent their spare time in spinning. The implements used in the cotton manufacture remained nearly as simple as those of the Homeric age, save that weaving had been facilitated by the use of the fly-shuttle " (4). Abram (19), comparing the position of women in the later Middle Ages with that of women to-day, writes :—" A surprisingly large number of callings were open to women, and they availed themselves freely of openings in agricultural and industrial pursuits. A much larger proportion of them than of the women of the present day appear to have been engaged in agriculture, and in rough unskilled labour." Down to 1842 women and children were employed continuously in coal mines.

The way has already been referred to in which the introduction of mechanical power made possible the exploitation of cheap female labour on processes previously carried on by men, and finally led to the protective measures of the Factory Acts ; it needs no repetition. Sufficient has been said to establish that the work of woman has been accepted by the race throughout the ages, and that in England she was employed on heavy labour before the industrial revolution.

The opinion expressed by Ellis (22, p. 520) is of interest when considering woman's capacity for modern industrial life. He writes :—" Savagery and barbarism have more usually than not been predominantly militant, that is to say, masculine, in character, while modern civilisation is becoming industrial, that is to say feminine in character, for the industries belonged primitively to women, and they tend to make men like women." There is no clear evidence that the character of the work carried out by women in our factories and workshops to-day is heavier or more strenuous than that to which they have always been accustomed.

III. Lack of Morbidity and Mortality Data.

Mortality data indicate that women resist disease better than men, and this fact appears even in the first year of life ; " tenacity of life, in fact, appears to be greater among women than among men, and I know of few facts in biology more remarkable " (6).

These data do not tell us the exact effect of industrial work upon women ; and there are in this country no mortality or morbidity data from which the effect of occupation upon women can be estimated. Such data, owing to the temporary nature of women's employment, are difficult to compile ; marriage and other domestic ties are constantly withdrawing women from occupation, who probably do not on an average remain under industrial influences for as long as ten years. While, however, this period is short compared with that of the male who continues to be employed all his life, it results in a larger proportion of the general female community having passed through a period of industrial life than is at any one time employed. Thus, if the average length of life ahead of females at fifteen years of age is a further forty years, only ten of which are spent in industry, then the number of females employed at any one time represents a much larger number of women who have in their time passed through the industrial mill ; and the influence of industrial conditions upon the female population is considerably greater than that which the actual number of employed women represents. The results which accrue are to be sought for at later ages of life ; but the difficulty of obtaining accurate statistical information is practically insuperable.

What information is available indicates that women in industry lose more time than do men ; the witnesses before the War Cabinet Committee on Women in Industry generally agreed that men are the best timekeepers, boys next, and women last ; and Loveday has shown (7) that lost time represents either sickness or a feeling of ill-being and fatigue prodromal to sickness.

Professor F. S. Lee quotes (5) the following figures from the Local Sickness Experience of Leipsic, which show that after the age of twenty years women suffer more sickness than men :—

TABLE 1.—*Cases of Sickness per* 100 *Persons.*

Age group.	Men.	Women.
Under 15	38·0	29·0
15—20	37·6	36·4
20—25	36·3	42·1
25—35	38·0	50·2
35—45	44·3	55·3
45—55	51·7	54·3
55—65	60·2	54·9
65—75	75·7	66·6

There is a tendency for sickness to affect different systems of the body in the two sexes ; and some indication is given in the appended table (5).

TABLE 2.—*Proportionate Sickness of the National Union of Clerks.*

Part affected.	1912—14.		1915—17.	
	Male.	Female.	Male.	Female.
Throat and chest . .	55·2	51·2	58·8	47·8
Stomach and abdomen .	11·1	6·8	9·2	15·0
Nervous system . .	9·1	13·7	10·0	13·4
Miscellaneous . .	24·6	28·3	22·0	24·0

IV. Physical Capacity.

Woman is not usually as tall or as strong as man. But she is not merely a smaller edition of the male ; she is built on rather a different model. Her trunk is proportionately rather longer, and her arms, legs, hands and feet shorter ; the fore-

TABLE 3.—*Strength of Males and Females contrasted.*

Strength in lbs. (drawing power).	Percentage of	
	Males.	Females.
150	·3	—
140	·3	—
130	·1	—
120	1·0	—
110	1·2	—
100	4·9	—
90	15·1	·4
80	19·8	·0
70	34·9	·8
60	16·7	2·1
50	4·6	10·4
40	·9	41·9
30	·2	40·7
20	·0	3·7
	100·0	100·0

TABLE 4.—*Relation of Strength to Weight in Males and Females.*

Age last birthday.	Average weight.			Average strength. (As of pulling a bow.)	
	Males.	Females.	Proportion of female to male.	Males.	Females.
15	102·7	104·8	102	52·2	29·6
16	119·0	112·7	95	58·2	31·8
17	130·0	114·9	88	67·8	33·9
18	137·4	117·7	86	74·2	38·9
19	139·6	123·7	89	76·4	40·8
20	143·3	123·2	86	77·9	42·0
21	145·2	121·2	83	80·2	41·9
22	146·9	124·2	85	81·7	42·9
23	147·8	126·4	86	79·7	38·5
24	148·0	120·6	81	80·9	39·2
25	149·2 ⎫				
26	151·7 ⎪ 152·3				
27	152·3 ⎬ 120·1	79	83·5	40·8	
28	153·9 ⎪				
29	154·2 ⎭				
30	159·8 ⎫ 162·0	121·1			
35	164·3 ⎬			77·5	46·2
40	163·1 ⎭	118·6			
50	166·1	—	—	76·5 ⎫ 38·1	
60	158·1	—	—	74·6 ⎭	

arms and legs are proportionately shorter relative to the upper arms and thighs ; and the whole lower extremity is shorter relative to the upper extremity (21). The claim is made (22, Chapter XVI.) that structurally woman is not so differentiated as man, that she exhibits fewer and less marked variations from the mean, is nearer to the child, and represents the more stable portion of the race. Pearson dissents (28) from this claim that there is any less variability among women, and the researches upon new-born infants of Montague and Hollingworth (27) are in agreement with his view that there is no difference in variability between the sexes. The question is here, perhaps, of no great fundamental importance. What concerns us is that anatomically woman possesses certain structural characteristics, and these characteristics are held to affect her capacity for activity. Efforts have been made to measure the physical capacity of the two sexes by strength tests and athletic achievements.

Strength.—Vernon, when giving evidence before the War

Cabinet Committee on Women in Industry (5), put in the above data (see Tables 3 and 4) from the report of the Anthropometric Committee of the British Association.

These figures suggest that women, even when of the same weight, only possess a little over one half the physical power of men.

Where women have been employed on the same work as men, say in brickmaking, their output on the average does not exceed three-fifths that of men, and this proportion probably represents not unfairly the relative physical capacity of the two sexes.

Thomas quotes (2, p. 21) the following strength tests, expressed in kilograms, made on 2,300 Yale students, and on 1,600 women of Oberlin College :—

	Back.	Legs.	Right forearm.
Men .	153·0	186·0	56·0
Women .	54·0	76·5	21·4

Athletic Capacity.—Thomas gives the following comparison of athletic records :—

	Yale. (Men.)	Vassar. (Women.)
100-yard dash . .	$10\frac{2}{5}$ seconds.	13 seconds.
Running broad jump .	23 feet.	14 feet $6\frac{1}{2}$ inches.
Running high jump .	5 feet 9 inches.	4 feet $2\frac{1}{2}$ inches.
220-yard dash . .	$22\frac{3}{5}$ seconds.	$36\frac{1}{4}$ seconds.

Vernon has also contrasted (5) certain athletic records of the two sexes :—

		Man.	Woman.
Swimming	100 yards .	59·0 seconds.	75·4 seconds.
	300 yards .	3 minutes 30 seconds.	4 minutes 25·4 seconds
	Plunging .	82 feet 7 inches.	60 feet 0 inches.
Longest golf driver		395 yards. / 388 yards.	254 yards. / 234 yards.

Lack of Training.—The structural differences already referred to between the sexes go some way to explain this lack of female athletic excellence. But the physical inferiority of women here shown is probably exaggerated, since only a few women devote as much time to athletic exercises as do men, and practice is known to have a marked influence both on muscular activity and on performance. Nevertheless, in considering the capacity of women to-day for industrial work it has a definite significance, since most women up to the time they enter factory life will have lived a more or less sedentary or domestic life without the habit of active and regular exercise.

This lack of physical training, rather than lack of structural physical capacity, is of great importance in relation to industrial activity and fatigue. Employers should be mindful of it, and let the new worker down lightly at first, while she is becoming acclimatised to factory life and learning to use her muscles. Such training, in tempering the wind to the shorn lamb, is needed throughout the labour world, but is especially needed for female labour.

Possibly, lack of physical power is the reason why females react more readily even than males to the interpolation of short rest pauses during long spells of work, and also to intervals for taking light refreshment, such as a cup of tea.

Liability to Hernia.—In one respect woman possesses an anatomical advantage over man, owing to the occlusion of the inguinal canal which renders her practically free from one of the serious dangers associated with the strain of heavy work, viz., the danger of inguinal hernia. Woman is, it is true, more liable to femoral hernia ; but this condition is comparatively rare.

What she gains in this respect, however, the multiparous woman, with relaxed pelvic ligaments, loses from her tendency to procidentia or vaginal hernia, and to umbilical hernia. This tendency should be guarded against by not employing on heavy work women who have borne several children.

Liability to Fatigue.—Women generally are suited to work of a more continuous character than are men, but whether they tire sooner or not is difficult to answer with certainty. Ellis (22) states, " When women are working at their own natural level of energy, they tire less quickly than men do when working at their natural level of energy ; but when women attempt to work at the masculine level of energy they tire very much more rapidly than men." We incline to agree with the opinion here quoted, but recognise that the problem does not lend itself to simple experiment.

In order to test it the process investigated would require to be repetitive and so light as to be well within the physical capacity of both sexes, but men are seldom employed on such light work, and even then, failing a physiological test of fatigue, when the output of one or other group fell off, the observer, if the falling off occurred among males, could not be certain whether it was due to physical tiredness, that is, fatigue, or to psychological tiredness, that is, *ennui*.

V. Physiological Characteristics.

The Blood.—As organic life passes from cold-blooded to warm-blooded animals, from low forms to higher, possessing greater activity, the blood changes its characters, and, according to Thomas, " rich, red blood characterises the forms of life fitted for activity and bursts of energy " (2). This author has looked into the question of the existence of any differences between male and female blood, seeking therein for an indication of the respective capacity of the two sexes for physical work. He writes as follows :—

" In his exhaustive work on the blood Hayem has given a summary of the results of the investigations of chemists and physiologists on the differences in the composition of the blood in the two sexes. Contrary to the assertion of Robin, Hayem finds that the white corpuscles are not more numerous in women than in men, and he also states that the number of hæmatoblasts is the same in the two sexes. All chemists are agreed, however, that the number of red corpuscles is greater in men than in women. Nasse found in man 0·05824 of iron to 100, and in woman only 0·0499. Becquerel and Rodier give 0·0565 for man, 0·0511 for woman, and Schmidt, Scherer, and others give similar results. Welcker (using a chronometer) found between the corpuscles of man and woman the relation of 5 to 4·7, and Hayem confirmed this by numeration. Cadet found in woman on the average 4·9 million corpuscles per cubic millimetre, and in man 5·2 million. More recently Korniloff, using still another method—the spectroscope of Viercrdt—has reached about the same result. The proportion of red blood corpuscles varies according to individual constitution, race and sex. In robust men Lacanu found 136 red corpuscles in 1,000 ; in weak men, only 116 in 1,000 ; in robust women, only 126 in 1,000 ; and in weak women, 117. . . . There is no more conclusive evidence of an organic difference between man and woman than these tests of the blood. They permit us to associate a high specific gravity, red corpuscles, plentiful hæmoglobin, and a katabolic constitution " (2).

Evidence, as quoted, with respect to the blood points to woman being rather less fitted than man for a life of physical activity and bursts of energy, but the data are far too scanty to warrant firm conclusions.

Varicose Veins.—Many processes entail long periods of standing, and the claim has been made that such work is especially detrimental to women because of their tendency to develop varicose veins. Long periods of standing do have this effect, and every effort should be made to study each process to ascertain how far standing is an absolute necessity, and whether without interference to the work seats cannot be provided for regular or, at any rate, intermittent use. The frequency with which varicose veins occur in young adult males and females is possibly not very different. Data on this point, derived from hospital out-patient departments, where the bulk of patients seeking treatment for pronounced varicose conditions are women, are misleading, because the importance of a varicose condition is greater to the female on account of the tendency to phlebitis and phlegmasia alba dolens at childbirth, as the majority of the cases are in multiparous women.

Whatever be the relative frequency of varicose veins in the two sexes, the relative importance of the condition is far greater for the woman ; every effort should, therefore, be made to relieve her from the necessity of standing during prolonged operations. This is important when organising her industrial work.

Nutrition.—The work of Du Bois made it probable that the energy transformation going on when a person is resting is not equal in men and women of the same bodily dimensions. If the heat liberated from the body of a resting man be compared with that set free by a woman of the same age, weight and height, the man is usually found to exceed the woman to the extent of some 5 to 8 per cent. Benedict and Harris (36) have also found a sexual difference.* Women have a greater tendency to put on fat than men. This fact is recognised in standards of art wherein the rounded contour of the female form is accepted to be more graceful than that of man. Here is an outward expression of woman's greater power of endurance and reserve energy ; she possesses a greater amount of reserve material to call upon. Ellis (22) quotes from Bischoff the following relation of muscles to fat in a man of thirty-three, a woman of twenty-two, and a

* They found that the basal heat production per square metre of body surface per diem was 75—77 calories less in women than in men ; no difference could be detected between male and female infants.

boy of sixteen, all of whom died accidentally and in good physical condition :—

	Man.	Woman.	Boy.
Muscle . . .	41·18	35·8	44·2
Fat . . .	18·2	28·2	13·9
Percentage of fat .	30·6	44·1	23·9

Women, probably as a result of this physiological fact, are more casual than men about their food, and are inclined to rely too much on such unsubstantial diet as tea, bread and butter, sweets, pastry and tinned fruit. "Most working women," writes Dr. Janet Campbell (15), "have never acquired the habit of taking solid and regular meals, partly because when food is not abundant the woman goes short rather than the man." Woman cannot continue to live on her reserves always, and her tendency to attempt the impossible requires to be counteracted when she is regularly employed. Digestive disturbances are not unusual among working women (though not so common as among domestic servants and sedentary women), and the common causes, writes Dr. Campbell, " are dietetic, e.g., insufficient, unsuitable, or improperly prepared food, the persistent use of certain unwholesome articles of diet, such as strong tea, unduly rich substances or food containing excess of carbohydrates " (15, p. 149). If industry employs women, and desires their work, cognisance must be taken of this sex tendency, and it must be guarded against. For this reason the provision of substantial and adequate food through industrial canteens is even more necessary for women than for men.

If nutrition is supervised, the above mentioned tendency is no bar to the employment of women.

Menstruation.—The chief trouble the industrial woman has to face is menstruation, which affects her for two or three days in each month. According to Howell (16), " At the time of or in the period just preceding the menstrual flow there is usually a more or less marked sense of ill-being or despondency, and a diminution in general efficiency. On the other hand, Mrs. Hollingworth, who leans to the view that the periodic incapacity of woman is a legend originating with males, but based upon no reliable or expert knowledge, has, after close investigation, in which motor fatigability was specially considered (30), concluded that " careful and exact measurement does not reveal a periodic mental or motor inefficiency in normal women ; the variability of performance is not affected by physiological periodicity, and no agreement is established between curves plotted for pulse, blood pressure, temperature, caloric radiation, etc., and the curves of work for the mental and motor traits tested." Lee (20, p. 59), remarks in comment, "Notwithstanding this conclusion, apparently justified from the results that were obtained by the methods used, one of my graduate students, Miss Epstean, in an investigation of the total strength of ten healthy young women, conducted by means of almost daily tests with the spring balance method extending over five months, reveals an average loss of muscular strength of about 5 per cent. during the menstrual days." While the exact effect upon physical activity (see also *infra*, p. 234) would appear to be *sub judice*, most women undoubtedly do not feel so well at these times, and due allowance should be made for the fact. The natural tendency not to speak of the matter to a male is one reason for employing women doctors, welfare supervisors and charge hands at factories where many women are at work.

Menstruation is a normal function, and the question to be answered is whether it is adversely affected by industrial work. While there is not to-day any sufficient body of statistical data to throw light on this question, a reasonable reply can be given. Physicians have long recognised that cases of dysmenorrhœa among better class patients are benefited and often cured by a course of physical exercises, such as cycling, tennis or golf, the result being due, apparently, to more vigorous circulation of the blood and an increase in muscular tone. The observation is no new one, for Ramazzini, in 1700, wrote, "Besides the profits of weaving, women generally reap this advantage from it, that their menstruation is easy ; for it rarely happens that women thus employed have their menses suppressed. . . . So that when young women complain to me of the irregular or inordinate discharges of their menses, I generally advise them to consult with working women, or those employed in weaving, rather than with physicians " (33). Investigations during the war among female munition workers, many of whom had not previously been engaged upon regular physical work, pointed in the same direction ; menstruation, notwithstanding long hours of work, tended to be more regular and less painful. But where long hours were associated with unusually heavy work, that is to say, where physical fatigue was a pronounced factor, some increase in dysmenorrhœa occurred.

The opinion expressed by Dr. Mock, an industrial surgeon of long experience in America, is of value : " Constant standing is, undoubtedly, fatiguing to most women workers, but of the two evils constant sitting is the worse. The congestion of the pelvic organs by this practice, and the tendency toward constipation because of lack of exercise, causes many pathological conditions to develop in the generative organs of women. The congestion and constipation also tend to develop hæmorrhoids. Backaches, pains in the legs and many ill-feelings can be traced to constant sitting. The ideal work for woman will enable her to stand part time and sit part time. If she can move about while at work it is even better. In the departments where the work permits this I have found at least 50 per cent. less absenteeism on account of dysmenorrhœa than in those departments where the girls sat constantly at work " (31).

The conclusion may be drawn that well organised industrial employment is not detrimental to menstruation and may be beneficial.

Anæmia and Digestive Disturbances.—Closely associated with menstrual troubles is the condition of anæmia, which is much more prevalent among young women than young men, and is frequently associated with amenorrhœa, and also with menorrhagia. Anæmia is not, however, only to be found among girls industrially employed ; on the contrary we incline to the view that it is less prevalent among them than among domestic servants and others who live a less regular life. Many authorities have held that constipation is the most frequent cause of anæmia ; and constipation is less frequent among females taking regular exercise and living an ordered day than among those whose exercise is irregular and mealtimes too frequent. One of us, while working at a hospital in an industrial area, frequently pointed out that the cases admitted of serious anæmia and gastric ulcer were always domestic servants. There was a fair proportion of female labour in the district employed for poor pay and long hours at heavy work, making chains and bricks, and at galvanising hollow ware, but anæmia was rare among these workers and gastric ulcer non-existent. It should, however, be pointed out that these workers, in addition to the advantages arising from regularity of life, were employed in places often open to the air, where the general ventilation and movement of air were good, and that anæmia is more prevalent among girls employed at sedentary work in ill-ventilated and badly-lighted workshops. Improved ventilation and the admission of more daylight and sunshine, associated with opportunities for exercise, do much to improve such conditions ; still better results will be attained by the provision and regular use of satisfactory sanitary accommodation (see p. 341).

Anæmia is more prevalent among women than men, but the

underlying causes do not appear to be aided more by industrial occupation than by other modes of life.

Respiration.—Two types of respiratory movement are recognised, abdominal due to contraction of the diaphragm, and costal wherein movement of the ribs is the distinguishing factor. At rest the normal type of breathing in the male is abdominal ; but during exertion respiration become costal as well. Breathing among women of the white races is costal in character, even when at rest, and Hutchinson considered that it indicated a secondary sexual characteristic. Later observations, however, among white women who habitually wear loose clothes, and Indian and Chinese women who never use stays, have shown that in these women breathing is normally abdominal like that of a man, and supports the view that costal breathing in the female is the result of fashion, and is in no way a sexual characteristic.

There can be little doubt that women who carry on manual work would be well advised to wear loose clothing ; for as a result of costal breathing the number of respirations taken by a woman is slightly greater than that of a man ; while her basal metabolic activity, measured by consumption of oxygen and production of carbonic acid, is less than that of a male of equal weight (*vide, supra,* p. 224). Given this alteration in dress, breathing supplies no reason against the industrial employment of women.

Shock.—The extent of shock, following upon trauma, varies with different forms of life. Max Bartels has expressed it : " the higher the race, the less the tolerance, and the lower the culture-condition in a given race, the greater the tolerance " (2, p. 36).

Here again, as in the case of the blood, woman is claimed to be less differentiated than man, and to sustain shock better. Ellis (22) quotes from Legouest the following figures in support of this view :—

Amputations.	Males.	Females.
Cases. . . .	1,244	284
Deaths . . .	441	83
Percentage of deaths .	35·5	29·3

The balance, 6·2 per cent., is in favour of women and does not provide any justification for excluding women from employment on account of any increased risk run through sustaining injuries.

Maternity.—No precise data have been collected which throw light on the influence of physical labour on maternity. In so far as industry supplies healthy exercise, its influence may be beneficial. But attention should be paid to Ellis's remark : " I have noticed that well-developed muscular and athletic women sometimes show a very marked degree of uterine, as well as vesical, inertia in childbirth, while on the other hand the processes of parturition are often carried out in the most admirably efficient manner in fragile women who show a minimum development of the external muscles." In support of this observation one of us recalls attending in her confinements a finely developed patient among the first flight of lawn tennis players ; each confinement was long and tedious, followed by serious *post partum* hæmorrhage ; while, in contrast, the confinements of another well-to-do patient, lame from infantile hemiplegia, were rapid, easy, and without complication. Probably the explanation lies in the difference between the voluntary and involuntary muscular systems ; development of the voluntary muscles does not necessarily affect the involuntary muscles.

The fact of woman's potential or actual motherhood, writes Dr. Janet Campbell (3) " necessarily governs to a large extent her industrial power, efficiency and value. It wholly prevents absolutely equal competition in industry, and though undue weight should not be given to possible impairment of the maternal function which may arise from circumstances connected with the nature of the employment, it cannot be disregarded if women are to be employed under the conditions most appropriate to them, not only as individuals, but also with a view to the future and well being of the race as a whole." Industry in accepting female labour as part of its organisation is bound to accept woman as a woman with her sex responsibilities, and to take steps to this end. Possibly at some future time the industrial employment of married women and the mothers of young children may be curtailed ; but difficulty must arise in limiting the opportunity for earning a livelihood for the unmarried mother and the widow left to provide for a young family. Certainly, to-day, a responsibility rests with those who employ female labour ; this was recognised during the war in this country, and also in France and in Germany. The responsibility is twofold : (1) on behalf of the expectant mother ; and (2) on behalf of the children of working mothers.

" Care of the Expectant Mother." The only restriction placed to-day in this country on employment in relation to pregnancy is the prohibition (sec. 61, Factory and Workshop Act, 1901), which lays down that " an occupier of a factory or workshop shall not knowingly allow a woman or girl to be employed therein within four weeks after she has given birth to a child." The International Labour Conference, held in 1919, at Washington, has recommended women should not be employed for six weeks before and six weeks after childbirth, and should be paid full wages during this time ; but at present there is no restriction on the employment of pregnant women, and the custom has been for them to continue at work right up to the time of confinement.

Previous to wartime the work undertaken by women was, for the most part, sufficiently light to permit of this custom ; but when women were called upon to undertake heavier tasks this was felt to be injudicious, and many managers dismissed pregnant women as soon as the condition was obvious. We consider such dismissal wrong ; it does not benefit the pregnancy, since miscarriages generally occur in the earlier months before the condition is definitely recognised ; a reasonable amount of active exercise for a pregnant woman is beneficial rather than the reverse ; the expectant mother requires not less but rather more earnings for the next four or five months to feed herself well and lay by for her confinement ; she should be encouraged to regard her condition as normal and physiological ; she requires for the next few months more sympathetic consideration. Instead of dismissal lighter work should be found which after the seventh month should be of a sedentary character. Just before the cessation of hostilities the Ministry of Munitions were developing for munition workers a scheme whereby a light employment depôt was established, where overalls and gloves were made and mended and other sewing work was done by expectant mothers drawn from several factories in a district. The hours of work were shorter than normal, and the workers were paid on a time basis. Milk was given in the morning, a good meal mid-day, tea in the afternoon, and a rest room provided. The health of the women was supervised by a sympathetic matron, who inquired into the home conditions and arrangements made for confinement. The women readily availed themselves of these facilities ; lost time was negligible, and work was so well done that the depôt was a financial success.

"Care of the Children of Working Mothers." Such a depôt should have attached to it a breast-feeding nursery, and the women after confinement should, if they intend to resume industrial work, be induced to return with their babies to the depôt, and continue on light work, time being allowed out of working hours for breast-feeding until the babies are weaned,

This scheme of establishing a light employment depôt for several factories or even for a district has advantages compared with that followed in France where each factory was called upon to provide a breast-feeding nursery, the mothers being employed at their usual work for the normal hours of the factory.

We recognise that maternity must be a serious handicap to the industrial employment of women, and feel that married women with families should so far as is possible be relieved of any necessity to seek employment. Their contribution to the community is amply fulfilled in the production and upbringing of healthy children, the greatest source of wealth a nation can possess.

When social conditions lead to their employment, and in order to meet the need of the unmarried mother, we advocate the establishment in industrial districts of light employment depôts with nurseries attached.

General Resistance to Disease.—The statement that woman is less resistant than men to environmental conditions and toxic influences has been made so often that it has passed into occupational literature almost unchallenged. But when the evidence upon which it is based is sought for it is found to be flimsy and open to other interpretations ; and the whole question calls for careful consideration. On *a priori* grounds (dangerous grounds upon which to build a conclusion), since woman, as has been pointed out, is claimed to be the more stable of the two sexes, possessing a greater anabolic surplus, she might be expected to be more resistant.

Certainly mortality statistics justify the contention that she is more resistant, and possesses greater longevity. The greater strain and stress of male life has, however, been blamed for the inferior position of males as compared with females in mortality rates ; and the suggestion is made that if females were exposed to similar risks they would succumb equally readily. We have already, when discussing tuberculosis, seen reason to give modified support to this suggestion. But reference to the data given below shows that up to the age of ten years, while the exposure of the two sexes to risk must be considered about equal, the male mortality is in proportion as much in excess of the female as at any later age. At later ages the risks associated with childbirth in the case of adult females may also be fairly set against the occupational risks of the male. We have been unable to satisfy ourselves that there is any statistical proof of woman possessing any general inferiority in succumbing to disease compared with males.

Death rates per 1,000 among males and females in England and Wales, 1838—87 (17):—

Age period.	Males.	Females.
0 . .	70·1	60·3
5 . .	7·9	7·7
10 . .	4·4	4·6
15 . .	6·2	6·7
20 . .	8·3	7·9
25 . .	9·5	9·5
35 . .	13·1	12·1
45 . .	18·9	15·6
55 . .	32·8	28·0
65 . .	67·6	59·8
75 . .	147·7	134·3
85 and over .	313·5	288·1
All ages .	22·8	20·8

Morbidity data on the other hand definitely indicate that working women suffer more sickness than men, and that cases of illness are more prolonged. The tendency to be sick, like the tendency to death, varies with age, and is twice as great at forty-five years of age as at twenty-five ; statistics of morbidity must, therefore, always be distributed according to age. Lee (5) quotes the statistics of the Local Sickness Experience of Leipsic given on p. 218.

Rusher (37) gives the following figures from Sutton's Friendly Society Records :—

Ages.	Rates of sickness per member per annum.		
	Males.		Females.
	1856–60.	1861–70.	1856–75.
20—29	0·902	0·973	1·092
30—39	0·988	1·022	1·490
40—49	1·448	1·500	2·107
50—59	2·557	2·632	2·695
60—69	6·407	6·402	6·688

The female sickness in both is in excess of the male from age twenty to age fifty-four, i.e., during the period of the menstrual function. How far morbidity arises out of, or is dependent upon this function has never been settled. Should this interpretation be correct, then, after allowances have been made as indicated under the heading, menstruation, morbidity data do not fully support the claim that women are less resistant to disease than men.

The statement is not infrequently made in relation to lead poisoning that females exhibit a sexual proclivity to plumbism. We hold that the effect of plumbism in causing miscarriage and still-birth is a sufficient reason for excluding females from exposure to lead dust ; but we do not feel satisfied that there is evidence that they fall victims more readily than men. When women (who by long employment had become more or less acclimatised, more or less immune to the influence of lead) were quite wisely prohibited from work in white lead beds in 1897, and their place was taken by non-acclimatised men, a great rise of cases of plumbism occurred affecting the men. Later, as the causation—the inhalation of lead dust—became more fully recognised and guarded against, the case incidence fell almost to vanishing point. When twenty years later, during the war, owing to the scarcity of male labour, the employment of women at this work was again permitted temporarily, and non-acclimatised women took the place of acclimatised men, no rise in the case incidence occurred. It was confidently expected that a rise would occur because the new workers were non-acclimatised, not because they were women ; and the absence of any significant rise was at once a tribute to the efficacy of the precautionary measures now adopted and to the resistant powers of women. On the completion of the war, the men resumed their old work ; during the period of war service they had lost their acquired immunity ; more cases of poisoning were now reported among the men than occurred when the women took over the work. The existence of greater activity in the industry in the post-war period must be remembered when considering this evidence ; but after due allowance has been made it supports the view that women are not more susceptible to lead poisoning than men.

We are unaware of any scientific evidence in support of the alleged sexual proclivity, and regret that a case, sound in itself, should be supported by unsound arguments.

VI. Psychological Aptitude.

The Brain.—The prevailing weight of the human brain varies in the male between 46 ozs. and 53 ozs., and in the female between 41 ozs. and 47 ozs. There are some differences in the two sexes in the rate of growth of the brain ; that of a woman reaches maximum weight between fifteen and twenty years of age, then it declines until about the fiftieth year. The brain of a man is nearly at its maximum at twenty years of age, but continues to increase up to about thirty-five ; then it also declines until about the fiftieth year. In both sexes there is an increase again between fifty and sixty years of age, and then a rather rapid diminution with advancing years. According to Topinard (8) the brain of an average woman between twenty and sixty years of age is from 126 to 164 grams less in weight than that of an average man ; and from sixty years of age onwards from 123 to 158 grams less.

These data are of general interest, but cannot be held to establish any useful comparison between the mental capacity of the two sexes. The female brain bears about the same relation to the body weight as does that of the male ; but the weight of the brain is a very poor measure of intelligence, and other tests are required to detect any characteristics distinguishing the sexes. Miss Thompson has investigated (9, p. 182) the question by laboratory experiments, and as a result has expressed the opinion that " the psychological differences of sex seem to be largely due, not to difference of average capacity, nor to difference in type of mental activity, but to differences in the social influences brought to bear on the developing individual from early infancy to adult years. The question of the future development of the intellectual life of women is one of social necessities and ideals rather than of the inborn psychological characteristics of sex."

Mrs. Hollingworth sums up (29) the question of sex mentality thus : " There exist no scientific data to show (i.) differences in average intellect ; (ii.) differences in mental variability ; (iii.) special causes of intellectual inefficiency affecting one sex but not the other ; (iv.) differences in effective or instructive equipment, implying a ' natural ' division of labour. The division of labour between the sexes, which has existed through historic times and still persists, originated, so far as we know, in physiological, not in psychological differences."

Psycho-neuroses.—When referring to the psychological characteristics of women we must not leave unnoticed the supposedly heavier incidence upon them of psycho-neuroses—by which we understand functional disorders of the intellectual and emotive sphere not traceable to an organic basis. Chief of these is hysteria, once, as its names implies, believed to be a peculiar privilege of women. That this disorder is not confined to women was clearly pointed out 250 years ago by Sydenham, but he admitted a greater prevalence amongst women, actually saying that " if we except those who lead a hard and hardy life, there is rarely one who is wholly free from them (hysterical complaints)." Were the cure of hysteria so simple as is hinted at in the sentence quoted, it would follow that the matter is of slight importance to the student of industrial life. Modern research has, however, not guaranteed so easy a remedy, but has much widened the connotation of hysteria, and displayed the grave damage to efficiency and happiness wrought by the psycho-neuroses, of which popularly conceived hysteria is only one.

The starting point of recent investigations was furnished by the work of Bruer and Freud, published in 1895 (24), which promulgated the hypothesis that the origin of a hysteria could be traced to some psychic injury of which the victim might be no longer conscious, but the effects of which remained and displayed themselves in strange forms. A fanciful analogy may be of service : In passing down a certain street, one is subjected to an unpleasant experience. The nature of the experience is forgotten, perhaps even that anything at all occurred is forgotten, but there remains a vague distaste for that street. Thus far we have nothing uncommon or unusual. A stage further and we may take pains to avoid the street without being able to say why. This would be set down as a harmless idiosyncrasy, and one's friends would quote the parallel case of Dr. Johnson. But when we find that, on the days of the week which would naturally take us to this quarter of the town, we have shooting pains in the leg, and, *a fortiori*, when we are afflicted with a permanent paralysis which prevents us from walking down that or any other street the stage of fully developed and incapacitating illness has been reached. A whole conglomerate of symptoms has now formed like a cluster of limpets upon the submerged and forgotten rock of incident which happened in the street long before.

In these general analogical terms the hypothesis, however valuable in the explanation and treatment of psycho-neuroses, cannot seem of peculiar importance in this chapter. The reason of its peculiar importance is that, in the experience of the physicians who have especially attended to the subject, the original injury—the street incident of our parable—is commonly sexual. In a few cases, a gross sexual trauma, *e.g.*, assault sustained in childhood ; in some, an unexpected or perhaps brutal revelation of the physical mechanism of sex ; in others sexual incidents of more complex ætiology ; but, in a majority of cases, something sexual is claimed to be the starting point. Now, should it happen that, in the after-history of the person, circumstances hinder the free play of the normal sex impulse, the probability that this process of accretion to a psychic foreign body will go on, is strengthened. Let us change the metaphor entirely. In the castle of life there is a locked door which most will open sooner or later. Before it should be opened, some have peeped through the keyhole; others have heard of what is in the chamber. Both classes have been affected; most very little, but a few a great deal, and these are a prey to nightmares and phantasies. Of this minority some will be cured when the door is opened, and each delay in opening makes the cure harder, the undergrowth of morbid phantasy thicker. Hence, we should expect that the frequency and gravity of the psycho-neuroses of common life would be somewhat greater amongst young women whose occupations place an obstacle to marriage than amongst their sisters.

Such we believe to be the case and we, therefore, felt ourselves justified in mentioning the subject, since judiciously handled at an early stage, psycho-neuroses, otherwise incurable, may easily be relieved. In the psychology of every-day life nothing is too trivial to merit notice; a laughable minor eccentricity, a stammer, a trick of speech, may have more to do with a later incapacity— a stiff arm or a lame leg—than one supposes. Here we see another argument for an educated sympathetic and observant welfare supervisor where female labour is employed.

We have mentioned this subject with considerable hesitation, since, while we have evidently no space to summarise what is rapidly becoming a great body of special literature, brief reference is eminently liable to be misleading. We do, however, think it right to observe that (i.) those who trace a majority of psycho-neuroses to the existence of a sexual *motif*, do *not* suppose that the cure of such conditions is obtained by simply prescribing marriage; (ii.) they do *not* suppose that sexual continence is harmful to a majority or even a large minority of young adults; and (iii.) they do *not* advocate the inculcation of sex knowledge by associations of amateur biologists, eugenists, and other well-meaning members of the middle classes upon factory workers, whether young men or young women.

In so far as industrial employment raises for women any barrier to marriage which it does not raise for men, so far it influences the occurrence of female psycho-neuroses; but we are of opinion that industry does not in fact raise for women a barrier to marriage sufficient to make this matter an important reason for the non-employment of women. The numerical inequality of the sexes, with its predominance of women, is a far more potent influence among a monogamous population.

Industrial Experience.—Experience of those who are accustomed to deal with women in employment is probably more valuable as an indication of their psychical capacity than any measurements and tests yet applied. The impression gathered from discussing the question with many factory managers may be summarised as follows :—Women are more industrious than men ; they will continue more steadily at monotonous and constant repetition work, but they show less initiative and inventive faculty. The male tends to devise a short cut to save himself labour ; the female to be content with her daily round and common task. A boy, after acquiring proficiency at one process loses interest, and wants to be transferred to another ; a girl will remain satisfied where she is. Thomas ascribes such characteristics to innate tendencies arising during the evolution of the race, and dependent on underlying anatomical differences. " Man's most immediate, most fascinating and most remunerative occupation was the pursuit of animal life. The pursuit of this stimulated him to the invention of devices for killing and capture, and this aptitude for invention was later extended to the invention of tools and of mechanical devices in general, and finally developed into a settled habit of scientific interest. The scientific imagination which characterises man in contrast with women is not a distinctive male trait, but represents a constructive habit of attention associated with freer movement and the pursuit of evasive animal forms. The problem of control was more difficult, and the means of securing it became more indirect, mediated, reflective and inventive ; that is, more intelligent.

" Woman's activities, on the other hand, were largely limited to plant life, to her children, and to manufacture, and the stimulation to mental life and invention in connection with these was not so powerful as in the case of man. Her inventions were largely processes of manufacture connected with her handling of the by-products of the chase. So simple a matter, therefore, as relatively unrestricted motion on the part of man and relatively restricted motion on the part of woman determined the occupations of each, and these occupations in turn created the characteristic mental life of each. In man this was constructive, answering to his varied experience and the need of controlling a moving environment, and in woman it was conservative, answering to her more stationary and monotonous condition " (2, pp. 293–4).

Effect of Woman on Industry.—Industry has exerted and is continuing to exert such a profound influence upon the conditions of life, that reference may here fairly be made, not merely (as above) to the way in which industrial occupation may affect women, but also to the influence women may exert on industry. In Chapter II. attention was drawn to the influence the industrial employment of women has already had upon factory legislation. There are those who hold that in the mind of woman, to whom the race is more than the individual, lies the psychic centre for the future. " Developing civilisation is being driven by causes which are inherent in a direction which is inevitable. Evolution will follow the line of maximum power. It is this question of power which will ultimately control everything. And the significant fact towards which we have to turn is that the qualities through which maximum power must express itself in the long sequences of the social integration, the qualities, that is to say, for which civilisation cries aloud now with the living hunger of a type in evolution, are precisely those which are most characteristically represented in the mind of woman " (23). If this opinion, which cannot be hastily brushed aside, be accepted, then industry, which is claimed to have been primitively developed by woman and which, we hold, has, as have schools, great power in cultural inheritance, will benefit from the mind of woman ; an influence which can only be fully exerted through her industrial employment.

The conclusions which emerge are that :—

(i.) The mentality of women is as useful as that of men ;

(ii.) The occurrence of psycho-neuroses is not a sufficient reason for the non-employment of women ;

(iii.) Women possess certain characteristics of value to modern industry with its tendency to specialisation and repetition work ; and

(iv.) The influence of the employment of women upon industry has already, through legislation, been beneficial, and may be needed in the future if industry is to exert for the benefit of the community the influence which lies latent within it.

VII. Other Considerations.

Life outside the industrial establishment, quite apart from the advantages and disadvantages discussed above, demands special consideration in the case of the woman. From time immemorial woman has performed the work of the home, cooking, cleaning, mending, washing, bedmaking, and the care of children ; frequently the employed woman after leaving home in the morning and on return in the evening after work has to perform a multiplicity of household duties, not perhaps onerous in themselves, but which, when added to the day's toil, considerably deplete her energies.

This point became manifest to the Health of Munition Workers Committee, when investigating the question as to whether during the pressure of war, nightwork for women should be carried on for long periods, or should alternate with daywork every other week. The output of women on continuous night-shifts was found to be inferior to that of women on alternate night and day-shifts. The Committee concluded (18) that "women on continuous nightwork are likely to perform domestic duties, which, when they work alternately in the two shifts, is impracticable; and this extra domestic strain may account for the inferior results of their industrial activities." In the case of men the inferiority of continuous night-shifts, though present, was less striking. "Men do not naturally take so much part in domestic work as women, and the temptation to burn the candle at both ends is, from this point of view, smaller. On the other hand, the incitement to devote the time, which should be given to sleep, to amusement is certainly as intense among men as among women, so that some inferiority might be anticipated."

This question of woman's domestic work cannot wisely be neglected; yet the ordered routine of industrial work seldom permits women being employed for shorter hours than men. In some processes entirely performed by women this could be done; but, in fact, industrial organisation is conservative and prefers to insist that all workers shall commence and leave work together. The onlooker, however, fails to appreciate the necessity, and the point should be faced, that, to allow for home-work, women's period of work should be shorter than men's; and advantage might be gained if on one day in the week, say Saturday, the employment of women were entirely abandoned.

VIII. Summary.

Productivity is the key-note of the times. Every nation is calling for increased production to repair the enormous destruction the Great War has brought upon the world's wealth, i.e., its surplus production. No nation can afford to leave any source of energy unused, and certainly not half its population, unless an overpowering racial reason exists.

We have attempted in this chapter a consideration of what innate obstacles there are to the employment of women; and the evidence indicates that :—

(1) Woman throughout the centuries has been accustomed to physical labour at least as onerous as that of modern industry.

(2) There is a lack of accurate information as to the effect of occupation on women.

(3) Woman represents the more stable portion of the race.

(4) In proportion to her size she is not so powerful as a man.

(5) Similarly her athletic capacity is less.

(6) Possibly the two previous instances of proportional inferiority are largely due to lack of training.

(7) Woman is less liable than man to hernia.

(8) Woman is possibly less fitted than man for a life of physical activity and bursts of energy.

(9) Varicose veins are more serious in women than in men.

(10) Habits of nutrition, if supervised, are no bar to the employment of women.

(11) Menstruation is not adversely affected by moderate physical work; but special consideration should be given to women during its occurrence.

(12) Anæmia is benefited by regular occupation.

(13) Differences in respiration supply no reason against the employment of women.

(14) Shock is not worse borne by women than men.

(15) Industry should, especially if married women are employed, make suitable provision for the pre-maternal and post-maternal periods.

(16) There is no clear evidence that woman is less resistant than man to environmental conditions and toxic influences.

(17) Mentally women are in their sphere as useful as men.

(18) The occurrence of psycho-neuroses is not a bar to the employment of women.

(19) Women possess certain characteristics of value to modern industry with its tendency to specialisation and repetition work.

(20) The influence of the employment of women upon industry has, through legislation, been beneficial.

(21) Consideration should be given, when arranging the hours of work for women, to the drain upon their energies entailed by carrying on domestic duties in addition to industrial work.

IX. Conclusion.

We hold that the opinion expressed by Ellis (22) calls for support :—

" The hope of our future civilisation lies in the development in equal freedom of both the masculine and feminine elements in life. . . . We are not at liberty to introduce any artificial sexual barrier in social concerns. The respective fitness of men and of women for any kind of work or any kind of privilege can only be ascertained by actual open experiment. The militant side of primitive culture belongs to the men ; the industrial belongs to women."

Further, after the evidence given above has received careful consideration, we find ourselves able to accept the statement made by Professor F. S. Lee (5) :—

" In the matter of women in industry it is necessary to accept the fact that men and women are not identical, and that men are better fitted for certain kinds of industrial occupations, while women are better suited to others. At the same time, training has tended to give a wrong conception of, rather than accentuate, these physiological and psychological differences, and the result has been that the possibilities of women's work have not hitherto been clearly realised."

X. Bibliography.

1. *The Cambridge Modern History.* Vol. XII., p. 762.
2. Thomas, W. I. *Sex and Society.* R. G. Badger. Boston.
3. *Report of War Cabinet on Women in Industry.* (Cd. 135.) 1919.
4. Hunt, W. *The Political History of England.* Vol. X., p. 271. Editors, W. Hunt and R. L. Poole. Longmans, Green & Co. 1905.
5. *Report of War Cabinet on Women in Industry.* Appendices and Summaries of Evidence. (Cd. 167.) 1919.
6. Campbell, H. *Nervous Organisation of Man and Woman*, p. 121. H. K. Lewis. 1891.
7. Loveday, T. "The Causes and Conditions of Lost Time." *Health of Munition Workers Committee. Interim Report on Industrial Efficiency and Fatigue.* (Cd. 8511.) 1917.
8. Topinard, P. *Eléments d'Anthropologie Générale.*
9. Thompson, Helen B. *The Mental Traits of Sex.* The University of Chicago Press. 1905.
10. Rogers, T. E. Thorold. *Six Centuries of Work and Wages.*
11. Lipson, E. *The Economic History of England*, p. 97. A. and C. Black, Ltd. 1915.
12. *Ibid.*, p. 300.
13. *Ibid.*, p. 316, *et seq.*
14. Unwin, G. *Industrial Organisation in the Sixteenth and Seventeenth Centuries*, p. 134. 1904.
15. *Final Report, Health of Munition Workers Committee*, p. 146. (Cd. 9065.)
16. Howell, W. H. *Textbook of Physiology.* W. B. Saunders Co.
17. Extracted from *Elements of Vital Statistics*, p. 101. A. Newsholme. 1892.
18. *Health of Munition Workers Committee. Interim Report.* (Cd. 8511.) 1917.
19. Abram, A. *English Life and Manners in the Later Middle Ages.* G. Routledge & Sons. 1913.

20. Lee, F. S. *The Human Machine and Industrial Efficiency.* Longmans, Green & Co. 1918.

21. Ranke, J. " Beitrage Zur Physischen Anthropologie der Bayern." *Beitrage zur Anthropologie und Urgeschichte Bayerns,* Vol. VIII.

22. Ellis, Havelock. *Man and Woman.* 5th Edition. Walter Scott Publishing Co., Ltd. 1914.

23. Kidd, Benjamin. *The Science of Power.* Methuen & Co., Ltd. 1918.

24. Freud and Breuer. *Ueber Hysterie.* 1895.

25. Frazer. *The Golden Bough.* 3rd Edition. *The Magic Art.* Vol. I., p. 140.

26. *Op. cit.* Vol. II., p. 204.

27. Montague and Hollingworth. *American Journal of Sociology.* 1914.

28. Pearson, Karl. " Variation in Man and Woman." *Chances of Death and other Studies in Evolution.* 1897.

29. Hollingworth, H. L. *Vocational Psychology.* Appleton & Co. New York. 1919.

30. Hollingworth, L. S. *Functional Periodicity.* Teachers' College, Columbia University. 1914.

31. Mock, H. E. *Industrial Medicine and Surgery.* W. B. Saunders & Co. Philadelphia. 1919.

32. Green, J. R. *A Short History of the English People.* Illustrated Edition. Macmillan & Co. 1892.

33. Ramazzini, B. *The Diseases of Tradesmen.* 2nd English Edition. 1746.

34. Frazer, Sir J. G. *Folk-lore in the Old Testament.* Vol. II., p. 343. Macmillan & Co. 1918.

35. Gibbon, E. *Decline and Fall of the Roman Empire.*

36. Harris, J. A., and Benedict, F. G. *A Biometric Study of Basal Metabolism in Man.* Carnegie Institute. 1919.

37. Rusher, E. A. " Historical Memorandum on Standard Sickness Tables in the United Kingdom." *Industrial Fatigue Research Board.* 1920.

PART III

CHAPTER X

THE FEEDING OF THE INDUSTRIAL WORKER

I. Introduction. II. Energy Value of Food : Energy Value of Diets ; Industrial Expenditure of Energy ; Energy Requirements and Wages ; Importance of a Diet Sufficient in Energy. III. The Importance of the Constituents of a Dietary. IV. Effect of Climate and Occupation upon Diet. V. The Importance of Food Accessory Factors (Vitamines) :—Fat-soluble A ; Water-soluble B ; Anti-scorbutic Factor ; Origin of Vitamines ; Vitamines in Workers' Food.

I. Introduction.

ALTHOUGH before August, 1914, a not negligible proportion of the inhabitants of these islands was underfed, as the researches of Mr. Rowntree demonstrated (12), the economic and scientific aspects of the problem of feeding the labouring population acquired through stress of war a peculiar importance. The evils bred of war have not yet abated, there is small reason to expect that in the lifetime of this generation the task of feeding the inhabitants of Europe will become easy or fail to occasion great anxiety. We have here nothing to do with these larger issues, nor is it even our business to give an account of the general science and art of human nutrition. We must, however, briefly expose such of the scientific principles as are of cardinal importance to employer and operative. Food is to be studied from two points of view, the mechanical and the physiological. From the mechanical point of view we regard man as a machine, subject to the law of all machines that when work is performed fuel must be consumed ; that no *more* energy can be got out than is put in ; that we can in no wise create energy. From the physiological point of view we observe that not only are the sources of energy available to the human body limited in number, but that quite apart from the demands of external work performance, particular combinations of chemical elements are needed to prevent the disintegration of the machine. Thus it comes about that while carbohydrates, proteins and fats are all available sources of fuel, deprivation of proteins, however much energy be offered in the guise of fats or carbohydrates, is fatal. Further, other substances not sources of energy in any measurable sense and of unknown chemical structure, the " vitamines," are

16—2

not less essential to healthy existence. Our general problem, therefore, resolves itself into three problems :—

(1) What is the quantum of energy needed ?

(2) How much protein and of what kind should be given ?

(3) How are we to ensure an adequate supply of " vitamines " ?

II. Energy Value of Food.

The first of these questions has engaged more attention than the others, and there is a good reason for this. Owing to the comparatively restricted choice of dietetic constituents, the fact that sugar and margarine or butter are almost the only important sources of dietetic energy which are destitute of protein, it would be very difficult to contrive a dietary which, adequate from the energetic side, would be inadequate in respect of protein. Hence the aphorism :—" Take care of the calories and the protein will look after itself." This aphorism is, however, like most epigrams only part of the truth ; in particular it pays no heed to our third question ; still it is much more than half the truth.

There are two ways of determining what is a diet of sufficient energy value. The first is to ascertain the value of the diets of representative samples of persons engaged in various tasks and preserving health and strength over a sufficiently extended period. The second is to measure directly the expenditure of energy by persons engaged in the several occupations. Given a series of standard chemical analyses, the former is a purely statistical, but the latter a statistico-experimental, inquiry.

Energy Value of Diets.—In the statistical study of dietaries the unit of reduction is the large calorie, or quantity of heat needed to raise the temperature of a kilogramme of water through a range of $1°$ on the Centigrade scale from $15°$ C. to $16°$ C. It is supposed, and the supposition is just, that the only sources of energy in the diet which need be considered are the proteins, fats and carbohydrates. The energy equivalents of unit masses of these proximate principles are deemed to be the complete heats of combustion of the fats and carbohydrates, and the heat of combustion of a typical protein less the heat value of incompletely oxidised waste products of protein metabolism which leave the body unutilised. In general the energy value is expressed in terms of the dietetic constituents *as eaten* or, perhaps more commonly, as submitted to the process of cooking. Hence the diets do not represent the energy actually liberated within the body and capable of exploitation by the human machine.

Between swallowing and assimilation a loss occurs, small in

the case of sugar and most fats, but large in some articles of diet. There is a still greater loss in preparation (cooking). An average discount of 10 to 13 per cent. must be allowed to bring purchased to the dimensions of available energy.*

TABLE 1.—*Women's Hostels.*

Hostel or canteen.	Numbers catered for.	Grammes per head daily.			Calories daily.	Cereal ratio.	Bread per week.	Report dated.
		Protein.	Fat.	Carbo-hydrates.				
							lbs. ozs.	
A	2600	110·4	113·3	414·8	3207	48·6	8 4	24.3.17
B	9	101·9	90·9	465·0	3166	56·0	8 4	14.7.17
C	520	159·1	203·9	791·6	4154	25·2	3 13	26.6.17
D	100	104·9	128·0	366·2	3122	41·8	6 0	28.7.17
E	22	69·1	69·9	295·3	2144	40·1	5 10	14.7.17
F	600	125·8	171·4	350·6	3547	29·5	5 12	21.7.17
G	4595	98·0	119·4	363·9	3004	33·2	2 8	13.6.17
H	151	125·4	130·9	436·0	3519	28·4	4 4	30.6.17
I	40	117·3	110·3	395·8	3130	36·9	5 0	23.6.17
J	370	95·8	126·8	291·8	2768	41·1	5 0	29.4.17
K	441	115·9	137·0	427·8	3503	46·4	5 10	13.5.17
L	7230	132·7	156·2	476·6	3951	39·7	6 4	30.6.17
M	57	146·0	244·4	386·3	4455	15·8	3 8	30.6.17
N	262	119·2	114·2	462·8	3448	49·3	7 3	15.6.17
O	105	102·1	123·4	283·2	2727	29·7	4 14	13.6.17
P	105	121·5	151·9	528·2	4076	36·6	6 3	11.8.17
Q	370	109·4	138·5	326·5	3075	29·9	4 1	31 8.17
R	42	104·3	139·6	465·0	3632	35·4	4 1	4.9.17
S	35	135·1	214·3	381·9	4113	23·5	4 0	25.8.17
T	1150	121·0	152·8	395·6	3539	28·3	3 11	30.6.17
V	46	118·1	151·4	625·1	4455	46·6	9 13	1.9.17
W	363	112·5	121·6	455·6	3460	44·5	7 14	1.9.17
Average		115·7	141·3	408·4	3463	36·7	5 8	

In Table 1 are shown the energy values of a series of diets supplied in English munition workers' hostels during the year 1917, and in Table 2 similar reductions of other diets. The arithmetical reduction has been effected on the lines above indicated ; in addition the diets of women in Table 1 have been reduced to " man " values by multiplying the woman's diet by 0·80, a fraction taken to represent the average relation between the needs of an adult man and those of an adult woman, founded partly upon statistical, partly upon experimental study. Further investigation has slightly modified the older values of equivalents; those now usually adopted are reproduced in Table 3, and these were employed in computing Table 2.†

* It is convenient to call the energy of the food as determined from analysis of the diets, gross calories, and that really available to the tissues, net calories.
† Hence Table 1 slightly exaggerates the value of the women's diets.

TABLE 2.—*Energy Values of Diets consumed by various classes before the War (Greenwood and Thompson).*

Source of data.	Calories per " man " per diem.
Mr. Rowntree's York families—	
Wages not more than 26*s*. . . .	2,574
Wages more than 26*s*. . . .	3,590
Servant-keeping class . . .	3,807
Board of Trade industrials—	
Wages less than 25*s*. . . .	2,670
Wages 25*s*. to 30*s*. . . .	2,879
Wages 30*s*. to 35*s*. . . .	3,036
Wages 35*s*. to 40*s*. . . .	3,034
Wages over 40*s*.	3,330
Agricultural labourers—	
Northern counties	3,085
Midland counties	2,868
Eastern counties	3,037
Southern and south-western counties .	3,067

Mr. Rowntree's data were published in 1902, the industrial and agricultural data relate to sample censuses in 1903–4. They are discussed by Dunluce and Greenwood (3), but the present reduction is that yielded by the new reduction factors and published in the *British Medical Journal* (13) by Greenwood and Thompson.

TABLE 3.—" *Man* " *Reduction Factors.*

Age.	Energy need (that of an adult man is taken as 1·00).
0—5 years	0·50
6—10 years	0·70
Over eleven years—	
Males	1·00
Females	0·83

The data relate to persons employed in a variety of occupations, but the majority were engaged upon industrial tasks of what may be called a moderate degree of physical severity. The average energy value of the diets is about 3,500 calories per diem. This figure has long been taken as a norm of physiological energy needs, corresponding to 3,100 to 3,200 calories actually available in the body. Still, long before the war there had not been wanting physiologists who thought that this norm exceeded the true requirements, and the exigencies of wartime focussed attention upon their arguments. Statistical averages of diets do not, *primâ facie*, seem to deserve much respect. We all know people who consume excessive quantities of food without any obvious ill-effects ; we are all sensible of the immense influence of custom upon habits of both eating and drinking ; many have enjoyed a green old age in spite of attending city dinners. When, in addition, we note the sources of error in the data; the introduction of more or less conjectural factors of reduction to a standard of comparison; lack of information as to either the external conditions or the precise character of the work performed, it will be admitted that there is room for doubt.

Industrial Expenditure of Energy.—On this account it is proper to measure directly the energy expended in various kinds of physical work. In two departments of activity, viz., the cost of pedalling a bicycle, and the energy expended by soldiers in marching and carrying out various military exercises, the researches of Benedict and Cathcart (16) and of Cathcart and Orr (2) have provided us with numerous data. In the industrial field the workers have been less successful, since the measurements are technically somewhat difficult and require time. The best accredited results are those of Becker and Hämäläinen, of Rosenheim, and of Greenwood, Hodson and Tebb (4). In Table 4 we reproduce some of the results reached by the last-mentioned investigators, and in Table 5 the conclusions provisionally reached by an authoritative committee of the Royal

TABLE 4.—*Actual Expenditure of Energy per Square Metre of Body Surface per hour of Women engaged upon the undermentioned Processes in a Munition Factory* (4).

Operation.	Number of Experiments.	Number of Persons.	Calories per square metre per hour.
Light turning . . .	37	8	96
Turning and finishing .	36	8	112
Tool setting . . .	25	5	124
Heavy turning . . .	21	5	123
Forging	20	4	114
Cleaning and drying . .	20	5	182
Gauging	19	4	154
Labouring . . .	14	5	184
Stamping	12	2	127
Walking and carrying .	11	3	161
Finishing copper bands .	6	2	128
Shell hoisting (with pulley).	5	1	129

These are observations made by the method of respiratory calorimetry. Note the vastly greater expenditure of energy on labouring (unskilled work of collecting and wheeling away rubbish) than upon semi-skilled work, such as light turning, or skilled work, such as tool setting.

TABLE 5.—*Daily Food Requirements of typical Occupations as estimated by the Food (War) Committee of the Royal Society* (7).

MALES.

	Calories.
Tailor	2,750
Bookbinder	3,100
Shoemaker	3,150
Metal worker	3,500
Painter	3,600
Carpenter	3,500
Stonemason	4,850
Woodcutter	5,500

FEMALES.

Hand seamstress . . .	2,000
Machine seamstress . . .	2,200
Charwoman . . . 2,900—3,600
Bookbinder	2,300
Typist	2,100

These figures are only to be regarded as rough approximations (see the Report of the Committee for details).

Society (7), and based upon the experimental findings of Becker and Hämäläinen. It is not without interest to observe that the average value* inferred differs little from the conventional 3,500 calories of the text-books. One of us was led to the same point by wholly different data. The French physiologist, Amar (8), published some years ago a series of experiments upon the energy expenditure of Arabs pedalling a stationary bicycle. These observations were numerous enough to permit of mathematical graduation by a formula connecting the energy requirements of the body with the thermal equivalent of the work done and the worker's body weight. When an estimate of the mechanical equivalent of a day's work was framed and its calorie equivalent for a seventy kilogramme man deduced from the formula, it appeared that a little under 3,200 net calories (or rather more than 3,500 calories in purchased food) were necessary (5). Hence, so far as our present experimental knowledge goes, there seems little reason to distrust the teaching of dietetic statistics, despite their manifold imperfections.

Some physiologists have, however, argued that it is possible to alter the plane of metabolism ; that one may become accus-

* Cathcart and Orr (2) reached 3,574 net (say 3,900 gross) calories for the mature army recruit, whose *physical* work is probably above the average factory requirements.

tomed to a lower intake, and that the physiological machine is capable of adaptation to a more economical style of living. This matter was the object of a prolonged research carried out under the supervision of Dr. Benedict of the Carnegie Institute (1). The result was to show that healthy college students could maintain active life for several months upon a diet yielding fewer than 3,500 calories, and that they could do so without giving any sign of physical detriment. But the experiment, notwithstanding the care and accuracy with which it was carried out, took place in conditions so remote from those of ordinary industrial life, and was on so small a scale, that it does not seem to us to weaken the inference from the other statistical and experimental results which we have mentioned.

In a matter of this kind to generalise from particular observations is hazardous. In criticising dietetic statistics we omitted a rebutting argument of the greatest importance. The real case against dietetic faddists, is expressed in the old saying that there is always some one wiser than even M. de Voltaire—*c'est tout le monde*. In these matters, the average experience of a sample of the population neither greatly oppressed by *res angusta domi*, nor seduced by the temptations of material luxury, is likely to be a reasonably good guide. A common habit of eating is the survival of generations' experience. It is not, therefore, surprising that there should be a concordance between what men have been observed to eat and what direct observation suggests they need. This is not to say that experimental observations are otiose. On the contrary, many more are required for the following reasons.

Energy Requirements and Wages.—Greenwood, Hodson and Tebb (4) inferred from their experiments upon female munition workers that the daily needs would be covered by diets yielding (in gross calories) 2,800, 3,100, 3,500 and 3,800 calories *per diem*. They remarked :—" One important inference may be drawn from these figures. The energy requirement of the lightest class is about 74 per cent. of the heaviest. But the remuneration of the kinds of work included in our heaviest class is much less than that of several operations needing many fewer calories. If we suppose that so small a sum as 10s. would purchase an adequate weekly diet for a member of the lowest class, then, assuming that the one and a half non-working days require the same allowance, which we may put at 1,800 calories *per diem*, for all classes, the total weekly needs are 16,615 calories and 21,538 calories, so that the worker in the heavier class must spend nearly 13s. a week. The data collected by the Board of Trade in 1904 showed that for families in receipt of less than

25s. weekly, 67·3 per cent. of total outgoings were expended upon food, the proportion only falling as low as 57 per cent. in families earning 40s. or more weekly. Even in the families of the poorest class studied by Rowntree, where the expenditure upon food was estimated to provide less than a maintenance diet, 51 per cent. of outgoings were for food. The Working-classes Cost-of-Living Committee (14) which reported in 1918, provided data from which the following percentages have been calculated. These figures refer to families composed of 4·57 'men.' Let us now suppose that the average earning, viz., 75s. 5d. per week is adequate to maintain the minimum standard of comfort in such a family, and that the principal wage earner is a 'man' occupied as in our lowest class. Dividing the

TABLE 6.—*Proportional Expenditure upon Food of Industrial Workers. (Deduced by Green-wood, Hodson and Tebb from the data of the Working Classes Cost of Living Committee, Cd. 8980 of 1918.)*

	Percentage of total expenditure devoted to the purchase of food.	
	1914.	1918.
Skilled workers . .	54·8	60·6
Semi-skilled workers .	56·2	63·4
Unskilled workers .	56·7	64·9

mean income by 4·57 and multiplying by 0·6 (on the assumption that the expenditure upon food is now about 60 per cent. of total outgoings), we find that the cost of food per 'man' is almost exactly 10s. a week. If then the wage earning 'man' of a family similarly constituted in all other respects is in our heaviest physiological class, the general standard of living can only be maintained if the gross family income be increased by nearly 3s. When it is remembered that the subsidiary earnings of other members of the family (which have always been relatively more important in the lower grades of manual labour) must be reduced by the new educational proposals, the grave importance of taking into account the physiological element of working class expenditure is manifest. In any scientific appraisement of the income needed to maintain an agreed upon standard of life, it is essential to determine the minimum expenditure necessitated by the occupation of the wage earner."

Importance of a Diet sufficient in Energy.—The period which has elapsed since the above words were written has increased the gravity of the problem and contributed nothing to its solution. In a few moments we shall have to speak of other aspects of the subject, to point out that " calories " are not everything ; *but wanting " calories," we lack everything.* Something more than petrol is required to run a motor car, but no mechanical skill can

TABLE 7.—*Requirements in Calories of a Sedentary Worker under different Conditions of Temperature and Wind Exposure. (Calculated by Greenwood and Thompson from Lefèvre's Experimental Results ; the subject was a Clothed Man, weighing 65 kilogrammes.)*

Temperature.	Air current of 1 metre per second.	Air current of 3·5 metres per second.
— 31° C.	6,000	7,400
+ 5° C.	4,500	5,200
+ 10° C.	3,400	4,100
+ 15° C.	2,600	3,100

The energy is expressed as calories in food, *i.e.*, as gross calories. The results have no pretension to accuracy, but they bring out the enormous influence of exposure to cold and illustrate the danger of neglecting this factor when diets are assigned.

run it without petrol. The need of calories for the human engine is fundamental, no subtle arguments, no appeal to a specialised experience, no invocation of half-comprehended factors such as " vitamines " must be allowed for an instant to obscure this truth. Heavy manual work *does* require more food than black-coated " brain " work. The ill-clad girl who travels to her work on foot or outside a motor omnibus *does* need more calories than her sister in the motor brougham,* and the difference of need is expressible in money and represents a substantial difference.

The retribution of neglect in this matter is slow but sure. An underfed industrial population does not collapse suddenly.

* The effect of exposure to cold is brought out in Table 7.

As a writer early in the last century put it :—" It is a popular saying, that hunger will break through stone walls, by which it is implied, that its calls cannot be resisted and that the most difficult obstacles will be overcome to satisfy it. This may be true of hunger induced by sudden fasting occurring to persons in good health, but it is very far otherwise when an individual is suffering gradually and becoming exhausted by slow degrees from a long continued deficiency of food or the use of a very impoverished diet. In such cases, when the health begins to decline, mental obtuseness and diminished sensibility follow ; all the sensations are blunted, and the feeling of hunger being feebly experienced, no very strenuous efforts are made to allay it " (9). In short, the consequences of under-nutrition are a slowly progressive decline of efficiency. Unless the deficit is qualitative as well as quantitative, there will be no dramatic incidents. Morbidity will increase, but there will be no new or strange diseases, merely an increased toll taken by the customary kinds of sickness:

This branch of the subject is so commonplace, it offers so few scientific novelties, such scanty occasions for the exercise of intellectual ingenuity, that we cannot expect the reader to be greatly interested. We must, however, reiterate that unless the quantum of energy in the form of attractive and digestible food is supplied, all other applications of hygiene to the lives of industrial workers are mere trifling. Having dealt with the quantitative side of the energy problem, we are to consider the form in which the " calories " should be offered.

III. The Importance of the Constituents of a Dietary.

Each of the three fundamental foodstuffs yields energy to the body ; the continued proportion of the yields of carbohydrate to protein to fat is approximately $1 : 1 : 2 \cdot 1$; but it is not a matter of indifference how the calories are furnished, i.e., what proportions of the proximate principles are chosen, so long as the right number of calories is secured. Although the body as an energy transformer has some analogy to a motor car or a steam engine, the analogy is imperfect. The nature of the fuel supplied affects the working of the machine and sets in motion processes which do not directly contribute to the performance of mechanical work. In other words, equal numbers of calories offered by way of proteins, fats and carbohydrates are not equally useful for transformation into mechanical energy. The quantity diverted is greatest in proteins and least in carbohydrates ; in technical language, the specific dynamic energy of proteins is maximal, *i.e.*, a larger proportion of the calories rendered up in their decomposition is necessarily liberated as inconvertible heat energy. For this reason the brunt of the energy supply for work should be borne by carbohydrates. "A large meat diet, apart from its content of fat, is of no special advantage for the performance of muscular work, and is a distinct disadvantage when this work has to be accomplished at a high external temperature " (7).

As experimental work has not revealed any very great difference between the specific dynamic energies of fat and carbohydrate, there might seem no special advantage in taking fat in the diet at all, provided enough calories are furnished by the carbohydrate. Practical experience, however, has made it evident that the diets of heavy manual workers ought to contain a large amount of animal fat. Possibly this depends upon the higher yield of heat per unit mass ; possibly on the vitamine content of fats ; but however this may be, the fact is certain. The rule proposed by the Food Committee of the Royal Society (7) is that not less than 25 per cent. of the total calories of the diet should come from fat. Protein is, of course, still more important. This substance must be supplied in the food since it is the essential constituent of the living cells and cannot be synthesised in the body from simpler nitrogen-containing substances.* Nature provides a wide range of proteins, but these are not of equal value to the body. Broadly speaking, proteins of animal origin are more valuable than vegetable proteins ; the protein of milk, for instance, is twice as valuable as that of wheat. Hence the minimum ration of protein is larger when the source is vegetable than when animal food is taken. As a practical rule, we may say that the average " man " needs 70 to 80 grammes of protein daily, an amount contained in 2 lbs. of bread, in 1 lb. 2 ozs. of meat, in 10 ozs. of cheese and in 10 eggs. As remarked above, a diet providing sufficient calories will rarely or never fall short in protein ; if the energetic needs are satisfied the protein requirements are almost sure to be.

IV. Effect of Climate and Occupation upon Diet.

Appetite controls diet, and appetite is largely controlled by metabolic activity. which is greater in cold weather than warm. In hot climates where but little heat is required to maintain the

---

* This statement is not *strictly* true, because under special conditions protein can be synthesised from simpler decomposition products ; and all ingested protein is, in the process of metabolism, split up into such bodies and reconstituted ; but the necessary cleavage products are themselves highly complex and would be more difficult to provide in a diet than native proteins.

body temperature, physical exercise cannot be indulged in to the same extent as in temperate regions, for fear of heat stroke. Comparatively little food is required, and a native student in Singapore is content with 1,500 calories daily (23). In such climates cereals, such as rice, form the staple diet ; food, therefore, is cheap, and wages are proportionately low. But energy cannot be got from the human machine unless it is first put into it, and here lies the explanation of the saying that cheap labour is expensive labour. If workers have to do heavy physical work they must consume an adequate amount of food. Railway engineers know this, and are said always to calculate that the labour required for constructing a mile of track costs the same all the world over ; an object lesson on the point occurred in Sicily a few years ago when railway extension was being carried out. The native navvies worked so much slower than the imported British workmen that serious delay resulted ; these natives were unaccustomed to eat much meat. The contractor noticing this fact began to pay them partly in money and partly in meat, with the result that the output of work went up almost to that of the British gangs. Thus was reversed the command of Paul that " if any would not work, neither should they eat."

Different industries as well as climates call for different types of food, and any one accustomed to travel through the various industrial districts of this kingdom, can observe how the main industry of the district is represented in the types of provision shops in the town. In Lancashire, in the cotton districts for instance, there is a noticeable scarcity of butchers' shops, while grocers' shops are in evidence. This may be ascribed to the way in which the cotton industry is carried on in the great mills, which are warm and often humid to allow cotton thread to work properly. Operatives exposed many hours of each day to such conditions, which somewhat resemble those of tropical countries, find that their appetites require tempting and do not demand butcher's meat. This matter will be alluded to later, p. 291, when the influence of ventilation comes under discussion. The failure of cotton operatives to attain normal stature, referred to on p. 291 (a failure recognised in wartime by the enlistment of the " bantams "), and ascribed to adverse physiological conditions and lowered metabolism, may possibly be due to a diet during adolescence deficient in accessory food factors, such a diet as the conditions of work render acceptable to the appetite.

In the Black Country the workers, though exposed often to the heat of iron from the furnaces, are employed in shops open to the air, and carry out more physical exercise associated with much wear and tear on their tissues. In this part of the country the prevalence of butchers' shops is a noticeable feature in the towns. These two instances are extremes between which an ordinary agricultural market town stands. In such a town the demand is much more for cereal foods, bread and confectionery shops being more to the front. The agricultural labourer requires a plentiful supply of energy for his open air life, but has less need of repair material than industrial workers on heavy work.

V. The Importance of Food Accessory Factors (Vitamines).

Finally, we come to accessory substances or " vitamines," and cannot do better than quote the findings of the Royal Society Committee (7). " Practically all fresh foods contain small traces of substances whose chemical nature has not been determined, but which are essential for the maintenance of health or for the production of growth. In their absence growth may cease, repair of wounds may be interrupted, or various diseases, such as scurvy, beri-beri, or pellagra, may be produced. A diet composed of preserved meats and dried vegetables infallibly leads in the course of a few months to disorders of nutrition. This generally takes the form of scurvy. Beri-beri may occur when the diet is too limited in scope, and is deprived of part of its normal constituents. Thus, this disease occurs in Chinese labourers fed on polished rice, but disappears when the polishings of the rice are added to the food. The growth " vitamine " is present in especially large quantity in the fats of milk. It is partly on this account that milk is of such vital importance for the nourishment of children. No child's diet can be considered .satisfactory in which milk or milk fat is not present."

The study of definite diseases has led to the discovery of vitamines ; but these factors have further interest, for " there are some grounds for believing that the accessory food factors are concerned in the processes of tissue formation and repair, and we should therefore expect larger amounts to be necessary after exercise than after periods of rest. Whilst there is as yet practically no experimental evidence upon this point, there are indications based upon human experience that the demand for the three accessory factors is greater when work is being accomplished. This probability should be borne in mind when the dietaries or rations of those engaged in severe manual work, such as soldiers and labourers, are being considered " (10). An instance may be given from the report here quoted. During the war, in a camp in Scotland, scurvy attacked eighty-seven men. " In this instance the first cases to develop and a large majority of those showing severe symptoms were among a small section of the inmates who were engaged in hard manual work for a few hours daily." This report goes on to state :—" One point of practical importance concerned with the slow development of these deficiency diseases is the certainty that long before the symptoms of the acute disease can be diagnosed there will be a general, ill-defined departure from good health which may defy diagnosis, but which will seriously lower the well-being and efficiency of the individual."

The substances here referred to are known as accessory food factors or vitamines (10). Three distinct and separate factors have now been shown to exist : (i.) fat-soluble A or the anti-rachitic factor ; (ii.) water-soluble B, or the antineuritic (anti-beri-beri) factor ; and (iii.) the antiscorbutic factor.

Fat-soluble A.—The absence of this vitamine from an other-wise ample dietary appears to cause rickets in childhood, while its introduction into the dietary prevents this disease. The exact effect upon adults of the absence of this body from food is not yet clearly understood, but there can be no doubt that adults fed on a diet in which it is not present would lose strength and vigour and be more susceptible to disease ; interest attaches to the fact that articles of diet containing this substance have for years been recognised as of paramount importance when dealing with consumptive patients. This vitamine is found associated with fats, especially with butter, cod-liver and other fish oils, cream, mutton and beef fat ; it is also present in eggs, germinating seeds and fresh green vegetables, but it is absent from lard and vegetable oils, such as olive oil, cotton seed oil, coco-nut oil, and linseed oil, and also from white flour, cornflour, custard powders and white fish. This body is only moderately resistant to heat, and exposure to boiling point for four hours, destroys it.

Water-soluble B.—This food factor has been especially studied in connection with the occurrence of beri-beri. Further, among a community fed on a dietary deficient in this vitamine, some members of which succumbed to beri-beri, a widespread abnor-mality in knee-jerks and other nervous reflexes was found among the apparently healthy. " This is an important observation, as it shows definitely that normal health may be undermined by a deficiency in diet before any symptoms are apparent to the casual observer or to the individual himself " (10). This body occurs plentifully in the seeds of plants, the eggs of animals and in yeast. It is also found in meats, beans and peas, and ger-minated seeds, and to a smaller extent in fresh vegetables and flour. It is absent from fats, white flour, custard powders and beer. This vitamine stands exposure to heat fairly well, and ordinary cooking which does not exceed boiling point, does not seem to impair its properties ; but it is damaged by alkalis, and for this reason green vegetables should not be boiled with sodium carbonate.

Anti-scorbutic Factor.—The absence of this vitamine from a diet is associated with another disease, namely, scurvy ; if introduced into the food it cures the disease. It occurs plentifully in fresh cabbages, raw swedes, orange juice, lemon juice, and tomatoes ; and of all the vegetables the family of the cruciferæ, which includes the cabbages, seems to contain them most plentifully. Thus, the old legend that plants with a cruciform arrangement of the flower possess special virtue in the service of mankind receives scientific support. It is found in germinated seeds, root vegetables and lime juice, and it is only present to a minor degree in milk and fresh meat. It is destroyed by drying ; is sensitive to high temperatures, thus twenty minutes in boiling water seriously impairs it, and exposure for an hour merely to hot water has a similar effect. Fresh vegetables, *e.g.*, cabbages, should, therefore, be cooked by exposing them for a short time to a high temperature, rather than for a longer time to a lower temperature. The process of tinning meat destroys this vitamine.

Origin of Vitamines.—The accessory food factors at present known to exist are ultimately derived from vegetables. The animal body does not appear to possess any power of constructing them ; but an analogy within the body to vitamines is to be found in hormones, the internal secretions of the endocrine glands. When found in animal flesh or fat, vitamines have reached there from the consumption of vegetable food, from which they have been absorbed and stored up until required. Fat-soluble A. is stored in adipose tissue ; the amount so stored is considerable and is only comparatively slowly exhausted ; therefore a diet may be free from this factor without obvious results ensuing for several weeks. Water soluble B. also is stored in the tissues and gradually drawn on as necessity arises. The anti-scorbutic factor, on the other hand, is not long retained in the tissues and should, therefore, always be present in food.

Vitamines in Workers' Food.—The industrial importance of food accessory factors depends upon two circumstances, the first is that " carried food," the food brought by the workers to the factory, is likely to contain a large proportion of preserved meats and other articles free of " vitamines." The second is that butter is unlikely to resume its place in the dietary for many years—if ever. The vast bulk of the margarine on the market is vegetable margarine without any vitamine value.

Further, fresh fruits, such as apples, oranges and bananas, are sure to be very scarce and dear for some time to come. It is, therefore, necessary, for those organising industrial feeding to pay special attention to the supply of green vegetables, to ensure that the methods of cooking are not such as to destroy the " vitamines," and to encourage the use of bread more nearly approximating to the war bread than to the æsthetically desirable and physiologically improper article which used to adorn the afternoon tea-table and may, perhaps, reappear.

We have now expounded the general physiological principles which should inform the practice of industrial catering. We have no doubt that the extension of the canteen system, which received such an impetus during the war, will be a valuable instrument in securing the necessary conditions. At the same time we are alive to the fact that a part, perhaps the larger part, of the commissariat problem is domestic and not capable of direct control. In the sphere of home life we can do little directly, a great deal indirectly. The economic factor is, of course, paramount. It is idle to prescribe diets if the workers have not the wherewithal to purchase them. This matter, however, is not within the scope of a treatise upon industrial hygiene. Given the necessary economic conditions, much is attainable by education. The general principles of dietetics, not even excepting the mysterious " calories " which a Minister of State once admitted to be beyond his comprehension, can be explained to any industrial worker of sufficient intelligence to be fit for industrial work at all. The duty lies with those responsible for welfare and hygiene in factories to see that such explanations are given.

(See end of Chapter XI. for Bibliography.)

CHAPTER XI

FOOD AT THE FACTORY

I. Introduction. II. Facilities Provided. III. Canteen Premises: Site; Extent; Payment; Canteen Suggestion Box; Reading Box. IV. Canteen Management: Canteen Committee; Finance: The Manager. V. The Menu. VI. Finally. VII. Bibliography.

I. Introduction.

THE consideration given in the previous chapter to the quantity and quality of food required by those doing industrial work raises the further question as to how steps can be taken to ensure that an adequate supply is consumed. The facts already stated would be of little practical value if means were not available for controlling, in part at least, the food eaten by workers. In the past this important matter has received scant attention in the great majority of factories; but during the war a great advance was made. Industrial canteens were erected at which, at the time of the armistice, over a million meals a day were being served. Previously the workers were left to fare for themselves; the result was not satisfactory.

Food brought by the Workers.—The custom prevailed, indeed, in many places still prevails, for workers, who lived too far away to return home for their mid-day meal, to bring food with them, and in some factories facilities were provided for heating such carried food. This custom is not good; industrial canteens are rapidly supplanting it. Carried food is often deficient in quantity; even when adequate from this point of view, it is frequently made up of remnants from the domestic table, which do not become any more appetising from confinement in a bundle for several hours, possibly since the previous evening. The gross energy values found (15) in four samples of carried food were as shown in the table on p. 260.

The additional amount of food taken at home cannot be readily ascertained, but the probability is that where the supply of carried food is inadequate and unappetising, the domestic menu will also be badly managed. " Experience indicates that for a large class of workers home meals are hurried and, especially for women workers, too often consist of white bread and boiled tea. A worker starting the day with a bread and tea breakfast, and walking or travelling for an hour or more to work, cannot

| Ingredients. | Weight in grammes. | | | | Calories. |
| | Gross. | Dry. | | | |
		Protein.	Fat.	Carbo-hydrate.	
(1) Meat . . .	87 ⎫				
Potato . .	100 ⎬	29·5	34·9	93·7	871
Pastry. . .	36 ⎭				
(2) Rabbit . .	112 ⎫	51·5	54·2	104·4	1,143
Pastry. . .	215 ⎭				
(3) Roast pork . .	70 ⎫				
Yorkshire pudding	72 ⎬	32·8	14·4	77·2	590
Potatoes . .	128 ⎮				
Cabbage . .	94 ⎭				
(4) Roast beef . .	78 ⎫				
Potatoes . .	64 ⎬	30·4	4·7	30·8	295
Cabbage . .	71 ⎮				
Haricot beans .	50 ⎭				

remain for long an efficient worker ; and probably much broken time and illness arise from this cause " (15).

Where no canteen or messroom is provided—and this group of factories still represents the majority—the workers take their food how and where they can. Often they tend to hide from onlookers so as to escape displaying the scanty provender they are allowing themselves. In other cases workers have been seen broiling their rasher of bacon on a red-hot horse shoe, or heating their can of stewed tea at a furnace.

Economy, comfort and cleanliness are all absent from such picnic meals, which rapidly lose any charm of novelty when taken day after day in the average environment to be found in industrial establishments.

II. Facilities Provided.

Every stage is to be found, from a complete lack of facilities up to the most modern development of the canteen ; these stages may be stated thus : (i.) a room may be set aside (usually inadequate as to cleanliness, lighting, heating and cheerfulness) in which workers may eat their carried food ; (ii.) the room may be fitted with a boiler to supply hot water, and a hot cupboard for warming food ; (iii.) the room may be rather better, with tables and chairs, and attendants provided to cook the food brought ; (iv.) a further advance

brings us to a canteen at which hot and cold food is supplied ;
(v.) lastly, there is the modern canteen combined under the
same roof with facilities for rest and recreation, *e.g.*, reading
room, billiard tables and gymnasium. While a case may be
made out for only providing in special instances (i.), (ii.), or
(iii.), according to the number employed, the character of the
work, or the nearness of the workers' homes, the ideal to aim
at in every case is (v.). A word of warning is required here ;
if an industrial canteen is to be a success, nothing less than the
best must be provided. Forms to sit on, plain tables to sit at
and rough earthenware to eat off, may fail entirely to attract
even a so-called rough class of labourer ; or if they do not fail,
only call forth rough treatment, breakages, and bad manners ;
while separate chairs, clean table cloths, flowers, good cutlery
and china, well chosen pictures and window curtains, nearly
invariably meet with the response they deserve, and so prove
economical in use while raising the whole tone of the factory
personnel. Give workers a canteen to be proud of and the canteen will soon be proud of its workers.

III. Canteen Premises.

Those about to construct a canteen will, we apprehend, not
be likely to rely entirely on information, however full, to be
found in this volume. We therefore, anticipating that reference
will be made to the explicit details given elsewhere (see Bibliography (17), (18) and (19)), only propose to refer to a few
guiding principles.

Site.—The choice is important ; if possible the windows
should face south and look out over a bowling green or a culti-
vated plot of ground on which meals may be taken in summer.
We recall one excellent canteen, where ground space was not
available, built on a flat factory roof ; it caught all the available
sunshine, and had an interesting outlook over an industrial
town ; some 8 feet, left between the outside factory walls and
the walls of the canteen, formed a parade which was much
appreciated in summer by the workers, and decorated by them
with evergreen bushes planted in wooden tubs. The position
chosen should be as central as possible to avoid waste of time in
transit from some outlying section of the works. Some advantage is gained by a ground floor site isolated from the rest of the
factory, with separate access for delivery of food.

Regard must, however, be had to convenience for drains,
water supply, and gas or electric light mains.

Extent.—The accommodation provided must include (i.) a

dining room, with serving counters of ample size, so as to avoid crowding ; the floor space required will vary with the number to be seated, for seventy persons about 11 square feet per person will be required, but for 300 persons, if the tables are well arranged, 8 square feet per person may be enough ; the window area should be ample, with a glass space not less than one-tenth of the floor area, and plenty of ventilation should be allowed for by hopper openings ; (ii.) a well-equipped kitchen ; the following scale is useful :—

No. of diners.			Size of kitchen.
100	.	.	. 20 feet by 15 feet.
300	.	.	. 25 ,, 20 ,,
400	.	.	. 30 ,, 25 ,,
500	.	.	. 35 ,, 25 ,,
1,000	.	.	. 50 ,, 30 ,,

(iii.) a scullery opening out of the kitchen, with a hatchway from the dining room for dirty plates; (iv.) store rooms and larder, the larder should face north and be well ventilated with perforated zinc panels to keep out flies ; (v.) a manager's office ; (vi.) sanitary accommodation, which in some cases may advantageously be combined with the lavatory and cloakroom installation of the factory ; (vii.) a paved yard for waste bins.

The first-aid station and rest rooms may often be usefully and economically constructed as part of the canteen block.

Service.—Probably the most important factor in deciding the popularity of a canteen is rapidity of service. In this respect an industrial canteen differs essentially from any other restaurant supplying mid-day meals, where the customers drop in one after another over a period of one and a half to two hours. Here, within three minutes of work stopping the whole number of customers present need to be served instantly. Maintenance of a staff of waitresses adequate to deal with such a rush, which only lasts a few minutes, would place an unnecessarily heavy charge on the expenses. The usual method adopted is to put the helpings out before-hand on the plates, place the plates on a heated counter within the serving hatch, and cover each plate with a metal cover so that others can be stacked on them. The workers then approach the serving hatch in single file behind a barrier, hand over their tickets, obtain their helpings, and take them to their seats. In a well-organised canteen, with adequate service within the hatch, every one should be served within ten minutes. Great advantage is gained by serving meat at one hatch, puddings at another, and tea or coffee at a third.

Where orders have been placed before, hand service can also be expedited by placing the food, a few minutes before the hooter goes, on the tables ready. Whatever method of service be decided upon, it is imperative that no money be paid at the serving time.

Payment.—The simplest plan is to sell tickets or tokens in batches sufficient for a week or more, the purchase of which can be effected at other times than the meal rush. There will, however, always be some extra persons who will require to buy their tickets at a ticket box before approaching the serving counter. All tickets, as handed in, should be dropped through a slit into a locked box.

Canteen Suggestion Box.—The provision of a suggestion box (see also p. 207) in the canteen for the reception of ideas and of complaints is useful. Suggestions made should be submitted to the canteen committee, referred to later, for consideration and action if thought advisable.

Reading Box.—A library in connection with a canteen is worth consideration, but another valuable and less ambitious institution is a reading box (21); in structure it is simple—just a large empty box. In this box are placed daily papers and magazines no longer required by any member of the firm or by the workers themselves. The habit of bringing picture papers and out-of-date magazines for deposit in the canteen reading box is readily developed. Scientific journals, dealing with engineering, the particular industry carried on, gardening, dressmaking, fashions, and the like, are useful material eagerly seized on. Catalogues and technical literature form valuable contributions; most firms receive more than are looked at in the office and consign them to the waste-paper basket; yet they represent the best effort of those who send them; under the proposed scheme they are read by the workers who, not infrequently, find therein matter valuable to the works and ideas which find their way into the general suggestion box. The keynote should be that everything placed in the reading box can be taken away by any one who likes. Once instituted, the employer will be astonished to find how the box is cleared daily, while he has at his disposal a ready means for directing the workers' line of thought into any desired channel. Education can be advanced, and inventive faculties stimulated.

Tea Trolleys.—A valuable adjunct to a canteen is the institution of tea trolleys. similar to those to be found on railway platforms, for conveying into the work places hot tea and light refreshments. The value of a light meal during a long morning spell, or more particularly in the mid-afternoon, to work has been remarked upon by investigators of output. The progress of work is hardly affected as the trolley goes by and each worker obtains what is desired. Judged by their popularity among the workers tea trolleys are a conspicuous success, a sufficient reason of itself for maintaining them ; they have also the effect of putting an end to promiscuous tea taking which, in some establishments, has definitely interfered with order and discipline.

IV. Canteen Management.

The employer should not burden himself with details of management, they should rather be delegated to a committee and an expert staff.

Canteen Committee.—Canteen management is skilled work, and must be entrusted to an expert. But, if everything is left in his hands, sooner or later suspicion is bound to arise that undue profits are being made ; the best step to take is to appoint an advisory committee of the workers, and place them in charge of all canteen affairs. The duties of such a committee are numerous ; not only will they examine accounts, but they will be responsible for order and discipline, organise concerts and entertainments to occupy the last half of the meal time ; they will consider complaints, put down pilfering which is liable to become a serious matter, and express the workers' fancies in the matter of new dishes. We feel strongly that co-operation with the workers through a canteen advisory committee possessing inside knowledge and responsibility is practically a necessity. Any one familiar with the history of " tommy-shops " and the Truck Acts, will require no argument to convince him on this matter.

Finance.—A canteen should always be made to pay its way. Well disposed firms, recognising the value to the workers of good food, may feel inclined to give financial support ; but this tendency should be resisted, otherwise workers look upon this support as money which should more legitimately have been distributed as wages. An effort should rather be made to secure a small profit to be placed at the disposal of the canteen committee for use as they think fit, whether for additional comforts in the way of pictures, table decoration, library, recreation, or entertainments.

The Manager.—The management must be entrusted to a skilled person who understands the importance and methods of book-keeping ; and his proceedings should in his own interest be checked from time to time by calling in the aid of an accountant accustomed to auditing the books of hotels and restaurants. He should know (i.) the value of bin cards ; (ii.) how to conduct portion-analysis ; (ii.) how to adjust the supply of *leading-lines*, *e.g.*, joints, and of other more paying commodities, such as tea and puddings ; (iv.) the proportion of the turn-over, not exceeding 25 per cent. spent on wages ; and (v.) how to adjust his selling prices so as to obtain a gross average profit of $33\frac{1}{2}$ per cent. on the buying prices. These are matters upon which other publications should be consulted (see (20)).

V. The Menu.

Energy supplied in food should be distributed as follows :— One-fifth should be derived from protein, one-quarter from fat, and about one-half from carbohydrates. The caterer in arranging his menu on scientific lines will require to know not only on general lines the amount of energy, as expressed in calories, a mid-day meal should contain, and the proportion of this energy which should be supplied in the form of protein, carbohydrate and fat ; but the actual amount of energy and the form in which it exists in common articles of food. The facts are stated in the following table :—

	Protein.		Fat.		Carbohydrates.		Total calories per lb.
	Grms. in 1 lb.	Calories per lb.	Grms. in 1 lb.	Calories per lb.	Grms. in 1 lb.	Calories per lb.	
Beef* (imported)	58·97	241·8	108·86	1012·4	—	—	1254·2
Mutton* (imported)	40·82	167·4	158·76	1476·5	—	—	1643·9
Pork	45·36	186·0	181·46	1687·6	—	—	1873·6
Fresh fish	45·40	186·1	4·50	41·9	—	—	228·0
Dried fish	88·90	364·5	24·20	225·1	—	—	589·6
Lard (refined)	—	—	453·60	4218·5	—	—	4218·5
Butter*	·45	1·8	371·95	3459·1	—	—	3460·9
Margarine*	·45	1·8	381·00	3543·3	—	—	3545·1
Sugar	—	—	—	—	444·50	1822·5	1822·5
Syrup	—	—	—	—	323·90	1328·0	1328·0
Jam*	—	—	—	—	317·52	1301·8	1301·8
Green vegetables	7·26	29·8	1·72	16·0	19·00	77·9	123·7
Mixed vegetables	3·45	14·1	·68	6·3	18·10	74·2	94·6
Fresh fruit	2·27	9·3	·91	8·5	54·40	223·0	240·8
Apples	1·40	5·7	1·40	13·0	49·00	200·9	219·6
Bananas	3·60	14·8	1·80	16·7	64·70	265·3	296·8
Potatoes* (raw)	9·07	37·2	—	—	90·72	372·0	409·2
Bread*	31·75	130·2	·45	4·2	217·73	892·7	1027·1
Flour*	45·36	186·0	6·80	63·2	340·20	1394·8	1644·0
Oatmeal	73·00	299·3	32·70	304·1	306·20	1255·5	1858·9
Milk*	13·61	55·8	13·61	126·6	20·41	83·7	266·1
Rice, sago, cornflour.	36·40	149·2	3·02	28·1	356·07	1459·9	1637·2
Sausages*	40·82	167·4	81·65	759·3	68·04	279·0	1205·7
Bacon	43·00	176·3	272·20	2531·5	—	—	2707·8
Dried peas, beans, lentils	108·80	446·1	6·80	63·2	272·20	1116·0	1625·3
Fresh peas and beans	12·92	53·0	1·13	10·5	37·88	155·3	218·8
Eggs (one egg weighs 2 ozs.)	54·40	223·0	43·10	400·8	—	—	623·8
Cheese	113·40	464·9	136·00	1264·8	11·30	46·3	1776·0

* In calculating the entries of this table, the calorie equivalents of 1 gramme of protein of carbohydrate and of fat have been taken as 4·1, 4·1 and 9·3. The analyses used in the items marked with an asterisk refer to substances on the English market in the last year of the war ; other analyses were, for the most part, pre-war.

Suggestions are given on p. 266 as to the way in which food may be combined to give in the mid-day meal somewhere about one-third of a daily dietary of 3,000 calories, that is, one-third of an average daily dietary for a *woman* worker (15). The total daily dietary for a male worker on the same scale would require to amount to 3,750 calories, that is to say, his mid-day meal should approximate to 1,250 calories.

Suggested Dinners for Munition Workers.

Speci- men.	Ingredients.	Weight in grammes.				Calories.
			Dry.			
		Gross.	Pro- tein.	Fat.	Carbo- hydrate.	
No. 1.	Meat pudding . .	120				
	Potatoes . .	200				
	Cabbage . .	120	32·0	52·1	178·4	1,346·0
	Pudding (jam roll) .	160				
No. 2.	Roast beef . .	78				
	Yorkshire pudding .	110				
	Potatoes . .	200	44·3	32·3	122·2	983·0
	Cabbage . .	140				
	Apple pie and custard	171				
No. 3.	Liver . . .	80				
	Bacon . . .	20				
	Potatoes . .	200	53·6	25·3	158·4	1,101·7
	Peas (preserved) .	134				
	Sago pudding . .	250				
No. 4.	Roast beef . .	110				
	Potatoes . .	182				
	Cabbage . .	77	40	30	101	837
	Syrup roll . .	120				
No. 5.	Roast beef . .	80				
	Potatoes . .	200				
	Peas . . .	150	33·4	25·0	132·8	1,002·6
	Currant pudding .	136				

The next table given sets out a weekly dinner menu as suggested by the Canteen Committee of the Central Control Board (17).

Weekly Dinner Menu.

Monday.	Tuesday.	Wednesday.	Thursday.	Friday.	Saturday.
Scotch broth.	Pea soup.	Mutton broth.	Lentil soup.	Vegetable soup.	Tomato soup.
Roast beef. Sausages and mashed potatoes.	Boiled mutton. Curried beef and rice.	Roast pork. Irish stew.	Boiled beef and carrots. Tripe and onions.	Roast mutton. Steak and kidney pie or pudding.	Liver and bacon. Potato pie.
Stewed fruit. Ginger pudding.	Stewed fruit. Jam roll.	Stewed fruit. Rice or sago pudding.	Stewed fruit. Apple tart.	Stewed fruit. Bread and butter pudding.	Stewed fruit. Raisin pudding.

Examples may also be of value taken from menus actually provided by two firms with good welfare departments representing two different types of industry (see pp. 268–9). Although the exact amounts served could not be ascertained, the amount of meat in the menu for the cotton operatives would appear to be less than for the engineering workers, just as would be anticipated from our remarks on p. 254.

VI. Finally.

A factory canteen, apart from its primary object of supplying wholesome food under favourable conditions, has in it great possibilities as a social institution, where workers meet, make friends, and learn to be part of, and take part in, the life of what should be a valuable humanising influence—their industrial home.

VII. Bibliography.

1. Benedict, Miles, Roth and Smith. *Human Vitality and Efficiency under Prolonged Restricted Diet.* Carnegie Institute. Washington. 1919.

2. Cathcart and Orr. *The Energy Expenditure of the Infantry Recruit in Training.* Stationery Office. 1919.

3. Dunluce and Greenwood. *Medical Research Committee. Special Report Series, No.* 13. Stationery Office. 1918.

4. Greenwood, Hodson and Tebb. *Proc. Roy. Soc. B.,* XCI., p. 62. 1919.

5. Greenwood and Thompson. *Proc. Roy. Soc. of Medicine* (Section of Epidemiology and State Medicine), XI., p. 61. 1918.

6. Lusk. *Elements of the Science of Nutrition.* 3rd Edition. London. 1917.

7. Royal Society (Food, War Committee). *Report on the Food Requirements of Man.* Harrison & Sons. London. 1919.

8. Amar. *Le Rendement de la Machine Humaine.* Paris. 1910.

9. Howard. *An Inquiry into the Morbid Effects of Deficiency of Food,* p. 28. London. 1839.

10. " Report on Present State of Knowledge concerning Accessory Food Factors (Vitamines)." *Medical Research Committee. Special Report Series, No.* 38. 1919.

11. *Physiology and National Needs.* Edited by W. D. Halliburton. Constable & Co., Ltd. 1919.

12. Rowntree. *Poverty : A Study of Town Life.* 1902.

13. Greenwood and Thompson. *Brit. Med. Journ.* August 10th, 1918.

14. " Working Classes." *Cost of Living Committee.* (Cd. 8980.) 1918.

15. Hill, L. E. " Investigation of Workers' Food." *Health of Munition Workers Committee. Memo. No.* 11. (Cd. 8370.) 1916.

16. Benedict and Cathcart. *Muscular Work, Metabolic Study.* Washington. 1913.

17. " Feeding the Munition Worker." *Canteen Committee of the Central Control Board (Liquor Traffic).* 1916.

(*Continued on p.* 270.)

Factory Dinner Menus.

Day of week.	Cotton mill.	Engineering factory.			
		Hostel menus.		Specimen canteen menus.	
		Men.	Women.	Men.	Women.
MONDAY	Irish stew. Currant pudding. Rice. Tapioca.	Mutton chops. Boiled ham. Roast mutton. Irish stew. Cabbage, potatoes. Peas. Fig pudding. Pineapple custard.	Roast beef. Roast potatoes. Cabbage. Gooseberry tart. Stewed apricots. Custard.	Thick mulligatawny. Minced lamb and green peas. Roast sirloin beef. Ribs of beef. York ham. Pressed beef. Lettuce salad. New potatoes. Baked beans. Blanc mange and jam. Stewed figs and rice.	Thick mulligatawny. Minced lamb, green peas and new potatoes. Roast sirloin beef and two vegetables. York ham. Rib of beef. Pressed beef. Salad. New potatoes. Heinz baked beans. Blanc mange and jam. Stewed figs and rice.
TUESDAY	Cold ham. Potatoes. Custard tart. Rice, sago.	Roast veal and bacon. Steak and onions. Cabbage, potatoes. Jam pudding. Sago pudding.	Roast veal and ham stuffing. Peas, potatoes. Gooseberry tart.		

WEDNESDAY	Potato pie. Rice. Tapioca.	Stewed veal and peas. Roast beef. Roast mutton. Cabbage, potatoes. Stewed figs. Custard.	Roast beef. Cabbage. Potatoes. Baked jam roll.
THURSDAY	Roast meat. Potatoes. Plain suet and jam. Rice. Tapioca.	Boiled veal and parsley sauce. Roast beef. Steak and kidney pudding. Turnips and potatoes. Pineapple, rice. Suet pudding and jam.	Stewed veal and parsley sauce. Cabbage, potatoes. Bread pudding with raisins. Custard.
FRIDAY	Boiled fish. Potatoes. Stewed gooseberries and custard. Rice. Sago.	Boiled beef. Dumplings. Roast mutton. Cabbage, potatoes. Raisin pudding. Stewed fruit and custard.	Roast beef. Cabbage. Potatoes. Date pudding.
SATURDAY		Irish stew. Boiled ham. Roast beef. Roast mutton. Cabbage, peas. Potatoes. Date pudding. Stewed fruit and rice.	Veal and ham pie. Steak pie. Boiled cod and parsley sauce. Potatoes. Haricots. Marmalade pudding. Boiled custard.

18. " Canteen Construction and Equipment." *Health of Munition Workers Committee. Memo. No. 6.* (Cd. 8199.) 1916.

19. " Mess Rooms and Canteens." *Home Office Paper.* 1918.

20. Hall, M. J. " Food at the Works." *The Industrial Clinic.* Bale, Son and Danielsson, Ltd. 1920.

21. Gilbreth, F. B. *Fatigue Study.* George Routledge & Son. 1916.

22. *Board of Trade. Report of an Enquiry by, into Working Class Rents.* (Cd. 6955.) 1913.

23. Hill, L. E. " Food Values in Relation to Occupation." *The Industrial Clinic.* Bale, Son and Danielsson, Ltd. 1920.

CHAPTER XII

THE USE OF ALCOHOLIC BEVERAGES BY THE INDUSTRIAL WORKER

I. Introduction. II. Physiological Effect of Alcohol. III. Psycho-physiological Results. IV. Rise of the Spirit-drinking Habit. V. Contrast between Industrial and Convivial Drinking. VI. The Charm of Alcohol. VII. Conclusion. VIII. Bibliography.

I. Introduction.

WE have entered upon the preparation of this chapter with reluctance; few subjects are more difficult to handle and few are more interwoven with strands of prejudice, of bad reasoning and of deliberate falsehood. Study of the literature of this subject will convince the most optimistic that the time when grave problems of social hygiene will be discussed dispassionately is indefinitely remote. Such a student will discover vulgar cupidity masquerading as love of liberty or regard for the rights of the working man; he will also find " bigotry, self-conceit, an insolent curiosity, a meddlesome temper, a cold-blooded criticism, founded on a shallow interpretation of half perceptions, a monstrous scepticism in regard to any conscience of any wisdom, except one's own; a most irreverent propensity to thrust Providence aside and substitute one's self in its awful place." Small wonder that many well fitted to elucidate the problem shun it and devote their energies to subjects which have not excited so many and so ignoble passions. It is, however, impossible for us wholly to avoid a consideration of the use of strong drink in a book devoted to the hygiene of industry; in the following pages we shall set out such facts and inferences as are, in our opinion, important to the student of industrial hygiene.

II. Physiological Effect of Alcohol.

We must, to begin with, refer to the *rôle* of alcohol in the physiological processes of the human body. This subject needs but little space, because a clear and adequate account has been rendered in the report of a committee appointed during the war by the Central Control Board (Liquor Traffic) which the reader, if he has not already done so, should study carefully (1). The essential results are these :—(*a*) Both ethylic alcohol itself and other substances present in alcoholic beverages are capable of oxidation in the body, and thus render available to its cells the biotic energy which it is a principal function of food to supply ;

(*b*) therefore, alcohol itself and alcoholic beverages have a restricted right to be termed *foods ;* (*c*) but this right *is* a restricted one because other actions of alcohol upon the systems of the body come into play after a quite small amount has been ingested, and may rapidly counterbalance the advantages in respect of energy supply by disadvantages of greater or less moment ; and (*d*) as a source of energy for the body, within the restricted limits mentioned, alcohol is neither more nor less valuable than other oxidisable substances.

We may conclude from these facts that for the normal man or woman alcohol as a source of energy cannot compete with the ordinary means of stoking the human engine which we discussed in the chapter on diets (see Chapter X.).   There is reason to suppose that in certain diseases, especially diabetes mellitus where the body cannot use carbohydrates, the fact that a fraction of the needed energy can be derived from alcohol is of importance in treatment ; but this has no relevance to the case of a healthy man.   In truth the physiological conclusions which we have just reached are concordant with the common experience of life. Nobody makes, or ever has made, a practice of drinking alcohol for the sake of its food value.   Arguments that beer, wines, and spirits are foods are usually *ex post facto* rationalisations, *i.e.*, attempts to give a reasoned explanation of actions the motives of which lie deeper than the little stratum of our conscious thoughts.   We explore this deeper region a few paragraphs further on ; first we have to notice some simple physiological or rather psycho-physiological results.

III.   Psycho-physiological Results.

Many observers have attempted to measure the effects upon the performance of skilled or semi-skilled movements of ingested alcohol.   The interpretation of such experiments is always hard because, as we shall soon see, the main action of alcohol is exerted upon the highest functions of the psycho-neural apparatus, and because it is extremely difficult to disguise from the subject of the experiment the fact that he has taken a dose of alcohol. In the most recent series of experiments any attempt at disguise was abandoned, but the subjects of the experiment were mostly trained observers.   An account of the work is contained in a recent report of the Medical Research Committee (2) drawn up by Dr. Vernon.   From these we quote a series of experiments made by one of us.   A passage consisting of nine Latin hexa-meter lines was learned by heart, and each day's experiment consisted in typing the passage four times before and four times after dinner.   A comparison was instituted between the results of typing after dinner when alcohol was and was not taken. When a single glass of port wine was drunk (containing 18·5 c.c. of absolute alcohol) there was no appreciable difference either in the speed or accuracy of the typing. When the quantity was increased to two glasses (37 c.c. of absolute alcohol) there was an increase in the number of mistakes amounting to nearly 80 per cent.

Another series of experiments was made using, not a typewriter, but an adding machine, *i.e.*, an instrument that the subject had not used with such frequency and regularity as the type-writer—there it was found that a smaller quantity of alcohol was associated with deterioration. " If the alcohol experiments with food be compared against a mean of non-alcohol experiments made before and after, the deterioration, measured in terms of mistakes, amounts to 42 per cent., whilst a similar comparison in the fasting experiments shows a deterioration of 74 per cent." (2, p. 55). In this series 15·3 c.c. of absolute alcohol in the form of claret were taken with food or 19·4 c.c. without food.

Many similar experiments carried out by Dr. Vernon, Dr. Sullivan and others led to similar results. Dr. Vernon summarises the conclusions of the whole inquiry in the following terms :—" Alcohol produced some effect in all of the individuals tested by the typing and adding-machine methods. The degree of effect depended largely on whether the alcohol was taken on an empty stomach or with food, for on an average it was about twice as toxic under the former conditions as under the latter. In the foodless experiments, one subject made 88 per cent. more typing mistakes after she drank 11·2 c.c. of alcohol. Another subject increased his adding-machine mistakes 74 per cent. after taking claret containing 19·4 c.c. of alcohol ; another increased her typing mistakes 156 per cent. after drinking sherry containing 22 c.c. of alcohol.

" In some subjects a moderate dose of alcoholic liquid, taken with food, produced no measurable reaction. Such a non-reactive dose amounted to one glass of port (= 18·5 c.c. alcohol) in a male subject, and to 4 ozs. of port (= 22 c.c. alcohol) in a female subject.

" The effect reached its maximum half an hour after taking alcohol on an empty stomach, and might completely disappear in two hours. When the alcohol was taken with food, the effect was slightly longer in reaching its maximum.

" When alcohol (30 c.c.) was taken in 5 per cent. strength, the effect produced was about three-fourths as great as when it was taken in 20 per cent. or 40 per cent. solution. A similar difference was observed when taking diluted brandy (10 per cent. alcohol) and neat brandy (37 per cent. alcohol) " (2, pp. 59—60).

Dr. Vernon's conclusions receive support from Dr. Edward Mellanby, who was led by a series of experiments on dogs to infer that " whereas alcohol, when present in low concentrations in the body, undergoes combustion at a more rapid rate during exercise than at rest, and therefore supplies a greater amount of energy to the active organism, at higher concentrations it is only oxidised at the same rate in the resting and active animal.   In other words, the greater the toxic action of alcohol the more limited is the increase in its rate of combustion by exercise, and the closer do the rates of combustion of alcohol in the active and resting states approximate.   Alcohol at high concentrations seems not only to have this self limiting action on its own oxidative process, but, if fatigue is a true indication of diminished or partial oxidation, to extend its baneful and detrimental influence to the limitation of the oxidation of other combustible material " (3, p. 48).

Vernon in another publication (7) gives reasons, based on an investigation made into factory records, for holding that consumption of alcohol increases the prevalence of industrial accidents ; a result to be anticipated from the increase in errors which occurred in the experiments referred to above.

The numerical details of these different inquiries are, of course, without exactitude, but the general trend of the results leads to the conclusion that quite small doses of alcohol diminish the accuracy with which skilled or semi-skilled neuro-muscular processes are carried out.*   Hence, we may conclude that :—

(1) Alcoholic beverages as a food, offer the normal adult no advantages over less equivocally designated foods ; and

(2) As preliminaries to work, they either do nothing or harm.

IV. Rise of the Spirit-Drinking Habit.

We have, as a nation, always had the reputation of hard drinkers, as exemplified perhaps by Hamlet's criticism of the Danish revels :—

> " But to my mind—though I am native here
> And to the manner born—it is a custom
> More honoured in the breach than the observance.
> This heavy-headed revel east and west
> Makes us traduced and taxed of other nations ;
> They clepe us drunkards, and with swinish phrase
> Soil our addition."

* McDougall & Smith (8) using a different method reach conclusions in agreement with those of Vernon & Mellanby with regard to dilution.

Nevertheless, intemperance as a serious national vice of the working classes seems not to be older than the second decade of the eighteenth century. The only spirit in common use in the seventeenth century was brandy, but it was too costly to be popular, and the habit of spirit drinking remained the privilege of the rich until the next century, when the distillers began to produce whisky and gin (6). " It was not," says Lecky, " until about 1724 that the passion for gin drinking appears to have infected the masses of the population, and it spread with the rapidity and violence of an epidemic. Small as is the place which this fact occupies in English history, it was probably, if we consider all the consequences that have flowed from it, the most momentous in that of the eighteenth century—incomparably more so than any event in the purely political or military annals of the country. The fatal passion for drink was at once, and irrevocably, planted in the nation. The average of British spirits distilled, which is said to have been only 527,000 gallons in 1684, and 2,000,000 in 1714, had risen in 1727 to 3,601,000, and in 1735 to 5,394,000 gallons. Physicians declared that in excessive gin drinking a new and terrible source of mortality had been opened for the poor. The grand jury of Middlesex, in a powerful presentment, declared that much the greater part of the poverty, the murders, the robberies of London, might be traced to this single cause " (4, Vol. 2, p. 101). By 1751 the estimated consumption of spirits reached 11 millions of gallons, and in that year Hogarth's engraving of Gin Lane was published with its inscription, " drunk for a penny, dead drunk for two-pence, clean straw for nothing," and the illustrious Fielding declared that " gin was the principal sustenance (if it may be so called) of more than 100,000 people in the metropolis."

Legislation was carried in 1751, which seems to have had some effect. Heberden, writing in 1801, remarked that " dropsy," which, as a cause of death in the London bills of mortality, had attained remarkable dimensions between 1718 and 1751, immediately diminished. " Still," to quote Lecky again, " these measures formed a palliative and not a cure, and from the early years of the eighteenth century gin drinking has never ceased to be the main counteracting influence to the moral, intellectual and physical benefits that might be expected from increased commercial prosperity " (4, vol. 2, p. 104).

These historical notes have not been interpolated at random. The point to mark is that the consumption of intoxicants, particularly spirits, began to be excessive in the generation which witnessed the birth of modern industrialism, and, as

18—2

Lecky remarks, the attendant evils have been prominent ever since. Industrialism and intemperance may not be cause and effect, but the variables are correlated ; to explain their connection we must digress into statistics.

V.   Contrast between Industrial and Convivial Drinking.

Dr. W. C. Sullivan, in his valuable essay on alcoholism (5), pointed out that, judged by the number of arrests for drunkenness, Durham was easily the most intemperate county in England.   The annual arrests per 100,000 (1891—1900) were 2,228·8 in Durham, 1,543·8 in Northumberland, 1,012·9 in South Wales, and below 1,000 in every other county ; the metropolitan police district had only 748·7, the industrial West Riding of Yorks only 644·1.   Now these " drunk and disorderly " counties are the great coal fields of England and Wales, so that we might expect to find that coal miners die at exceptionally heavy rates of diseases supposed to be caused or exacerbated by alcohol.

The direct contrary is found.   Taking the mortality of all males in England and Wales from alcoholism and diseases of the liver as 100, the mortality of coal miners from these causes was fifty-one in 1900–2.   In the following decennium the mortality of all males from these causes declined considerably, but the decline amongst miners very nearly kept pace with that amongst all males, and in 1910—12 coal miners had only 57 per cent. of the standard mortality.   Dr. Sullivan further pointed out that in seaports, although the convictions for drunkenness were less numerous than in the mining districts, the death rates from alcoholism and from diseases of the liver were very much higher. The occupational group of dock labourers dies from these causes at a very high rate indeed ; at a rate of 167 per cent. of the standard in 1900—02 and of 187 per cent. of the standard in 1910—12.

The conclusion plainly follows that in the social pathology of alcoholism, drunkenness in the police court sense has not the same effects as other methods of indulgence.   A study of the industrial habits of the two groups of employed persons we have mentioned at once makes the distinction clear.   Dr. Sullivan writes as follows of coal mining (and one of us can confirm his impressions from personal observation) : " In this industry the conditions that determine the drinking habits of the workers are uniform and distinctive to a degree, which we do not find in any other occupational group.   Whatever differences exist between the coal fields of one district and those of another, and however these differences may affect the methods of working, they are as nothing compared with the characters that are shared in common, and which, from our point of view at all events, make all coal mines essentially alike. Of these characters, besides the general similarity in the muscular work involved in coal getting, the most important are the constantly large scale of the operations, which prevents those contrasts between large and small employers so frequently met with in other trades ; the length of the spells of work which, owing to the difficulty of access to the place of labour, are more prolonged than in other industries, and finally, the extreme danger of drunkenness in the pit, a danger which, as it affects many interests, leads to a correspondingly rigorous supervision of the sobriety of the individual workman. . . . By the circumstances under which he works the miner is practically cut off from all access to liquor during the eight or ten hours which he spends in the pit. . . . In the result, therefore, the coal miner has, at most, an opportunity for having a single dose of alcohol before he gets to work, and as its stimulant effect does not last long he speedily realises that beer is a ' muddling ' thing to work on " (5, p. 106).

Conditions are very different in riverside labour. Besides the regular intervals for breakfast and dinner, a general practice used to be to sanction pauses, " bever times," one in the forenoon and one in the afternoon. A docker would take a " livener " of half a quartern of rum before starting work, or perhaps a glass of " four ale " ; at breakfast he might drink a pint of ale ; from one to three half-pints would be the allowance at the first " bever time " ; dinner would be the occasion of another pint or two ; the second " bever time " would correspond to the first, and on knocking off work another pint or two might be imbibed (5, p. 80).

The two instances we have selected are, of course, extremes ; they illustrate, however, a fundamentally important distinction which can be used with more or less success to grade all forms of industry. The distinction is between what in a mild form is convivial excess, in an extreme form drunken debauch, on the one hand, and the practice of using alcoholic beverages continuously, what Dr. Sullivan happily terms industrial drinking, on the other.

Both practices lead to enormous social evils, but they are not equally relevant to the subject of this treatise. With regard to the former we have nothing to say. Crimes committed under the influence of alcohol, actions falling short of legal criminality which have destroyed the chance of happiness and embittered the lives of so many, *these* are topics which more skilful writers than we have many times described.

VI. The Charm of Alcohol.

The less dramatic circumstances of industrial drinking are more properly our business. We pointed out in earlier paragraphs that the use of alcohol never improves and often deteriorates industrial efficiency and that, as a " food," it cannot compete with less attractive articles. What virtues does it possess which endow it with such powers of attraction ? The answer has been given in the following words—" the secret of its charm, its well-nigh universal attraction for the human race is a sense of careless well-being or bodily and mental comfort. In so far as this sense of well-being is of bodily origin, it is no doubt largely due to a flushing of the skin with blood that abolishes all sense of chill, but it is due also in part to a blunting of the sensibility to the small aches and pains and a thousand hardly distinguishable sense impressions which, except in those in perfect health, contribute to tip the balance of bodily feeling-tone to the negative or unpleasant side. In so far as this effect is primarily mental, it results from the blunting of those higher mental faculties which lead us to ' look before and after and pine for what is not,' and harass us with care for the future and a too sensitive self-consciousness for the present " (1, p. 31). If we recall the conditions of factory labour in the days of the industrial revolution, even in the last generation, even in some industries in the present generation, we shall not find it hard to recognise the " thousand sense impressions " which do very decisively tip over the balance of bodily feeling-tone to the negative or unpleasant side.

These facts having been grasped, the industrial phenomena of alcoholism appear in their proper perspective. Hedonism is, doubtless, a poor ethical creed, but in practice we are all hedonists in greater or less measure. If the conditions of our lives are such that the task of the moment is irksome and anticipation of future pleasure but faint, we shall certainly try

> " . . . . Something to snatch
> From dull oblivion, nor all
> Glut the devouring grave."

When positive increments of happiness are excluded, some decrement of present misery, by a blunting of the psychic sensitiveness to the discomfort of environment, is afforded by a narcotic drug. This is the real case in favour of alcohol as a beverage ; it *does* increase the agreeableness of life as lived by a majority in the past and a very large minority in the present. The addiction of the labouring classes to drink should be regarded not as an opportunity for gratifying the desire to preach at other people, which is so common in the half-educated middle and upper classes, but as a protective reaction to the stimulus of conditions which have deprived millions of positive opportunities to lead full and happy lives. The business of the hygienist is not elaborately to refute factitious arguments in favour of the physiological merits of alcoholic beverages or to waste words over the " selective " value of alcohol as a factor of racial evolution, but to point out that all the conditions (discussed in other chapters of this book), which improve the moral and material conditions of labour in factories diminish the motive of industrial drinking and must, *pro tanto*, restrict its amount.

VII. Conclusion.

The industrial problem of alcohol is not *sui generis*, but part and parcel of the whole question of industrial-social organisation. Hence, we can only refer to the other chapters of this book in which we have incorporated suggestions of a general kind. The conclusions now to be expressed are these :—

(1) Physiologically, alcohol is never required by a healthy man, whatever his occupation.

(2) Industrially, alcohol never improves and usually impairs efficiency.

(3) But owing to its narcotic action it diminishes the present discomfort of work carried on in depressing conditions, in itself uninteresting and holding out no pleasurable anticipations of the future ; hence, in badly conducted industries the attraction of alcohol is immense.

(4) This present alleviation of misery is purchased at the cost, *inter alia*, of an enhanced general death rate.

(5) The reduction of industrial drinking is indissolubly connected with the general hygienic and sociological amelioration of industrial conditions.

VIII. Bibliography.

1. *Alcohol, its Action on the Human Organism.* H.M. Stationery Office. 1918.

2. Vernon, H. M. " The Influence of Alcohol on Manual Work and Neuro-Muscular Co-ordination." *Medical Research Committee. Special Report, No. 34.* 1919.

3. Mellanby, E. " Alcohol, its Absorption Into and Disappearance From the Blood under Different Conditions." *Medical Research Committee. Special Report, No. 31.* 1919.

4. Lecky. *History of England in the Eighteenth Century.* Popular Edition, 7 Volumes. 1913.

5. Sullivan, W. C. *Alcoholism : A Chapter in Social Pathology.* Nisbet, London. 1906.

6. Traill, H. D., and Mann, J. S. *Social England,* Vol. V., pp. 180–1. Cassell & Co., Ltd. 1904.

7. Vernon, H. M. " An Investigation of the Factors Concerned in the Causation of Industrial Accidents." *Health of Munition Workers Committee. Memo. No.* 21. (Cd. 9046.) 1918.

8. McDougall, W., and Smith, M. "The Effects of Alcohol and some other Drugs during Normal and Fatigued Conditions." *Medic. Research Council. Spec. Rep. No.* 56. 1920.

CHAPTER XIII

REASONS FOR AND METHODS OF VENTILATION

I. Introduction.

HEALTH is more affected by atmospheric conditions than by any other influence. From the moment the new-born child utters its first cry, until life finally ceases, he is directly and immediately dependent on the atmosphere he breathes for continued existence. Records of sickness and of mortality clearly show that the nearer atmospheric conditions are to those of the open country, the better is the health of the population ; and that the more these conditions are modified owing to urbanisation and industrialisation, the more pronounced is the ill-effect upon general health.

The effects are manifested on the very threshold of life. Chadwick (1) states :—" In the space of four years, ending in 1784, in a badly ventilated house, the Lying-in Hospital in Dublin, there died 2,944 children out of 7,650, but after freer ventilation the deaths in the same period of time, and in a like number of children, amounted only to 279." Brend (2), after close investigation into excessive infant mortality, has recently concluded :—" The excess is due to some factor or factors in industrial towns, the centres of large cities, and mining areas, of which possibly the most important is the polluted state of the atmosphere " ; and supports this conclusion by pointing out that the causes of death to which the excess is due are mainly respiratory diseases, and to a lesser extent enteritis, which are most prevalent in crowded, smoky industrial and mining districts.

The effects are manifest also in adult life, as was pointed out by Chadwick in 1842. He presents the conditions of tailors' work in London at that time ; eighty men in a room 16 or 18 yards long and 7 or 8 yards wide, lighted by skylights, sitting nearly knee and knee, with an atmosphere in summer 20 degrees higher than outside, and the perspiration so running from them as to spoil the clothes they worked at ; while in the winter things were worse, and in the very coldest nights large thick tallow candles melted and fell over from the heat. The smell was intolerable and men fainted at the work. Few of such men reached fifty years of age, and out of 233 tailors who died in 1839 in the Metropolis, 123 died of disease of the respiratory organs, of whom 92 died of consumption ; only 29 died of old age, and Chadwick states " we may be profoundly confident that the greater proportion of them were not journeymen but master-tailors." He further wrote : " Of that which in these instances appears to be the main cause of premature disease and death, defective ventilation, it is to be remarked that until very lately little had been observed or understood even by professional men or men of science."

Nor is this relation between ventilation and disease confined to men. Rossignol (3) states that "previous to 1836 the mortality of the French cavalry horses varied from 180 to 197 per 1,000 per annum. The enlargement of the stables and the increased allowance of air, has reduced the loss in the present day to 24·2 per 1,000. In the English cavalry (and in English racing stables) the same facts are well known. The annual mortality of cavalry horses (which was formerly great) is now (1895) reduced to 23·7 per 1,000."

Intimate as the connection undoubtedly is between ventilation and general well-being and physical efficiency, investigations (19) aimed at determining what, if any, influence ventilation exerts upon mental work have entirely failed to establish any clear connection. Is this the reason why ventilation in the average clerical office is so hopelessly lacking ?

Further evidence as to the importance of ventilation, especially in connection with industrial life, is unnecessary ; but the aim and object to be attained by ventilation, whether in workplaces or elsewhere cannot be grasped without an understanding of the composition of the atmosphere and of the way in which the human body depends upon and reacts to atmospheric conditions ; while the means to be adopted cannot be approached until the aim to be attained is settled.

II. The Air.

The influence exerted upon health by air depends upon (i.) its chemical composition ; (ii.) its physical properties ; and (iii.) its impurities. The physiological functions concerned are (a) breathing carried on by the respiratory apparatus which depends on the chemical composition of the air ; (*b*) heat regulation, carried on mainly by the skin ; and (*c*) resistance to infection.

(i.) *Chemical Composition.*

For practical purposes average air may be taken to contain in every 10,000 parts :—

Oxygen	2,094
Nitrogen	7,809
Argon	94
CO_2	3
Helium, Krypton, Neon, Xenon and Hydrogen	} Traces.

These gases are not chemically combined, but exist as a mechanical uniform mixture, the uniformity of which is maintained by the diffusion of gases. There are also present aqueous vapour and traces of ammonia, organic matter and ozone.

Nitrogen, which forms so large a proportion of the air, is an inactive gas which only comes to form part of living matter by indirect means. Hill claims (25) that " the so-called ' active oxygen ' of fresh country air is not ozone but nitrogen peroxide, probably formed by ultra-violet rays of sunlight causing the direct union of nitrogen and oxygen." Electric discharges may cause nitrogen to combine with oxygen to form oxides, which when washed down by rain can be assimiliated by plant life ; or it can be converted into nitrogenous compounds by nitrifying bacteria. Nitrogen takes no part in respiration except as a diluent of oxygen.

Argon similarly is an inert gas which takes no part in the chemistry of life ; and the same remark applies to helium, krypton, neon, and xenon.

Oxygen is the active constituent of air without which life could not exist. It is the agent which makes combustion possible. Combustion, *i.e.*, the union of oxygen with other elements to form oxides—of which the ordinary coal fire is a good instance—is accompanied by the freeing of energy ; and the katabolic processes of life, which represent internal combustion, set free energy required for maintaining the body temperature and for performing work, and result in the formation of simple compounds of oxygen, such as water, carbon dioxide and urea, waste products from which no further energy can be obtained. Although the presence of oxygen in the air breathed is a necessity of life, the amount present is not (within limits) of paramount importance, as the living organism regulates its own consumption.

Respiratory Exchange.—Expired air, in ordinary breathing,

contains about $16\frac{1}{4}$ per cent. of oxygen, but this readily varies between such limits as 15·5 per cent. and 18·3 per cent. in accordance with the depth and frequency of the respirations. When the partial pressure of the oxygen (which we have seen is normally about 21 per cent. of an atmosphere) is reduced suddenly and greatly, as happens when an aviator ascends to great altitudes or in the less dramatic incident of " mountain sickness," the amount of oxygen rendered available for the cells is insufficient and death may follow unless the precaution of inhaling oxygen is observed. Conversely, if the pressure of the oxygen is very greatly increased the gas acts as poison. Animals placed under fifty atmospheres of pure oxygen (i.e., nearly 240 times the pressure of oxygen in the ordinary air) are instantly thrown into convulsions and die ; and in five atmospheres of oxygen convulsions occur within a few minutes ; prolonged exposure to much lower pressures, but pressures a great deal higher than that of the ordinary air, say 1·8 to 2 atmospheres of pure oxygen, cause a fatal pneumonia. These facts are of importance in the regulation of aviation, and, to a less degree, in connection with deep diving, but have no direct interest in ordinary industrial work, wherein lack of oxygen is never the cause of evils associated with imperfect ventilation. Interest, however, attaches to the recent work of Dr. J. S. Haldane (23), who has pointed out that while under normal conditions oxygen reaches the blood by diffusion through the epithelium lining the pulmonary alveoli, " the physical laws of diffusion do not explain the phenomenon of blood-oxygenation when the subject is making a special demand on oxygen supply either because he is doing physical work or because, as an airman or mountaineer, he is breathing rarefied air." He considers " the evidence strongly supports the view that the epithelium is not a mere porous diaphragm, but that the living cells from which it is built possess the faculty—which they exercise at need—of secreting oxygen from the air and of handing it forward at enhanced pressure to the blood." This attribute of secretion can be developed and improved by physical training, and was found to be present among practical miners. " When, during muscular exertion, a far larger amount of oxygen has to be taken, there is not time for the hæmoglobin to become fully saturated by diffusion alone if ordinary air is breathed, and, unless the epithelium lining the alveoli actively passes oxygen inwards, the arterial blood is imperfectly saturated with oxygen, and this makes the breathing faster and tends . . . to exhaust the breathing power. But the activity of the epithelium can be increased by practice. Hence, in men who are accustomed to muscular exertion, there is no deficiency of oxygen in the arterial blood when ordinary air is breathed until exertion is pushed to the utmost." If persons who are industrially employed are more or less in physical training, this capacity to secrete oxygen from the air, regardless of the pressure of oxygen present, makes of less moment the absolute amount in the atmosphere of workplaces.

The percentage of carbon dioxide in the expired air varies in the same fashion as does that of oxygen, but inversely ; and corresponding to an average oxygen percentage of 16·25, we are likely to have a percentage of carbon dioxide of about 4·21. Carbon dioxide is, so far as the exploitation of biotic energy is concerned, a waste product, but the presence of this gas in the blood is of importance in the normal regulation of respiratory movements. Haldane has shown that the percentage of carbon dioxide in the alveoli of the lungs varies very little indeed in the same person under different conditions ; when the percentage increases, the amount of carbon dioxide in the blood, flowing through the part of the central nervous system—the medulla oblongata—from which impulses governing the movements of the muscles of respiration are discharged, is necessarily increased. The consequence is that this so-called centre is stimulated into discharging stronger or more frequent impulses to the muscles. The breathing becomes quicker and deeper, the ventilation of the alveoli is increased and the percentage of carbon dioxide diminishes ; thus the tension in the blood falls, the respiratory centre is no longer stimulated and the frequency and depth of respiration reduced. This is the normal way in which the movements of respiration are controlled. Carbon dioxide is formed during all katabolic processes, and particularly during muscular contraction when energy is released to do work ; it is then carried away by the blood to the respiratory centre, where it stimulates the deep and rapid breathing associated with active exercise. Under abnormal circumstances, for instance, when the pressure of the oxygen in the air breathed is much reduced (to less than 13 per cent. of an atmosphere or a little more than half the usual pressure) the respiratory centre is excited by lack of oxygen, and there is deep breathing without any increase of the percentage of carbon dioxide in the alveoli or blood ; but this is an abnormal condition. Many experiments have demonstrated that the mere presence of a large proportion of carbonic dioxide in the air respired does not do any injury ; the rate and depth of the breathing is increased, and that is all ; it is only when the pressure of carbonic dioxide reaches a level which could not be attained save in a hermetically sealed chamber, that the force and frequency of respiration needed to reduce the percentage in the alveoli to the level tolerated by the respiratory centre would become dangerous to life. Hill and one of the writers, in experiments upon the effects of compressed air, frequently allowed the amount of carbon dioxide in the air they breathed to reach 1·8 per cent. of an atmosphere (4), that is, much more than is found even under conditions of extremely defective ventilation, without suffering any inconvenience at all. The still common belief that ventilation is needed to keep down the percentage of carbon dioxide, is a pure superstition.

Carbon Dioxide as a Measure of Ventilation.—The importance ascribed by the hygienist to the amount of carbon dioxide present in the air of an occupied room has passed through various phases which may be thus summarised :—When chemistry became an exact science and the interchange of gases in the lungs was first demonstrated, attention was concentrated on the gaseous condition of the atmosphere, and air was deemed to be bad or good as more or less carbon dioxide was present. This view was so far accepted that standards of carbon dioxide were fixed, such as twelve parts per 10,000, which should not be exceeded. The advocates of such standards as proof of satisfactory atmospheric conditions had, however, to modify their opinion when it was found that an atmosphere containing larger amounts of carbon dioxide, amounts such as are never met with under ordinary conditions, produced no ill-effects when breathed. The claim was then put forward that carbon dioxide was a useful measure of other poisonous emanations given off during respiration ; but careful investigation has quite failed to establish the existence of such emanations, and so this claim also fails. Still the hygienist has clung to carbon dioxide estimation, probably because it is a reasonably easy estimation to make, and he now claims that the existence of an unusual amount of carbon dioxide in an inhabited room is an indication of lack of air change. While this is certainly true there can be little doubt that for this purpose alone carbon dioxide estimation would never have been originated. The changes of opinion above mentioned have taken place as knowledge has advanced as to the physiological influences of the atmosphere. The composition of the air met with ordinarily in houses and factories, so far as it contains more or less oxygen or carbon dioxide, is now recognised to be an unimportant factor.

The general conclusion is that the chemical composition of the air of occupied rooms and workplaces is adequate for all the needs of respiration ; and that the ill-effects which are associated with bad ventilation do not depend upon any alteration in the balance of oxygen and carbon dioxide present.

(ii.) *Physical Properties.*

Air possesses definite physical characteristics—temperature, humidity, and movement—the importance of which upon health is coming to be more and more recognised. These characteristics owe their importance to the way in which they influence the heat regulating mechanism of the body, and, as this mechanism reacts to the resultant influence exerted at any moment by the combined effect of the temperature, humidity and movement of the air, these three characteristics have to be considered together. Of the three, however, temperature is in itself the most important. Exposure to sufficiently low temperature is the cause of frost bites ; rapid movement of the air accentuates the effect, but rapid movement alone, unless the air is cold, will not produce the effect. Similarly, exposure to sufficiently high temperatures may cause heat stroke, an effect which is hastened if the hot air is saturated with moisture but delayed if the air is moving and dry ; but exposure to still air, however saturated with moisture, will not produce heat stroke unless the temperature is sufficiently high.

Temperature.—Great extremes of temperature are not experienced in industrial work ; ice chambers for cold storage represent the lower limit reached, and work before furnaces and in unloading kilns the upward limit, but in these cases dryness and movement of the air so ameliorate the position that temperatures approaching 135° F. are endured without any immediate harmful result. As is pointed out later, such high temperatures cannot be safely endured if the air is humid, indeed, a wet bulb temperature of 78° F. represents a danger point for carrying on active work ; and such high wet bulb temperatures exist in certain tin mines in this country and occasionally in cotton mills.

The human body is warmer than its usual surroundings, and like any other warm body gives off heat to these surroundings, either by conduction through direct contact with them, or by radiation, just as heat leaves a fire or the sun ; heat is also carried away from the body by convection due to air, warmed by contact, moving on and being replaced by cooler air. The body is not, however, confined, as is a piece of hot iron, to these three ways of losing heat ; it possesses a fourth— evaporation—due to its power of secreting moisture on its surface in the form of sweat, and this last way is the most important. The body, in fact, so far as heat-loss is concerned closely resembles a wet-bulb thermometer, but the temperature of such an inanimate instrument varies with that of its surroundings, while that of the body does not. The temperature of the body is maintained by katabolic processes or internal combustion ; the energy so released is manifest either as external motion or as heat. Helmholtz estimated that 7 per cent. of the energy released in the body is represented by mechanical work, and that of the remainder about four-fifths are lost by radiation, conduction and evaporation from the skin, and the remaining one-fifth by expired air and excreta. Such an estimate is, of course, approximate and subject to variations, dependent especially on the amount of mechanical work done.

The energy is obtained ultimately from food, and the intake of food and the output of energy as heat and work normally balance one another in such a way that the body in health maintains within small limits a constant temperature which varies about a mean of 98·4° F. During sleep the temperature may fall below 97° F., and during hard exercise may rise as high as 103° F. ; but the tendency always is in health to return to about 98·4° F., and this is effected by a heat-regulating mechanism, of which the skin is the main executive agent, assisted by the lungs. If the temperature falls, the blood vessels of the skin contract and allow but little blood to reach the surface ; the skin becomes cold and pale, the secretion of sweat ceases, and at the same time respiration is slower and not so deep. Heat is now only lost from the skin surface by conduction, radiation and convection, and, to a minor extent, through expired air.

If, on the other hand, the temperature rises, the cutaneous blood vessels dilate, the skin becomes warm and flushed, the secretion of sweat is active, and respiration is quicker and deeper. Heat loss by conduction, radiation and convection is increased, and an important new influence is introduced— evaporation of moisture from the skin.

Humidity.—Heat loss is nearly entirely dependent on the condition of the air ; if the air is warm, the loss is less rapid than when it is cool ; if it is humid the evaporation of sweat is less active than when it is dry ; if it is stagnant, the loss is less rapid and evaporation slower than if it is moving. Attention has been particularly directed by Haldane and others to the influence of atmospheric humidity upon body temperature. The body has been found to react to the effect of temperature as recorded by the wet-bulb thermometer, *i.e.*, to the capacity of the air to absorb moisture. The body is able to regulate its heat loss by lessening or increasing the flow of blood through the skin, associated with a concomitant decrease or increase in secretion of sweat until the wet-bulb thermometer reaches about 78° F. At this temperature prolonged physical work becomes impracticable because the body temperature rises steadily until, unless the work is stopped, heat apoplexy threatens. At about 88° F. wet-bulb, even at rest the body temperature rises steadily, and it is impracticable to remain long in such air. If, however, the air is moving rapidly more heat-loss by evaporation and convection occurs, and the danger limits of temperature mentioned are extended upwards for several degrees. Note, it is not the temperature of the air, nor its relative saturation with aqueous vapour, nor the absolute percentage of vapour present, which is the determining factor, but the temperature as read on the wet-bulb thermometer.

While these upward danger limits of wet-bulb temperatures are of great importance, long before they are reached the effect of warm humid atmospheres upon the body is considerable. This subject has been carefully investigated in relation to the process of weaving cotton cloth, which calls for a humid atmosphere to prevent the cotton threads from breaking. The conclusions arrived at by Pembrey and one of the writers (6) have an important bearing upon the enervating effect of humid warmth and the need for ventilation in other places than cotton mills.

" The influence of the warm moist atmosphere is to diminish the difference between the internal temperature of the body and that of the peripheral parts. The tendency is to establish a more uniform temperature of the body as a whole, and to throw a tax upon the powers of accommodation, which is indicated by the low blood pressure (see Table 1), notwithstanding the rapid rate of the pulse.* This is exactly the condition which would explain the discomfort and low state of health of which many of the weavers complain.

" During work, heat is produced by the contraction of the muscles, and a rise of internal temperature up to a certain optimum is an advantage to the worker. If, however, the air is hot and moist, the worker must send more blood to the skin to be cooled and must sweat in order to prevent his temperature from rising too high. Hot moist air is not favourable for the cooling of the blood or the evaporation of sweat. Muscular work, by creating the need for a greater and faster supply of blood to the muscles, increases the rate of the heart's action. If, at the same time, more blood must be sent to the skin to be cooled, then an extra amount of work must be done by the heart. The regulation of the distribution of the blood is effected by the nervous system. A warm skin diminishes the tone of the muscles, lowers the exchange of material in the body, and

* The original paper should be consulted for observations on the pulse.

TABLE 1.—*Blood Pressure of Workers.*

Arranged in age periods showing in millimetres of mercury the maximum systolic blood pressure (1) of males at work with the wet bulb thermometer recording less than 60° F. (*a*) in the tinplate trade, (*b*) in grinding metals, and (2) of certain weavers at work with the wet bulb thermometer recording 70° F. or over.

Age period.	Males employed in								Weavers.				
	The tinplate trade.				Grinding metals.								
	Persons examined.	Lowest reading.	Average.	Highest reading.	Persons examined.	Lowest reading.	Average.	Highest reading.	Sex.	Number of observations.	Lowest reading.	Average.	Highest reading.
(1)	(2)	(3)	(4)	(5)	(6)	(7)	(8)	(9)	(10)	(11)	(12)	(13)	(14)
20 to 24 inclusive.	155	110	151	200	176	85	143	210	F. F. M.	6 7 5	85 85 115	105 104 127	125 110 145
25 to 29 inclusive.	115	110	158	215	151	105	152	200	F. F. M. M. M. M.	7 8 4 8 8 8	90 80 100 80 80 80	100 96 118 92 110 96	120 110 125 110 125 125
30 to 34 inclusive.	92	120	158	210	182	110	159	220	M.	7	100	126	150
35 to 39 inclusive.	109	115	160	210	168	90	155	210	M.	8	95	106	115

depresses the appetite, and the natural tendency is for the nervous system to become less active, and for muscular work to be diminished. In a weaving shed, however, the machine sets the pace, and the worker must neglect the dictates of his sensations, which are the natural guardians of his health and well-being. He must strive as far as possible to accommodate himself to the adverse conditions of heat and moisture. Some workers can respond to the demand better than others, but all must have their powers of accommodation taxed when the temperature of the wet bulb rises much above 70° F. It is not surprising, therefore, that at the end of a day's work many of the weavers complain that they have no energy left, have no great desire for food, and need only drink and rest. The need of food for the production of heat in the body is diminished in a warm moist atmosphere, but food is needed for supplying the energy for work, and for the growth of the body.

" As a class, the weavers appear to be small in stature, spare in build, thin in the face, pale in complexion, and have a wearied look. Many of them complain that their appetites are poor and require tempting, and that they suffer from indigestion. These conditions cannot be explained otherwise than by the prolonged exposure to the effects of the warm, moist atmosphere in which the weavers work, for they are not seen in outdoor labourers of either sex, or in weavers of jute,* who may earn far less wages and have much inferior dwellings, or in workers in other industries in Lancashire."

One of the writers compared the blood pressure of weavers at work with that of other operatives (see table), and showed how much lower on an average it was for the weavers (6). He also observed on himself a rapid rise of pulse rate to 104—116 while making observations in an atmosphere giving wet-bulb readings of over 72° F., a point which was further brought out by observations upon the operatives, especially those who indicated by a rise of mouth temperature their inability to accommodate their heart-regulating mechanism to the conditions. Dr. Legge, using a large number of observations, compared the average pulse and respiration rate of operatives with mouth temperatures of 100° F. and over, with those of operatives with temperatures of 99° to 99·9° F., and found in the former an average pulse of 101 and respiration rate of 23, and in the latter a pulse of 89 and respiration rate of 20. These differences are not in themselves considerable, but when regard is had to their maintenance for a long working day, for day after day and week after week, they represent a heavy tax thrown on the economic working of the body, and partly explain the poor physique of the cotton operative who has in the past started work young, possibly as a half-timer at twelve years of age. School records show that Lancashire juveniles at that age do not differ much in physique from juveniles in other parts of the country, yet by the time they are eighteen years of age they have failed to attain the average height of the artisan class by some inch and a half or more.

Movement.—Attention has been directed, particularly by Dr. L. E. Hill (7), to the importance of air movement in relation to health. The nerve endings in the expansive area of the skin originate by far the largest group of impulses which are constantly affecting the central nervous system. Response to these impulses decides whether the skin is flushed or pale, whether secreting sweat or dry and cold, and whether the nasal mucous membrane is taut or soggy. A cold skin depleted of blood is an incentive to muscular activity, while at the same time the blood stream is diverted to the muscles and deeper

* A humid warm temperature is not required for weaving jute.

structures.   A hot perspiring skin contra-indicates physical exertion and draws the blood to the surface to allow of heat loss.   Healthy metabolism depends on sufficient physical exercise, and an influence as ubiquitous as air acting through the skin, either as an incentive or otherwise, must play an important part.   Hill says, " the evaporative power of the atmosphere has a far-reaching effect, not only on the comfort of the skin, but on the respiratory membrane, the absorption of water from the gut, and the renal secretion.   The ceaseless variation in the rate of cooling, evaporation, absorption of radiant energy, as in outdoor conditions, relieves us from monotony, stimulates tone and metabolism.   Indoors the conditions are generally uniform, monotonous and unstimulating.   In closed artificially heated rooms, cooling and evaporative powers are very greatly reduced by the lack of the vastly freer ventilation which pertains out of doors even on calm days."   In pressing forward this point of view he removes the whole question of ventilation from supposed injurious chemical products of respiration (which, as we have pointed out, are inadequate to explain the need) to movement of air of suitable temperature and humidity.   Stated baldly, a fully occupied room could be well ventilated by properly arranged movement of the air without introducing air from outside ; but such internal movement of air without the introduction of air from outside would be difficult to arrange, and in practice the air movement advocated necessitates change of air.   We agree with Hill in pressing the importance of air movement, but before agreeing that the whole question of ventilation is covered by this factor, desire to know whether expired air may not possess certain physical rather than chemical properties different from those of inspired air ;   some unpublished work suggests that this may be the case.   Whether this ultimately prove to be so or not, we are undoubtedly on sure grounds in advocating ventilation by air movement as recommended by Hill and in effecting this movement by introducing fresh air into factories (see also (26)).

The next question arises as to what amount of air movement is required ;   to this question Hill has devoted much careful and prolonged research.   He has designed an instrument (see Fig. 17) to measure comparatively and approximately the rate of heat loss of the body under varying conditions.   In use, the bulb is dipped into warm water until the alcohol rises just to the safety reservoir, then the instrument is placed in the air to be tested, and the time the alcohol takes to fall from $100°$ F. to $95°$ F. (i.e., through $2\frac{1}{2}°$ F. above and below normal body temperature) is observed with a stop watch ;   the instrument is called a katathermometer because it is a meter of falling temperature (κατά down, θερμός heat). By this means the amount of heat lost by radiation and convection is ascertained. But the

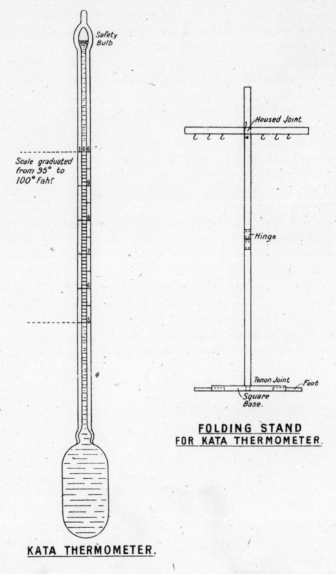

Scale graduated from 95° to 100° Fah!

KATA THERMOMETER.

Safety Bulb

Housed Joint

Hinge

Tenon Joint Foot

Square Base.

FOLDING STAND FOR KATA THERMOMETER.

Fig. 17.

human body, which is practically always sweating, though perhaps not visibly, also loses heat by evaporation and resembles a wet-bulb thermometer rather than a dry-bulb ; so the kata-thermometer is also used wet ; for this purpose a muslin glove is passed over the bulb before it is dipped into warm water. The instrument so used gives the cooling power by radiation, convection and evaporation, and the difference between the rates of cooling of the instrument used dry and wet represents the cooling due to evaporation. Thus the instrument is a suitable means for measuring the physiological efficiency of air movement. Each instrument, owing to slight differences in size of bulb, thickness of glass and the like, possesses a "factor" of its own, for which allowance has to be made before readings can be compared ; this standardising factor is stated on the stem. The factor divided by the number of seconds the kata takes in cooling from 100° F. to 95° F. represents the standard cooling power, *i.e.*, the heat loss in milli-calories per square centimetre per second ; in practice several readings, from 3 to 5, are taken, and the average of these readings is used as the time taken to cool ; thus, if the factor stated on the instrument be 520, and the average time taken by the dry katathermometer to fall be 76 seconds, the cooling power of the atmosphere would be taken as 520 divided by 76, that is to say, 6·8 milli-calories per square centimetre per second. Experience has determined that comfortable conditions are represented if the standard cooling power of the dry kata is not less than 6 when sedentary work is pursued, and not less than 7 for work involving medium physical exertion, and that the wet-kata cooling powers should for such occupations be not less than 18 and 20 respectively. The following figures (8) may be quoted :—

Place.	Temperature in degrees Fahr.		Cooling powers.		Evaporative power.
	Wet bulb.	Dry bulb.	Wet kata.	Dry kata.	
Brass foundry (good)	60	72	24	7·3	16·7
Machine shop (bad).	61	72	15	4·6	10·4

Here the dry and wet bulb readings in the two workplaces are practically identical, but the kata readings bring out physiological differences.

Rubner holds that every hindrance to heat loss either reduces bodily exertion or causes the exertion to be done under a feeling of oppression and a burden of weariness. Therefore, the production of sweating must be most energetically countered by adequate conditions of environment. The first objective of ventilation, then, is to prevent visible sweating by securing a

comfortable rate of cooling by convection ; for, as Hill puts it,
" it is the high cooling rate of bracing days which gives the
desire for, and joy in, the taking of muscular exercise. In the
tropics work must be done at the expense of the sweating
mechanism. Living on a low metabolic level and low protein
diet, *e.g.*, 1,600 calories and 60 grammes protein, the native does
not do more than a fraction of the work performed by an ordinary
Englishman " (7, p. 56).

Energy which should be devoted to muscular work is wasted
when it is diverted to cooling the body by sweating ; and the
aim of industrial ventilation should be to stimulate the desire
for physical work, the desire for healthy activity. The employer
by having regard to this physiological fact in arranging ventilation will secure greater efficiency and output ; the worker by
working in a healthy atmosphere will have increased comfort,
enjoy better health, and do more work with less fatigue.

The desiderata have been described (8) as—
" (*a*) Cool rather than hot ;
   (*b*) Dry rather than damp ;
   (*c*) Diverse in temperature in different parts, and at different
        times, rather than uniform and monotonous ; and
        (which is intimately connected with this diversity)
   (*d*) Moving rather than still."

Extreme cases of inefficient ventilation are to be found in tin
mines, where, owing to the hot moist atmosphere, the strain on
the heat-losing mechanism is so great that practically no energy
is left over for work (9) ; and also in the Rand gold mines, where
observations with the wet kata indicate worse physiological
conditions than on the closest of days in Ceylon (7). In steel
rolling mills, also, much energy is expended in sweating, and
output and comfort have been increased by installing air-douches
to cool the men (10). Further instances might be quoted grading
down from heavy labour through medium work, *e.g.*, cotton
weaving (*vide* p. 289), to sedentary occupations, such as that of
tailoring, described by Chadwick (*vide* p. 281). Hill states (7)
that, " *to keep down loss of heat by evaporation*, the tailor will be
right in still air at 15° C., and requires a breeze of more than
one mile per hour at 27° C. The carpenter, metal worker, and
painter will be right in still air at 0° C., and need a wind of more
than one mile an hour at 22° C., two miles at 25° C., and nine
miles at 30° C. The stonemason a wind of more than one mile
an hour at 10° C., two miles an hour at 15° C., nine miles an hour
at 24° C."

He holds that the physiological mechanism regulating the
temperature of the body is adapted particularly to ward off the

effect of heat, and that danger from heat is greater than danger from cold, since the latter in temperate climates can be warded off by increased exercise and warmer clothing. Hill has set out fully (7) the facts and observations upon which his opinion is based ; our purpose is served by recognising (a) the end to be attained, viz., a moving and bracing atmosphere, and (b) the means for ascertaining whether the end has been attained, viz., the use of the katathermometer.

(iii.) *Impurities.*

The reader will see that so far no case has been made out, by appeal either to the chemical composition or to the physical properties of air, for the introduction of fresh air ; although a strong case exists for adequate movement of air of suitable temperature and humidity. Yet a general agreement exists that the introduction of fresh air into occupied rooms is necessary. The evidence is not clear why this is so ; but the suggestion has been put forward (20, p. 84) that air becomes impure due to various ill-defined volatile substances arising from human beings, *e.g.*, gases from the intestinal canal, and emanations from sebaceous secretion, especially when personal hygiene is defective.

Various gases, CH_4, CO_2, H, N, and H_2S, have been detected in intestinal gases eliminated per rectum, and they may be tainted with the disagreeable odour of skatol and indol, which are normally present in the lower bowel. These gases which arise from bacterial fermentation of proteids may not be actually harmful, but they undoubtedly create a feeling of discomfort and make the air taste stuffy to any one coming in from outside. Nothing definite is known concerning emanations from the skin ; but white men find repugnant the odour associated with a place occupied by coloured men, while coloured men similarly dislike the odour connected with white races. These gases and odours undoubtedly make an atmosphere unpleasant and so limit its refreshing qualities ; possibly they do more and are the origin of headaches and lassitude ; certainly they should be removed, and this can only be done by introducing fresh clean air.

The atmosphere, apart from its chemical or gaseous composition, contains impurities in the form of particles of various kinds which undoubtedly, when inhaled, exert an important influence upon health ; but measurement of this influence is difficult to carry out, since other adverse conditions, either physical or due to volatile substances, are frequently associated with the presence of particulate impurities.

We have already pointed out that in relation to infant mortality

the most important factor for consideration may be a polluted
state of the atmosphere such as is found in smoky industrial
towns; for while the mortality for 1914 per 1,000 births in

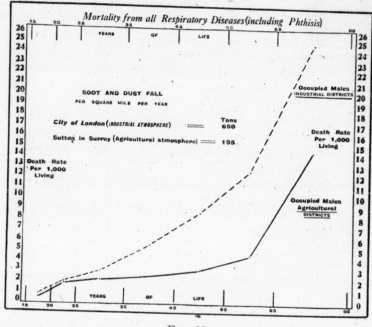

FIG. 18.

Roscommon, Cavan and Leitrim was about 40, that in Barnsley
was 153, in Burnley 158, and in Ashton-under-Lyne 184 (2).

Some measure of the effect of particulate impurities on adult
life can be obtained by comparing the mortality through life

TABLE 2.

RELATION OF ACUTE LUNG DISEASES TO FOG City of Manchester		
Period	Fog Days	Death Rate Per 1,000 from Acute Lung Diseases
1896-1900	36 ·8	5 ·04
1901-1905	23 ·4	4 ·28

from respiratory diseases experienced by males living in the
country with that of those living in industrial districts (see
Fig. 18), and also by noting the effect of fog upon the death
rate from acute lung diseases (see Table 2).

Particulate impurities in air may be divided into two groups ; the first containing particles capable of exhibiting the phenomena of life, *i.e.*, germs ; the second containing particles which do not possess this property.   Both are important.

Germs.—The probability of ill-health arising under factory conditions from air-borne microbic infection rests upon definite evidence, for the air of occupied rooms is known to contain micro-organisms greater in number, as the rooms lack cleanliness and are overcrowded.   Thus Carnelly, Haldane, and Anderson (18) found in Dundee in two-roomed dwellings ten micro-organisms per litre of air in the cleaner dwellings, twenty-two in dwellings of average cleanliness, and sixty-nine in dirtier ; but in one-roomed dwellings they found eighteen in the cleaner, forty-five in the average, and ninety-three in the dirtier ; while the outside air in Dundee contained only 0·8 micro-organisms per litre.   The increase noted was mainly due to bacteria, and not to moulds ; the proportions being one mould to three bacteria in outside air, one to twenty in two-roomed dwellings, and one to forty-eight in one-roomed dwellings.   Few determinations have been made of factory air, but the average of thirty-nine analyses, made chiefly among printers', book-binders', tailors', and milliners' workrooms, gave 8·0 bacteria and 2·2 moulds, or 10·2 micro-organisms per litre of air.   These figures prove that bacteria are present in the air of occupied rooms, and so can be inhaled.

All germs are not pathogenic, and estimation of the number present at any time in the air is no certain indication of danger arising from infection.   For this reason we consider it sufficient to recognise that air-borne infection does take place ; and that " a certain propinquity is required in order that the infected saliva spray sneezed, coughed, or spoken out may be distributed from a ' carrier ' to another victim.   It has been shown that a zone within one metre of a consumptive patient is particularly dangerous for guinea-pigs, kept within cages and exposed to saliva spray infection, and this is particularly so when doors and windows are shut in winter.   Out of doors folk do not crowd so closely, and the ventilation is very much greater ; even on the calmest day the air is not still, and convection currents are at work ; the saliva spray is blown away, and the infection cannot be massive, as it may be indoors or in railway carriages, where the atmosphere is comparatively still " (7, p. 142).   Examples taken from the report just quoted may be instanced from war-time experience : the incidence of infective pharyngitis and epidemic catarrh on a troopship was ten times as great upon the men on three badly ventilated decks as upon those on a

well-ventilated deck (11) ; Canadian troops when moved from
the discomforts of tent life on Salisbury Plain into huts succumbed to an epidemic of sore throats and catarrhs ; a sick
rate of 7·9 per cent. in an artillery unit was reduced to 1·5
per cent. in six weeks by better ventilation of tents and
sunning and airing of bedding, while that of other regiments
trebled.

Hill stresses (7, p. 148) the importance of infection through the
nasal mucous membrane ; in a warm atmosphere it becomes congested, swollen, and covered with mucus, a veritable trap for
germs ; on now passing into cold air the membrane becomes pale
and contracts, in this way imprisoning the germs caught on the
surface. He writes :—" In those who live out of doors not only
is the membrane kept taut, but the flow of arterial blood through
it is rapid, for the inhaled air has to be warmed up and moisture
rapidly evaporated from the membrane, so as to saturate this
air at body temperature. Thus more lymph comes out into the
membrane from the blood-vessels, and this contains protective
substances. Offensive bacteria are either washed away or
destroyed and thus kept out. On the other hand, a membrane
covered with thick secretion, and congested, offers a medium
more suitable for the bacteria to settle and grow on, for it is
boggy and stagnant, not flooded with fresh lymph, particularly
when vaso-constriction takes place on passing from an over-hot,
moist atmosphere into the wintry outside air. The ciliated cells,
white corpuscles, and lymph may be chilled and the velocity of
vital reaction reduced when the blood-vessels constrict. Colds
may not always be a question of reinfection, but of lowered
resistance to the strains of pneumococci or streptococci which
people happen to carry in their noses. Stagnant conditions of
the nose and its sinuses may exalt the virulence of organisms,
and so spread infections. Epidemics may thus be started by
carriers whose humoral conditions are altered by unhealthy
environment."

All diseases which may be air-borne, such as ordinary " colds,"
sore throat, bronchitis, influenza, measles, cerebro-spinal fever,
are in their spread largely influenced by the moist, heated
atmospheres of indoor life ; if factory workers congregated
together in large numbers in one establishment are not to
continue to contract them and distribute them wide cast to their
homes, steps must be taken to introduce adequate ventilation
scientifically planned, and also to place workers so that they
do not sit in rows *facing* one another on either side of narrow
work benches, and so that at least 4 feet of sitting space is
allowed to each.

Inorganic Particles.—The influence of inorganic particles when inhaled varies with the size and nature of the particles. Particles must be of a certain minuteness to be inhaled at all ; fairly large particles, especially if light, may gain access to the upper air passages ; but no particles exceeding 10 μ in diameter have been found in the alveoli and lung tissue. Inhalation of dust particles gives rise to a group of diseases known as pneumonoconioses, which has been fully dealt with by one of us elsewhere (12 and 13). Some members of the group, *e.g.*, bronchitis and pneumonia, are indistinguishable from the same diseases as they occur in the general population ; a short summary of present knowledge is, therefore, here given ; but full discussion properly belongs to a work on diseases of occupation.

Only particles which are insoluble in the fluids of the body when carried into the air passages remain as foreign bodies either to stimulate the ciliated epithelium to overaction for their expulsion, or, if they gain access to the lymph channels, to give rise to a proliferation of connective tissue ; thus dusts of ivory, horn, bone, and other animal structures, and of calcium sulphate (plaster-of-Paris and alabaster), of limestone, and of oxide of iron are not associated with pneumonoconioses in the way that dusts of vegetable husks, emery, glass, sandstone, and flint are. Generally speaking, dusts are more injurious as their chemical composition differs from that of the human body, or from the elements of which the body is normally composed, whence it follows that animal dusts are less injurious than others. Dust formed from the husk of vegetable fibres tends to cause a typical form of asthma associated with bronchitis. Bronchitis is *par excellence* the chief of the pneumonoconioses, and follows upon inhalation in excess of practically every form of dust which is insoluble and non-colloidal. Pneumonia, although its association with dust inhalation is not so marked as in the case of bronchitis, may result from inhalation of the same dusts that cause bronchitis. Phthisis as determined by dust inhalation is a distinct disease ; and is only associated with exposure to dust of uncombined silica, as for instance the dust of flint, sandstone, quartz, quartzite, granite, and buhrstone ; it occurs as a secondary infection implanted upon a condition of pulmonary fibrosis or silicosis ; its correct name is tubercular silicosis. This disease occurs exclusively in middle-aged workers, and appears to belong to that group of tuberculosis named by Brownlee " middle-age type " (14).

The interest of inorganic particles lies for this chapter in the steps which are needed to prevent their inhalation by the application of localised ventilation.

III. Methods of Ventilation.

The aims to be attained by ventilation have now been stated, viz., (a) to maintain an atmosphere sufficiently moving to be bracing, sufficiently warm to avoid undue loss of body heat, sufficiently cool and dry to permit of the working of the heat-regulating mechanism of the body, sufficiently free from microbic content to avoid the spread of infection ; and (b) to prevent injurious particles generated in industrial processes from gaining access to the air.

These objects must be attained (a) through *general ventilation* by introducing fresh air to minimise the spread of infection, and by so arranging the ventilation that dry-kata readings are not less than six for sedentary work, and seven or more for more active labour, and wet-kata readings are not less than eighteen or twenty respectively ; and (b) through *localised exhaust ventilation* on the principles stated later.

(a) General Ventilation.

General ventilation may be effected by natural means, such as windows and chimneys ; or by mechanical means brought about by the use of revolving fans of suitable design.

Natural Means.—Factories in the early days of industrial development were frequently converted dwelling houses ; and workplaces possessed fireplaces and chimneys. Chimneys, even when no fire is burning in the grate, act as ventilating shafts of great value ; usually, as the room is warmer than the outside air, they function as upcast shafts, but occasionally in summer the direction may be reversed. Where there are no special openings for incoming air, sufficient generally gains access at ill-fitting window sashes or under doors ; and even where these chinks and crannies are tightly closed, a certain amount of air will come in through walls—an amount which is increased if the wind is blowing, but diminished if a large proportion of the wall space is composed of tightly glazed window glass, and if the walls are painted so as to be practically air-tight. In a room of 1,400 cubic feet with a boarded floor above and only one outside wall, when all openings were closed up, the chimney draught was found, when there was no appreciable wind, to be 4,450 cubic feet per hour, giving a rate of air change of once in three to five hours (15, Appendix II.). Small rooms in this respect have an advantage over large ones in possessing a proportionately larger area of wall surface. " The surface increases as the square, and the capacity as the cube, of any corresponding diameter for rooms of the same shape. Thus an increase of eight times in the capacity will correspond to increase of only four times in the surface. Very large rooms, when unprovided with openings for ventilation, may thus contain very foul air, although the air space per person is very large " (15, p. 110). This is an important point in view of the modern tendency to construct large work-rooms, which, since they often provide an air space per worker far in excess of the minimum of 250 cubic feet laid down in the Factory Acts, may be expected to be satisfactory ; thus in contrast to the small rooms referred to above may be quoted a spinning room of 91,500 cubic feet, occupied by only nine persons, in which the windows were tightly glazed, and the walls painted ; here the rate of air change was found to be not more than about once in twenty-four hours.

The structure of the roof, in addition to that of the walls, has an important influence upon ventilation ; in a church and a hall of relatively large size with easily permeable roofs the air was changed about once in three hours ; while in a cotton weaving shed of 388,800 cubic feet with a roof almost air-tight (as it was covered by an asphalted water tank) the rate of air change was only about once in twenty-nine hours.

Another factor, in addition to windage, which may affect the exchange of air through walls is the difference between the inside and outside temperature ; a difference of about 18° F. (the inside being the higher) has been found associated in a weaving shed with ventilation about three times as great as when there was no difference. The value of windows, even though not open to air movement, should be noted. Warm air coming in contact with the glass kept cool by the outside air is cooled ; it then becomes heavier and falls to the floor. In this way a steady circulation of air occurs, which is prevented by covering the windows with blinds or curtains. This effect can often be demonstrated on a winter evening, if a sitting-room feels unduly warm, by drawing back the curtains and pulling up the blinds, when in a few minutes, as the air circulates more freely, the oppressive feeling in the room disappears. In modern factories the sides of which are often largely formed of window lights, this influence upon the movement of air in workrooms is considerable and does much to prevent the air becoming stagnant. Generally speaking, " in small rooms, provided there is an open chimney, no gas burning, and an air space of not less than 1,000 cubic feet per person, the ventilation may often be fairly sufficient without open windows or other special means of ventilation. With a good coal fire burning in the grate the ventilation is likely to be fair, even with only 400 cubic feet of air space per person. The larger the size of the room, however, the greater becomes the need of special openings for ventilation; and in rooms of over 5,000 cubic feet open windows or special ventilators are nearly always necessary unless the air space per person is very large or the roof is very permeable to air" (15, pp. 110—111).

Mechanical Means.—While a small room with a comparatively large outside wall area, a chimney and windows, may possibly be reasonably ventilated without having recourse to mechanical means for introducing fresh air and removing tainted air, the same cannot be said for the large apartments which form the greater part of modern factories. Here fireplaces and chimneys are non-existent, as the room is usually warmed by pipes or radiators heated with hot water or steam. The problem to be solved is how to change the air of such large apartments sufficiently frequently without creating unpleasant draughts, or unduly lowering the temperature; so long as these two points are avoided, the more rapid the change of air, the better will be the effect. The problem then comes to be to ascertain what frequency of air change is possible; and much help can be obtained from the schemes adopted in relation to the process of coating the canvas-covering of aeroplane wings and bodies. The object of the process is to coat the fabric with a cellulose skin; and a dope composed of a solution of cellulose compounds in various volatile spirits is used. After the dope is applied the spirits evaporate and leave the cellulose behind. The fumes arising cause unpleasant symptoms—headaches and sore throat; when tetrachlorethane was one of the solvent spirits used, its fumes caused serious poisoning among the workers who breathed them, associated with gastric disturbances, jaundice and liver destruction, the typical symptoms of toxic jaundice. The removal of these fumes became a matter of urgent necessity; but the temperature of the rooms had to be maintained between 65° and 70° F. to promote sufficiently rapid evaporation of the spirits; and local draughts had to be avoided or the varnish dried in patches. Localised exhaust ventilation was found impracticable owing to the large surface of the aeroplane wings varnished at one time. The difficulties have been finally overcome by constructing rooms with large exhaust fans placed at the floor level in one wall, while air passing over hot pipes is admitted through hoppered openings situated in the opposite wall at a height of 8 to 10 feet above the floor. As the end in view is moving large volumes of air, low pressure, so-called "propeller," fans are used. Thirty or forty changes of air per hour in doping rooms were obtained by these means without the creation of any appreciable draught and with advantage to the drying of the material.

We appear in this plan to have approached near to the ideal way of ventilating and at the same time maintaining a reasonable temperature in workplaces. The rapidity of air change required in doping rooms, though advantageous, is in excess of that absolutely necessary for health and comfort when sedentary work is in progress ; a change of air, varying with the time of year, equivalent to from six to ten times the content of the room every hour, may be sufficient.

Ventilation by Extraction.—The method referred to above of sweeping air through a room by drawing air out and allowing fresh air to take its place is the one which generally is simplest in action and most readily installed. Propeller fans (see Fig. 19), owing to their capacity for moving large volumes of air with but little expenditure of power, provide the most suitable means available.

TABLE 3.—*Speed and Output of Propeller Fans.*

Diameter (inches).	Speed range (revol. per minute).		Output range ($k = 0·6$*) (cubic feet per minute).	
	Minimum.	Maximum.	Minimum speed.	Maximum speed.
12	1,300	2,100	780	1,260
15	1,050	1,685	1,230	1,970
18	850	1,400	1,720	2,835
20	760	1,265	2,110	3,510
24	630	1,050	3,020	5,040
25	610	1,015	3,310	5,510
30	510	840	4,780	7,875
35	440	715	6,550	10,640
36	425	700	6,890	11,340
40	380	625	8,440	13,890
42	360	590	9,260	15,180
45	340	550	10,760	17,400
48	320	525	12,290	20,160
50	305	510	13,240	22,140
54	295	490	16,130	26,790

* k is a constant, the value of which varies somewhat according to the construction of the fan, but is in practice usually about 0·6 ; if the value of k reaches 0·7 or more the output range will be higher.

The fan power required in each case is a matter for an engineer, but some idea may be gathered from the following data. A 4-foot propeller fan should discharge not less than 12,000 cubic feet of air per minute, or 200 cubic feet per second (see table). The horse-power required may be calculated from the formula—

$$\text{Horse-power} = \frac{Q^3}{D^4} \times 0\cdot0000115$$

where Q = quantity of air in cubic feet discharged per second; and D = diameter of fan in feet. In the instance given of a 4-foot fan the horse-power required to drive it would be—

$$\frac{200^3}{4^4} \times 0\cdot0000115 = 0\cdot36 \text{ horse-power.}$$

This expenditure of power is slight compared with the volume of

Fig. 19.—Cross Ventilation of Dope Room.
(Extraction fans at floor level.)
Ventilating and Heating Plant by Sturtevant Engineering Co., Ltd., London.
Reproduced from (24).

air moved which would be sufficient to change six times an hour the air of a room 15 feet high, 100 feet long, and 80 feet wide. " The air-delivery by a propeller fan varies in direct proportion to its rate of revolution, while the power needed to drive it varies as the cube of its velocity. Hence for a given expenditure of power much more air is propelled with a low than with a high rate of revolution. In practice, however, it is best to run a fan at a considerable velocity ; otherwise the flow of air may easily be greatly diminished, or even reversed, by the influence of wind " (16, p. 4).

The best position for a fan extracting air is at or near the floor level. Openings for admitting air should be placed at not less than 8 to 10 feet from the floor in the wall opposite to that in which the fan or fans are placed ; the area of the openings should be distributed as far as may be to ensure that the incoming air reaches every part of the room. They should also be fitted with hoppers on the inside to prevent any down draught.

Propeller fans will not work effectively against any pressure ; and resistance, either to the air delivered, or by constriction of the air inlets, may diminish the efficiency of a propeller fan almost to nothing, even though considerable power is being expended in maintaining its rate of revolution ; attention, therefore, must be paid to the openings for admitting air, and to the discharge side of the fan.

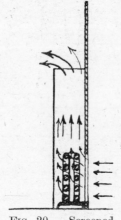

The provision of ample inlet openings for admitting air to a room is important, not only to ensure that the fan is in no way baffled, but to prevent the air entering with a velocity exceeding 250 feet per minute. A velocity above that limit, even though the air is warmed, may create an unpleasant sensation of draught. The standard to aim at is that " the minimum total inlet area should be at least three times the total disc area of the extraction fans " (24). In cal-culating this area, allowance must be made for any obstruction offered for a battery of hot pipes used for warming the incoming air, or by any filtering material used for removing dust—such material in industrial towns quickly becomes choked and requires frequent attention.

FIG. 20. — Screened Inlet with Heater. Reproduced from (24).

Provision must also be made for free discharge of air from the fan. For this purpose the opening on the discharge side, if not direct into the outside air, must be rather larger than the fan both in breadth and height, and there should be no obstruction in front of the opening. Should the opening be exposed to the wind, which will easily overcome the power of the fan, it should be carefully shielded. The output of a fan can be measured by taking a series of readings with an anemometer held on the delivery side within 1 foot of the fan ; but the efficacy of the work it is doing is best ascertained by having recourse to kata-thermometer readings taken inside the room.

Ventilation by Impulsion or Plenum.—The construction of premises or the requirements of special processes may necessitate

a reversal of the exhaust method of ventilation ; and fresh air
may have to be driven into the workplace. This system is
known as plenum ventilation. It may be needed to introduce
fresh air into the centre of capacious rooms, such as are to be
found in many modern factories ; in these rooms the width may
be too great to ensure sufficient air movement in all parts with
exhaust fans and air inlets in the walls ; or again where there
is exposure to great heat, as before furnaces in rolling mills
or in the manufacture of glass, cool air may be needed locally
as a douche for the workers. Plenum ventilation is usually
effected by driving air through channels or ducts which open

Fig. 21.—Cold Air Plenum for Glass Works.
Ventilating Plant by Sturtevant Engineering Co., Ltd., London.
Reproduced from (24).

in desired positions. However well planned, these ducts offer
resistance to air movement, and the air should be driven
forward by centrifugal or pressure fans, i.e., by fans which will
move the air against pressure. In mines where complicated
underground workings have to be ventilated, fans are used
which will maintain a pressure of 12 inches on a water gauge ;
but in factories, fans capable of giving pressures of $2\frac{1}{2}$ inches
or less are usually employed. Pressure fans require more power
than propeller fans for moving the same amount of air ; when
the volume of air to be moved is the object rather than the
rate of removal, economy is effected by running the fans slowly
and having large ducts.

    Air driven into a room will tend to find its way out through
any openings there are, but the efficiency of the ventilation will

be impaired if definite exits are not provided.   The best position for these exits is low down in the walls and so arranged that the incoming air sweeps through the room before reaching them.

Each room will present problems of its own ; neither exhaust nor plenum alone may suit the case ; but the principles described for ventilation by exhaust or by plenum apply equally when for any reason the two methods have to be used in combination. Air may stagnate in certain parts of large rooms supplied with an adequate amount of fresh air by the plenum system, unless localised exhaust fans are installed.   Or again, when sufficient fresh air is being introduced advantage can be obtained from the use of paddles fixed on revolving shafting to create air movement and waft otherwise still air into the general circulation.

(b) Localised Exhaust Ventilation.

The principles involved have been set out by the Health of Munition Workers Committee (8) with which one of us was associated, and we feel we cannot do better than reproduce here that Committee's statement.

The essentials of localised exhaust ventilation are : (a) a duct along which a flow of air is maintained in a definite direction ; and (b) a localised opening or openings in this duct, through which sufficient air is admitted to allow the flow of air to be maintained.   The air so admitted carries with it any dust or fumes the removal of which is desired ; and this action may be made effective for the purpose of removing from the atmosphere of workplaces of (1) dust ; (2) heated fumes such as arise from melting scrap lead and other poisonous materials ; or (3) volatile vapours and gases such as are evolved when india-rubber is vulcanised and in certain chemical processes.   The principles underlying effective action differ for each of these purposes.

Removal of Dust.—The removal of dust is best effected by an air current produced by mechanical power, preferably by a pressure fan, and so arranged as to prevent the dust particles escaping from the place where they are produced into the general atmosphere.   For this purpose the openings in the ducts should terminate in hoods shaped so as to envelop, as far as practicable, the seat of origin of the dust.   In the case of dust from a revolving wheel the hood and duct should be so placed as to intercept the dust which is thrown tangentially from the wheel, and to catch dust which would otherwise fall to the ground ; the dust then comes under the influence of the air current in the hood and is drawn into the duct, while the air current itself is assisted by the air thrown off by the wheel.   The heavier dust particles, especially of abrasive materials, may be allowed to fall into a receptacle at the bottom of the hood and removed at intervals. In this way only the lighter particles are carried through the ducts and the wear and tear on them and on the fan is thus minimised. Where dust is created by manual labour the operative should stand or sit facing the opening of the hood, so that the current of air draws the dust away from him.

Removal of Heated Fumes.—The removal of heated fumes may often be effected without using mechanical power if the area of

FIG. 22.—Pressure Fan. Reproduced by permission of Messrs. Keith and Blackman.

the fume-producing surface is not too large, but to secure this the duct should be vertical, of ample diameter and height, and surmounted by a suitable wind cowl, while the lower end should open gradually into a bell-mouthed hood. The lower end of the hood should envelop and extend below the place where the heated fumes originate. The opening to the hood should only be large enough to permit of necessary manipulations. The errors usually found in this form of exhaust ventilation are (i.) the opening to the hood may be too large and air currents in the workplace carry the fumes away before they come under the influence of the draught; (ii.) owing to the sides of the hood too nearly approaching the horizontal, the area within the hood may be too small; (iii.) the height of the upcast shaft or vertical duct may be insufficient; and (iv.) provision may not be made to avoid down draught due to wind. The natural draught in such hoods can often be supplemented by means of a jet of compressed air discharged up the shaft.

Removal of Volatile Vapours.—Volatile vapours such as those given off when fabric is waterproofed with rubber solution, are difficult to localise. If, as is usually the case when noxious vapours have to be dealt with, the vapour is heavier than air, the openings to the duct must be at the ground level and as near as practicable to the place where the vapour is given off. The air current must be so arranged that large volumes of air are drawn away, and ample openings for incoming air must be arranged at a moderate height in the workroom.

Air Inlets.—Factors essential to any form of localised exhaust ventilation are the distribution and size of openings for air coming into the workroom generally. To obtain an interchange of air and so secure general ventilation these openings should be placed as far as possible from the exhaust openings, preferably on the opposite side of the workroom; to avoid draughts, such openings should be of ample area (*vide supra*). The supply of incoming air may, in some cases, be ensured by the use of a pressure fan driving in air through well distributed openings.

Faults to Avoid.—In practice the efficiency of exhaust plants is frequently found impaired by lack of attention to details: (i.) the hood to collect dust may be too small, in which case dust flying from a wheel is not intercepted; (ii.) the shape of the hoods may be faulty, in which case dust accumulates on areas having an inclination towards the throat less than the angle of rest of the dust; or, in the case of heated fumes, the expanding gases rebound and escape from the hood like smoke from a badly-constructed domestic chimney; (iii.) the duct opening may be so small that dust collects there and blocks the opening; (iv.) the inlets to the workplace may be insufficient to admit freely the amount of air required, in which case the air flow in the ducts is slowed, and, if a fan is being used, power is wasted in overcoming unnecessary resistance; (v.) bends in the ducts if too sharp impede the flow of air; (vi.) where dust is being dealt with, dust-settling chambers of insufficient size or with insufficient openings may have been provided; (vii.) insufficient attention may have been paid to the plant erected; hoods detached from ducts, holes broken into ducts, and ducts blocked with every kind of *débris* have been found in well-planned installations and in places where considerable power is being expended to drive exhaust fans.

Types of Fan.—Generally speaking, where a keen draught, as for the removal of dust, is required, pressure fans should be employed; since these fans, though requiring more power to drive, can work against considerable pressure, smaller ducts may be used. Where, on the other hand, large volumes of air, as for the removal of vapours, are to be moved, volume or propeller fans can be more economically employed; but with such fans attention to the sectional area of the ducts is of great importance; the ducts must never be constricted at any point, the total area of the openings must be considerably greater than that of the fan, and all sharp bends in the ducts must be avoided; further, the delivery side of the fan must not be impeded or so placed as to be exposed to the action of wind.

Maintenance.—Nearly every workplace where localised exhaust ventilation is required presents special problems of its own for the solving of which technical advice may be necessary, but adherence to the principles above enumerated will effect great improvement. In particular, wherever an exhaust system has been installed the duty should be placed on some responsible person of testing and reporting

FIG. 23.—Reproduced by permission of Messrs. Keeling & Walker, Stoke-on-Trent.

to the management at stated intervals on the efficiency and maintenance of the installation.

Further information as to the construction of ducts and hoods will be found in the Home Office paper on ventilation in factories and workshops (24); in the second report of the Departmental Committee on Ventilation of Factories and Workshops (17); and, especially in relation to the use of propeller fans, in the report of the Departmental Committee on Earthenware and China (22).

IV. Respirators.

Exhaust ventilation cannot always be employed to prevent dangerous dust escaping into the air, as for instance in stonemasons' work, or in filling and emptying silica-brick kilns. Recourse must then be had to respirators. The majority of respirators sold have one fundamental fault ; shaped like a dog's muzzle they contain a space in front of the mouth and nose in which the last part of the expired air is retained. This air is of necessity rebreathed, and the wearer must breathe rather deeper to get rid of the normal amount of carbon dioxide. For this reason these respirators cause breathlessness on exertion and are to be condemned. Probably no form of perfect respirator can be devised, but the one here illustrated is designed on scientific principles as laid down by Sir H. Cunynghame (21), and is open to fewer objections than any other.

V. Bibliography.

1. *Report of Poor Law Commissioners into the Sanitary Condition of the Labouring Population of Great Britain*, p. 107. 1842.

2. " The Mortalities of Birth, Infancy and Childhood." *Medical Research Committee. Special Report Series, No.* 10. 1917.

3. Notter and Firth. *Theory and Practice of Hygiene.* 1896.

4. Greenwood, M. " Physiological and Pathological Effects which follow exposure to Compressed Air." Arris and Gale Lectures. *British Medical Journal.* April, 1908.

5. *Departmental Committee on Humidity and Ventilation in Cotton Weaving Sheds.* Minutes of Evidence. (Cd. 4485.) 1909.

6. *Departmental Committee on Humidity and Ventilation in Cotton Weaving Sheds.* Second Report. (Cd. 5566.) 1911.

7. Hill, L. E. " The Science of Ventilation," Part I. *Medical Research Committee. Special Report Series, No.* 32. 1919.

8. " Ventilation and Lighting of Munition Factories." *Health of Munition Workers Committee. Memo. No.* 9. (Cd. 8215.) 1916.

9. *Report on the Health of Cornish Miners.* (Cd. 2091.) 1904.

10. Vernon, H. M. " The Influence of Hours of Work and of Ventilation on Output in Tinplate Manufacture." *Industrial Fatigue Research Board. Report No.* 1. 1919.

11. *British Medical Journal*, Vol. I., p. 257. 1919.

12. Collis, E. L. " The Effect of Dust in Producing Diseases of the Lungs." *Proc. Seventeenth International Congress of Medicine.* Section XVIII. 1913.

13. Collis, E. L. *Industrial Pneumonoconioses.* Milroy Lectures (1915). H.M. Stationery Office. 1919.

14. Brownlee, J. " An Investigation into the Epidemiology of Phthisis in Great Britain and Ireland." *Medical Research Committee. Special Report Series*, Parts I. and II., No. 18, 1918 ; Part III., No. 46, 1920.

15. *Departmental Committee on Ventilation of Factories and Workshops.* First Report. (Cd. 1302.) 1902.

16. *Departmental Committee on Ventilation of Factories and Workshops.* Second Report, Part I. (Cd. 3552.) 1907.

17. *Departmental Committee on Ventilation of Factories and Workshops.* Second Report, Part II. (Cd. 3553.) 1907.

18. Carnelly, Haldane and Anderson. *Philosoph. Trans.*, B. 1887.

19. Thorndike, E. L., McCall, W. A., and Chapman, J. C. *Ventilation in Relation to Mental Work.* Teachers' College, Columbia University. 1916.

20. *Health of Munition Workers Committee*. Final Report. (Cd. 9065.) 1918.

21. *Royal Commission on Metalliferous Mines and Quarries*. Second Report, Appendix F. (Cd. 7476.) 1914.

22. Pendock, C. R. *Report of Departmental Committee on Earthenware and China*, Vol. II., Appendix XLVIII. (Cd. 5278.) 1910.

23. "Second Report of the Mine Rescue Apparatus Research Committee." *Department of Scientific and Industrial Research*. H.M. Stationery Office. 1920.

24. *Ventilation of Factories and Workshops*. Home Office. H.M. Stationery Office. 1920.

25. Hill, L. E. "The Science of Ventilation," Part II. *Medical Research Council. Special Report Series, No. 52*. 1920.

26. Huntington, E. *Civilisation and Climate*. Yale University Press. 1915.

CHAPTER XIV

LIGHTING

THE effect upon industrial efficiency exerted by the lighting of workplaces is considerable ; a greater amount of better and more accurate work is done where illumination is adequate. Yet, although lighting has this important aspect, the attention paid to the subject during industrial development has not been commensurate with the need ; with this aspect, however, we are hardly concerned, except in so far as improved facilities for work react beneficially upon the well-being and psychology of the workers ; but lighting has also other aspects to which the Committee (1) on Lighting in Factories and Workshops drew attention in 1915. They point out " the recognition that defective illumination may be a contributory cause to accidents, may be injurious to the health and eyesight of workers, and may exercise a prejudicial effect on the output and quality of work, has led to a general interest in the question of industrial illumination."

I. Effect upon General Health.

There is no evidence that want of light *directly* produces any specific effect upon general health ; Arctic explorers do not report any peculiar effect upon general health associated with prolonged absence of sunlight during the winter months ; the same holds good for miners, who work for years underground during the day, and their ponies and horses who for years spend all their lives in mines. Nevertheless unsatisfactory illumination exerts in several indirect ways a definite harmful influence on general health, and a direct harmful influence on eyesight.

Sunlight is known to be inimical to the life of most pathogenic organisms ; a gelatine plate evenly sown with micro-organisms, covered with a photographic positive, and set to incubate in sunlight, will present a living reproduction of the picture, owing to the growth of organisms being densest where least light penetrates, and least where most penetrates. The tubercle bacillus in particular may be instanced as a micro-organism of which the vitality is destroyed by direct sunlight and much impaired by exposure to daylight. While daylight is harmful to microbic life, it stimulates a healthy skin reaction, and exerts a beneficial effect which is in danger of being overlooked due to the prominence given to atmospheric influences, especially when " open-air " life is under discussion. This effect is clearly demonstrated in plants, which decline to flourish in the absence of light. The introduction into workshops of hardy plants and ferns, which is sometimes practised, is a sound proceeding ; apart from adding a touch of beauty, they provide a useful test of light and air. Where plants refuse to live, human beings should only be called upon to exist under exceptional circumstances. The more daylight, therefore, there is in the rooms where workers are congregated together, the less is the chance of the spread of infectious diseases and the better will be their general health. Adequate illumination also discloses the presence of accumulations of refuse and dirt, which, when disturbed as workers pass to and fro, infect the air with the microbes they harbour. Where food is prepared, such as in fruit preserving factories and bakehouses, the presence of refuse is undesirable in the interests of manufacture, and adequate lighting is required by statute.

II. Effect upon Eyesight.

The influence exerted by light upon eyesight has two extremes. The first, due to the absence of sufficient light, causes a special disease known as nystagmus. This disease is characterised by unsteady gait, headache, and curious oscillatory movements of the eyeball ; it practically only occurs among coal miners, and among those miners who work with safety-lamps ; it is not found among miners working with naked lights. The glass which surrounds the light of a safety-lamp becomes dimmed with smoke as work proceeds, while coal dust collecting on the gauze curtails the air supply to the light. This disease, which is extremely distressing, entirely incapacitates a man from continuing as a miner ; if not too far advanced he may recover after prolonged absence from underground work, but the condition frequently reappears if he resumes his old occupation. Llewellyn estimates that to-day 6,000 miners are disabled each year through this disease, with a cost through compensation of £1,000,000 a year to the industry. The introduction of a safety-lamp giving greater illumination would rapidly lead to the disappearance of this disease ; every effort is being made to produce a lamp which, while possessing the advantages of the present safety-lamp, will give an illumination of 0·1 foot-candles * at the working face.

The second, due to exposure to intense light and heat, causes a special form of cataract, posterior polar cataract, first described by Legge among glass workers. It also occurs among other workers, *e.g.*, those exposed to the rays of molten metal. The prevalence of cataract in India is also generally ascribed to exposure to excessive sunlight.

Description of these two diseases belongs to a work on Diseases of Occupation rather than to one on general industrial health, therefore more than passing reference to their existence is omitted. Between these two extremes light exerts an important influence upon the eyesight of workers, grading from exposure to the intolerable brightness of arc welding, through the glare of badly arranged illumination, to eyestrain at fine work due to insufficient light.

Glare.—Glare is defined as follows by the Committee :—

" (i.) The effect of looking directly at a bright source of light, such as an arc lamp, so that the observer is for the time being prevented from seeing other objects properly. He is temporarily dazzled and his vision is impaired for a short period after the light has ceased to enter his eyes.

" (ii.) The effect which is produced by the presence of one or more bright sources of light towards the edge of the field of vision so that the rays enter the eye obliquely from them. An observer may never look directly at such sources of light, but he is nevertheless troubled by their presence near to the object to which he is looking. This is the commonest form of glare. Both the above forms of glare (i.) and (ii.) are directly attributable to the presence of unshaded sources of light.

" (iii.) The effect which is produced when the surface of cloth, metal, paper, or other material being worked upon is shiny or polished, and reflects light directly from some source into the eyes of the worker. Many satin cloths, for instance, have a ' sheen ' or a power of regular reflection of light which causes work with such materials to be very trying unless the worker is so placed with reference to the source of light that none of the rays can be directly reflected from the material into his eyes."

Glare causes " annoyance, headache, and other trouble and, often, eventually, diminished ability to see." This statement may be accepted, even though no accurate determination has

---

* For definition of a foot-candle see top of page 322. On the Continent the "meter-candle," about one-tenth of a foot-candle, is the unit of measurement.

been made as to the extent to which exposure to various forms of glare is associated with these manifestations.

III. Insufficient Light.

The pupil of the eye dilates in dim light and contracts in strong light. Similarly it dilates for distant vision, while the act of accommodation for near vision carries with it constriction of the pupil ; the act of narrowing the pupil is of value to near vision, since, by diaphragming the lens, the definition is improved and more exact vision, such as is needed for close work, is obtained (6). Should, however, illumination be insufficient, the pupil will tend to dilate in order to admit more light, an act which in its turn will be countered by the necessity to accommodate for near vision. Thus, deficient light, especially for near work, leads to a constant struggle, an important factor in the complex of " eyestrain." The effect of eyestrain due to defective lighting is well recognised among workers upon delicate operations such as sewing, and fine engineering work ; headache and nervous irritability result, while both the quality and quantity of output suffer. Whether or not fine eye-work long continued under defective illumination actually impairs visual acuity has never been definitely ascertained. Opinions expressed on this subject are open to attack, because we cannot be sure that the defects revealed by examination did not exist before the work was undertaken ; the prevalence at any eye infirmary of refraction cases coming from occupations such as lace making and weaving, is no certain evidence that these occupations have caused the trouble. The proportion of ocular defects present among school children is known, but there is no guide to what normally exists among adults at various periods of life. Without such a standard for comparison, the observation that at certain processes such as embroidery and tailoring, the use of spectacles is unusually prevalent, only establishes a certain prevalence of ocular defects among those workers ; but the prevalence of these defects is in itself a sufficient reason why special attention should always be given to the illumination provided. The human eye was not evolved for long continued fine industrial work, and every possible assistance in the way of adequate and satisfactory light should be given to enable it to meet this demand upon its capacity.

IV. Influence of Light on the Occurrence of Industrial Accidents.

Illumination in daylight hours may generally be taken to be better than that when artificial light is employed, and Wilson and

Paterson (2) have investigated the incidence of notified industrial
accidents during these two periods. They found that this class
of accident was generally 29 per cent. more frequent during the
hours when artificial light was used, and that the increase was
especially great in the case of accidents due to " persons
falling," see table. An appeal to accidents in the mining
industry showed that, although an increase took place in the dark
winter months, it was not a seasonal one ; as here the accident
rate underground in the winter was less than in the summer,
while on the surface the rate was greater in the winter than in the
summer.

Computed Rate of Notified Accidents in 1913 : (a) *During
Daylight, and* (b) *during Artificial Light.*

Causation.	Accident rate per hour.		Percentage difference.
	Daylight.	Artificial light.	
Machinery moved by mechanical power	16·62	19·64	18
Molten metal	2·58	2·96	15
Struck by falling bodies . . .	9·43	12·46	32
Persons falling	7·16	12·32	71

Vernon, however, has pointed out (3) that the method of
investigation adopted is liable to sources of error, such as the
temperature factor, which may account for an excess of accidents in winter months, since these months are not only dark,
but also cold, and more accidents occur in cold weather than in
warm. He investigated during wartime the frequency of minor
accidents in engineering factories, comparing night-shifts with
day-shifts, and concluded that lighting had very little influence
upon this class of accidents, but did influence accidents to the
eye. He found accidents to the eye more frequent by night, and
that the frequency increased with the inadequacy of the lighting.
" An attempt to trace the relation between inadequate illumination and accidents has also been made in the United States.
Mr. R. E. Simpson," writes Mr. Gaster, " quotes statistics
obtained by the Travellers Insurance Co., who estimated that of
91,000 accidents studied in 1910, 23·8 per cent. were due to

imperfect illumination. After eight years' work this proportion has been reduced to 18 per cent., but even so it is estimated that during this period the services of 108,000 men for one year have been lost through preventable accidents. . . . *The prevention of industrial accidents due to faulty lighting is thus a measure which is amply justified on economic grounds alone, besides being, of course, a measure which ought to be taken in the interests of humanity.*"

There are, however, so many other factors at work determining the causation of accidents, such as length of hours, rapidity of work, and the varying psychology of the workers at the beginning and end of the working spell, that any statistical estimate as to effect of illumination can only be approximate; indeed, evidence is hardly required to establish the case, that in the absence of adequate light, muscular action is less accurate and more liable to error.

V. Economic Value of Illumination.

The economic value of lighting hardly falls within our purview, but interest attaches to certain results which have been obtained. Witnesses before the Lighting Committee (1) reported in one instance that the output for daylight hours was 12·3 per cent. above that for the hours of artificial light ; and in another that an increase of earnings of 11·4 per cent. followed the installation of improved illumination. Gaster (5) quotes a valuable experiment in progress in America where " improved illumination resulted in an increased output ranging from 8 to 27 per cent. in different departments when the illumination was increased three times, *i.e.,* from 4 to 12 foot-candles. In another case, where the illumination was twenty-five times the inadequate value originally employed, increases in output of from 30 to 100 per cent. were observed. On a conservative estimate it was concluded that an *increased cost of lighting amounting to not more than 5 per cent. of the pay-roll would lead to an increased production of quite 15 per cent.*"

Lighting at pre-war prices used to cost in a typical machine shop about 0·3 per cent. of total cost of production, and about 1 per cent. of the wages bill, and Gaster remarks, " only a very small improvement in output would be needed to compensate for the cost of better lighting, quite apart from the other advantages referred to previously, such as better health of employees, less fatigue and nerve strain, etc., all of which are difficult to assess commercially."

An interesting comparison has been made (8) between hourly

curves of output in silk weaving (*a*) during December, when the
use of artificial light was at its maximum, averaging sixty-nine
minutes in the morning and eighty-five minutes in the afternoon ;
(*b*) during February, when artificial light was used on the
average sixty-one minutes in the morning and forty-seven
minutes in the afternoon, and (*c*) during April, when no artificial
light was used. The curves of output were of the saddle-back
type, but, as less artificial light was used, they became flatter,
and ran at a higher level, that is to say, the early and late hours
of the day were comparatively more productive, even though
the output of the midday hours was higher. " There was a
considerable fall in the rate of production during periods of
artificial lighting, and this drop was of the order, in magnitude,
of 10 per cent. of the rate of output which would have been
reached during these periods if there had been natural lighting.
It is worth while to emphasise the fact that this loss is not due
to working under *insufficient* electric light ; " the illumination
is stated to have been in excess of the standards proposed later.
The greater output in the midday hours is of interest : " It is
probable that the slower pace under which work is performed
under artificial light is continued unconsciously for a while in
natural light, and acceleration only takes place gradually, also
that fatigue, sufficiently developed to affect the rate of output,
sets in at an earlier hour after a spell of artificial lighting than
during a day of natural lighting."

An American Division Committee have summarised (7) the
advantages of good lighting as follows :—

(1) Reduction of accidents.
(2) Greater accuracy in workmanship.
(3) Decreased waste of material.
(4) Increased production for the same labour cost.
(5) Less eyestrain.
(6) Better working and living conditions.
(7) Greater contentment of the workmen.
(8) Better order, cleanliness and neatness in the plant.
(9) Easier supervision of the men.

VI. The Measurement of Illumination.

The amount of illumination at any given point may be measured
by using a photometer, a simple form of which is shown in the
diagram. It consists of a case containing an electric light of
known brightness (L), which can be moved along a calibrated
scale (H) nearer to or farther from a white surface (S_2) ; and an
eyepiece of which the field of view is partly occupied by S_2.   A

white surface (S_1), in every way identical with S_2 is placed at the point where the illumination is to be measured ; and then looked at through the eyepiece, when its brightness is directly compared with that of S_2. By moving L, the brightness of S_2 is then altered until it coincides with that of S_1. The illumination of S_2, which is now identical with that of S_1, is then read off on the

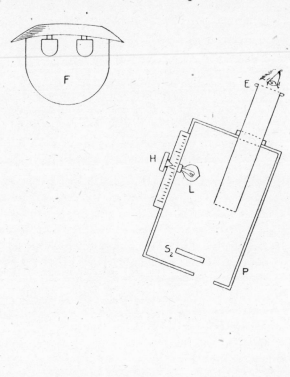

FIG. 24.—Diagram of Photometer.

scale H. The use of two surfaces S_1 and S_2, identical in every way, is the foundation of all photometers, because different materials reflect different amounts of light according to the nature and colour of their surface, that is to say, they have a different surface brightness, e.g., the surface brightness of white blotting paper is high, that of black cloth is low. Rough or matt surfaces diffuse light in all directions, but highly polished surfaces hardly diffuse light at all but reflect it according to the laws of reflection.

Light is usually measured in " foot-candles " in this country, and on the Continent in " meter-candles." The value of a meter-candle is roughly $\frac{1}{10}$ that of a foot-candle. " One foot-candle may be defined as the illumination produced by the light source of one standard candle at a point of a surface one foot from the source, and so placed that the light rays from the source strike the surface at right angles." If the light source be increased to thirty-two standard candles the illumination at the point on the surface becomes thirty-two foot-candles ; but if the surface be now removed 4 feet away, the illumination diminishes by the square of the distance and becomes $\frac{32}{16} = 2$ foot-candles.

VII. Natural Lighting.

Natural light, if adequate in amount, is always, from the health point of view, to be preferred to artificial illumination, and every effort should be made in the interest of economy as well as of health to ensure that work is carried on for as long as possible by natural light. The amount which penetrates any workplace depends on (i.) the structure of the factory with regard to the position and area of window space, the transparency of the glass, and its relation to adjacent buildings ; and (ii.) the amount of daylight present which varies with time of day and the season of the year. The relation the light reaching any place inside a building bears to the amount of light outside at any moment is known as the " daylight factor," and is usually expressed in the form of a percentage ; thus, " the daylight factor for roof-lighted buildings such as weaving sheds is of the order of 2 per cent.," that is to say, that only 2 per cent. of the light which would reach any definite spot if the roof and walls were removed is actually found to be reaching it. " At the centre of some workrooms depending entirely on lateral windows the factor falls as low as 0·01 per cent., which means that the light reaching the point in question is only $\frac{1}{10000}$ of that which would reach it if walls and roof were removed." This daylight factor for any point is practically constant whether the outside light is considerable or meagre ; but investigations have shown that the amount of light it represents is too frequently surprisingly small, and that the outside light must be considerable to allow this factor to be adequate. Apart from temporary fluctuations due to the presence or absence of clouds, the amount of daylight varies greatly at different times of the year and at different times of the day (see Fig. 25) ; indeed the vacillations of daylight are so rapid that care must be exercised when estimating the daylight factor to make the inside and outside observations simultaneously. An illumination of one foot-candle is a reasonable one to aim at for the general lighting of a workroom, although where fine processes are not concerned artificial light may not be necessary until the illumination falls below 0·5 foot-candle ; a 0·2 daylight factor may be considered low for a factory of modern construction. In order to obtain 1 foot-candle illumination with this daylight factor, the amount of daylight must be not less than 500 foot-candles. Reference to Fig. 25 shows that, approximately, this amount of

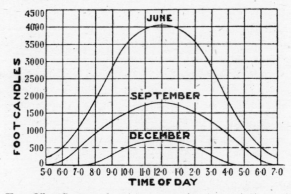

FIG. 25.—Curves showing approximate variation of daylight from 5 a.m. to 7 p.m. on average days in June, September and December.
Reproduced from *Report of Departmental Committee on Lighting* (1).

daylight is present in June from 6 a.m. to 6 p.m., in September (and February) from 7 a.m. to 5 p.m., but in December only from 10 a.m. to 2 p.m. Taking the period of factory employment as eight hours plus one hour for dinner, the work may start at 8 a.m. and cease at 5 p.m. During four months of the year, unless the daylight factor exceeds 0·2 per cent., 1 foot-candle of natural illumination is not available at the commencement and end of work ; and recourse must be had to artificial light, or to increasing the daylight factor. There are, however, on an average 25 foot-candles of daylight at sunrise or sunset, that is to say, from 8 a.m. to 4 p.m. in December ; and, if the daylight factor be increased to 2 per cent., by no means an unattainable standard, an illumination of at least 0·5 foot-candles may be obtained with natural light during working hours throughout the year, except for the last hour, 4 p.m. to 5 p.m. during a few weeks in December.

Much can be done to admit more daylight into the average factory by attention to details inexpensive compared with the price of artificial light. The size of windows can be increased by widening them and extending them up as near the ceiling as possible. The height of a window, however, is, for equal area, more important than its width, not only because of the greater sky area subtended, but because of the angle of incidence of the light. Vertical extension is required particularly in converted dwelling-houses, but the windows of old factory buildings also are frequently quite unnecessarily small and low. Obstruction of light outside by other buildings may be minimised by whitewashing the walls and using reflectors ; obstruction within can be avoided by the removal of boxes and packing cases thoughtlessly stored so as to block the light. Regular cleaning of windows is a simple expedient, but it is seldom adopted, and windows are frequently to be seen so opaque with grime that nothing less than soaking with strong acid could make the glass again transparent ; meanwhile, with bright sunshine outside, work inside is proceeding by gas flares. One reason why window cleaning is not carried out more often is faulty construction of casements, which, especially in the case of extensive modern window lights, is such that access to the outside for cleaning purposes is quite impossible without ladders from below or ropes from above ; some factories even rely on the occasional visit of the local fire brigade to clean their windows. All window casements should be made to pivot inwards. Greater value can be obtained from the light which does enter through keeping ceilings white by frequent lime washing, which is particularly valuable for the sloping ceilings of saw-tooth roofs, whence much light is reflected on the work below, while the walls of workplaces and also the painted parts of machinery should be white or light coloured,* and preferably of a surface which can frequently be washed down and kept fresh.

The American Committee consider (7) that natural illumination calls for consideration as follows :—

(1) The light should be adequate for each employee.

(2) The windows should be so spaced and located that daylight conditions are fairly uniform over the working area.

(3) The intensities of daylight should be such that artificial light will be required only during those portions of the day when it would naturally be considered necessary.

(4) The windows should provide a quality of daylight which will avoid a glare due to the sun's rays and light from

* Some authorities advocate keeping machinery parts black in order to obtain contrast.

the sky shining directly into the eye, or where this does not prove to be the case at all parts of the day, window shades or other means should be available to make this end possible.

(5) Ceilings and upper portions of the walls should be maintained a light colour to increase the effectiveness of the lighting facilities from window areas. The lower portion of the walls should be somewhat darker in tone to render the lighting restful for the eye. Factory green or other medium colours may be used to good effect.

VIII. Artificial Lighting.

Daylight, while it may with great advantage be far more used than it is to-day, must be supplemented or replaced for certain processes, and on dark and foggy days, by artificial light. This source of illumination is entirely under control, and should, therefore, always be adequate. Nevertheless, far too little attention is paid in industry to the amount of light provided ; the position of lights in relation to work ; the maintenance of the sources of light, or to modern improvements in lighting. The use of antiquated gas burners vitiating the air and giving a minimum of illumination, of broken gas mantles, of electric light bulbs encrusted with dust, is to be found in many factories. A lighting system, possibly efficient when first installed, is too frequently left to itself to become quite inadequate for want of attention. No one is detailed to look after it, large bills are paid for gas burned to little purpose, or for electric current which is carried to worn out lamps or to illuminate the filaments of darkened glass bulbs. Economy could often be effected and illumination increased by paying an attendant for the purpose. Artificial lighting falls under two headings—(i.) general illumination, and (ii.) local illumination. (This distinction does not hold good for daylight illumination where local illumination is part of the general.)

General Illumination.—A standard of lighting should be adopted which will illuminate the whole " working area " of the factory sufficiently for rendering visible dirt and *débris*, and for purposes of safety, that is to say, for allowing obstacles and moving machinery to be plainly seen. This standard, when supplemented by local illumination, may reasonably be lower than that aimed at for minimum daylight illumination ; but when the general illumination serves also for the carrying on of work, at least the same minimum standard, from 0·5 to 1·0 foot-candles, should be fixed. This standard is not difficult to attain if modern fittings are used, such as high-pressure gas or gas-filled electric lamps. The source or sources of light should be so placed that the illumination does not fall below the standard in any part of the working area, and is as far as possible equally distributed. By *working area* is understood " that portion of the floor occupied by, and in the immediate neighbourhood of, the machines, benches, plant or material, at which the operatives stand or sit in the execution of their work, and includes the gangways and alleys between and around such working places." The placing and shading of lights requires consideration, and must be so arranged that light does not fall on the eyes of the workers when at work or looking horizontally across the room. Further, if powerful lights, such as arc lamps, are used they must not be placed too low down, or dense black shadows, possible sources of danger, may be formed. Staircases and passage ways, not part of the working area, but through which persons may pass, should also be illuminated on a definite standard (not less than 0·1 foot-candle), which should be carefully supervised and maintained. And factory yards and approaches should be so lighted that roads, paths, pools of water and corners can be easily distinguished ; the lights should be not less than 10 feet high in order to avoid glare, and should be surmounted by reflectors ; here a standard of at least 0·05 foot-candle should be maintained.

General illumination, like general ventilation, should be entirely outside the control of the operators, and placed in the hands of some responsible person, otherwise what is at every one's fancy to use is no one's duty to maintain. " A few months' neglect," says Gaster, " may result in a loss of as much as 50 per cent. of the working illumination, and cases are on record where, by merely making good defects and cleaning lamps and appliances, the available illumination was doubled " (5).

Local Illumination.—Standards of illumination for special processes are difficult to lay down, as the light required must vary, not only with the process, but often with the material which is being dealt with ; thus more light is required for sewing dark cloth with dark thread than for light coloured cloth. Certain principles should, however, be adhered to : All light must be so placed as to illuminate the work rather than the worker ; localised illumination which falls on the workers' eyes and foreheads must be avoided ; it causes irritation from

FIG. 26A.—A Bad Example of Lighting for a Lathe.

The shallow reflector does not sufficiently cover the filament, and much of the light falls in the eyes of the worker, causing glare, instead of upon the work where it is actually needed. Glare of this description is highly inconvenient to the worker and adds greatly to the fatigue of work, while the unduly shallow nature of the reflector means that a lamp of higher consumption has to be used than would be the case if the light were properly directed. The arrangement is detrimental in two ways: it causes eyestrain and wastes electricity.

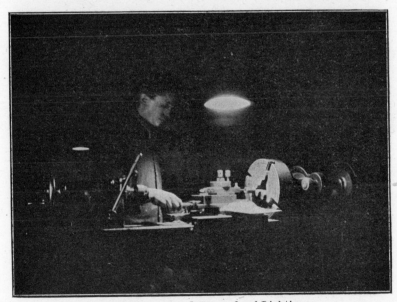

FIG. 26B.—A Good Example of Lighting.

The reflector covers the lamp, and directs the light downwards on the work. The face of the worker is in partial shadow, and his eyes are not dazzled by the view of the bright filament. Owing to the concentrating action of the reflector the maximum effect is obtained from the lamp. It is, however, also desirable to ensure that the light strikes the work at the best angle, so as to avoid direct reflection of light off the polished surfaces into the eyes of the worker, which would give rise to eyestrain.

Reproduced from *British Industrial "Safety First" Association.* *Technical Pamphlet No. 1.* December, 1919.

light rays, and is also frequently unpleasant owing to the heat it radiates, while throbbing and headache, entirely preventable, result (see Fig. 26A).   A small movable light for each worker is better than a more powerful light acting for several; electric lights with suitable shades are especially useful for this purpose ; an excellent example is provided by the use at sewing machine work of small glow lamps placed in bell-shaped reflectors ; these lamps are adjusted within a few inches of the needle on the opposite side of the machine to the worker ; the machine keeps all light from reaching the worker, and the reflector keeps it from worrying a worker on the opposite side of the table

FIG. 27.—Localised Illumination.
Reproduced by permission of Messrs. Wallwin & Co.

(see Fig. 27). Individual electric glow lamps may also be used in a similar way in engineering works. Localised illumination may advantageously be placed under the control of each operator to arrange according to his own convenience, always presuming that he does not thereby inconvenience his neighbours ; should a light be out of order the worker should immediately bring it to the attention of the light overseer. Lights should be so placed as to avoid casting extraneous shadows on the work.

IX. Standards of Illumination.

The Departmental Committee make (1) the following recommendations, but in considering the standards proposed it must be kept in mind that they are *minimum* standards put forward with a view to their adoption as legal requirements, and that the aim should be in every case to provide illumination well in excess of these standards :—

(1) There should be a statutory provision—

    (*a*) Requiring adequate and suitable lighting in general terms in every part of a factory or workshop, and

    (*b*) Giving power to the Secretary of State to make Orders defining adequate and suitable illumination for factories and workshops, or for any part thereof or for any processes carried on therein.

(2) Over the " working areas " of workrooms the illumination measured on a horizontal plane at floor level shall be not less than 0·25 foot-candle, without prejudice to the illumination required for the work itself.

(3) In all parts of iron foundries in which work is carried on or over which any person is ordinarily liable to pass, the illumination measured on a horizontal plane at floor level shall be not less than 0·4 foot-candle.

(4) In all parts of factories and workshops (not included under recommendation 2) over which persons employed are liable to pass, the illumination measured on a horizontal plane at floor level shall be not less than 0·1 foot-candle.

(5) In all open places in which persons are employed during the period between one hour after sunset and one hour before sunrise, and in any dangerous parts of the regular road or way over a yard or other space forming the approach to any place of work, the illumination on a horizontal plane at ground level shall be not less than 0·05 foot-candle.

(6) There shall be power for the department to allow exemption in individual cases.

(7) All external windows of every workroom shall be kept clean, on both the inner and outer surfaces.

The Council of National Defence in the United States has recommended (7) the minima given in the following table :—

	Foot-candles at the work.	
	Ordinary practice.	Minimum.
(a) Roadways and yard thoroughfares .	0·05— 0·25	0·02
(b) Storage spaces	0·50— 1·00	0·25
(c) Stairways, passageways, aisles . .	0·75— 2·00	0·25
(d) Rough manufacturing, such as rough machining, rough assembling, rough bench-work	2·00— 4·00	1·25
(e) Rough manufacturing, involving closer discrimination of detail . . .	3·00— 6·00	2·00
(f) Fine manufacturing, such as fine lathe work, pattern and tool making, light-coloured textiles	4·00— 8·00	3·00
(g) Special cases of fine work, such as watch-making, engraving, drafting, dark-coloured textiles	10·00—15·00	5·00
(h) Office work, such as accounting, type-writing, etc.	4·00— 8·00	3·00

X. Bibliography.

1. *Report of Departmental Committee on Lighting in Factories and Workshops.* (Cd. 8000.) 1915. The contents of this section are largely drawn from this Report, and paragraphs in inverted commas, if not otherwise indicated, are extracts from it.

2. *Op. cit.*, Appendix IX.

3. Vernon, H. M. " An Investigation of the Factors Concerned in the Causation of Industrial Accidents." *Health of Munition Workers Committee. Memo. No.* 21. (Cd. 9046.) 1918.

4. Collis, E. L. " Eye Injuries caused by Occupation." *The Ophthalmoscope.* 1915.

5. Gaster, Leon. " Industrial Lighting and its Relation to Efficiency." *Journ. Roy. Soc. Arts.* 1920.

6. Howell, W. H. *Textbook of Physiology.* W. B. Saunders Co. 1917.

7. " Code of Lighting for Factories, Mills and Other Workplaces." *Report of Divisional Committee on Lighting, Council of National Defence.* U.S. Public Health Reports. January 24th, 1919.

8. Elton, P. M. " A Study of Output in Silk Weaving during the Winter Months." *Industrial Fatigue Research Board. Report No.* 9 (*Textile Series, No.* 3). H.M. Stationery Office. 1920.

CHAPTER XV

WASHING ACCOMMODATION. SANITARY ACCOMMODATION.
DRINKING WATER. WORKING CLOTHES. CLOAK ROOMS.
SEATS.

I. Washing Accommodation.

Introduction.

THE saying that cleanliness is next to godliness lacks in precision through not stating which virtue should be practised
first ; but the value of washing as a means to acquire health
certainly dates back to the time of Naaman. Nevertheless the
importance of washing was not fully appreciated in mediæval
England ; the *Liber Niger,** for instance, states that the barber
was to be in attendance every Saturday night for fear the King
desired to cleanse his head, legs or feet. Washing utensils
occasionally occur in lists of furniture in the houses of nobility,
but evidence suggests that the sons of toil remained unwashen
well into the nineteenth century.

We get a sidelight given us in 1700 from Italy by Ramazzini (9),
an advocate for cleanliness of the body. He wrote : " In the
beginning of brickmakers' fevers, a bottle of sweet water would
prove highly beneficial for washing off the nastiness adhering to
their bodies. And the pores of the skin being relaxed and opened
a discharge of the febrile heat would be procured ; but at present
baths are not so much used as formerly. In ancient Rome it
was customary for tradesmen, after the labours of the day, to
repair to the public baths, where they at once removed the
sordes and weariness their bodies had contracted ; for which
reason they were less subject to diseases than our modern
tradesmen " ; another passage runs " it would certainly be
convenient for them to use baths, to wash off the dusty filth
which sticks in the skin along with the sweat, but now that

---

* *Liber Niger* in *Ordinances and Regulations for the Government of the
Royal Household.* Soc. of Antiquar., 1790.

baths are in disuse, the poor workmen are deprived of that
benefit ; for we must not think that these ancient builders of
cities and compilers of laws, were at all that charge and magnificence of building, not only in great cities, but even in lesser
towns, in making public baths only to gratify the luxury and
effeminacy of women and idle fellows, but likewise for the sake
of tradesmen and hard workers, that they might have an opportunity of washing off the filth of their bodies, and refreshing
their weary limbs at a small charge " ; yet again he urges
tradesmen to " endeavour to wipe off the matter which hinders
perspiration, and correct the noisome smell which attends them,
by washing and rubbing their bodies with a sponge dipped in
hot muscadine-wine ; and, by way of precaution, upon all Holy
days, I would advise them to wash themselves at home in sweet
water, and walk abroad in clean linen."

The extent to which public baths were used in the heyday of
the Roman Empire, referred to above, may be gathered from the
fact that the baths of Diocletian at Rome provided accommodation for 18,000 people to bathe at the same time ; those of
Antoninus Caracalla, which were even larger, were 1,840 feet
long and 1,476 in breadth ; there were many others in the city ;
and the establishment of public baths was customary throughout
the Empire in important towns, such as Pompeii, and in distant
provinces, such as Britain.   For the most part these baths were
erected for the people by the emperors ; and architecture was
carried to an extreme point of magnificence in their construction ;
a point not rivalled to-day at English and Continental Spas,
where the accommodation is only at the disposal of the well-to-
do.   " Agrippa bequeathed his gardens and baths to the Roman
people, and assigned particular estates for their support, that
the people might enjoy them gratuitously."   Roman baths
generally " stood among extensive gardens and walks, and often
were surrounded by a portico.   The main building contained
extensive halls for swimming and bathing ; others for conversation ; others for various athletic and manly exercises ; others
for the declamation of poets and the lectures of philosophers ; in
a word, for every species of polite and manly amusement.   These
noble rooms were lined and paved with marble, adorned with
the most valuable columns, paintings and statues, and furnished
with collections of books for the sake of the studious who resorted
to them " (13).   The Romans instituted their system of baths
in this country 1,600 years ago ; their ruins exist to-day to
interest the antiquarians of imperial Britain.

The following words of Mr. Handley, medical officer of
Chipping Norton Union, although reported nearly eighty years

ago by Chadwick (1), still remain worthy of consideration when the construction of artizan dwellings is urgent and the provision of pit-head baths continues to be exceptional :— " When the smallpox was prevalent in this district, I attended a man, woman, and five children, all lying ill with the confluent species of that disorder in one bedroom, and having only two beds amongst them. The walls of the cottage were black, the sheets were black, and the patients themselves were blacker still ; two of the children were absolutely sticking together. It was indeed a gloomy scene. I have relished many a biscuit and glass of wine in Mr. Grainger's dissecting-room when ten dead bodies were lying on the tables under dissection, but was entirely deprived of appetite during my attendance upon these cases. The smell on entering the apartments was exceedingly nauseous, and the room would not admit of free ventilation."

Even to-day the provision of washing accommodation at mines and at factories is unusual ; miners, workers in foundries, smelting works, chemical and manure factories, dock side labourers, and indeed those employed in nearly every variety of manual occupation, still carry away with them the dust and dirt of their toil. They find themselves shunned by fellow passengers in trains and trams, a form of invidious class distinction better avoided. They arrive soiled at their homes, seldom provided with baths, where the housewife already has all she can do to keep the premises tidy and clean. Small wonder then that the hygiene of the skin is neglected by the working class population when their employers, by neglecting to make provision for removing the evidences of employment, appear to them to pay so little heed to so obvious a requirement. Employers often maintain, and maintain with justice, that, when provided, washing accommodation is abused rather than properly used. This very fact is in itself eloquent testimony to the existence of uncleanly customs, adoption of which the employers should never have permitted. In this matter, however, the conservatism of the worker can be overcome with but little patience. One of us recalls visiting a factory where excellent accommodation had recently been provided to comply with the requirements of Home Office Regulations applying to a dangerous trade. Vigorous complaints were made of torn towels, stolen soap and broken basins. At a revisit only six months later the information was elicited that the previous week there had been a threatened strike because the water for washing was not warm. At another factory where the new washing accommodation was on the ground floor and the canteen on the first floor, the manager told how at first he had himself to stand at the bottom of the stairs and turn the workers back to wash, and how he no longer had to do so, because if an unwashed worker went up to the canteen his fellows kicked him downstairs.

The position as it exists in relation to the provision of public baths in the United Kingdom has been fully set forth in a recent valuable report (14) issued by the Carnegie Trust, while the social aspect of the case, with special reference to the mining industry, has been ably discussed by Chappell and Lovat Fraser (15). These authors, after pointing to the " colour-bar " conferred by their occupation on miners, conclude that colliery baths would :—

    (1) Improve the health, comfort, safety and moral purity of the miner himself and his family.

    (2) Increase the miner's efficiency, effect economies in the working of the mines, and improve the conditions of safety.

    (3) Give greater comfort to the non-mining population who have to use public cars and trains and to frequent places where miners gather in their mining clothes.

    (4) Add to the miner's self-respect and improve his status in the eyes of the general public.

The Need.

The skin considered as an organ of the body presents a larger surface for the reception of, and for reacting to, impulses from the outside world than any other organ. Reference has been made to the important part it plays in reacting to atmospheric conditions of temperature, humidity and movement of air. Its duty of acting—mainly through the power of secreting sweat— as the main heat-regulating agency of the body is perhaps its most important health function. But the skin also possesses other important duties. It acts as a protective envelope, preserving the underlying tissues from microbic invasion. It acts as an organ of excretion for the elimination (a) of carbon dioxide, especially when the sweat glands are active ; and (b) through the sebaceous glands, of certain fatty substances which, if allowed to accumulate, trap micro-organisms and tend to decompose, so giving rise to unpleasant odours and a liability to the formation of pustules and dermatitis. It acts as an organ of protopathic and epicritic sensibility for the appreciation of touch, heat, cold, and pain ; in this connection its sensitivity is of more importance to skilled manual workers than to any other class of the community ; but these workers who particularly need this sensitivity are precisely those whose work, by exposure to dust and dirt, interferes with its acuteness. The skin, for the adequate carrying out of these functions, must be kept clean, a matter which is not always fully appreciated either by the industrial population or by their employers.

The Standard.

The standard of the accommodation which must be provided in certain dangerous trades laid down by the Home Office is as follows :—The washing conveniences should be under cover, and maintained in a cleanly state and in good repair.

There should be either—

(a) A trough with a smooth impervious surface (fitted with a waste pipe without plug), and of such length as to allow at least 2 feet for every five persons, and having a constant supply of water from taps or jets above the trough at intervals of not more than 2 feet ; or

(b) At least one lavatory basin for every five persons, fitted with a waste pipe and plug, or placed in a trough having a waste pipe, and having either a constant supply of hot and cold water or warm water laid on, or (if constant supply of heated water be not reasonably practicable) a constant supply of cold water laid on, and a supply of hot water always at hand when required for use by persons employed.

This standard was adopted during the war for factories where high explosives, such as T.N.T. were manipulated. At one of these factories, where great stress was laid upon personal hygiene and every worker had to change completely on commencing and leaving work, a serious explosion occurred causing several deaths and many injuries. Nearly every wound healed by first intention, and there was not a single case of serious sepsis ; a result ascribed by the medical staff to the cleanly condition of the workers' skin.

Apart from the value of washing to preserve the healthiness of the skin, it is particularly necessary in certain industries ; in those exposing the workers to contact with such poisons as lead, arsenic, mercury and their compounds, which may be conveyed from unwashed hands to food and so swallowed ; in engineering shops where contact with cooling fluids and lubricating oils may cause dermatitis ; in the gutting of fish, in salt mines, and in gut scraping, where contact with strong brine may cause painful indolent ulcers and dermatitis, and in the manufacture of bichromate of potash, and its use in tanning, where similar troubles occur.

What to Provide.

In view of the hard usage which the accommodation provided is likely to receive, special consideration should be given to its design. Every effort should be made to attain strength and simplicity combined with economy of space.

Basins and Troughs.—Traps on the waste pipe should be avoided. Plugs should not be provided ; even though attached by chains they become lost when, as is inevitable sooner or later, the chains break ; then the pipe opening is stuffed up with anything within reach and becomes choked ; moreover, even when all is in order they allow opportunity for several

FIG. 28.—Washing Trough with Spray Taps.
Reproduced by permission of Messrs. Shanks & Co., Barrhead.

workers to use the same water. Ordinary taps readily get out of order and are best replaced by water sprays which are economical of water and give the advantage of washing in running water ; when work ceases an attendant can turn on the water, adjusting the warmth by a mixing cock, when it flows from all the sprays, but there is advantage in having at least one spray fitted with its own tap for use at any other time. When sprays are being installed, they should be so placed that if desired a douche for the head, neck, and arms, can be indulged in. When basins and washing troughs are placed against walls, soapsuds soil the walls and render cleanliness difficult. A useful form of washing trough is shown in the illustration. It is economical of space, saves plumbing, and, being placed centrally, leaves the wall space for cloak-room accommodation, whether hooks or lockers. Note that the floor slopes towards the open drain channel, an arrangement which facilitates floor washing.

Soap.—The accessories for washing call for some consideration. Soap, if supplied in tablet form, is found to disappear with alarming rapidity, and can be more economically provided in the form of powder, fluid or paste. The paste form is most favoured, and may be placed either in an open box, or in a locked box with a hole in the bottom whence a supply of soap can be extracted by inserting a finger. A further device has also been

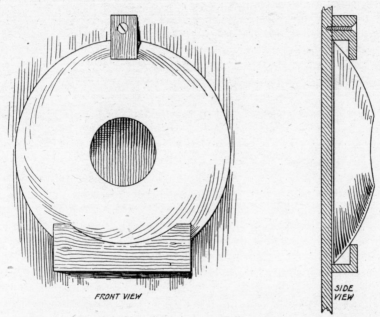

FRONT VIEW   SIDE VIEW

FIG. 29.—Container for Jelly Soap.

seen in use, which is shown in figure. It consists of a glazed earthenware container of the shape and size of a saucer with a hollow base. The container is charged with soap paste and then fixed against a flat board.

Nail-brushes.—Nail-brushes, even though chained in position, are frequently removed ; this difficulty may be overcome by providing large brushes say 18 inches by 4 inches fixed in position so that they drain into the washing trough. These brushes are used by rubbing the nails and hands against the bristles instead of the more usual reverse procedure.

Towels.—Clean, dry towels must be provided ; and the best plan is to supply a separate towel for each person washing, just as is done at hotels and clubs. Sometimes, while the workers are learning good manners, in order to avoid loss of towels, roller towels fastened in position are provided ; in this case the towels should be about 15 square feet in area ; each towel should serve nine workers, and be renewed before the next washing time ; but separate towels are always to be preferred.

Bathing Facilities.

Baths, even though more seldom provided than washing accommodation, are to-day, owing to housing conditions, a real necessity in many industries where there is special exposure to heat and dust, such as in coal mining and work at hot kilns, furnaces and rolling mills.

Douche Baths.—The simplest, most efficient and economical form is that of douche baths ; the falling water exerts a more refreshing and stimulating effect than is obtained by total immersion. This form of bath has been advocated for pit-head baths (2), and is already in use in some factories. Where women are employed, in order to avoid wetting the hair, the spray can be arranged to flow from a ring which is passed over the head, or from a nozzle attached to a flexible pipe. The following further details stated by the Health of Munition Workers Committee (3) should receive attention :—

" *Cubicles.*—The cubicles in which the baths are placed should be arranged to secure privacy. In order to reduce the time which each worker spends in the cubicle it may be possible to arrange for the workers to dress and undress partly outside the cubicle, but at any rate in the case of women some provision for dressing, including a seat and pegs, must be provided inside the cubicle. Where this is done the size of the cubicle should not be less than 3 feet wide by 4 feet deep. The walls should ordinarily not be less than 6 feet high. A space should be left between the floor and the walls of the cubicles sufficient to permit of drainage and cleaning.

" *Cleaning.*—The building and fittings should be so constructed as to facilitate the maintenance of absolute cleanliness. Square corners, ledges or rough inner surfaces should be avoided. Wood should be used only for seats, and for this purpose hard wood should be employed with spaces between the wood for ventilation. The walls and partitions (and this applies also to lavatories and sanitary conveniences) should always have smooth and curved surfaces which can be readily washed down and cannot be used for writing on. Enamel tiles and bricks or enamel metal sheets may be used for this purpose ; any initial cost thus incurred is soon recouped by saving in cleaning and lime-washing.

" *Water.*—The water used should be of adequate purity and should not be liable to cause injury to the health of the workers

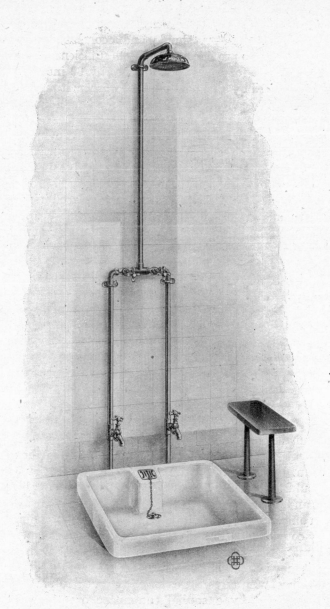

FIG. 30.—Douche Bath.
Reproduced by permission of Doulton & Co., Limited.

or to yield effluvia. It will generally be found preferable for the temperature of the water to be regulated by an attendant

22—2

rather than for the temperature of each bath to be regulated separately by the worker. A temperature of about 100° F. is usual. A thermometer should be placed in a convenient position so that the attendant can readily correct variations of temperature.

"*Soap and Towels.*—A simple and economical method of supplying soap is to provide small tablets sufficient for one bath. A convenient size for towels is 25 inches by 60 inches. When the baths are used by a large number of workers it may be found convenient and economical to provide a small laundry for washing them.

"*Drying of Clothes.*—The conditions of employment which render the provision of baths specially important often also make it desirable that facilities should be available for the drying of clothes. If only cloakroom pegs or lockers are provided for the damp clothes, hot water pipes should be placed immediately beneath them. A preferable plan where a large amount of clothing has to be dried is to suspend the clothes from the roof of the building by a chain or string securely fastened at the lower end. The heat of the building produced by the hot-water pipes for the baths causes a good current of air in the roof, which satisfactorily dries the clothes and prevents any disagreeable odour. The interior of the building may with advantage be maintained at a level temperature of about 70° F. This adds to the comfort of the workers and effectively dries the clothes. Ventilation can be obtained by the provision of ventilators in the roof or by the use of fans."

Maintenance.

" The maintenance of lavatories and baths is almost as important as their construction. This should be made the definite duty of an appointed officer acting under the Welfare Supervisor, who should keep the lavatory clean, control the supply of nail brushes and soap, and arrange that dry clean towels are available. Such an officer may also usefully be employed in attending to the sanitary conveniences and in supervising the cloakroom. While the ultimate responsibility for upkeep must rest with the employer, it may be found, at any rate in the case of baths, that the workers may, with advantage, be encouraged to participate in the management by a special committee or otherwise. The question of the payment to be made for baths will also need careful consideration ; in some cases at any rate the workers may prefer to make some small payment. Where periodic baths are of special benefit to health and efficiency, it is found desirable to allow workers time for bathing within working hours."

II. Sanitary Accommodation.

Construction.—Types of sanitary accommodation are discussed in books on general hygiene ; but one or two details may be specially mentioned in reference to installations for industrial establishments. These details are shown in the illustration given. Construction should be simple and strong :—

(i.) White enamelled pedestals with a good sized floor-base are preferable.

(ii.) Circular wooden seats, even if of the hinged lift-up type, are better avoided ; seat pads fixed on the rim of the pedestal are better ; care must, however, be taken in using such pads, that the opening of the pedestal is not too large ; for this reason pedestals previously fitted with a lift-up seat can seldom be fitted with seat pads.

(iii.) Each pedestal should have its own flush tank and its own trap to the drain ; an automatic flush common to several pedestals is objectionable, while several seat openings over one trough, periodically flushed, is a stage worse.

(iv.) Traps should be constructed so that they can be easily cleaned out.

(v.) The chain to the flush tank should be strong and durable.

(vi.) The floor upon which the pedestal is fixed should be of smooth impervious material to facilitate washing.

(vii.) The walls of each cubicle should have a smooth enamelled surface, formed by preference of glazed bricks ; scribbling on the wall is thus avoided.

The Standard.—The standard adopted by order under section 9 of the Factory and Workshop Act, 1901, is as follows :—

" (*a*) Not less than one sanitary convenience shall be provided for every twenty-five females.

" (*b*) Not less than one sanitary convenience shall be provided for every twenty-five men provided that—

" (i.) Where the number of males exceeds 100 and sufficient urinal accommodation is also provided, it shall be sufficient if there is one sanitary convenience for every twenty-five males up to the first 100 and one for every forty after.

" (ii.) Where the number of males exceeds 500, and proper supervision and control is exercised by a special officer, one convenience for every sixty men need only be provided in addition to sufficient urinal accommodation.

" (*c*) The accommodation must be arranged and maintained so as to be conveniently accessible at all times to all persons employed.

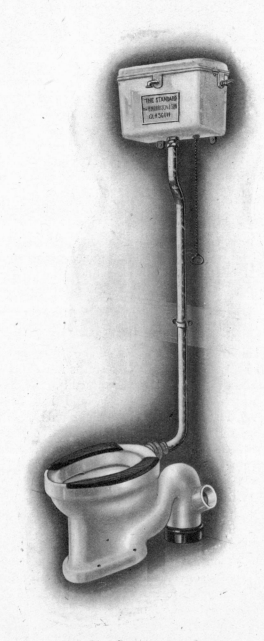

FIG. 31.—Sanitary Convenience.
Reproduced by permission of W. B. Morrison & Son,
Glasgow.

" (*d*). Every sanitary convenience must be kept in a cleanly state, sufficiently ventilated and lighted, and must not communicate with any workroom except through the open air or through an intervening ventilated space.

" (*e*) Every sanitary convenience must be under cover and so partitioned off as to secure privacy, and if for the use of females must have proper doors and fastenings.

" (*f*) Where persons of both sexes are employed, the accommodation for each sex shall be so placed that the interior shall not be visible, even when the door of a convenience is open, from any place where persons of the other sex have to work or pass ; if the convenience for one sex adjoin those for the other, the approaches must be separate."

One matter, frequently neglected, is worthy of note where women are employed : A receptacle, of simple material such as cardboard, which can easily be removed and incinerated, should always be provided for sanitary towels ; it should be placed on a shelf about 5 feet from the floor. Lack of attention to this simple detail leads to frequent blocking of drain pipes.

III. Drinking Water.

Opportunities should be afforded for drinking water as needed. All the functions of the body, respiration, the assimilation of food, heat regulation through sweating, elimination of waste products through the kidneys or by the bowels, require water. If too little is drunk " staleness," to use an athletic term, and constipation result. Normally about two and a half pints should be taken daily. The position has been summed up in the United States (6) as follows :—" Since so much body water is lost under conditions which provoke free perspiration, it is important that an ample amount of water be drunk to replenish the tissues thus deprived of their normal water content. Without this their proper functions will be hampered, and health and efficiency cannot be expected. The worker should be furnished with an abundant supply of water together with drinking facilities which are clean, attractive, and placed so as to be conveniently accessible at all times. The water should never be below 55° F. in temperature, as the drinking of cold water is likely to cause gastro-intestinal disorders. The jet sanitary fountain is the best drinking facility. Though under ordinary conditions the amount of heat lost in bringing the temperature of water up to that of the body is small, this amount, by judicious drinking, can be increased. Water should be drunk in small quantities and at frequent intervals, not in large quantities at infrequent intervals."

The Standard.—An order has been made in this country under the powers of section 7, Police, Factories, etc. (Miscellaneous Provisions), Act, 1916, by which " in all factories and workshops in which twenty-five or more persons are employed provision shall be made at suitable points, conveniently accessible at all times to all persons employed, for :—

" (*a*) An adequate supply of wholesome drinking water from a public main or from some other source of supply approved in writing by the local authority of the district in which the factory or workshop is situated, which shall be either laid on or contained in a suitable vessel ;

" (*b*) (Except where the water is delivered in an upward jet from which the workers can conveniently drink) at least one suitable cup or drinking vessel at each point of supply, with facilities for rinsing it in drinking water."

Drinking Fountains.—Drinking fountains such as that shown in the illustration have been devised to meet these requirements. Care, however, should be taken in their construction, for investigations have disclosed that a vertical jet of water may become infected from a case of septic throat or of influenza, and continue infected, somewhat in the way that a light ball placed on such a jet remains suspended in position. In one investigation (7) 58 per cent. of cultures taken from drinking fountains during an epidemic of influenza were found to be contaminated. The remedy is simple : the jet should be directed from the nozzle at an angle of about 15°, and be of such length that the lips of the drinker do not touch the side of the fountain.

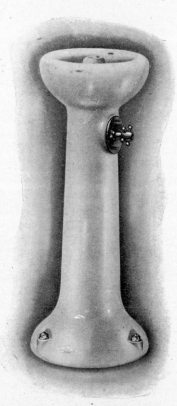

FIG. 32.—Drinking Fountain.
Reproduced by permission of Messrs. Shanks & Co., Barrhead.

IV. Working Clothes.

The rule when undertaking any kind of occupation is to " dress the part," and it should be strictly observed in industrial occupation. Here, however, observance can only be effected by the use of suitable working clothes separate and distinct from ordinary wearing apparel. The provision of working clothes by employers is called for under certain factory regulations aimed at safeguarding the worker against accident or injury to health ; but such provision is not to-day generally the custom in industry. We hope that ere long it may become the rule, especially as under section 7 of the Police, Factories, etc. (Miscellaneous Provisions), Act, 1916, powers exist to require such clothing where it appears to be necessary for securing the welfare of the workers. Working clothes or overalls are required for three reasons : (i.) to enable personal cleanliness to be attained, (ii.) to conduce to safety, and (iii.) to protect other clothing.

Personal cleanliness is important, not merely on account of the *amour propre* which goes with it, exerting a valuable psychological effect, but for health reasons. The wearing of working clothes enables the worker to leave his work tidy, and is a direct incentive to wash before leaving. A clean skin, which, as has already been pointed out, is a valuable asset, carries out better its physiological functions of sweating and temperature regulation ; and it is better able to resist nfection and heal rapidly when wounded. Attire only worn during working hours can be supervised and kept clean ; and thus there can be avoided at least one form of industrial dermatitis due to dirty cuffs of overalls rubbing infected oil and grease into the skin of the forearm in engineering shops.

The pattern of working clothes when supplied by the employer can be regulated, and thus loose-fitting tunics, loose neckties and aprons, and loose hair (among women)—prolific causes of serious accidents—can be got rid of. Mr. W. Sydney Smith, when dealing with this matter in relation to transmission machinery, recommended (4) that (i.) " every person employed or working in a room or place *within reach* of unfenced *transmission machinery* in motion in that room or place shall wear close-fitting clothing : aprons or neckties with loose ends shall not be worn by such persons ; (ii.) every female employed or working in a room or place *within reach* of *transmission machinery* in motion in that room or place shall have her hair fastened up, confined in a net, or otherwise secured." His reasons for these recommendations have been referred to in the chapter dealing with accidents.

Workers, especially when employed at dusty or dirty processes, at processes entailing exposure to acids or caustic liquids, to wet, to excessive heat, or exposure to weather, must have their clothing as well as themselves protected.

The wearing of working clothes has also another advantage. Workers generally dress in accordance with the weather ; their clothes are often too heavy and warm for hot and laborious processes.   As a result they sweat unduly, which in itself throws undue strain on their energies ; and when work is over they leave the factory for what may be a journey of half an hour or more on a cold day clad in damp underclothing.   The chilling which results adds to the natural tiredness following work, predisposes to muscular rheumatism and reduces resistance to possible infection.   A change room and suitable clothing to wear while at work are valuable means for improving health and efficiency and lessening lost time and sickness.

For Women.—Special attention, due to the employment of women during the war on many processes not previously undertaken by them, has been given (5) to the type of protective clothing which is suitable in each case for female operatives ; and the illustration (p. 354) shows types of costumes recommended for wear.   Further information with regard to these costumes is to be found in the appendix to this chapter.

For Men.—Protective clothing for males has received less attention, but all the reasons just given for the wearing of protective clothing apply with greatest force to male workers, who, to a far greater extent than women, are called upon to undertake arduous processes involving to an unusual degree exposure to heat, weather, dirt, and burning liquids ; a miner in a wet mine, smelters of metals, brickmakers, stonemasons, patent fuel workers, stokers, provide instances in point.   We are of opinion that working clothes should be regularly worn and discarded on leaving work.   Thus the labourer would learn the value to health of cleanliness while at work, would cease to carry home with him the grime of his toil, and would no longer find himself a pariah avoided by others on entering a tram, bus or train.   A king does not always wear his crown.

V. Cloak Rooms.

Provision of cloak rooms, which may now be called for under section 7, Police, Factories, etc. (Miscellaneous Provisions), Act, 1916, is needed for the accommodation of clothing put off during working hours, and for working clothes at other times.   Cloak rooms should be placed with convenient access to the washing facilities.   A good arrangement is for the workers to have to pass through the lavatory as they leave the factory in order to enter the cloak room where the working clothes are deposited and ordinary attire is resumed.   A cloak room should provide (i.) separate accommodation for each worker so arranged that working clothes and ordinary attire are not in contact ; for this purpose hanging pegs should not be less than 18 inches apart ; (ii.) means for drying garments ; hot water pipes at the floor level placed beneath the pegs or lockers are useful for this purpose ; another effective device is to suspend the damp clothing from a long rod or board which is then hauled up to the ceiling (*vide supra*, p. 340) ; (iii.) supervision by an attendant of the garments left, or control by locks, the keys of which are retained by the workers, in order to prevent pilfering—nearly always a source of serious annoyance until proper etiquette is established.

These desiderata may be obtained in several ways. The simplest is rows of pegs with hot-water pipes at the floor level, the room being kept locked except just before the commencement and at the cessation of work. Separate lockers may be provided for each worker, ventilation being arranged for by openings at the top and at the bottom above hot-water pipes. A third useful device is to hang the garments at one end of a pole which is then elevated and hung up so that the garments are out of reach ; a separate pole is provided for each worker ; the lower end of the pole is placed in a slot and locked in position, or a number of poles are locked in position by one lever controlled by the attendant.

Cloak rooms and provision for drying clothes call for special consideration for miners. The subject has been well dealt with by Chappell and Lovat-Fraser (15) ; their book, which contains illustrations of several useful devices, should be consulted by any one constructing cloak room accommodation.

VI. Seats.

Seats may not at first sight appear to be intimately connected with health ; but they are of considerable importance, first to eliminate unnecessary fatigue, secondly to correct faulty posture at work, thirdly to minimise aching feet and any tendency to varicose veins and flat feet. Consideration is more likely to be given in the future than in the past to the provision of sitting accommodation, since the subject is now included in two Acts of Parliament, one dealing with seats for shop assistants, and the second section 7 of the Police, Factories, etc. (Miscellaneous Provisions), Act, 1916. Under the powers conferred by the second, an order has been made calling for the provision of seats for those engaged upon the turning of shells. The mere provision of some sort of seat, although it might technically comply with the letter of the law, would, however, not be in accordance with the spirit. Sitting accommodation has in the past been little studied, so much so, that factory seats have been likened (10) to coffins, as things which the maker does not need, the purchaser does not use, and the user has no opportunity to speak about.

Seats may be required for two distinct purposes: (i.) for rest; (ii.) for work. Many processes which entail constant standing provide periods during which an operative is not actively occupied. Some foremen object to workers being allowed to sit down at these periods on the ground that seats suggest idleness and tend to slackness; these disciplinarians wish for parade ground smartness in the workshop. But let them remember that military preciseness required for saluting the colours does not represent the work-a-day procedure of warfare, whether in the trenches, with the guns, or on the march; and that where efficiency is the objective, superficial smartness contributes but little to discipline and less than nothing to output. The Health of Munition Workers Committee in their final report pointed out (12) that " the object of the provision of seats is not to secure that all work should be done seated, since a sedentary life has its own disadvantages, but rather that means should be provided for varying the position wherever possible, and for occasional use when work necessitates a standing position." While in the same report Dr. Janet Campbell remarks :— " The provision of seats and the use made of them unfortunately appears to depend too much on the caprice or prejudices of individual managers and foremen, who do not yet realise that, if suitably used, seats reduce fatigue and do not encourage habits of idleness and slackness."

Seats for Rest.—The processes concerned in the turning of shells may be instanced. Here a worker may have merely to watch a lathe for half an hour or more while the outside is being removed from the rough casting of a large shell; or, by way of contrast, work at a multi-tool capstan lathe may keep the operative constantly and actively employed, and the only opportunity for a pause is when the supply of material for any reason slackens or the tools require setting. A large rough casting can be watched as carefully by a worker sitting down as standing up, but the process of constant standing without activity is productive of static fatigue. The pioneer of industrial medicine, Ramazzini, spoke (9) of this matter in 1700 :—" In general those who stand at work are subject chiefly to varices, or swellings in the veins, for the tonic motion of the muscles retards the course of the blood, upon which it stagnates in the veins and valves of the legs. . . . Hence the blood, that returns from the arteries into the veins, does not receive the necessary force from the impulse of the arteries to make it rise in a perpendicular line ; so that, for want of the due impulse to back it, it stops and produces varices in the legs." Human beings are not constructed for maintaining the erect posture except during muscular activity ; this activity squeezes forward the blood in the veins and assists circulation. When it is absent the pressure of the blood in the veins, especially of the legs, is considerable, and the circulation not only of the blood but also of the lymph slows down ; aching feet result, and, if idle standing is insisted on over weeks and months, varicose veins and flat feet follow. Seats should be provided to obviate static fatigue. Investigation, moreover, has shown that at many lathe processes short periods of from three to four minutes frequently occur during which time a seat can be used with advantage ; that supplies of material from time to time run short ; and that broken tools or other machinery difficulties also provide further opportunities for resting. There is also the further case of the operative on a multi-tool capstan lathe who feels that a rest-pause is needed to enable him to maintain the pace he finds most suited to himself ; he must either rest or slow down to a pace at which he is less efficient.

The turning of shells is not an isolated process in this connection. An instance is quoted (16) where " instructions were given that a number of girls were to stop work and sit down at five minutes to every hour, except the last hour of the day, for a five-minutes' rest. A few months later the figures of their output were carefully examined—six cases were selected in which all variable factors could be eliminated, i.e., the girls chosen were employed during both periods on the same article, the same machine, and had been working constantly without days off.

" In no case did their output show less than a 6·4 per cent. increase, and in four out of six it showed over 10·9 per cent. This means an increased production of, roughly, 180,950 pieces per annum."

Seats should be provided for processes at which (i.) periods of inactivity as long as three minutes occur ; (ii.) the supply of material cannot be continuously guaranteed ; (iii.) machinery delays are inevitable ; (iv.) the operatives control the pace ; and (v.) where short rest-pauses are introduced.

Seats for Work.—Seats required for rest purposes in shape and construction call for no special thought ; but seats for work are entirely different and call for consideration under two headings —seats for sedentary work, and seats for work usually done standing.

Seats for sedentary work should be designed to fit the worker for the work in those cases where the reverse cannot be effected.

A simple case may be taken, that of sedentary work at a table.
An observer may see in almost any factory a row of workers
seated on one long bench; the tall with bent backs almost
sprawling over the table, the short, with their feet hardly touch-
ing the ground, reaching up to their work. Clearly equally
efficient work cannot be expected. The height of work benches
and tables as well as of chairs here calls for consideration; and
Gilbreth points out (10) that " at almost no cost factory workers
can have their workplaces and chairs designed or altered for their

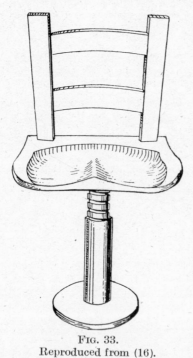

individual measurements, and in
the majority of cases should have
tables or benches made for working at standing height, and chairs
arranged to maintain the elbows
the same height above the floor
while either sitting or standing.
This is not intended to convey
the idea of sanction or approval
of the too common book-keepers'
chair, with its inhuman round top
and its opportunity for the book-
keeper to imitate a woodbine
around and through its legs and
rungs." The provision of separate
chairs suited to each worker is not
a difficult matter; but the sitting
height, that is the length of the
body, rather than the standing
height, should be the measure
to go by. Seats are sometimes
provided the heights of which
can be adjusted, like a music

FIG. 33.
Reproduced from (16).

stool (see Fig. 33); and we have noted in such cases that the
heights at which the seats are adjusted are as numerous as the
workers using them. Each seat should have a back, and the
object should be that each worker should sit comfortably.
The process concerned will determine the exact relation of the
height of the table to the worker; this may be measured with
regard to the level of the elbow when the arm is bent and held
by the side. In the case of short workers foot rests should be
provided, either on the chairs or on the table. Vibration from
machinery is often considerable in factories and adds materially
to the onset of fatigue. Much can be done to minimise its effect
by providing the legs of chairs with rubber soles, or even, as
designed by Gilbreth (8), with springs.

The arrangement and spacing of seats provided for sedentary work are matters equally as important as their construction, but for a different reason. Much lost time occurs among operatives due to the spread of infectious complaints which include all kinds of sore throats, influenza, phthisis, pneumonias, cerebrospinal meningitis, scarlet fever, measles, diphtheria, and, most important of all, the "common cold." These diseases travel from one person to another by direct infection due to projection of germs into the air by an infected person or a carrier during acts of coughing, sneezing and speaking, to be inhaled by a neighbour. Wherever persons are brought together risk of infection is present; but the risk can be lessened by spacing, that is to say, by keeping them a reasonable distance apart, and allowing for this purpose at least 4 feet for seating each person. The provision of separate chairs for each worker rather than a bench is a great help in this matter, as the temptation to crowd workers more closely together, and any tendency on the part of the workers themselves to sit close together, is thereby countered. Another important point is *not* to place workers in rows facing one another across a narrow table or work bench; this plan, which is all too usual, provides every facility for infection. A table on the opposite sides of which workers are to sit should be at least 4 feet wide.

There remains yet the third group—chairs for use at processes which are usually carried on standing. Greater thought and ingenuity is required in devising this group of chairs; but the trouble taken will be fully repaid in improved output. When attention is directed to the matter, but few processes which entail the operative standing for long periods in one position will be found for which a chair cannot be devised. The height of the chair should be such that a bent elbow will be at what has been found to be the best level in relation to the work, whether that work be at a lathe, a power press, or a vice. Foot rests and backs should form parts of such chairs; for, as Spaeth writes (11): "A moment's consideration will make it clear that the higher we get from the floor the more attention and energy we have to give to maintaining our balance. In the case of a high stool without back and arms the waste of energy becomes considerable. The types of defence reactions that are developed by workers who are forced to sit on high stools are most interesting. Some hook their feet about the table or stool legs; others arrange temporary foot-rests under the tables, using boxes or discarded chairs; still others wedge themselves tightly between the stool and table tops. A practical solution of this problem is either to scrap the old stools and install a simple type of saddle-seated

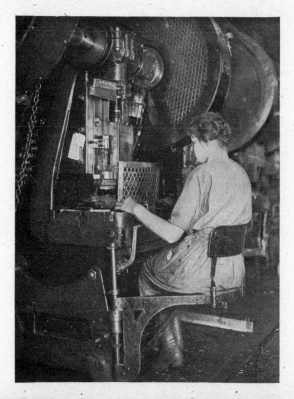

Fig. 34.—Swinging Seat for Press Operators. It swings under the press
out of the sweeper's way and when not in use.
Reproduced from *Factory*, the Magazine of Management, by
permission of A. W. Shaw Co., Ltd.

stool with a back and foot-rest, or to convert the old stools into reasonably comfortable seats by screwing a broad seat and low back on to the old stool top." Workers often prefer to work part-time sitting and part-time standing, and there is advantage in this preference; therefore, the chairs should be capable of being easily pushed on one side when not required (see Fig. 34).

Chairs intended for factory use should be well built in order to stand the wear and tear. Appearance should not be so much studied as suitability.

VII. Bibliography.

1. *Report of Poor Law Commissioners into the Sanitary Condition of the Labouring Population of Great Britain*, pp. 253–4. 1842.

2. *Report of Departmental Committee on Washing and Drying Accommodation at Mines*. (Cd. 6724.) 1913.

3. "Washing Facilities and Baths." *Health of Munition Workers Committee. Memo. No.* 14. (Cd. 8387.) 1916.

4. Smith, W. Sydney. *Fencing and Safety Precautions for Transmission Machinery.* H.M. Stationery Office. 1913.

5. *Protective Clothing for Women and Girl Workers.* H.M. Stationery Office. 1917.

6. United States Public Health Service. *Report No.* 50, Vol. XXXII. Washington Government Printing Office. December 14th, 1917.

7. Pettibone, Borgorl and Clark. *Journal Bacteriology*, Vol. I., p. 471. 1916.

8. Gilbreth, F. B. and L. M. *Fatigue Study.* Geo. Routledge & Sons. 1916.

9. Ramazzini, B. *The Diseases of Tradesmen.* Translated by Dr. James. 2nd Edition. 1746.

10. Gilbreth, F. B. and L. M. "Unnecessary Fatigue." *Journal Industrial Hygiene*, Vol. I. March, 1920.

11. Spaeth, R. A. "The Prevention of Fatigue." *Journal Industrial Hygiene*, Vol. I. January, 1920.

12. *Final Report, Health of Munition Workers Committee.* (Cd. 9065.) 1918.

13. Pompeii. *The Library of Entertaining Knowledge*, Vol. I. Charles Knight. 1833.

14. *Report on Public Baths and Washhouses in the United Kingdom.* Carnegie U.K. Trust. 1918.

15. Chappell, E. L., and Lovat-Fraser, G. A. *Pit Head and Factory Baths.* Welsh Housing and Development Association, Cardiff, 1920.

16. *Seats for Workers in Factories and Workshops.* H.M. Stationery Office. 1920.

VIII. Appendix.

Reproduced from (5).

PART I.

There are two main types of protective clothing in general use :—

The overall suit—Type A.

The trouser or knicker suit with tunic—Type B.

One or other of these types will as a rule be suitable wherever the work is dusty or dirty, or where women are employed on or near machinery not of a specially dangerous character.

Special types will be required in cases where there is exposure to acids or alkalis (Type C); excessive wet (Type D); machinery involving special risk (Type E); excessive heat (Type F); or where the employment is in the open air (Type G).

The full descriptions of the several types are as follows :—

Type A.—Overall dress and cap; also apron in some cases. No outside pockets—sleeves to fasten closely at wrists.

Type B.—Trouser or knicker suit with close-fitting coat or tunic, and leggings. No outside pockets.

D   D   G   F   B   C   C   E   A
(without apron)   (without apron)

FIG. 35.—Group showing Various Types of Protective Clothing.
Reproduced from (5).

Type C.—Overall dress or trouser suit of woollen material (baize, etc.); cap; leather apron (with bib); and high-topped waterproof boots or leather or flannel leggings, or puttees covering the open tops and lace-holes of clogs or boots. Gloves, in some cases, of rubber. Goggles where there is risk of splashing.

Type D.—Overall dress or trouser suit; cap; apron (with bib) of waterproof material such as rubber, oilskin, mackintosh, pegamoid or leather; and high-topped waterproof boots, or leggings or puttees covering the open tops and lace-holes of boots, or clogs.

Type E.—Boiler suits; cap. No outside pockets—sleeves to fasten closely at wrists.

Type F.—Thin overall dress or trouser suit; cap. The material may be cotton, drill, or jean, etc., or linen, of thickness according to need.

Type G.—Weatherproof coat or trouser suit and clogs; waterproof cap ("sou'wester").

PART II.

Process. (1)	Nature of risk. (2)	Type of clothing recommended. (3)
1. *Aeroplane works.* Doping	Varnish . .	A, with apron.
2. *Boot and shoe making.* Skiving, buffing and trimming.	Dust . . .	A.
3. *Brick works.*	(1) Dust and dirt (2) Exposure to weather.	A. G.
4. *Cement works* . . .	Dust . . .	A or B.
5. *Chemical processes.* (a) Acids . . .	(1) Acid burns . . (2) Wet . .	C. D.
(b) Alkali . . .	Caustic burns .	C.
(c) Ammonium nitrate .	Wet (deliquescence of salt).	D.
(d) Chlorate . . .	Burns . .	A or B. Fireproofed material, washed daily.
(e) Phenol . . .	Burns . .	D, with gloves and goggles where there is risk of splashing.
(f) Bleaching powder .	Burns . .	C.
6. *Engine house* . . .	Danger from machinery.	E.
7. *Fellmongering, tanning and currying.* (a) Lime and tan pits .	Wet . . .	D.
(b) Dry processes . .	Dust . . .	A.
(c) Oiling skins . .	Oil . . .	D.
8. *Food production.* (a) Aerated water bottling and beer bottling.	Wet . . .	D.
(b) Bacon curing . .	Wet . . .	D, with clogs.
(c) Bread baking. . .	Dust . . .	A.
(d) Brewing . . .	Heat . . .	F.
(1) Fermenting (cleaning vessels).	(1) Ladder climbing.	B.
(2) Barrel washing .	(2) Wet . .	D.
(e) Confectionery (starch room).	Dust . . .	A.
(f) Cocoa grinding . .	Dust . . .	A.
(g) Milk drying . .	Heat . . .	F.
(h) Fish curing . .	Wet and salt .	D, with long sea boots and sou'-wester cap.

23—2

Process. (1)	Nature of risk. (2)	Type of clothing recommended. (3)
8. *Food production*—continued.		
(*i*) Flour milling . .	(1) Ladder climbing and oiling machinery.	B or E.
	(2) Dust . .	A.
(*j*) Gut scraping and preparation of sausage skins.	Wet and offensive material.	D.
(*k*) Ham boiling . .	Wet . . .	D, with clogs.
(*l*) Jam making (boiling house).	(1) Wet . .	D.
	(2) Stickiness .	B.
(*m*) Malting :		
(a) Steeping . .	Wet . . .	D.
(b) Spreading on floors	Damp and active work.	B.
(*n*) Pickle making . .	Wet and vinegar.	D.
(*o*) Sugar refining . .	(1) Great heat .	F.
	(2) Stickiness .	B.
	(3) Wet . .	D.
(*p*) Tea packing . .	Dust . . .	A.
(*q*) Tripe dressing . .	Wet and offensive material.	D.
9. *Gas works.*		
(*a*) General . . .	(1) Heat . .	F.
	(2) Fine dust .	A or B (G if in open air).
(*b*) Coke washing . .	Wet . . .	D, with clogs.
(*c*) General labouring .	Wet weather, outdoor.	G.
10. *Glass works.*		
(*a*) Grinding and polishing	Wet . . .	D.
(*b*) Handling and carrying	Sharp edges (cuts)	A (stout leather apron and palm shields, clogs or strong boots).
(*c*) Washing . . .	Wet . . .	D.
(*d*) Mixing . . .	Dust . . .	A and B.
(*e*) Packing . . .	Dust (straw, etc.)	A.
11. *Hair.*		
(*a*) Sorting . . .	Dust . . .	A.
(*b*) Washing and drying .	Wet and dirt .	D.
(*c*) Packing . . .	Dust . . .	A.
12. *Kapok, feather and down stuffing.*		
Hand processes . .	Dust . . .	A. Veil to protect eyes, nose and mouth.
13. *Labouring.*		
(*a*) Outdoor . . .	Exposure to weather.	G.
(*b*) Indoor . . .	Active and heavy work.	B.

Process. (1)	Nature of risk. (2)	Type of clothing recommended. (3)
14. *Laundry work and job dyeing.*		
(a) Wash-house . .	Wet . . .	D.
(b) Dye-house . . .	Wet . . .	D.
(c) Dry cleaning . .	Burn, benzene .	A. Fireproofed material.
15. *Linoleum.*		
(a) Stoves . . .	Heat and ladder climbing.	B, of thin material.
(b) Whiting department .	Dust and heavy work.	B.
(c) Cork department .	Dust . . .	A.
16. *Metal processes.*		
(a) Acetylene welding .	Burns . .	Drill overall dress, leather or asbestos cloth apron, tinted glass goggles and gauntlets.
(b) Aluminium (manufacture or use).	Fine dust . .	B or A.
(c) Battery house (cleaning and preparing accumulators).	Acid . . .	C.
(d) Crane driving . .	(1) Ladder climbing.	E or B, with cap.
	(2) Mill gearing .	E or B, with cap.
(e) Electric welding .	Burns . .	Drill overall dress, leather or asbestos cloth apron, leather gloves, goggles, and screen.
(f) Electro plating . .	Wet . . .	D.
(g) Engineering . .	(1) Dirt and dust, oil.	D or A, with impervious apron.
	(2) Wet and oil .	D.
	(3) Revolving or projecting machinery parts.	A or B.
(h) Forges and foundries .	Burns . .	Trouser suit, boots without laceholes or with special tongues, and leather leggings to knee; cap.
(i) Galvanising . .	(1) Acid . .	C.
	(2) Wet . .	D.
(j) Grinding and turning .	Wet and metal particles.	D, with goggles in some cases.
(k) Moulding and core making; cleaning. .	(1) Dust . .	A or B.
	(2) Particles of metal or scale.	A, with leather gloves and clogs. Goggles in some cases.

Process. (1)	Nature of risk. (2)	Type of clothing recommended. (3)
16. *Metal processes*—continued.		
(*l*) Pickling . . .	(1) Acid . .	C.
	(2) Wet . .	D.
(*m*) Tinning . . .	(1) Acid . .	C.
	(2) Wet . .	D.
(*n*) Shipyard processes (general).	(1) Exposure to weather.	G.
	(2) Climbing .	B or E.
(*o*) Painting . . .	Climbing . .	B or E.
17. *Millgearing.*		
Work on or about . .	Danger from machinery and climbing.	E.
18. *Oil seed crushing.*		
General	(1) Great heat .	F.
	(2) Oil and dirt .	D.
19. *Paint and colours* . .	(1) Dirt (paint) .	A, with apron.
	(2) Climbing .	B, with apron.
20. *Paper making.*		
(*a*) Pulp trucking . .	Wet . . .	D.
(*b*) Machine work . .	Danger from projecting or revolving machinery parts.	E or B.
21. *Paper and rag sorting.*		
Sorting and grinding .	Dust . . .	A.
22. *Potteries.*		
(*a*) Dry processes . .	Dust . . .	A.
(*b*) Wet processes . .	Wet . . .	D.
23. *Rabbit skins or hatters' furriers.*		
(*a*) Sorting . . .	Dust and offensive material.	A.
(*b*) Pulling . . .	Dust and offensive material.	A.
(*c*) Drying . . .	Dust and offensive material.	A and F.
(*d*) Carrotting. . .	Wet Acid . .	D.
(*e*) Cutting and other machine work.	Dust . . .	A.
24. *Rope or twine making* .	(1) Dust . .	A.
	(2) Danger from machinery.	B.

Process. (1)	Nature of risk. (2)	Type of clothing recommended. (3)
25. *Rubber works.* General	(1) Danger from projecting or revolving machinery. (2) Heat . . (3) Wet . .	B. F. D.
26. *Sand blasting.* (*a*) Inside chamber . .	Dust and grit .	B or E, with helmet and breathing tube.
(*b*) Outside chamber .	Injury to hands .	Gloves.
27. *Saw-milling and wood-working.* (*a*) General . . .	(1) Dust . . (2) Climbing . (3) Danger from machinery.	A. E or B, with cap. B or E, with cap.
(*b*) Fire-lighter making .	Burns, naphthaline	C. Fireproof apron.
28. *Slag wool.* . . .	Dust . . .	A, with veil.
29. *Soap making.* (*a*) Boiling . . . (*b*) Cask filling . . (*c*) Dry soap packing .	Dirt . . . Dirt . . . Dust . . .	B, with clogs. B, with clogs. A.
30. *Stoking*	Heat and dirt .	B or F.
31. *Textile and allied processes.* (*a*) Cotton doubling (wet).	Wet (or heat) .	Waterproof apron with bib.
(*b*) Flax spinning . .	Wet . . .	Waterproof apron with bib.
(*c*) Jute spinning . .	Dust . . .	A.
(*d*) Wool washing and finishing.	Wet . . .	D.
(*e*) Bleaching . . .	Wet . . .	D.
(*f*) Dyeing . . .	Wet . . .	D.
(*g*) Chrome dyeing . .	(1) Wet and chrome ulceration.	D, with rubber gloves where hands are immersed in chrome solutions.
(*h*) Brattice cloth preparing	Wet . . .	D or F.

PART IV

CHAPTER XVI

LABOUR TURNOVER OR INDUSTRIAL WASTAGE

I. Introduction. II. Effect of Labour Turnover. III. Methods of Investigating Industrial Wastage. IV. The Value of Investigation. V. Prevention of Industrial Wastage :—Selection of Workers ; Care of the Employed. VI. Bibliography.

I. Introduction.

THE supply of labour in the past has for the most part been adequate to meet the demand ; but during and since the war the condition has altered, labour is both less plentiful and more costly. Employers are coming to realise how workers have been accustomed to drift from factory to factory or from mine to mine ; but even yet they hardly appreciate the magnitude of this drift or labour turnover, the economic loss of this industrial wastage. Astonishment is often expressed at the discovery that a turnover of 100 per cent. per annum is quite ordinary, which means that to maintain a *personnel* of 1,000 workers, 1,000 new workers require to be engaged every year, and that a turnover of 400 per cent. is only somewhat unusual.

The industrial hygienist, while regretting the loss of efficiency and wasteful expenditure of wealth thus caused, looks at the subject from a different angle ; to him a high rate of leaving at any industrial concern suggests the existence of conditions ill-suited to the human machine ; for him labour turnover represents industrial " deaths " (even though the individual concerned may and usually does come again into industrial life at another factory) and plays the part taken by mortality in vital statistics ; while, when excessive in early weeks of employment, industrial wastage has the same importance to industry that infantile mortality has to the general community. Such premature labour turnover is as much an indication that something is wrong with industry, as a high infantile mortality is of something wrong with social life.

Certain investigations have been made into the subject in America. Thus Mr. Willits (1) after examining data for the period 1907—15, referring to a particular shop in a carpet mill, found that 48 per cent. of the men and 38 per cent. of the women remained in the service of the firm less than ten weeks. Mr. Alexander (2) conducted another inquiry on a larger scale; the figures he collected showed there were in the establishments investigated 38,668 persons employed on January 1st, 1912, a number which rose to 46,796 by December 31st, an increase of 8,128. He found that in order to effect this increase no less than 44,365 persons were engaged, which meant that 36,237 had dropped out of employment during the twelve months. That is to say, five and a half times as many people had to be engaged as constituted the increase in the number employed at the end of the period.

An investigation conducted (3) in relation to munition workers in this country provided for one old-established firm the following data :—

Month.	Number employed.	Number started.	Number left for various reasons.	Number left without reason.	Number employed at end of month.
June . .	4,340	622	138	253	4,571
July . .	4,571	695	48	87	5,131
August . .	5,131	464	67	220	5,308
September .	5,308	578	174	45	5,667
October .	5,667	1,054	236	248	6,237

Hence at this factory during the five months 3,413 women were engaged; if no workers had left the total number employed would have reached $(4,340 + 3,413 =)$ 7,753; but in fact, by the end of October, the *personnel* totalled 6,237; so that 1,516 had left, a number representing 44·4 per cent. of the number engaged. The data of Table 7 show that this state of affairs is not peculiar to war time. The cause of leaving was only known with regard to 663, or 43·7 per cent.; the balance had simply vanished (4).

Professor F. S. Lee of the Public Health Service of America quotes (5) an instance where out of 10,434 employees who left, 9,442, more than 90 per cent., left for reasons unknown to the company, and remarks that this experience is probably not exceptional.

Data from another factory (L. 7 in Table 8) showed that during the twelve months ending August 28th, 1916, an increase of 624 workers resulted from 1,031 new engagements amongst men, while an increase of 914 was obtained from 1,527 new engagements amongst women—percentages of 165 and 167 respectively—figures which compare favourably with those previously quoted.

Further information has recently been published in America (10) concerning labour turnover in two well-organised engineering factories mainly concerned with male labour. The first, which was employed on an eight-hour day and possessed good welfare conditions comparable to those, referred to later, of factory L. 7, experienced a similarly low labour turnover of 30 per cent. ; the second was employed on a ten-hour day, " with long hours of labour and low wages, averaging, even in 1918, piece rates of \$3.2 per day for men, and \$2.8 for women. It is not surprising to find the turnover at this plant nearly six times as high as at the eight-hour plant, that is, 176 per cent." At this second factory the welfare conditions compared unfavourably with those of the eight-hour plant.

II. Effect of Labour Turnover.

We point in Chapter XVII. to the cost to industry of labour turnover, but should remark the estimate there quoted, 35 dollars per person, is comparatively low. Alexander estimates it at 53·9 dollars for each new employee, while other American estimates vary from 10 dollars to two hundred. These estimates presumably include among other things spoilt material and loss in quantity and quality of output due to lack of skill in the new worker, which even for the simplest process does not disappear in less than three months.

The relation between fatigue and industrial wastage is referred to in Chapter V. There are also other ways in which an industrial concern is affected by an influx of new workers. For instance, evidence shows that such workers are more liable to sustain injuries than workers of long experience, and they also lose more time for sickness (see Chapter VIII.). With regard to the latter point, investigations show that the percentage of the time lost among a group of workers who leave at the end of three months' service rises rapidly during the last fortnight of service, a rise which is not found at that period among those remaining in employment, and that the same thing is also found if the period of service be taken at six months, or nine months ; in other words, the unrest which culminates in cessation of employment or industrial " death," definitely expresses itself in an increase of sickness.

The cost to the worker is certainly not less than that to the employer ; he may remain out of work for a time, so suffering

loss of wages; at new work he takes time in coming to his full
output, meanwhile he is earning less; if he sustains an accident
or falls sick, as he is more prone to do in early weeks at new
work, his financial loss is serious.

The following rough estimate may convey some idea of the
cost incurred to-day. There are some eight million workers in
our factories and workshops. Take labour turnover at 100 per
cent., and the cost to employers of replacement at the low figure
of £2 per head. We arrive at a total of £16,000,000. The cost
to the workers is not less than an equal amount. Hence, in
factories and workshops alone, without considering mines,
railways, transport, shipping, shop assistants, agriculture, or
clerks, industry bears an annual burden of over £30,000,000
due to labour turnover.

The study of industrial wastage is, then, clearly of importance
to the economics of labour. It is also important to the application of preventive surgery and medicine to the health of the
worker. Our next purpose is to discuss how industrial wastage
may be calculated.

III. Methods of Investigating Industrial Wastage.

If we wish to appraise the value of modifications of the routine
of industrial life, we should have some method of standardisation
comparable in form to the " corrected " death and morbidity
rates of vital statistics by means of which one factory can be
tested against another, or one year contrasted with another in
the experience of the same factory. To measure the consequences of recruiting labour from different social classes,
age groups or geographical districts, sometimes even to
judge the effect of hygienic reforms, we need a statistical
method.

An attempt has been made to furnish a common measure by
treating the employment statistics much as the actuary of an
insurance company handles its policies.

The method is simple enough. Provided we know the date of
engagement and the date of leaving of all employees in a factory
or industry who passed through such factory or industry over
an assigned period, we may proceed as follows. The probability
that an employee will leave in his first month (week, fortnight or
whatever time unit we please) of service will be the ratio of the
numbers actually leaving in the first month of service to the
total number of entrants less the number still at work, but only
having been at work less than half a month (since these have not
had on the average a month's " exposure " to the " risk " of

leaving). The chance of leaving in the second month will similarly be the ratio of the numbers leaving in that month to the entrants less the losses of the first month, the number of those employed less than half a month and the number of those employed less than one and a half months. Following out this process we can compute the probabilities of leaving in the first, second, third, etc., month of service.

To illustrate the nature and calculation of a wastage table we will take an imaginary example. Let us suppose that during the first six months of a year 700 boys had been engaged and that their cards were sorted out immediately on the expiration of the six months, it being found that 500 of the boys were still at work and that 200 had left, these totals being distributed as shown in Tables A and B. Then, in order to calculate the proportions leaving in each month of service, we proceed as set out in Table C. Obviously all the boys might have left in the first month of service, since they all either did so leave or remained at work for at least one month. Hence the chance of leaving in the first month is simply the number actually leaving divided by the total of the two tables. For the second month, those who left in the first month and those still at work, but only having been at work one month when the record was made, evidently had no chance of leaving in the second month and must be deducted from the first month's total to reach the number exposed to risk for the second month, and similarly for each subsequent month.

AFTER-HISTORIES OF BOYS ENGAGED BETWEEN JANUARY 1ST AND JUNE 30TH.

Record taken on July 1st.

TABLE A.—*Boys still Employed.*

Length of service.				Number.
1 month	.	.	.	50
2 ,,	.	.	.	100
3 ,,	.	.	.	150
4 ,,	.	.	.	125
5 ,,	.	.	.	65
6 ,,	.	.	.	10
		Total	.	500

A boy who has been at work more than two but less than six weeks is entered as having worked one month ; more than six but less than ten, two months, and so on.

TABLE B.—*Boys Left.*

Left in			Number.
1st month	.	.	. 100
2nd ,,	.	.	. 50
3rd ,,	.	.	. 20
4th ,,	.	.	. 15
5th ,,	.	.	. 10
6th ,,	.	.	. 5
		Total .	200

TABLE C.—*Wastage.*

Exposed to risk of leaving in	Number.	Actually left.	Per cent. Wastage.
1st month .	700	100	$\dfrac{100 \times 100}{700}=14 \cdot 3$
2nd ,, .	$700-100-50=550$	50	$\dfrac{100 \times 50}{550}= 9 \cdot 1$
3rd ,, .	$550-50-100=400$	20	$\dfrac{100 \times 20}{400}= 5 \cdot 0$
4th ,, .	$400-20-150=230$	15	$\dfrac{100 \times 15}{230}= 6 \cdot 5$
5th ,, .	$230-15-125= 90$	10	$\dfrac{100 \times 10}{90}=11 \cdot 1$
6th ,, .	$90-10- 65= 15$	5	$\dfrac{100 \times 5}{15}=33 \cdot 3$
7th ,, .	None exposed.	—	—

Such a wastage analysis places the factory in possession of much accurate information. It is usually found in the case of adults that the wastage of the first month is the heaviest—much as the death rate is heaviest in the first year of life, and for much the same reason—but if it appears that this " infantile mortality " is much heavier in one shop than in another, or for one year than for the previous year, then the inference may be drawn that the method of selecting candidates for employment needs revision. It may also be found that the rate of wastage shows a sudden increase after two or three months' service, indicating the effects of, perhaps, unsuitable hours and suggesting the need of inquiry. The method can be applied to persons of particular ages, tables of wastage among entrants from fourteen to fifteen years of age and of older persons being separately compiled and compared. It is also easy to calculate from the rates what percentage of 100 persons engaged will still be at work in the factory after any desired number of months. Thus, taking the example given, the percentage of persons still at work three months from engagement will be:—100 × ·857 × ·909 × ·950 = 74, or 26 per cent. leave within three months of entry (6).

If, in addition to the simple particulars of engagement and withdrawal, we have information as to sex, age, reason for withdrawal, etc., we may make minuter subdivisions.

TABLE 1.—*All Factories. Combined Ages.*

Months of service.	Exposed.	Numbers left.				Percentages.			
		Ill-health.	Other sufficient reason.	No sufficient reason.	Total.	Ill-health.	Other sufficient reason.	No sufficient reason.	Total.
0	36,736	407	633	1,632	2,672	1·108	1·723	4·443	7·274
1	30,736	318	449	1,065	1,832	1·035	1·461	3·465	5·960
2	26,382	216	387	975	1,578	·819	1·467	3·696	5·982
3	22,254	176	308	803	1,287	·791	1·384	3·608	5·783
4	17,995	150	220	599	969	·834	1·223	3·329	5·385
5	14,469	126	200	451	777	·871	1·382	3·117	5·370
6	11,798	88	135	368	591	·746	1·144	3·119	5·009
7	9,710	43	104	261	408	·443	1·071	2·688	4·202
8	7,856	33	63	179	275	·420	·802	2·279	3·501
9	6,091	40	49	125	214	·657	·804	2·052	3·513
10	4,863	19	30	83	132	·581	·917	2·537	4·034
11	3,309	15	22	53	90	·453	·665	1·602	2·720
12	1,956	6	8	24	38	·307	·409	1·227	1·943
13	1,685	4	8	11	23	·237	·475	·653	1·365
14	1,475	—	6	11	17	—	·407	·746	1·153
15	1,325	3	6	11	20	·226	·453	·830	1·509
16	1,123	—	6	10	16	—	·534	·890	1·425
17	1,011	1	3	2	6	·099	·297	·198	·593
18	890	2	6	9	17	·224	·674	1·011	1·910
19	788	1	3	6	10	·127	·381	·761	1·269
20	668	1	1	3	5	·150	·150	·449	·749
21	531	—	4	5	9	—	·753	·941	1·695
22	402	1	1	8	10	·249	·249	1·990	2·488
23	344	—	2	3	5	—	·581	·871	1·453
24	292	1	3	—	4	·342	1·027	—	1·370
Totals	204,689	1,651	2,657	6,697	11,005	·807	1·298	3·266	5·376

This method was applied upon a large scale to women employed in English munitions factories during the war, and Tables 1—5 summarise the results (7). Table 6 contrasts the experiences of two factories engaged upon similar work, one of which (L. 7) possessed a highly organised welfare system while the other did not. The columns headed L. 7 record the numbers actually lost in each month of service (0 means the first month, 1 the second, etc.) by L. 7, the column headed L. 1 gives the number which would have been lost had the wastage rates prevailing in L. 1

applied to L. 7. Table 7 contrasts the experiences of L. 1 (an old-established firm of high standing) before and during the war. In this table the form of the statistics has been assimilated to that of a life table, and it should be read as follows :—Of 1,000 entrants aged eighteen to twenty-two, 928 will still be at work after -one month from entry (peace time experience), 848 after two months, and only 668 will " survive " six months' labour.

TABLE 2.—*All Factories. Ages* 13—17.

Months of service.	Exposed.	Numbers left.				Percentages.			
		Ill-health.	Other sufficient reason.	No sufficient reason.	Total.	Ill-health.	Other sufficient reason.	No sufficient reason.	Total.
0	2,937	17	26	155	198	·579	·885	5·277	6·742
1	2,515	8	23	91	122	·318	·915	3·618	4·851
2	2,237	6	23	76	105	·268	1·028	3·397	4·694
3	1,936	12	19	68	99	·620	·981	3·512	5·114
4	1,666	6	19	52	77	·360	1·140	3·121	4·622
5	1,466	8	10	38	56	·546	·682	2·592	3·820
6	1,251	4	5	31	40	·320	·400	2·478	3·198
7	1,090	2	7	14	23	·183	·642	1·284	2·110
8	989	1	2	13	16	·101	·202	1·314	1·618
9	900	5	5	19	29	·556	·556	2·111	3·223
10	800	1	2	5	8	·125	·250	·625	1·000
11	735	—	4	4	8	—	·544	·544	1·088
12	663	—	2	3	5	--	·302	·452	·754
13	614	1	3	7	11	·163	·489	1·140	1·792
14	537	—	1	9	10	—	·186	1·676	1·862
15	473	—	2	4	6	—	·423	·846	1·268
16	402	—	3	4	7	—	·746	·995	1·741
17	360	1	2	1	4	·278	·556	·278	1·112
18	304	1	—	2	3	·329	—	·657	·987
19	270	—	—	3	3	—	—	·741	·741
20	235	1	—	1	2	·426	—	·426	·851
21	195	—	2	4	6	—	1·026	2·051	3·077
22	145	1	—	—	1	·690	—	—	·690
23	118	—	1	1	2	—	·847	·847	1·794
24	95	1	—	—	·1	1·053	—	—	1·053
Totals	22,933	76	161	605	842	·331	·702	2·638	3·672

Far from being an exceptionally heavy wastage rate this is small compared with that experienced in many industries.

An interesting point is brought out in Table 8, showing the proportion still " surviving " after three months' work in several factories, the work of which was physically heavy in those entered as " H," of a lighter character in those denoted " L." The wastage rate is, generally speaking, higher (the proportion of " survivors " smaller) in the " H " factories, but the difference increases with age as is brought out in the next Table 9, where the nine months' survivals are shown in each class of factory.

The explanation of this increasing disadvantage seems to be that the proportion of married women increases rapidly with age (in factories for which requisite data existed, less than 6 per cent. of the women under twenty-two were married, 28 per cent. of those aged twenty-three to twenty-seven, and more than 50 per

TABLE 3.—*All Factories. Ages* 18—22.

Months of service.	Exposed.	Numbers left.				Percentages.			
		Ill-health.	Other sufficient reason.	No sufficient reason.	Total.	Ill-health.	Other sufficient reason.	No sufficient reason.	Total.
0	14,395	135	165	542	842	·938	1·146	3·65	5·849
1	12,388	128	147	388	663	1·033	1·187	3·132	5·352
2	10,690	72	120	365	557	·674	1·123	3·414	5·210
3	9,056	75	117	300	492	·828	1·292	3·313	5·433
4	7,291	58	78	234	370	·796	1·070	3·209	5·075
5	5,869	43	85	172	300	·733	1·448	2·931	5·112
6	4,775	31	62	151	244	·649	1·298	3·162	5·110
7	3,937	12	48	116	176	·305	1·219	2·946	4·470
8	3,204	14	31	75	120	·437	·968	2·341	3·745
9	2,449	16	16	42	74	·653	·653	1·715	3·022
10	1,959	10	15	41	66	·510	·766	2·093	3·369
11	1,289	7	12	18	37	·543	·931	1·396	2·870
12	722	2	5	10	17	·259	·648	1·295	2·202
13	617	3	2	4	9	·483	·324	·648	1·459
14	557	—	4	1	5	—	·718	·180	·898
15	512	1	2	7	10	·195	·391	1·367	1·953
16	440	—	3	4	7	—	·682	·909	1·591
17	401	—	—	1	1	—	—	·249	·249
18	372	—	4	6	10	—	·995	1·493	2·488
19	326	—	2	3	5	—	·613	·920	1·534
20	279	—	—	1	1	—	—	·358	·358
21	218	—	2	—	2	—	·917	—	·917
22	166	—	1	7	8	—	·602	4·217	4·819
23	144	—	1	1	2	—	·694	·694	1·389
24	123	—	3	—	3	—	2·439	—	2·439
Totals	82,179	607	925	2,489	4,021	·739	1·126	3·029	4·893

cent. of those aged twenty-eight and upwards) and that although the married women can stand the strain of factory life (in war-time) nearly as well as unmarried women if the physical work involved is not very heavy, heavy work tips the balance over.

IV. The Value of Investigation.

The reader will, we think, perceive that this method of treating industrial statistics, a method which makes no demand upon his mathematical knowledge,* would, *if accurate data were compiled,* enable him to solve a large number of highly important problems. Obviously, an analysis of employment statistics in this way would enable the management to forecast the immediate future with some accuracy† when an industry is of such a character that the productive capacity of a plant depends upon the available force of employees who are trained workers. There are

TABLE 4.—*All Factories. Ages* 23—27.

Months of service.	Exposed.	Numbers left.				Percentages.			
		Ill-health.	Other suffi- cient reason.	No suffi- cient reason.	Total.	Ill-health.	Other suffi- cient reason.	No suffi- cient reason.	Total.
0	7,564	87	170	342	599	1·150	2·247	4·521	7·919
1	6,317	70	114	225	409	1·108	1·805	3·562	6·475
2	5,336	45	109	215	369	·843	2·043	4·029	6·915
3	4,441	34	68	175	277	·766	1·531	3·941	6·238
4	3,577	30	57	136	223	·839	1·594	3·802	6·234
5	2,798	32	46	86	164	1·144	1·644	3·074	5·861
6	2,251	19	23	72	114	·844	1·022	3·199	5·064
7	1,836	14	26	57	97	·763	1·416	3·105	5·283
8	1,431	8	17	37	62	·559	1·188	2·586	4·333
9	1,050	10	12	23	45	·952	1·143	2·190	4·286
10	792	5	5	9	19	·631	·631	1·136	2·399
11	509	2	3	14	19	·393	·589	2·750	3·733
12	267	2	1	5	8	·749	·375	1·873	2·996
13	226	—	1	—	1	—	·442	—	·442
14	192	—	1	—	1	—	·521	—	·521
15	168	1	1	—	2	·595	·595	—	1·190
16	144	—	—	1	1	—	—	·694	·694
17	127	—	1	—	1	—	·787	—	·787
18	103	1	1	—	2	·971	·971	—	1·942
19	94	—	—	—	—	—	—	—	—
20	83	—	1	—	1	—	1·205	—	1·205
21	63	—	—	1	1	—	—	1·587	1·587
22	42	—	—	—	—	—	—	—	—
23	40	—	—	—	—	—	—	—	—
24	34	—	—	—	—	—	—	—	—
	39,485	360	657	1,398	2,415	·912	1·664	3·541	6·117

few of even the simplest semi-skilled operations in which, as Vernon found (8) by statistical examination of output for the simple repetition process of turning aluminium fuze bodies, a maximum productivity is attained by learners within less than three months from initiation.

If workers, says Professor Lee, " do not remain long in the

* This does not apply to the subject of " probable errors " : *vide supra*, Chapter III.

† Naturally on the assumption of *rebus sic stantibus*, the method will *not* cope with labour unrest.

place which they have entered, it is because there is a lack of adaptation between them as human beings and their environment. This may relate to wages, length of working day, nature of the work and their fitness for it, danger of accidents, physical conditions of the factory affecting comfort and welfare, their foreman or their fellow workmen, or other features with reference to which they do not, or think that they do not, fit. Specific

TABLE 5.—*All Factories. Ages 28 and over.*

Months of service.	Exposed.	Numbers left				Percentages			
		Ill-health.	Other suffi-cient reason.	No suffi-cient reason.	Total.	Ill-health.	Other suffi-cient reason.	No suffi-cient reason.	Total
0	11,840	168	272	593	1,033	1·419	2·297	5·008	8·725
1	9,516	112	165	361	638	1·177	1·734	3·794	6·704
2	8.119	93	135	319	547	1·145	1·663	3·929	6·737
3	6,821	55	104	260	419	·806	1·525	3·812	6·143
4	5,461	56	66	177	299	1·025	1·209	3·241	5·475
5	4,336	43	59	155	257	·992	1·361	3·575	5·927
6	3,521	34	45	114	193	·966	1·278	3·238	5·481
7	2,847	15	23	74	112	·527	·808	2·599	3·934
8	2,232	10	13	54	77	·448	·582	2·419	3·450
9	1,692	9	16	41	66	·532	·946	2·423	3·901
10	1,312	3	8	28	39	·229	·610	2·134	2·973
11	776	6	3	17	26	773	·387	2·191	3·351
12	304	1	—	6	7	329	—	1·974	2·303
13	228	—	2	—	2	—	·877	—	·877
14	189	—	—	1	1	—	—	·529	·529
15	172	1	1	2	4	581	·581	1·163	2·326
16	137	—	—	1	1	—	—	·730	·730
17	123	—	—	—	—	—	—	—	—
18	111	—	1	1	2	—	·813	·813	1·626
19	98	1	1	—	2	1·020	1·020	—	2·041
20	71	—	—	1	1	—	—	1·408	1·408
21	55	—	—	—	—	—	—	—	—
22	49	—	—	1	1	—	—	2·041	2·041
23	42	—	—	—	—	—	—	—	—
24	40	—	—	—	—	—	—	—	—
	60,092	607	914	2,206	3,727	1·010	1·521	3·671	6·202

remedies are, therefore, indicated in specific cases, and a careful search for the causes and the application of the proper remedies should constantly be made by the employing company " (5).

So far as we are concerned, the most important use to which the data can be put is the compilation of rates of wastage due to sickness. For this purpose much greater accuracy in compilation is needed than was secured in wartime factories, which is why we do not comment upon the sickness columns in our tables.

All persons who asserted that they left their employment because of ill-health did not really do so, while some who left

TABLE 6.—*Observed Losses of Factory L 7 compared with those expected from experience of Factory L 1.*

	Under 22			23–27			Over 28			All ages.	
	L 7.	L 1.		L 7.	L 1.		L 7.	L 1.		L 7	L 1.
0	11	43·18	0	12	26·28	0	22	22·81	0	45	92·72
1	5	30·93	1	4	15·15	1	10	17·05	1	19	63·13
2	1	9·54	2	1	8·68	2	2	8·05	2	4	26·27
3	–	8·42	3	1	5·18	3	2	4·94	3	3	18·54
4	–	5·23	4	1	3·26	4	–	2·89	4	1	11·38
5	3	4·61	5	–	1·39	5	3	2·05	5	6	8·05
6	1	1·60	6	–	1·38	6	–	1·16	6	1	4·14
7	–	1·04	7	–	·96	7	–	74	7	–	2·74
8	–	·04	8	–	·03	8	–	·04	8	–	·11
9	–	·02	9	–	·04	9	–	·03	9	–	·09
10	–	·02	10	–	·02	10	–	—	10	–	·04
11	–	·04	11	–	—	11	–	—	11	–	·04
12	–	·04	12	–	—	12	–	—	12	–	·04
Over 12	–	—	over 12	–	—	over 12	–	—	over 12	–	—
Total	21	104·71	Total	19	62·37	Total	39	59·76	Total	79	226·84

for what—so far as our records are concerned—was a wholly insufficient reason may have been really sick. The investigation of the real wastage by ill-health is a task of the future, and all

TABLE 7.—*Numbers remaining at work out of 1,000 Entrants in accordance with various Rates of Loss.*

Numbers remaining after months.	L 1 Factory (War (time).	L 1 Factory (Peace (time).	L 1 Factory (Peace time, ages 18–22).	L 1 Factory (War time, ages 18–22).	L 1 Factory (War time, ages 13–17).	L 1 Factory (War time, ages 23–27).	L 1 Factory (War time, ages 28–).
0	1,000	1,000	1,000	1,000	1,000	1,000	1,000
1	917	921	928	902	929	921	911
2	868	855	848	853	881	860	877
3	826	795	800	813	841	811	830
4	791	749	754	778	799	777	807
5	757	703	710	749	764	729	781
6	730	658	668	727	739	696	742

we have attempted in this chapter is to show how the data, when obtained, may be used. The wastage rate in our tables of the first month of employment is higher than that of the succeeding months, just as in ordinary vital statistics the death rate of the

24—2

first year of life is a great deal higher than that of the immediately following years. Indeed, we should expect to be able to trace a complete formal analogy between an ideal industrial life table and an ordinary life table, to find that the death rate declines from a maximum in the first year of life and gradually increases in adult life to a second maximum in old age. Some "infant

TABLE 8.—*Three Months' Survival Rates.*

Factory.	Ages 18–22.	Ages 23–27	Ages 28–
L 4	84·16 ± ·83	81·08 ± 1·21	83·95 ± 1·06
L 5	93·60 ± ·74	94·12 ± ·71	89·50 ± 1·10
H 4	88·32 ± ·92	84·62 ± 1·81	81·65 ± 1·89
H 1	82·30 ± 1·67	72·88 ± 1·92	71·24 ± 1·23
H 8	66·27 ± 2·04	66·34 ± 2·86	66·93 ± 2·74
H 9	90·73 ± 1·40	86·81 ± 2·01	83·84 ± 1·56
L 3	85·75 ± ·73	81·50 ± ·98	86·07 ± ·67
H 2	81·03 ± 2·03	74·71 ± 2·00	66·56 ± 1·57
H 3	77·16 ± 1·53	64·76 ± 1·66	72·32 ± 1·14
H 5	87·89 ± 2·29	—	88·67 ± 1·74
H 10	85·71 ± ·52	82·70 ± ·86	81·01 ± ·78
L 1	81·32 ± ·71	81·07 ± 1·08	83·02 ± ·97
H 6	87·91 ± ·61	78·80 ± ·95	78·50 ± 71
L 2	77·45 ± 1·05	71·81 ± 1·16	80·92 ± ·80
H 7	82·65 ± ·59	77·55 ± ·70	75·65 ± ·92
L 8	74·70 ± 2·06	—	—
L 6 .	70·29 ± 2·77	64·70 ± 3·68	71·87 ± 2·26
L 7	95·34 ± ·78	90·92 ± 1·46	87·78 ± 1·38

mortality " is inevitable in any industry, since, however perfect the system of selection, some must be engaged who are unsuitable and quickly discover (or have pointed out to them) their unfitness. It is equally fitting that the old age "mortality"

TABLE 9.—*Nine Months' Survival Rates.*

Age Group.	L.	H	Difference
18–22	67·55 ± ·52	59·64 ± ·49	7·91 ± ·71
23–27	65·15 ± ·76	51·46 ± ·68	13·69 ± 1·02
28–	66·59 ± ·59	52·45 ± ·54	14·14 ± ·80

should again increase, because the longer the service the greater the proportion of withdrawals conditioned by socially proper motives, such as marriage, promotion, pensioning.*

But—here again the analogy to ordinary vital statistics is

* Our wartime statistics throw no light at all upon these matters ; the rates of leaving in later months are quite unreliable and in some cases, for instance, when the statistics only covered a few months, meaningless.

evident—an unusually high rate of "infant mortality" in factories can often be reduced, and its existence is usually a sign that the conditions of employment need attention. In the course of our official duties at the Ministry of Munitions we had several opportunities to prove the utility of such statistics in forming a judgment of and advising as to the improvement of local conditions. In general, a case exists for inquiry in any factory which suffers a large "infant mortality," and in which the wastage rates after a decline in the second month rise steadily and unmistakably in the third, fourth and immediately following months. In many cases, probably the majority, the explanation is not of medical interest. Thus the beginner, if not on his guard, may discover mares' nests; for instance, a great increase of wastage in the third month may merely depend upon a system of booking, absentees being struck off the register finally after an absence of a certain number of months. Local strikes or the closure of particular departments may lead to very strange statistical consequences. A moderate application of common sense and reasonable patience will overcome these difficulties. When, however, these obvious explanations have been exhausted it will sometimes be found that there remain matters to which the hygienist must give his attention.

The wastage rate from sickness is, in our opinion, the most important object of study. In the analysis of this it is not sufficient to attend only to gross percentages. We have already said that the sickness rates in our data are unreliable, but we may be permitted to use them as illustrations. In the general Table 1, the wastage assigned to ill-health is 1·1 per cent. of all entrants in the first month, 1 per cent. in the second month, and then declines irregularly, being less than 0·5 per cent. in all months after the 12th. Even if these figures accurately measure the wastage due to ill-health it would not follow that the conditions in the later months are more favourable, because : (a) the selective effect of the elimination of weakly persons due to the high rates in early months must, pro tanto, leave a healthier population ; and (b) the proportion of grave illnesses amongst the employees leaving owing to ill-health in the later months of service might be greater. In other words, a table of percentage wastage due to sickness is a starting point, not a goal, of hygienic inquiry.

We here repeat what we have said in Chapter VI., viz., that the industrial affinities of tuberculosis merit the closest study. We have remarked that general vital statistics point to a correlation between fluctuations of employment in industry and variations of the death rate from tubercular diseases. We have also shown that no simple or direct interpretation of this is yet possible. The moral is that more information should be collected. Is the proportional invalidity rate from phthisis a function of the length of employment in industry ? This is a most important question. A tabulation of phthisis rates by length of service would not suffice to answer it—we should have to allow for the effect of age itself, because the optimum age for the manifestation of phthisis is later than the usual age of entering a factory ; but a tabulation by length of service would at least give us information of essential value—indeed, one of the elements of our problem. So far as we are aware, no such data has ever been compiled on an adequate scale. The factory medical officer or welfare superintendent who intelligently practises the methods sketched in this chapter, and avails himself of the information which the improvement and co-ordination of the Medical Health Insurance Service under the Ministry of Health should afford, might make a substantial contribution to our knowledge of this subject.

V. Prevention of Industrial Wastage.

The existence of industrial wastage, recognition of its adverse effect and knowledge of how to measure it, would be of little more than academic interest if no means existed for its reduction. There is, however, evidence to show that it can be reduced, and reduced greatly, by means already tried. Attention, for instance, has been above directed to the favourable influence exerted by a highly organised welfare system, which included a preliminary medical examination of workers, upon the labour turnover of factory L 7 (see Table 6), and of an eight-hour plant in America. Measures to prevent labour wastage should be twofold, directed to diminishing " infantile mortality " through careful selection of workers, and also to prolonging the period of industrial life through care taken of those employed.

Selection of Workers.—The selection of workers may be considered from two points of view : (i.) the general health of the applicant ; and (ii.) the special fitness, if any, he possesses for the work to be undertaken. These points of view are by no means distinct ; for instance, an applicant with impaired circulation may on general grounds be unfitted for heavy physical work, but be considered able to undertake sedentary employment. Nevertheless general health should be the first consideration, and the medical organisation and methods which should be adopted for selecting workers on this account are discussed in Chapter XVII. An industrial medical officer should with experience become skilled not merely in eliminating those obviously unfit for any work, but in selecting workers fitted for particular processes ; for this purpose he should familiarise himself with all forms of work carried on in the concern to which he is attached. He may then with advantage tabulate the various processes and record against each group what disabilities should prohibit employment, and what special capacity is called for. He will soon find that for dusty processes, for instance, bronchitis is a disability ; for long standing, varicose veins ; for lifting weights, hernia ; for exposure to high temperature, impaired circulation. While on the other hand good vision will be required for fine work, such as sewing, drawing or linotyping ; good hearing for a shorthand writer ; good physique for heavy labour.

The next step he should take is to tabulate the qualities and capacities required ; then as each applicant comes before him the presence or absence of these qualities can be quickly noted, and the combination possessed by the individual ascertained ; after which the process requiring this combination is found by reference to the first table. He will, from such simple beginnings, find himself embarked not merely upon rejecting the unfit, but upon selecting the fit. He should, however, always be kept informed as to the result of his work by being provided with tables of labour turnover, corresponding to his classification of processes ; only in this way can he estimate the correctness of his method or the need for reconsidering his estimates.

Any one embarking upon this work who is dubious as to his skill in determining capacities and disabilities may be advised to proceed on the following lines. Let him ascertain from the foreman or the wage book who of those already employed are the best workers and who the worst at the processes concerned ; then let him examine the two groups and discover what characteristic distinguishes one from the other. In this way he may find some apparently chance characteristic which, though not actually of value to the process, is present in all or most of the best workers and absent from the worst. Then he may venture to pick as new workers persons possessing this characteristic.

The future may see a considerable development in the science of selection of workers, which is coming to be known as vocational selection ; for the moment, however, while its ultimate value to the productivity of industry and to the efficiency and health of the workers must, we think, be great, there is no sufficient body of data upon which to present here an accepted line of practice. The reader may with advantage consult the work of Muscio (9).

Care of the Employed.—Important as is the selection of workers in lessening labour turnover, of equal importance is the care of those already employed. The data we have already given show that with length of employment the field of endeavour is smaller ; industrial wastage becomes progressively less as industrial life lengthens. But workers increase in value to the employer in proportion to the length of their industrial experience ; the loss of a single experienced operative may be a more important matter than the loss of several recent recruits.

Supervision of the personal health and welfare of those employed, and of the hygienic conditions under which they work, provides the means for preventing this " adult industrial mortality." These matters are discussed in Chapter XVII. ; but stress may here be laid on the advisability (i.) of watching the wage list for signs of gradually diminishing earnings, an indication that energy is falling off, due in many cases to some reason medically remediable, which if not taken in time may lead to loss of the worker ; and (ii.) of inquiring closely into the circumstances connected with every impending notice to leave, or with every person who may have left without notice given.

VI. Bibliography.

1. Willitts, J. H. " Steadying Employment." *Annals American Acad. Polit. and Soc. Science.* May, 1916.
2. Alexander. " Proceedings Employment Managers' Conference." *U.S. Bureau of Labour Statistics, No. 227.* 1917. [Also cited in (1).]
3. Greenwood, M. " A Report on the Causes of Wastage of Labour in Munition Factories employing Women." *Medical Research Committee. Special Report Series, No. 16.* 1918. (The data quoted in this chapter and the method of reduction are fully discussed here.)
4. Greenwood, M. *Health of Munition Workers Committee. Final Report,* Appendix D, p. 163. (Cd. 9065.) 1918.
5. Lee, F. S. *The Human Machine.* Longmans, Green & Co. 1918.
6. *Handbook for Welfare Supervisors and Apprentice Masters,* pp. 104—108. Ministry of Labour. 1919.
7. Greenwood, M. " Problems of Industrial Organisation." *Jour. Roy. Stat. Soc.,* Vol. LXXXII., p. 186. 1919.
8. Vernon, H. M. " Statistical Information concerning Output in relation to Hours of Work." *Health of Munition Workers Committee. Memo. No. 12.* (Cd. 8344.) 1916.
9. Muscio, B. " Choosing the Worker." *The Industrial Clinic.* J. Bale, Sons and Danielsson. 1920.
10. " Comparison of an Eight-hour Plant and a Ten-hour Plant." *Public Health Bulletin No. 106.* Government Printing Office, Washington.

CHAPTER XVII

SUPERVISION OF INDUSTRIAL HEALTH

I. Introduction.

THE foregoing chapters will have shown how a new branch of
medical science has come into existence, a branch dealing with
the life and health of those industrially employed. Scientific
discoveries to be of practical use must be embodied in an art ;
and where the art, or technic, contrived for this new branch of
preventive medicine has been introduced into industry, results
have followed, beneficial not only to the health and welfare of
the workers, but also to the quality and quantity of output, and
to the economics of industrial management. In order to attain
ends so important to the industrial world in particular, and the
community in general, definite persons must be appointed to
carry out definite duties. Certain of these duties are strictly
medical, and must be placed in medical hands ; others can be
undertaken by trained nurses acting under medical supervision ;
dental treatment calls for qualified dentists, while certain
other duties more particularly social in character must be
entrusted to those who are specially trained in such work. A
condition of success in each case is the establishment of close
personal relations with the individual workers ; so that individual
conditions can become known through the medium of trained
experts appointed to advise the management, each in relation to
his own sphere.

II. Medical Supervision.

Industrialisation has modified the medical man's relationship
to his patients. When occupation was either on the land or in
the home the doctor knew from personal observation how daily
work was carried on, and was able to advise his patient accordingly ; to-day the position is different. The doctor and patient
still meet either in the surgery, when both are tired after a long
day's toil, or in the artisan's home ; but in neither case has the
doctor now an opportunity of acquainting himself with the
environment of the man's daily toil, although he is frequently

called upon to give advice upon the suitability of the occupation carried on, or even to state upon certificates that the malady suffered from has been caused or accentuated by occupation. Unfortunate results sometimes follow from the doctor putting his name to a statement made by the patient and certifying that symptoms are the result of exposure to some influence, possibly a poison, which the occupation does not really entail.

The medical man of to-day should acquire that knowledge of industry and its effect in causing or contributing to disease which can only come from direct personal observation. In the past some recognition had been given to this by sporadic efforts to establish medical supervision; as early as 1842 Chadwick (1) reported how Mr. John Smith, of Deanston, near Stirling, " retained the services of a medical gentleman to inspect the workpeople from time to time, and give them timely advice, and, as far as possible, prevent disease." Experiments like these were, however, few and did not represent any organised effort to establish a scheme of preventive medicine in relation to industry.

The Origin of the Certifying Factory Surgeon.—The art of preventive medicine in Great Britain was originated by Sir John Simon between 1855—65, when the importance of the industrial revolution to social life had attained public recognition. Attention has already been directed to the work done at that time by Greenhow upon the influence exerted by the industries of the country upon health; but the services of the profession already, some twenty years earlier, had been required in relation to factory employment. Simple though the early duties demanded were, they are of historic interest because they brought the profession directly into contact with industry; the Factory Act of 1833 laid down that no child under nine years of age might work in cotton mills, and that no child between nine and thirteen might work more than eight hours a day. The first factory inspectors who were appointed, since birth certification was not made obligatory until 1837, had no documentary evidence as to the age of the children to depend on; but they were permitted to call for a certificate from a surgeon or physician to declare any employed child was of " the ordinary strength and appearance " of a child of nine years of age. Certificates were, however, tendered from cow-doctors, dentists and others quite unqualified to give them; Mr. Rickards, inspector for the Manchester district, found it necessary to recognise only the certificates of certain medical men authorised by him for the purpose. His system was found to work well, and was adopted by other inspectors; in the Act of 1844 the appointment of certifying factory surgeons was definitely recognised (see also Chapter II.).

At this time the child seeking employment had to pay 6*d*. for his own certificate. Later the cost was shared between the employer and the employed, and finally was laid on the employer alone. The charge has remained 6*d*. per certificate,* although with the introduction of birth certification the duties laid on the factory surgeon have been profoundly modified.

Present Duties.—The surgeon is now no longer called upon to certify to the age of the juvenile as this is proved by the birth certificate which must be produced before him ; but he has now to examine the young person and certify that he " is not incapable by disease or bodily infirmity for working daily for the time allowed by law in the factory named in the certificate " ; he may examine the process at which the young person is to be employed, and he may qualify his certificate by conditions as to the work on which the young person is fitted to be employed. In order to assist a factory medical officer when acting as a certifying surgeon in carrying out his duties, a useful purpose may be served by dwelling upon some medical points to be paid attention to when making examinations. The suggestions made are based upon official experience.

Privacy should be ensured, and advantage is obtained from the presence of the welfare officer or nurse, who should undertake the duty of carrying out any instructions given by the surgeon.

The points to which attention should be paid are :—

(1) Auscultation of the heart and presence or absence of anæmia.

(2) State of the glands in the neck.

(3) Condition as regards tonsils and adenoids.

(4) Condition of the teeth.

(5) Infectious or contagious diseases, including pediculi capitis.

(6) Physical development.

(7) Mental condition.

(8) Hearing.

(9) Vision.

Defects disclosed should determine for any employment under consideration whether the person presented should be (i.) rejected, or (ii.) receive a certificate qualified as to conditions.

The objects to be aimed at in the examination have been well-stated (7) as—

(1) Avoidance of injury to the health, development, or bodily capacity of the individual inspected.

* The fee was raised to 1*s*. per certificate in March, 1920.

(2) Protection of the fellow workers, of whatever age or sex.

(3) Maintenance of legality : this directly protects the employer.

(4) Checking unfair competition, and protecting the more conscientious manufacturers from the less scrupulous.

A certifying surgeon should examine the heart with the chest bared. This procedure should not be restricted to occasions when appearance or a history of previous illness, such as rheumatic fever, suggests it.

Anæmia, particularly in girls, where the proposed employment necessitates standing or heavy physical work, should be a cause for rejection ; in such cases the employment may accentuate the condition, while the possibility of fainting when working among moving machinery is an important consideration.*

Physical examination of lungs on factory premises, unless a suitable ambulance room or rest room is available, may be restricted to cases where other manifestations, such as the condition of glands in the neck, suggest the possibility of tubercular infection. Glands of the neck, if discharging, should be a bar to indoor employment. A child or young person with distinct signs of incipient phthisis may be rejected, even if there is no actual inability to undertake the full time allowed by law for the proposed employment, should the surgeon consider such employment would be prejudicial to health. Consideration has already been given (see Chapter VI.) to the industrial treatment of phthisis.

Enlarged tonsils alone are seldom a sufficient cause for rejection ; even when adenoid tissue is clearly hypertrophied the surgeon should be satisfied that associated physical development unfits the child or young person for employment. Those suffering from these conditions certainly run a risk in crowded workrooms of catarrhal infection ; but action should generally be limited to giving advice. The surgeon may also be influenced by the presence of dust, or of artificial humidity or high temperature which necessitates extreme changes of atmosphere on leaving work and so predisposes to affections of the air passages.

Bad teeth and oral sepsis should be advised upon ; but only when the state of health consequent upon them renders the proposed employment injurious to the individual or entails infection to others should the surgeon consider them reasons for rejection. In carrying out his duties the certifying surgeon must have in mind that his legal powers restrict him to deter-

---

* The certifying surgeon must, of course, try to avoid a confusion between "functional" and "organic" heart trouble, and, to that end, endeavour to control by other methods the data of auscultation.

mining whether some special form of occupation is advantageous or disadvantageous for an individual ; he may nevertheless draw attention to and advise upon other matters, but he cannot enforce his advice by refusing to issue a certificate.

The presence of pediculi capitis may be a reason for rejection, especially when associated with an eczematous condition and enlarged glands.   Advantage may be gained by having instructions issued to the children before they are presented to the surgeon, which indicate how these conditions may be remedied. The following form may be taken as an example of instructions :—

" In order to pass the doctor it is necessary to have the head very clean.   The following is a good method of cleaning the hair :—

" (1) The hair to be well combed with a small toothcomb.

" (2) Wash the hair with carbolic soft soap.

" (3) Then soak the hair in brown vinegar and water, equal parts.   Then tie the hair up in a towel for half an hour.

" (4) Rinse well with hot water and borax.

" (5) Do not fail to use the vinegar."

Much can be done where half-time employment prevails by co-operation in this matter between the school medical officer and the certifying surgeon.   The homes of children who seek factory work are frequently not places where such treatment will be carried out, and, if a factory nurse is employed, she can do valuable work by quietly giving practical demonstrations to those refused by the surgeon.   Such instruction is often carried home to the benefit of a whole family.

Small size of a child is not of itself a sufficient cause for rejection ; regard must also be had to the work which is contemplated. The employment of children prevails mainly in the textile industry, and the overlooker of a cotton mill will seldom choose a child who is too short for the work.   The work includes such operations as (a) sweeping, (b) cleaning, (c) creeling, (d) tubing, (e) piecing, (f) doffing, and (g) bobbin sorting and collecting ; it is generally speaking of a light character.   Where heavier work is to be done, such as lifting or dragging tins or skips, qualifying conditions can be added to the certificate.   A short and wiry child may be more fitted for working in a cotton mill than a tall, flabby child.

The home circumstances of a child who is badly nourished should be taken into consideration.   The condition of the child may be caused by want of food, which is improved when the child becomes a wage earner.   Nutrition below normal may not then be a sufficient reason for rejection ; but if malnutrition is associated with anæmia rejection may be called for.   These latter cases will probably improve better by rest and treatment rather than by work.

The mentality of the person presented should always be considered, and the standard attained at school is a valuable indication.   Special Acts exist for dealing with defective and epileptic children up to the age of sixteen years ; and the surgeon should, when such cases come before him, refer them to the local education authority.   There is always the possibility that a mental defective may be attempting to obtain work in contravention of the Acts.

Where eyesight is defective the surgeon should ascertain that the employment is such as will not cause undue eyestrain. Monocular vision, however, should be a bar to work near machinery.   Children with eye defects, if called upon to do work requiring close attention, seldom become experts or able to earn reasonable wages.   A text-type is issued by the Home Office for use by surgeons.   Ability to read $D = 1\cdot75$ on the card supplied at one metre distance indicates a visual acuity which lies between $\frac{6}{9}$ and $\frac{6}{12}$.   The card may be useful as some guide as to when glasses are needed before a certificate can be granted for close work or work near machinery.   But while surgeons should make ample use of the power which they now possess of qualifying their certificates with conditions of labour, and they are empowered to state that the child or young person should not be employed upon heavy physical work or in the neighbourhood of moving machinery, yet they have no power of limiting the period of employment, or requiring that the individual shall, for instance, wear suitable spectacles.

The surgeon should keep in touch with the juvenile employment committee if such exists in the neighbourhood, or with any special advisory committee connected with the labour exchanges. Advantage is also gained if he is provided with the names of those who when leaving school are suffering from any serious defect such as heart disease, incipient phthisis, mental defects or impaired vision, so that when they apply for employment he may have this information at his disposal and so insure that suitable employment is undertaken.

The surgeon has in his power opportunities for safeguarding the health of the rising generation, and he should remember that he often has the chance of addressing the first word of encouragement to a child on his start in industrial life.

The duties above set out, when they are fully performed, make for an efficient supervision of those entering upon industrial life ; but, at best, they only establish a filter through which healthy young persons are admitted to employment ; they do not set up any method of supervision for ascertaining the effect of work upon health and physical development. And unfortunately the fee for which the surgeon has to perform his work is not sufficient to ensure that the work is conscientiously carried out.

Once this office of certifying factory surgeon was legally recognised, other duties were from time to time added, which to-day include investigating and reporting upon the causation of certain specified industrial diseases and poisonings, and septic poisoning resulting from accidental injuries ; examining periodically workpeople employed in certain dangerous trades ; examining, under the Workmen's Compensation Act, those suffering from certain scheduled industrial diseases and poisonings, and granting certificates accordingly.

While these duties are important in themselves, the value of medical men visiting industrial establishments has been considerable in other ways. Their advice has been sought on many points and their services have been retained in certain cases to supervise first-aid organisation and the general health of the workers. Action on these lines, however, has been left to employers to develop on their own initiative, and it has been the exception rather than the rule.

Recent Development.—A great impetus was given to factory medical service, as set out above, during the war, owing to the occurrence of poisoning from trinitrotoluene (T.N.T.), the high explosive used for filling shells, bombs, mines, hand grenades and other munitions of war. Immediate steps had to be taken to preserve the health of the workers, and to inspire confidence among them, in order to maintain the output. One of the most important steps taken was the appointment of whole-time medical officers, one for every 2,000 persons employed, entrusted with definite duties : to examine every applicant for work before engagement ; to inspect frequently the conditions of employment and the processes carried on ; to inspect every worker periodically, pick out those indisposed, and if necessary suspend them from work ; and to advise the management upon all medical matters arising.

The importance and value of the work became more and more obvious as it developed, not only in controlling T.N.T. sickness, but in many other medical questions which were found to be constantly referred to the medical staff. Managers discovered that a medical staff was invaluable, and at other factories where there was no special risk such as T.N.T. poisoning to combat, medical officers were called for. These officers living and working within the organisation of the factory were found able to render more valuable services than can a doctor who only sees his patients during busy consulting hours, or in the cottage home after health has broken down, and moreover has little knowledge of the daily life of the worker and of the industrial strain causing the breakdown.   Development on these lines may become more rapid in the immediate future than was possible during the war period owing to the sudden diminution in the supply of medical men available for civilian work.

For the moment development is in this country probably being rather hampered than helped by the office of certifying factory surgeon ; the employer is inclined to estimate the use of medical services from the work he sees done, and this work is confessedly as inadequate as the fee paid.   The service requires to be entirely reorganised ; closer touch should on the one side be established with the school medical service so that information as to past health can be at the disposal of the factory medical officer when examining for employment ; on the other side the scope of work must be enlarged to include adults, and the whole period of industrial employment.

Possibilities of the Factory Medical Officer.—Dr. Mock, an American industrial surgeon of considerable experience, has described fully (10) the scope of work and the organisation required in an establishment employing several thousands of workers.   We do not propose to repeat here what he has ably set forth ; but all factories are not on so large a scale, and a few instances of the way in which medical services have been utilised in this country may be of value to show the lines which development may take.   One engineering factory, employing some 2,250 workers, almost all men, engaged a medical officer working full time, who acted also as panel doctor for most of the employees.   He made a medical examination of all new workers, not merely of the juveniles ; absentees from work were followed up by him if they had not seen him before leaving work, and they again saw him before resuming work.   The medical officer's work included also supervision of dressings at the ambulance station, ordinary diagnosis of illness, minor surgical treatment and any attendance on the workers where necessary in their homes or at the neighbouring cottage hospital.   The number of patients seen varied from sixty to seventy-five a day.   The medical officer had quarters provided on the ground floor—any quarters approached by a staircase are unsuitable for the expeditious and humane treatment of sick and injured people— comprising (*a*) a waiting room ; (*b*) an ambulance room ; (*c*) a consulting room ; (*d*) an office for a clerk who deals with sick pay and compensation claims ; (*e*) two water closets.   The fittings of the ambulance room are dealt with later. Experience shows that if arrangements have been made for male and female cases to be seen at separate hours there is no need for a separate male and female waiting room. Emergencies that cut across this arrangement are few and far between.

A different plan was adopted at another engineering factory, where about 2,500 men and women were employed. The part-time services of a medical officer were retained. He attended the ambulance room daily from noon till one. He then saw cases of injury which had been held over for his inspection or had come up for redressing. He also examined at that time all workers before engagement, when any physical defects such as hernia, hydrocele, varicocele, varicose veins or heart trouble were entered in a book and the entry countersigned by the worker; in this way claims in respect of that particular defect at some later date were avoided. The medical officer also treated at his own house cases sent to him by the nurses on duty. Employees had to report every accident, no matter how slight, to the fore man, who passed the case on to the ambulance room. Workers were *in no case* allowed to treat any wound themselves. All wounds were dressed by nurses under the supervision of the medical officer, and patients were not sent to their own doctors, for the latter had not time for treating, and could not be expected to treat daily a large number of minor and *apparently* trifling injuries. Under the system adopted every wound, however slight, was dressed within a few minutes of its occurrence and properly cared for until healed.

TABLE 1.

PERIOD.	Average number of employees.	—	REPORTED ACCIDENTS.							
			All cases.	Losing no time.	Causing lost time.					
					Under two weeks.	Two weeks but under one month.	One month but under six weeks.	Six weeks but under six months.	Six months and over.	All periods.
First six months.	2,630	Number.	347	61	131	87	31	35	2	286
		Percentage.	13·2	2·3	5	3·3	1·2	1·3	0·1	10·9
Second six months.	2,550	Number.	494	215	157	88	21	13	0	279
		Percentage.	19·4	8·4	6·2	3·5	0·8	0·5	0	10·9
Third six months.	2,400	Number.	351	140	121	64	12	14	0	211
		Percentage.	14·6	5·8	5·0	2·7	0·5	0·6	0	8·8
Fourth six months.	2,400	Number.	411	190	129	63	22	7	0	221
		Percentage.	17·1	7·9	5·4	2·6	0·9	0·3	0	9·2

This scheme is of special interest because the effect was carefully watched (2), and is shown in the accompanying tables. The first table shows how the time lost on account of injuries was materially lessened. The gross increase in the number of accidents treated is of course a mere consequence of the rule that all accidents, however trivial, should be reported ; the important point is the reduction in total lost time through accidents. If we suppose that the average loss of time in the group under two weeks is one week, three weeks in the next group, five weeks in the next, sixteen in the next and thirty-four for those incapacitated more than six months, it appears that during the first six months 1,175 weeks were lost, 734 in the next, 597 and 540 in the following periods ; expressed as proportions of the average numbers employed, we have, 0·45, 0·29, 0·25, 0·23. The second

TABLE 2.—*Workmen's Compensation.*

Period.	Actual Compensation paid. A.			Medical expenses. B.			Heavy risk insurance. C.			Total A. plus B. plus C.			Cost if insured at usual rate.		
	£	s.	d.	£	s.	d.	£	s.	d.	£	s.	d.	£	s.	d.
First six months (1916)	516	16	3	177	14	7	156	5	0	850	15	10	1,125	0	0
Second six months (1916)	703	7	9	177	14	7	156	5	0	1,037	7	4	1,125	0	0
Third six months (1917)	655	17	4	177	14	7	156	5	0	989	16	11	1,125	0	0
Fourth six months (1917)	471	19	6	{177 14 7} {152 0 0}			156	5	0	957	19	1	1,125	0	0
Total for two years	£2,348	0	10	£862	18	4	£625	9	0	£3,835	19	2	£4,500	0	0

table shows that not only was this amount of illness saved, but that the saving was effected economically. The firm decided to carry its own insurance against accidents for all claims less than £100. The table shows the actual amount paid in compensation, the medical expenses and the insurance to cover risks over £100 ; and these three items added together come to considerably less than would have been paid on insurance at the usual rate. The second figure of medical expenses for the fourth period refers to the cost of paid professional nurses who were then substituted for voluntary attendants. Notwithstanding this alteration, in this period also a substantial economy was effected.

Yet a third instance is of interest where a group of factories agreed together to employ a medical man, paying him on a capitation basis of so much per 100 workers employed. The duties he was asked to undertake were to make not less than four health inspections of every part of each factory every year, and during these inspections to give attention to the following matters :—(*a*) The organisation of first-aid treatment ; (*b*) the keeping of personal records of health and progress of each worker ; (*c*) the condition of the sanitary conveniences ; (*d*) the cleanliness of the windows ; (*e*) the ventilation of each workplace ; (*f*) the temperature of each workplace ; (*g*) the cleanliness of each workplace ; (*h*) the prevalence of spitting ; (*i*) the provision of facilities for obtaining foods ; (*j*) the provision of drinking water ; (*k*) the provision of cloakroom accommodation ; and (*l*) the provision of washing conveniences. On the occasion of these visits the appointed doctor should be prepared to advise on any medical subject connected with the employment carried on and as to the health of any person employed about whom he is consulted. Any observations or instructions which he may give should be stated in writing before leaving the factory, and preserved for the information of the management and for reference at subsequent visits.

While these examples are of value to indicate how medical supervision can be organised, the simple principles which should be followed when establishing industrial medical service may be stated as follows. The service is required :—

(*a*) To inspect and grade all new workers ;

(*b*) To advise the management and particularly the Welfare Branch on working conditions in relation to the health of the workers ;

(*c*) To supervise the organisation of ambulance work both medical and surgical, and the professional work of the nursing staff ;

(*d*) To visit the establishment at frequent intervals for the purpose of seeing special cases of injury or sickness ;

(*e*) To inspect periodically every part of the premises and report on the hygienic conditions found ;

(*f*) To re-examine juvenile workers at periodic intervals in order to ascertain the effect of employment upon development ; and

(*g*) To re-examine workers who have been away ill before they resume full employment.

The Cost of Factory Medical Service.—The instance quoted above shows how one item of service, *i.e.*, adequate treatment of injuries, may bear the whole cost of medical service and yet leave a profit, with all else done on the credit side.

Mock has also tried to construct a balance sheet, and has taken another item of service for consideration, viz., the examination of applicants. He quotes figures from ten large concerns where " these examinations are not made for the purpose of selecting only the physically fit and refusing employment to all others, but are made for the following purposes :—(*a*) To prevent those with diseased conditions, making work of any kind dangerous to them, from going to work ; (*b*) to select proper jobs for those with certain defects where they can still be efficient and yet the work will not be hazardous to them ; (*c*) to prevent those with contagious diseases from mingling with the old working force." He claims that workers eliminated by these means may fairly be held to represent a saving in labour turnover, since ill-health or inefficiency would soon have led to their departure ; the cost of hiring and training a worker is placed at what he considers to be a low average figure of 35 dollars. He found that in ten large concerns 118,900 applicants were examined in one year, of whom 34·7 per cent. possessed disabilities which did not prevent suitable work being found for them, while 11,433, or 9·7 per cent. were definitely rejected. He calculates, therefore, that these rejections represented an annual saving of $(35 \times 11,433 =)$ 400,155 dollars in labour turnover. The method of estimation appears to be a legitimate one.

Next he ascertained the average cost per head per year of total medical service ; and found it worked out at two and a half dollars. The regular number of employees at the above ten concerns was 102,400, for which the total medical service came, on this estimate, to 256,000 dollars.

		$
Saving in labour turnover .	. . .	400,155
Entire cost of medical service	. . .	256,000
Annual profit from only one item of service .		144,155

The first instance (p. 385) makes no claim with respect to saving in labour turnover ; this latter instance makes no claim with respect to saved compensation ; neither claim anything for diminished lost time, for increase in quality and quantity of output, or greater safety to the plant, due to steadier work by employees more efficient through greater length of service and better health. There still remains on the credit side that unmeasurable asset—happiness, which Comte claims to consist in doing the work for which we are naturally fitted.

III. The Factory Nurse.

The appointment of this useful officer is an innovation in factory life of the last few years, and her advent has been practically synchronous with the establishment of factory ambulance rooms ; engaged originally to carry out first aid dressings and attend to cases of minor accident and illness, her usefulness has been found to cover a wider sphere. Before ambulance rooms were established and records were kept of minor injuries, there was but little knowledge of the number of injuries which occurred, but data for some factories are now available which show the work there is for a nurse to do. In twenty engineering factories, employing 42,700 workers, there were treated in one week when there were no special contributory causes, 9,393 cases, *i.e.*, approximately 22 per cent. of the workers were attended, a percentage which in one of the factories rose as high as 33·7. Slight though each injury may have been in itself, yet every case represented an interruption more or less prolonged in the work of the factory, and a potential starting point for sepsis and grave illness.

The frequency with which minor injuries occur varies considerably in different industries ; it is, for instance, less in the textile industry than in the engineering, but the occurrence of minor medical cases does not vary to the same extent. Of the numbers quoted above, from 10 to 20 per cent. were minor medical cases, sufficient in themselves to justify the need for the services of a trained nurse ; and it is here that the records give some indications of the wider duties she is called upon to perform. The ambulance room of a large factory tends to become not merely a first aid station for accidents, but also a centre to which gravitates any one and every one, without social distinction, from the manager to the newest apprentice, seeking relief from any of the numerous ailments which interfere with daily life ; the nurse has a unique opportunity for seeing and advising upon the preliminary symptoms, slight and often neglected, of illness, manifested in any member of the factory staff.

Work started in the ambulance room is generally found to be but the first introduction for the activities of a capable nurse. But she is not to be pictured controlling arterial hæmorrhage, dealing with frightful burns, or conducting other strenuous fights to ward off impending dissolution ; such spectacular events seldom do occur and should not occur at all. Rather she should be found investigating the origin of the troubles which have brought the workers to consult her, whether they lie at the door of the work, in the worker himself, or his home ; watching the wage sheets for any steady decline in earnings, an indication of lessening efficiency due to failing health ; establishing contact with the medical practitioners of the district, the hospitals and dispensaries, local nursing organisations, and health visitors, or possibly giving short health talks from time to time in the dinner hour. Pregnant workers for whom pre-natal supervision must be undertaken will be found consulting her ; from this follows infant welfare, the feeding and care of children of working mothers ; an industrial day nursery may be required or a crèche. Cases sent home from the ambulance room should be followed up and the suitability of the home for looking after illness ascertained. Information is thus acquired as to the housing conditions and social surroundings of the operatives which may go far to explain lost time and inefficiency during working hours.

There is no need to emphasise at length the sphere of activity of an industrial nurse ; but we feel confident that the establishment in factories of ambulance rooms by bringing nurses into industrial establishments is creating an important means for improving the health of the industrial worker. We are, however, in agreement with an industrial nurse who writes, "industry requires a good nurse with a knowledge of social work in addition to familiarity with methods of public health nursing " (9) ; mere training in first aid work for injuries and for sickness is inadequate. The nurse comes in intimate touch with the workers and has unique opportunities for educating them in the principles of health ; and, as the author just quoted says, " we must not forget that we cannot move people along the road of progress one bit faster than they see the need of being moved."

The Ambulance Room.—The Health of Munition Workers Committee recommended (3) the establishment of central dressing stations in factories, and made suggestions as to structure, equipment and supervision of such stations. These recommendations have been embodied in certain Home Office Orders (made in pursuance of the powers conferred under section 7 of the Police, Factories, etc. (Miscellaneous Provisions) Act, 1916) calling for the provision of ambulance rooms in certain classes of factories. The wording used is as follows :—

" In every factory to which this Order applies and in which the total number of persons employed is 500 or more, the occupier shall provide and maintain in good order an ambulance room.

" The ambulance room shall be a separate room used only for the purpose of treatment and rest. It shall have a floor space of not less than 100 square feet and smooth, hard and impervious walls and floor, and shall be provided with ample means of natural and artificial lighting. It shall contain at least—

" (i.) A glazed sink with hot and cold water always available.
" (ii.) A table with a smooth top.
" (iii.) Means for sterilising instruments.
" (iv.) A supply of suitable dressings, bandages and splints.
" (v.) A couch.
" (vi.) A stretcher.
" Where persons of both sexes are employed, arrangements

shall be made at the ambulance room for their separate treatment.

"The ambulance room shall be placed under the charge of a qualified nurse, or other person, trained in first aid, who shall always be readily available during working hours, and shall keep a record of all cases of accident and sickness treated at the room."

FORM 1.

Name : Check No. : Shop or Department :

Date.	How employed.		Time of arrival in ambulance room.	Surgical.			Medical.	Treatment or redressing.	Return to work or departure from factory with time.
	Usually.	At time of accident.		Time of accident.	Nature of injury.	How caused.	Nature of case.		

FORM 2.

Summary to include all Cases Attended at First Aid Posts or Ambulance Room.

Monthly Records for 19 .

Date.	Cuts, etc.	Septic.	Bruise.	Burn.	Sprains.	Eye.	Redressing.	Illness.	Total.	Remarks.
1. 2. 3. 4. 5. 6. 7. 8. 9. 10. etc. to 31.										
Totals.										

This summary should not take the place of records, but should act as a speedy and complete method of summarising all accidents. The card record should be kept in addition and a stroke entered on this form as each case comes under observation.

The provision here called for is not merely structural, stating the minimum requirements of an ambulance room, but also personal in relation to the attendants.   Further, the keeping of records of cases treated is definitely demanded.   No standard method of record-keeping has yet been laid down, and records are often incomplete ;   the reason for this is probably lack of appreciation of the value of records when used with intelligence. The forms here given show how the results of treatment may be ascertained ;   and a nurse who is watching her cases may get valuable information as to an undue frequency of accidents of a certain kind, or in one particular department.   The card system is undoubtedly the best form of record, a separate card being started for each worker on engagement.   A specimen card is here shown on which the subsequent history can be noted until recovery is complete.   The nurse then has immediately before her details of the occurrence of previous accidents or sickness, and if the cards are kept in alphabetical order, the time involved in finding the one required is inconsiderable.   Information can be extracted from the cards as any special point comes up for investigation.   Advantage may be gained by also keeping a summary of cases occurring each day, and for this purpose a record sheet such as is shown may be used (8).

The procedure the nurse will adopt in relation to treatment will vary with her training and the directions given her by the factory medical officer.   She should, however, always establish close touch with outside medical services ;   in some cases nurses effect co-operation by sending cases with a note to the out-patient department of the nearest hospital, or to a panel doctor, asking for help and advice ;   the patient returns to the nurse who carries out the treatment indicated—say, fomenting a septic wound for a week—and is then perhaps sent for further advice. In this way busy out-patient departments and panel doctors are relieved of routine dressings, and the patients avoid long waits for treatment.   The latter point, if the injury does not incapacitate the operative from work, is an important one, as a visit to a crowded out-patient department usually takes up at least half a day.

The factory nurse and the ambulance room were originally called into existence for treating accidents ;   but, as we have said, many medical cases come under observation as well.   Usually a supply of drugs and remedies are kept for such cases ;   but care must be exercised in limiting what is provided.   Any desire on the part of the nurse to be supplied with such drugs as phenacetin, chlorodyne, caffein, antipyrin and aspirin must be resisted.   Only a few simple drugs should be stored, such as castor oil, sal-volatile, ginger, bicarbonate of soda, and essence of peppermint. The nurse should be taught to rely on her own common sense, giving advice and not drugs ; she must remember that headache or abdominal pain may be the first signs of serious trouble, and that drugs, administered to give immediate relief, may mask symptoms required to establish a diagnosis ; and similarly that a gargle may temporarily remove from the throat signs of diphtheria. She will then be more ready to refer cases to her medical superintendent at that early stage, the importance of which is coming to be more and more appreciated. The duty of a nurse is not to provide temporary relief for every ailment by the promiscuous exhibition of drugs, but to seek out the underlying causes of the troubles she is consulted about, and ascertain whether these causes lie with the work, the worker, or home surroundings.

First Aid Organisation.—The Health of the Munition Workers Committee in the memorandum (3) already referred to, pointed out that in addition to an ambulance room, local first aid boxes were needed in big factories, placed in the workshops. Operatives employed on piece work grudge the time—half an hour or twenty minutes—involved in going to a central dressing station to have some apparently trifling scratch or abrasion attended to, but will readily allow a fellow worker to apply a simple dressing. In small factories where the numbers employed hardly justify the expense involved in providing an ambulance room and the services of a nurse, the first aid boxes have to do duty alone. The method of treatment to be adopted through these boxes has received careful consideration, and aseptic dressings are now called for. The wording of the Home Office Order in relation to them is as follows :—

" In every factory to which this Order applies and in which the total number of persons employed is twenty-five or more, the occupier shall provide, in readily accessible positions, ' First Aid ' boxes or cupboards in the proportion of at least one to every 150 persons.

" The number of ' First Aid ' boxes or cupboards required under this provision shall be calculated on the largest number of persons employed at any one time, and any odd number of persons less than 150 shall be reckoned as 150.

" Each ' First Aid ' box or cupboard shall contain at least :—

" (i.) A copy of the ' First Aid ' leaflet issued by the Factory Department of the Home Office.

" (ii.) Three dozen small size sterilised dressings for injured fingers.

" (iii.) One dozen medium size sterilised dressings for injured hands or feet.

" (iv.) One dozen large size sterilised dressings for other injured parts.

" (v.) One bottle of eye drops, and

" (vi.) Sterilised cotton wool.

" Each ' First Aid ' box or cupboard shall be distinctively marked, and if newly provided after the date of this Order shall be marked plainly with a white cross on a red ground.

" Nothing except appliances or requisites for First Aid shall be kept in a ' First Aid ' box or cupboard.

" Each ' First Aid ' box or cupboard shall be kept stocked and in good order, and shall be placed under the charge of a responsible person who shall always be readily available during working hours.

" A notice or notices shall be affixed in every workroom stating the name of the person in charge of the ' First Aid ' box or cupboard provided in respect of that room."

The instructions issued in the leaflet referred to above run :

FORM 923.   FACTORY DEPARTMENT.
    October, 1917.   HOME OFFICE.

FIRST  AID.

TREATMENT OF   MINOR INJURIES.

The following suggestions have the approval of H.M. Medical Inspectors of Factories in rendering first aid in factories and workshops so as to prevent subsequent septic infection or blood poisoning.

A SCRATCH OR SLIGHT WOUND.

Do not touch it.

Do not bandage or wipe it with a handkerchief or rag of any kind.

Do not wash it.

Allow the blood to dry and so close the wound naturally ; then apply a sterilised dressing and bandage.*

If bleeding does not stop, apply a sterilised dressing and sterilised wool, then bandage firmly.

If the wound is soiled with road dirt or other foul matter, swab freely with wool soaked in the iodine solution † and allow the wound to dry before applying a sterilised dressing.

A BURN OR SCALD.

Do not touch it.

Do not wash it.

---

* Minute wounds can be efficiently closed by applying collodion.

† An alcoholic solution containing 2 per cent. of iodine.

Do not apply oil or grease of any kind.

Wrap up the injured part in a large dressing of sterilised wool.*

An Acid Burn.

Do not touch it, or apply oil or grease of any kind.

Flood the burn with cold water.

Sprinkle it (after flooding) with powdered bicarbonate of soda.

Apply a sterilised burn dressing of suitable size.

However slight the burn, if the area affected is extensive a doctor must be consulted.

Do not remove any dressing, but, if the injured part becomes painful and begins to throb, go to a doctor at once.

Destroy all dressings which have been opened but not used ; they soon become infected with microbes and then are not safe to use.

Eye Injuries.

A Foreign Body.—Apply the eye drops, Solution No. 1,† to the affected eye-ball by means of the camel-hair brush in the bottle.

Do not try to remove any particle which cannot be brushed away.

Tie up with a clean handkerchief or bandage.

Go to a doctor *at once.*

An Acid Burn.—Brush the affected eye-ball thoroughly with Solution No. 2, ‡

Then apply Solution No. 1 in the same way.

Apply an eye-pad and tie up with clean handkerchief or bandage.

Go to a doctor *at once.*

Prevention is better than cure ; therefore, if your work entails danger to the eyes,

Wear Goggles.

Goggles have saved hundreds of eyes ; *thousands* have been lost for want of them.

Note.—Danger from minor injuries arises from blood poisoning which is caused when microbes infect a wound. The majority of wounds are at first " clean," that is they are not infected with microbes ; such infection usually occurs later and comes from hand-

---

* This would not exclude treatment by prepared paraffin or picric acid.

† Solution No. 1 :—Cocaine   .   .   . 0·5 per cent.
                Hyd. Perchlor.   .   . 1 in 3,000
               in castor oil.

‡ Solution No. 2 :—Sodium bicarbonate, 15 grains ; distilled water, 1 ounce.

Instructions to chemist for making eye drops :—Weigh 95 grammes of castor oil into a flask capable of holding twice the quantity. Add 0·5 gramme of powdered cocaine. Warm on a water bath till dissolved. While the solution is still warm (but not hot) add one cubic centimetre of a solution containing 3·3 grammes of mercuric chloride in 100 cubic centimetres of absolute alcohol. Mix the solutions by rotating the flask.

About half an ounce, or 15 c.c., of this solution should be supplied in a bottle from the cork of which a camel-hair brush is pendent in the fluid.

[The Secretary of State has issued a general permit to occupiers under the Defence of the Realm Regulations, 40 B, to purchase this preparation on condition that it is used for the purpose specified and no other and that it is kept in the custody of the occupier or of a responsible official nominated in writing by him.]

kerchiefs or other materials applied to stop bleeding or to wipe away blood, and, in the case of eye injuries, from efforts to remove fixed particles with unclean instruments. *It is better to leave a wound alone than to introduce microbes by improper treatment.* The congealing of blood is Nature's way of closing wounds against infection, and should not be interfered with.

Burns and scalds when the skin is not broken will heal if left alone ; all that is necessary is rest and a protective covering. When blisters form they must not be pricked, except under medical advice.

Rest is an important aid to healing. A short rest at first allows healing to commence and often saves a long rest later. An injured hand or finger can be rested in a sling, and an injured eye by a bandage, but an injured foot or toe can only be rested in bed.

ECZEMA FROM LUBRICATING OIL.

Dermatitis and eczema from oils and fluids used to lubricate and cool metals can best be prevented by cleanliness of (1) the overalls, and (2) the skin. All overalls should be washed weekly, and the hands and forearms daily in warm water before leaving the factory. Lanoline and castor oil ointment (equal parts) applied to the skin after washing is a help. When dermatitis and eczema occur washing should be stopped and a doctor seen at once.

The use of tincture of iodine as a disinfectant for minor injuries advocated in these instructions is of considerable importance. The majority of minor injuries, if left entirely alone, and only guarded from outside infection by the application of a dry sterilised dressing, will heal by first intention ; but nothing is lost by the use of iodine in every case before applying the dressing, and some surgeons follow this procedure. Dr. Mock, for instance, writes (10) :—" My own experience has absolutely convinced me that the immediate use of tincture of iodine to an injured part by the employee himself or by a fellow employee is the most important first aid procedure which can be adopted in industry. In 1909, when I first used iodine in every department of the industry with which I was connected, there was an immediate reduction of 28 per cent. in the number of infections the first month after this plan was installed." Iodine treatment is of undoubted value, but of equal value is the elimination of the washing of wounds which " is in itself a minor surgical operation requiring technical skill and training if the injured person is not to be subjected to unnecessary risk " (8). Elimination of washing and the use of sterilised dressings alone reduced septic cases by some 80 per cent. when introduced in a group of engineering factories. Washing " should not, therefore, be included in the first aid treatment, and the removal of dirt should be limited to the application of iodine solution which not only stops bleeding but also helps to disinfect the wound " (8). Other points relating to simple first aid treatment are clearly explained in the instructions reproduced above and need no further exposition.

Workers well drilled on the above lines can render useful service to their fellows; but the service should be organised and directed from the ambulance room.

The success of first aid boxes has not yet been so unequivocal as that of the ambulance rooms, partly owing to the fact that

No. 1.—Unsealing a Dressing.

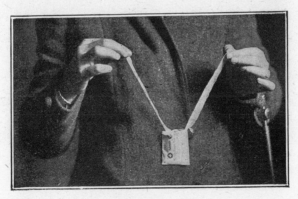

No. 2.—How to Open.
Fig. 36.
Reproduced from (8).

nurses, wishing every case to come to the central station, do not encourage their use, and partly because persons trained in older ambulance methods can with difficulty be persuaded simply to apply a dressing without some preliminary washing of the wound; but in time the first aid boxes should justify themselves. The factory nurse should organise the treatment given in the workshops, teach the simple methods to be employed, and be responsible for the actions of those placed in charge of the boxes.

These persons should be members of the factory ambulance corps, be trained in stretcher drill, and taught the principles of workshop ventilation and cleanliness. Thus there may be brought into existence an organisation of the workers responsible to the nurse for the general health of the personnel throughout

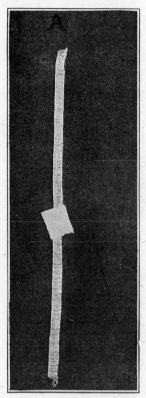

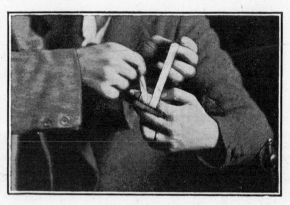

No. 4.—How to apply.

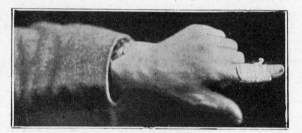

No. 3.—Unfolded
Dressing.

No. 5.—When finished.

FIG. 36 (continued).
Reproduced from (8).

the factory, each member keeping a watch over a group of workers.

In some factories members of the ambulance corps are remu·nerated to compensate them for any earnings they may lose through being called upon to render first aid.

A note should be made at each first aid box of each case treated, which can be sent later to the central station to be entered up. At a small factory where there is no central ambulance room the notes may be made in a case book containing headings similar to those set out above for separate cards.

IV. The Welfare Superintendent.

The duties carried out by the factory medical officer and by the factory nurse are purely medical; but there has come into existence recently in large industrial establishments a special

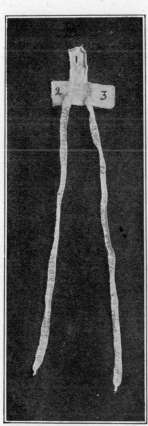

No. 1.—Unfolded Dressing
for Top of Finger.

No. 2.—How to apply.

FIG. 37.
Reproduced from (8).

department concerned with the welfare and health of operatives presided over by a welfare superintendent (also called welfare supervisor, labour superintendent, or, in the case of boys, apprentice master).   The importance of this department in the future organisation of industry can hardly be exaggerated.

Certain of the duties belonging to it have a direct relation to health ; and the person appointed should, where the services of

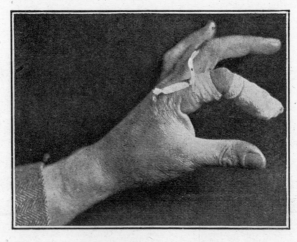

No. 3.—When finished.
FIG. 37 (*continued*).

a whole-time doctor are not retained, be responsible to the management for the work of the ambulance room and the first

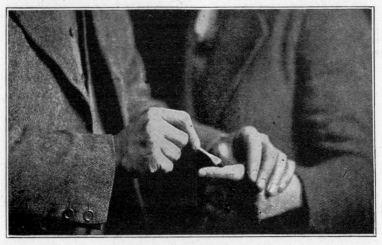

FIG. 38.—Application of Iodine.
Reproduced from (8).

aid organisation. This department maintains with the workers that personal touch so necessary in human affairs, which busy managers must delegate to others.

Where women and girls form a large proportion of those

employed, the post of welfare superintendent should be filled by a capable and intelligent woman, by preference one of good education, with sound training in the principles of hygiene and of social and industrial life. Where boys and men are concerned, a man with similar training and possessing experience in dealing with boys should be chosen. The duties to be undertaken by these officers will vary in different places, but the scope of the work may be gathered from the following suggestions :—The duties fall naturally under two headings. The first relates to obtaining a personnel whose health is fitted for the work of the factory ; the second relates to maintaining the personnel in health and vigour. Both these groups can again be subdivided according to whether activity is outside or inside the factory.

Obtaining the Personnel.—The welfare officer must come in touch with the workers on engagement. At some establishments the whole question of engagement is entrusted to this officer. At others, after sifting out the unsuitable, the remainder are submitted to the foreman to pick from. Certain matters must be attended to for the work of engagement to be adequately carried out. (i.) The officer must be familiar with the industrial processes carried on. Advantage is gained if he has familiarised himself with some of the processes by performing them personally. At one factory at least excellent results were obtained by calling upon every welfare officer, before undertaking the duties of the office, to act for a period as an operative. The familiarity so gained is of inestimable value for grasping the principles of accident prevention and the avoidance of poisoning in dangerous processes. (ii.) The officer must examine the previous history of applicants for work, and for this purpose keep in close touch with educational authorities and labour exchanges. (iii.) A register of available houses and lodgings in the district must be kept, so that the management can be informed of any lack of accommodation and the workers can be assisted to find lodgings. (iv.) Transit facilities must be looked into and the length of time taken to travel from various districts. The need for increasing train service, tram or motor service, or for suggesting moderation of factory hours to fall in with existing time-tables, must be under constant consideration. (v.) The officer must be present when the certifying factory surgeon or the factory medical officer conducts his examination and note any recommendations which are then made with a view to seeing that they are carefully carried out.

Maintenance of Health.—The duties falling under this heading are numerous and diverse. (i.) Personal records of each worker must be kept in which are noted the places of abode, progress in the factory, accidents sustained, time lost and sickness suffered. (ii.) Investigation into these records must be made ; otherwise their value will be lost. Investigations, for instance, into the causation of lost time should go a long way towards diminishing this cause of industrial worry ; one investigation in which factories were first grouped according to the amount of bad time-keeping experienced, and then regrouped according to whether the welfare work at these factories was considered to be good, medium, or bad, disclosed no single case of pronouncedly bad time-keeping among the factories where welfare supervision was good. (iii.) The officer must establish his position with the foremen, and induce them to take a personal interest in those who work under them, instead of regarding them as mere animate tenders of inanimate machinery. (iv.) The wage system in vogue at the factory must be carefully studied, whether payment is by time, by piece work, by the group system, by time and bonus, by premium bonus, or any other plan. Only thus can less intelligent workers have explained to them how they are paid. The officer must, however, have nothing whatever to do with fixing the rates of payment. (v.) An acquaintance is necessary with the principles of canteen management and the energy value and suitability of food ; further, attention should be paid to the fancies, often local, of the workers in relation to food. (vi.) The sanitary conveniences, lavatory accommodation, and cloak rooms must be inspected, kept clean and tidy, and supplied with soap and clean towels. The actual work will lie with others, but the responsibility will lie with the welfare officer, who must be prepared to advise his firm as to the best structural provision to make for each of these purposes. (vii.) The ambulance, rest room, and first aid organisation will require supervision, and close touch must be established between this department, the factory medical officer, and outside medical service. (viii.) The officer must pass through the workshops frequently and on the occasion of these visits take note of—

(a) The atmospheric conditions and need for ventilation.

(b) The temperature, especially when work is starting on cold mornings, or at mid-day when the shops may be over-heated and stuffy.

(c) The light, both natural and artificial ; much can be done to get windows cleaned and to rectify the position of lights which may be so placed as to be causing headaches.

(d) The posture of workers in relation to their processes and the provision of seats or stools, varying in height according to the stature of the workers.

(e) The advisability of providing seats where seats could be used but are not provided.

Care must be exerted in carrying out these duties not to invade the province of technical control, or even to appear to interfere with the prerogatives of the foreman. (ix.) The feelings of the workers and their confidence must be obtained if the work is to be effective. A means to this end is to be found in a welfare committee elected by the workers themselves. The welfare officer should be a member, possibly the chairman of such a committee. (x.) Where juveniles, especially boys, are employed, attention must be given to their continued education ; and for this purpose co-operation is needed with local education authorities with whom the duty lies to establish classes for general and technical instruction. An eye must also be kept on the efficiency of any apprenticeship scheme which may have been adopted at the factory. (xi.) The officer acting over the boys, who is sometimes known as the apprentice master, will have certain other special duties to undertake. Since, however, these are not part of health questions and can be easily ascertained elsewhere (4), we do not discuss them further here. (xii.) Where mothers of young children are employed, a necessity may arise for establishing a *crèche* for these children while their mothers are at work. If such an institution be in existence in the district, the officer may require to urge the mothers to take advantage of its facilities. (xiii.) Matters concerned with pregnancy (already dealt with on p. 229) will come within the province of the woman welfare supervisor, who may need to organise a light employment depot for nursing mothers, with a nursery attached. (xiv.) The inauguration of healthy recreation of all kinds must be one of the most important sides of welfare work, and this side will grow in importance with the tendency to shorten the hours of employment. The organisation of social clubs, institutions, girl guides, boy scouts, dances, concerts, summer camps, holiday homes, tennis, hockey, cricket, horticulture, and lectures form only a part of the work to be done in this direction. Recreation may cover the growing of vegetables in a few yards of waste ground in a factory, or the purchase of a piano to enliven the meal hour ; and may extend to the provision of playing fields and institutions for factories employing over 10,000 workers, or even the inauguration of extensive civic schemes.

The value of recreation on organised lines is immense. It possesses three aspects : (i.) It interferes with Satan's vocation of " finding mischief still for idle hands to do " ; (ii.) it provides mental interest and physical exercise different from those of working hours, and so tends to counterbalance any harmful effect due to occupation from muscular strain ; (iii.) it promotes through healthy rivalry that *esprit de corps* upon which patriotism is built. Interfactory competitions naturally spring up and affiliation develops, until something akin to the elastic athletic organisation of a university may evolve.

Health Committee.—We hope what has already been written will have made it sufficiently clear that the health of the industrial worker, if it is to be maintained, must depend more upon the worker himself than upon any one else. No individual can be compelled to be healthy. The services of the doctor, of the nurse, the welfare officer, and the dentist, the proper use of the welfare facilities which may have been provided, and indeed every effort to maintain the health of the workers, will fail unless the active and intelligent co-operation of the workers is obtained. This should be sought for by forming a health or welfare committee at an early date. The personnel of this committee should be elected by the workers themselves. Once elected, the duties, which are numerous, fall under the following three headings :—(i.) They should be responsible for the maintenance of order and discipline. Here the monitorial system of English public schools should be taken as the example to be followed. (ii.) Personal grievances, real or imaginary, should be referred to and considered by the committee. (iii.) The committee will be the executive authority acting probably through sub-committees for organising various recreational activities.

The committee may be presided over by the welfare officer. Indeed, at some factories this will be necessary, at any rate at first. A case of an unusual form of welfare committee may be instanced. It took the form of a parliament. Every twenty-five boys elected a member once every quarter, and these members in their turn appointed a prime minister and a cabinet. The welfare officer might reasonably become the speaker of such a committee.

Dismissal.—No worker should be dismissed or leave the factory without the knowledge of the welfare officer. Frequently, threatened dismissal of a useful worker, originating from some personal quarrel between foreman and workman, has by this means been avoided. The quarrel may be adjusted or the worker may be transferred to another part of the factory. Sometimes workers may be leaving on account of ill-health not otherwise known to exist, and lightening the conditions of work may enable a useful operative to be retained. Or, again, misunderstanding in relation to payment of wages may be explained satisfactorily.

The handing over of the transference of workers or their engagement entirely to the welfare officer is sometimes objected to by the technical staff; but there can be no objection to reference to the welfare officer of all cases of impending dismissal. Such references frequently go a long way to diminish labour turnover with its economic loss.

Staff required.—Perusal of the above suggestions shows how intimately the welfare department of any industrial establishment is associated with the health and welfare of those employed. Where the work is well organised its value is quickly demonstrated by the diminution in labour turnover or wastage of workers, and in better time-keeping. These two matters alone effect an economy in production sufficient to justify any management in establishing a welfare department.

Where 300 women and girls are employed there is work for the whole-time services of a welfare superintendent; and when the numbers reach 600 an assistant is required in addition. An increase of a further 450, making 1,050 in all, calls for a second assistant; and every increase thereafter of 600 in the personnel calls for a further assistant.

Where boys are employed, the work, as set out (4), will be seen to be more onerous, and 100 boys provide full-time work for an apprentice master, who requires an assistant when the number employed exceeds 400. Where the duties of the welfare department refer to men and boys, the numbers employed in relation to the number of officers may be counted as set out above for the case of women and girls.

Much might be written on the organisation of a welfare department, the scope of its work, and its relation to technical management on the one side, and to trade union activities on the other; but these matters hardly fall within the sphere of this book, which is concerned only with the health of industrial workers. Enough has been said to show how the welfare department of any industrial establishment, working with the factory medical officer, the nurse, and the canteen manager, forms an effective organisation for watching over the health of the employees. The management is amply repaid for the cost involved by improvement in the quantity and quality of output; the workers benefit in health and in contentment arising from increased capacity for earning wages.

V. The Dental Clinic.

Dental clinics were first established in factories to safeguard workers manipulating yellow phosphorus when that substance was permitted to be used in the manufacture of phosphorus matches; the fumes of the phosphorus affected those with decayed teeth and caused necrosis of the jaw, known as phossy jaw. When yellow phosphorus came to be used in the preparation of some munitions of war, these clinics again became a necessity; and they were also established for workers handling T.N.T. because this poisonous explosive set up gastritis difficult to distinguish from ordinary dyspepsia due to bad teeth. The improved standard of health among the workers which resulted fully justified the action taken, and convinced the management of the first factory where a clinic was started of its immense value, quite apart from the immediate purpose for which it was intended. For many years appointed surgeons carrying out periodical examinations of workers exposed to risk of lead poisoning have, apart from lowering the incidence of plumbism, achieved great improvement to the general health of the workers under their care by insisting on attention to the teeth. These results accord with the increasing attention which is steadily being centred upon the value to digestion and general health of a healthy condition of the teeth. Pyorrhœa, rheumatic arthritis, sore throats and inflamed cervical glands are some of the constitutional troubles now claimed to originate in oral sepsis; in addition, inflamed fangs cause toothache and neuralgia, which not only result in lost time, but seriously impair the efficiency and the working capacity of those continuing at work. The importance of food to industrial workers is dealt with elsewhere; but the advantage of an adequate dietary is lost if the workers, owing to the condition of their teeth, are dyspeptic. Some employers have recognised this, and have established successful dental clinics on factory premises, which can readily be done in connection with the ambulance room. Operatives appreciate these clinics, for they often find difficulty in obtaining efficient dental service, because the consulting hours of registered dentists generally coincide with the working hours; and they are compelled to seek unqualified and often entirely unskilled help.

Where such clinics are established the medical officer can readily direct applicants for work, as well as those already employed, whose dentition requires attention, to obtain treatment; indeed, a dental clinic as an adjunct to the work of an industrial doctor is necessary to make his work effective. The scope of work to be done may be gathered from a statement made by Mock (10) that among a staff of 5,000 employees when a dental clinic was started, 2,870 treatments were given to 2,707 patients in the first six months, and 3,383 treatments to 2,843 patients in the next six months. The same author notes that at another establishment during the first six months a dental clinic was opened 391 employees received treatment ; in the next twelve months 6,081, and in the next year 8,502. Such a rapid increase clearly indicates that workers fully appreciate and make use of a dental clinic. The Board of Education have recently dwelt upon the value of dental clinics in connection with schools ; there is no doubt that the dentition of adults equally requires constant attention.

The existence of an ambulance room and a trained nurse makes the installation of a dental clinic simple and comparatively cheap. The necessary chair and implements must be purchased, and arrangements made for the attendance of a qualified dentist at definite times. Some firms arrange finance so that extractions are free, while the workers themselves pay for other treatment ; or the workers may pay for all treatment. In consideration of the facilities provided the dentist is able to fix fees on a low scale. A dental clinic seldom fails to be an unqualified success.

VI. Bibliography.

1. *Report of Poor Law Commissioners on Sanitary Conditions of the Labouring Population of Great Britain*, p. 244. 1842.

2. *Dilution of Labour Bulletin.* Issued by Ministry of Munitions. November, 1917, and April, 1918.

3. " Sickness and Injury." *Health of Munition Workers Committee. Memo. No.* 10. (Cd. 8216.) 1916.

4. *Handbook for Welfare Supervisors and Apprentice Masters.* Ministry of Labour. 1919.

5. Collis, E. L. " The Protection of the Health of Munition Workers." *Journal of State Medicine.* 1917.

6. Collis, E. L. " Welfare Work in Factories." *Journal of Roy. San. Inst.* June, 1919.

7. Graves, C. A. " The Granting of Certificates of Fitness to Children and Young Persons employed in Factories and Workshops." *Brit. Med. Jour.* September 13th, 1902.

8. *First Aid and Ambulance at Factories and Workshops.* H.M. Stationery Office. 1919.

9. Wright, F. S. *Industrial Nursing.* Macmillan & Co. New York. 1919.

10. Mock, H. E. *Industrial Medicine and Surgery.* W. B. Saunders Co. Philadelphia. 1919.

11. *See, also,* Collis, E. L. " The Practice of Industrial Welfare and Health." *Lectures on Industrial Administration.* Sir Isaac Pitman & Sons, Ltd. 1920.

CHAPTER XVIII

RECLAMATION OF THE DISABLED

I.   Introduction.

ONE lesson learned from the war is that more can be done to fit a disabled man to work at a remunerative occupation than was formerly supposed possible. The subject had never been thoroughly gone into in this country, as, after our previous wars, the number of disabled was not sufficient to awake public feeling to the necessity for action. Owing to the many nations engaged in the war the problem of the disabled is now being worked out by each in its own way. Before 1914 the only nations with any system of training the disabled were Belgium, Sweden and Germany ; other nations, like ourselves, were content to deal with the training of crippled children, and to leave those crippled in industry, whether by accident or disease, to the cold mercies of inadequate benefits.

II.   The Extent of the Need.

The toll taken by industry every year is heavy, so heavy that were it not always with us, the national conscience would be aroused just as it is on behalf of the maimed soldier. The data given in Chapter VIII. gives some idea of the extent of industrial accidents. A census taken in 1918 of civilians in Wales disclosed that one in every 810 had lost one or more limbs. Dr. Mock writes from America (1) :—" If the casualty list from industry could be printed every day in our newspapers the people of this country would be appalled at its size. In one year from accidents alone it is over four times as large as the entire casualties among our troops on the battle fields in Europe. We have no record to show the number who are killed or disabled as the result of occupational diseases and diseases partially traceable to working conditions, but these undoubtedly are even more shocking." The same writer quotes statistical data prepared by Mr. Riddle, who concludes : "On the basis of those figures, it may be safe to assume that the total number of amputations suffered by men in Pennsylvania's army in the field of war will be considerably less than the total number of amputations suffered in Pennsylvania's industries over an equal period."

The extent of medical disablement cannot be fairly represented, but the effect of one disease alone, miners' nystagmus, may be instanced. Dr. T. L. Llewellyn writes (2) on this matter :— " At any given time since 1913 there have been 6,000 men disabled in England by miners' nystagmus. . . . The indirect cost to the nation cannot be calculated—it includes all the suffering and mental worry of the patients, and the effect of the loss of nearly three-quarters of a million tons of coal on the general industries of the country. The reduction in family income will be followed by a corresponding reduction in the size of the family, and the children already born will be thrown into the world at an earlier age to help their parents, and will have their own chances in life greatly diminished." Add to these cases the occurrence among miners in 1914 of 2,772 compensation cases due to beat hand, beat elbow and beat knee. The prevalence of these diseases is known because they are scheduled for compensation. We can only guess at the effect of other diseases. D. M. Holman, who has considered the matter, writes (1): " It is a very conservative estimate to state that annually 250,000 workers are, under present conditions, permanently thrown out of employment through accident or preventable disease in the United States alone. These men and women must be supported somehow. Part of them receive whole or partial support under the provisions of the Workmen's Compensation Acts, and while this solves in whole or in part their individual problem of existence it does so in most States only for a limited period, and after six or ten years of idleness, when their compensation ceases, they are left in a most pitiful condition. . . . This economic waste caused by the apparently enforced idleness of this vast army of men and women exceeds $100,000,000 a year of added burden, and amounts to not less than half a billion dollars annually, a figure that is constantly being increased by the addition of a quarter of a million cripples each year."

Steps taken to reclaim disabled soldiers have taught us much.

These steps are described in what follows, and indications are given of how the same thing can be done for disabled workmen.

III. Development due to the War.

Orthopædic surgery has made great advances in recent years, so that cases which ten years ago would have been regarded as permanently disabled for life are now by special treatment cured in a few months. It was not until 1907 that massage and electrical treatment were widely adopted by the big general hospitals in this country.   Owing to pressure on the beds the system used to be to put up fractures in plaster of Paris, and send them to a con-valescent hospital for six weeks ; when the plaster case was taken off, the man was given some liniment and left to cure himself as best he could.   In time perhaps he obtained a useful limb, if he had the perseverance to go on using the liniment.

How different was the system developed during the war under the guidance of Sir Robert Jones ! Men with bad wounds in their limbs were sent straight to special orthopædic hospitals, where they were attended to by specialist surgeons provided with costly apparatus.

It is now proposed that the orthopædic hospitals which are carried on by the Ministry of Pensions should be taken over by the Ministry of Health for civilian cases when their use by pensioners ceases.   The system of motor ambulances which is being set up throughout the country by the Red Cross Society and St. John Ambulance Association should remove all difficulty in taking any accident requiring orthopædic treatment to a special hospital, even from a remote country district.   Massage and electrical treatment after orthopædic operations are now considered so important by the Ministry of Pensions that centres have been established in big towns with clinics in small surround-ing towns ; men are thus able to get treatment without having to travel many miles.   The results obtained are remarkable compared with those of pre-war days.

Artificial Limbs.—Another branch of orthopædic work which has also been developed of recent years is the fitting of artificial limbs in special hospitals ; no doubt some of these hospitals will be retained for civilian use.   This subject never received adequate attention before the war, and was left too much to instrument makers.   The fitting of some artificial limbs was so unsatis-factory that surgeons preferred amputating at a site where a good stump could be obtained, and sacrificed part of the limb to do so ; thus they preferred to amputate just below the knee rather than just above the ankle.   Now, with the excellent artificial limbs used, such procedure would not be regarded as good surgery. Any attempt at describing fully the advances which have been made would extend outside the scope of this book. Certain principles, however, underlie the construction of appliances ; these have been formulated (3) by Amar as follows :—

" (a) To devise prosthetic appliances which can be firmly and strongly attached, without impeding the movements involved, or those of other articulations ;

" (b) To adapt these appliances, in respect of weight and dimensions, to the strength of the stumps ;

" (c) To fit appliances for the upper limbs with an organ of prehension which will permit of protracted and varied employment.

" These threefold conditions guarantee *strength, simplicity,* and a *good output* in prosthetic appliances, resulting in the always desirable employment of human energy in professions to which it might have seemed that the war cripple could never gain access."

The appliances now supplied for upper and lower limbs are so ingenious that many of the men are quite able to carry on their previous trades. In one case a man with a steel appliance for the arm seemed to have been specially meant for feeding a circular saw in a brush factory ; if the steel end did happen to get caught in the saw, no question of compensation arose and no report of an accident had to be rendered to the factory inspector.

Functional Re-education.—It is now realised that besides the accurate-fitting of an artificial limb a special course for re-educating the muscles working the stump is required, and several limb-fitting hospitals have been established. At the Prince of Wales' Hospital for Limbless Sailors and Soldiers at Cardiff a special garden has been prepared with uneven paths and obstacles so that men can train themselves in overcoming difficulties.

Medical Disablement.—In the first two years of the war about 66·5 per cent. were discharged disabled as the result of wounds and the remaining 33·5 per cent. as the result of disease ; but as the war continued and was carried on in unhealthy climates, and also the necessity arose of calling up older men, the number of those discharged as disabled by disease rose considerably.

Those disabled by wounds attract more attention, and perhaps receive more sympathy, than those disabled by disease ; yet the latter are often more to be pitied. A man who has lost a limb from wounds may enjoy perfect health for many years and

rightly be received as a hero wherever he goes ; but the man who
has valvular disease of the heart, nephritis, neurasthenia or
debility following malaria is constantly feeling out of health,
and in some cases his life may be shortened in consequence of
his disability.   Any scheme for helping must provide for those
who are medically as well as for those who are surgically disabled.
Medical disablement arises in civil life from the ordinary risks
of disease ; influenza, acute rheumatism, pneumonia, may leave
a man quite unfitted to follow his previous occupation, while the
anxieties associated with industrial life are a potent cause of
neurasthenia.

Occupational Training.—In cases where a pensioner's disablement prevents him following his pre-war occupation provision
has been made to train him for a fresh occupation.   It is found
that 80 per cent. of war cripples can be trained to carry on a
trade without special equipment, or by one man helping another ;
and that the remaining 20 per cent. may require some special
provision at factories.   As employers may not be inclined to
accept the latter, Government factories for providing them with
special employment on the lines of the Lord Roberts Memorial
Workshops may be necessary ; these factories should here-
after be maintained for disabled civilians.   A man should
always be encouraged to resume his previous occupation in which
he may have spent years in acquiring valuable experience ; and
the ways by which limbs adapt themselves functionally if trained
should be explained to him.

The Ministry of Pensions have provided convalescent centres
for the concurrent treatment and training of pensioners unfit to
follow their pre-war occupations, or only able to do so with
diminished earning capacity.   A man, having been recommended
for concurrent treatment and training, is sent to a centre and
given an opportunity of seeing the various courses of training,
and of selecting one for which he may be considered suitable by
the medical officer.   The training given is in general preparatory
to a course of training of the same kind under the Ministry of
Labour, when the man no longer requires treatment.   At these
convalescent centres ample provision is made for treatment
rooms, workshops, and lecture rooms ; the comfort and amusement of the men are provided for by common dining rooms,
dry and wet canteens, recreation rooms and libraries ; there are
also facilities for outdoor games.   The training is regulated
according to a man's physical ability, as determined by the
medical officer, and in all cases treatment is considered to come
before training.

Concurrent treatment and training are also carried out for

men living in their own homes in some large towns where orthopædic centres and municipal technical schools exist.

Cases of tuberculosis are dealt with in training colonies under the Ministry of Health; several colonies have been started where outdoor work is the chief feature.

For men not requiring further medical treatment, arrangements are made with the Ministry of Labour, Ministry of Agriculture and Fisheries, and the Board of Education.

The Ministry of Labour, in addition to arranging for industrial training, also by their Appointment Department arrange for professional and commercial training.

The Ministry of Agriculture and Fisheries arrange for training in dairy work, horticulture, market gardening, forestry, poultry farming and bee keeping.

The Board of Education arrange for training men as teachers in elementary schools.

IV. Re-education.

Nature has a wonderful way of adapting herself to circumstances. Re-education of the disabled should be directed to assisting nature in her efforts to make functional adaptation as perfect as possible. It should aim at making the disabled person a good wage earner, and an occupation should be chosen for which the disablement is the least handicap. For, as the Gilbreths, who have given much study to the question, put it (4), a cripple is not a cripple " during the period that he is at that work *the performance of which is not affected by the mutilation.*" What this means to the disabled can only be estimated by noting the joy a lame lad takes in swimming, a form of exercise in which his short leg is no particular drawback.

Psychological Influences.—Attention must not be paid exclusively to the local condition, but central control must also receive attention. Petrol and the magneto make the motor work, not the oil that lubricates the crank shaft. A man may receive massage and electrical treatment, but mentally he may be lethargic; he may have no wish to get well quickly; he is content with his compensation, sickness pay, or treatment allowances, and idles away his time smoking cigarettes, attending race meetings, football and cricket matches, long after the time when another man with the same disability returns to work. The latter perchance has a wife and family to maintain, and necessity speeds up the cure. In Italy, where compensation for an injury is paid in a lump sum, men return to work quicker than in other countries where compensation is paid weekly.

The length of time which elapses before a man returns to work bears a distinct relation to his receipts from compensation and one or more clubs. Some men are actually better off when on the sick list than when at work. A married man, the needs of whose family compel him to resume work before he is completely cured, is speeding up the cure and functional adaptation.

The rapidity with which compensation cases improve after their suit has been settled in the courts has often been noticed. Some cases are beneficially affected by relief from anxiety ; but in others there has been wilful prolongation of the symptoms pending the decision of the court. Therefore, where a man has exceeded the average time required to recover from his disability, he should appear before a medical board assisted by a trade expert, entrusted with the duty of determining whether treatment is on the right lines, and whether, if he cannot resume his usual occupation, he can do some form of light work which would improve his mental and bodily condition.

A medical board with experience and technical knowledge would have the advantage over a county court judge, who at present decides these cases ; they would often discover some real cause, possibly a psychological one, for the delay, which had escaped the notice of the man's medical attendant, and be able to suggest how by a slight operation or some other procedure recovery could be effected.

A man may suffer some anatomical loss, and yet in time may recover his industrial capacity. A man lost half his left hand including the third and fourth fingers in 1914, and as a high standard for a soldier was then required he received his discharge. Later, under the Military Service Act, he was called up and posted to a labour company where he was employed with a spade. His hand and forearm became so developed that he could work as well as any other man. He has a fixed pension for life of 8s. (eight shillings) a week. Such a case illustrates the difference between fixed pensions for war wounds and compensation for industrial accidents. The pensioner with a fixed pension cannot have it reduced, however complete functional adaptation is. The workman receiving compensation, on the other hand, is liable to have his case reviewed from time to time with a view to reduction ; and has further before him the fear that any improvement manifest upon which a reduction will be based may prove to be temporary and not permanent.

The Left Hand.—Training of the left hand when the right is disabled should be commenced as soon as possible. However ingenious an artificial hand may be, it can only perform a few of the functions of the real hand. Men can be trained to write with the left hand so that their writing cannot be distinguished from that of the right hand, but to do so some special training is required.

M. Tamenne, a Belgian who has had considerable experience in teaching men to write with the left hand, says (5) the man should :—

(i.) Place his forearm comfortably on the table so as to fatigue the hand as little as possible ;

(ii.) Practise writing between lines about 3·5 mm. apart ;

(iii.) Place the paper in a sloping position slightly to the left ;

(iv.) Try from the very beginning to give the usual slope to the letters ; and

(v.) Always take care that the hand is immediately below the point at which he is writing.

But while writing with the left hand is a subject which has received special attention, the part the left hand is going to play in the man's future career should also receive individual attention. A man can learn to shave himself, tie his tie with the assistance of his teeth, open a pocket knife, use a saw or hammer, or some of the special tools he may require at his future trade.

It has been strongly advocated that children should be trained to use both hands, so that they are prepared in the event of an accident to one hand ; but in an experiment made by the Japanese of training a number of children to use both hands equally the result was not satisfactory. No child trained in this fashion was ever so adept with either hand as a right-handed or left-handed child, and the results obtained were not proportionate to efforts entailed. The factor of necessity was missing in these children.

V. Surgical Disabilities of the Limbs.

Ankylosis and Stiffness of the Shoulder Joint.—If mobility of the scapula is retained total ankylosis at the shoulder joint may not seriously interfere with most trades provided the angle of fixation is favourable. The most favourable position is that of abduction at 60 degrees with a slight flexion. In such a position elevation can take place through the scapula so that brushing the hair is possible. For some occupations a fixed shoulder is not a serious disability. Thus, for example, little inconvenience would occur in the case of a worker at a bench, a typist, a postman ; but the disability would be serious for a house painter or an electric light fitter. For these latter a change of occupation would be necessary.

Many cases of limitation of movement at the shoulder are due to adhesions and tend to improve rapidly if the subject resumes work. Compensation in these cases should not be continued too long, in the man's own interest. The length of time men are off work after a dislocation of the shoulder varies a good deal. In some cases, age, or latent disease, may cause a simple sprain or contusion of the shoulder to be followed by a periarthritis, which may cause considerable stiffness and require prolonged treatment ; in others, the man drawing compensation and sickness pay may absolutely neglect to carry out any treatment himself and so prolong the case unduly. In civil practice, adhesions at the shoulder joint are a common cause of prolonged absence from work ; they can be avoided to some extent by early passive movements.

Muscular wasting, which occurs when a joint is kept immobile for a prolonged period, often does not receive sufficient attention. It has been found advantageous before breaking down adhesions at a joint to restore the muscular activity by massage and electrical treatment, so that the patient has power to carry on movements afterwards.

Ankylosis of Elbow Joint.—The most favourable position for fixation of the elbow joint is at a right angle or at an angle of 70 degrees. A man can then feed himself and use tools, whereas if fixed at an acute angle, viz., 30 degrees, he is severely handicapped. But to enable a man to follow his previous occupation of milking cows it has been found necessary to set the elbow at an angle of about 135 degrees.

Flail Elbow Joint.—A large number of elbow joints had to be excised during the war ; many of these are flail-like unless properly fitted with an appliance. A hinged appliance is necessary in these cases, but such appliances are difficult to keep in position when the condyles of the humerus have been removed. A hinged leather appliance which laces on the full length of the forearm and arm is in some cases quite satisfactory ; but it is often necessary to use an appliance which can be fixed at whatever angle is required for the working hand.

A fixed joint obtained by surgical means in some cases gives a more useful limb. This is done by inserting the lower end of the humerus between the bones of the forearm and fixing with a transverse bone peg, or by fixing the bones of the forearm to the humerus by lateral bone grafts.

Ununited Fractures of Arm.—Ununited fractures of the humerus, which some years ago used to cause permanent disablement, are now successfully treated by the step cut operation, or by a sliding bone graft ; thus a useful arm is obtained.

The use of bone grafts for joining fragments where there has been a loss of bone does not produce a strong limb, and a man must be warned as to the work he is fitted for. Thus a man with fractures of the radius and ulna where there had been a loss of 3 inches of both bones, had the bones joined together with grafts taken from the tibia. These were pointed at each end like cricket bails and thrust into the hollow of the shafts of the fragments. The result was good and the man was quite fitted for light work. Unfortunately he did not understand this and went back to his old work in which he had to lift heavy boxes, which resulted in fracture of both bones.

Limitation of Pronation and Supination of Forearm.—With regard to the position in which the radio-ulnar joints are allowed to become ankylosed, occupation must be taken into account. In some trades full supination of the forearm may be most suitable ; but generally the most favourable position is the mid position between pronation and supination. Where a man is disabled from following his previous occupation by an unfavourable position the surgeon can as a rule make the necessary alteration by an osteotomy of the radius.

The Hand.—In the case of the hand there is really no favourable position for ankylosis. If the fingers are immobilised in extension they are of little use and liable to injury. If immobilised in flexion they may serve to act as a hook ; but as usually only one or two fingers are fixed in that position they prevent the use of the hand in grasping. It may be desirable to remove them to gain a more important function of the hand.

Ankylosis of Hip Joint.—If ankylosis of the hip joint occurs in the extended position, while walking is easy, sitting is difficult ; but this difficulty can be overcome to some extent by the use of a special chair in which the seat is cut away on one side so that the weight is born on one buttock. The best position for ankylosis is one of very slight abduction with the thigh extended and very slight outward rotation. If the joint is fixed in flexion and adduction with internal rotation, the position of the sound limb is so interfered with in walking that an osteotomy may be necessary.

Ankylosis of Knee Joint.—Fixation with the knee extended is the favourable position for ankylosis except for occupations which require mounting ladders or steps. Many cases of fibrous ankylosis are so firm that without the aid of X-ray examination it is difficult to decide whether they are bony or fibrous. Cases of fibrous ankylosis of the knee and other joints have been successfully treated by prolonged ionization with sodium chloride. By this means the fibrous tissue about the joint becomes softened and absorbed.

Ununited Fractures of Femur.—By means of the caliper splint, ununited fractures of the upper end of the femur are now success-fully treated while the patient is able to walk about. This splint consists of a modification of Thomas's splint by which the weight of the body is transmitted from the closely fitting ring at the top to the ground by lateral iron rods which are fixed into the heel of the boot on each side.

VI. Stumps.

The condition of stumps is a frequent cause of delay in return-ing to work. This may arise from pain in the stump or incom-plete healing, both of which may require operative treatment. With a painful stump the pain is generally localised in the enlarged ends of one or more of the main nerves which can be readily felt. When a nerve is divided the axis cylinders grow out endeavouring to make connection with the other severed end. In time these axis cylinders form a tangle, which is known as a nerve bulb. If these nerve bulbs are in situations where they are not liable to pressure no painful condition may arise. When once they have become painful the only treatment is their removal. Their size can be limited by crushing the end of the nerve and applying a catgut ligature (6) ; or by stripping back the sheath of the nerve in the form of a cuff, and, having removed the denuded portion of the trunk, by covering the end with the sheath which acts as a limiting resisting membrane (7). Some-times the axis cylinders instead of forming a bulb spread out into the surrounding tissues when the whole stump may be painful and division of the nerve be required. Pain in some cases is due to a neuritis, apparently due to some toxic element, and is resistant to treatment. Pain may be due to a small nerve having become included in the scar ; it is then very localised, and can be cured by excision of the scar. Prolonged and delayed healing in many cases follows amputations which were septic, due to chronic osteitis of the bone followed by necrosis. A troublesome sinus calls for an X-ray examination which may disclose the presence of a sequestrum, a piece of shrapnel, clothing, or a non-absorbable ligature ; these objects must be removed. A scar should be movable and not adherent to the bone ; but in the arm, where there is no end bearing weight, a large adherent guillotine scar covering the end of the bone has not been found to cause inconvenience.

Stumps tend to shrink progressively. The muscles no longer having work to do gradually atrophy ; but the shrinking also depends on the pressure of the artificial limb. It may be a year before the shrinking ceases, and no further alterations are required in the shape of the appliance. The shrinking may cause a defective gait, as when the stump of a thigh amputation sinks down too far into the bucket. Bony spurs or an occult abscess may be a source of pain requiring operative treatment.

The industrial capacity of the victim of amputation will depend on whether the stump is adapted to carry an artificial limb, and the requirements differ in the upper and lower limb. In the upper limb the anterior and external surfaces to which the appliance is attached are of more importance than the terminal extremity.

VII. Artificial Limbs.

The Leg.—Great advantage is gained in cases of amputation of the lower limb by getting the patient to walk about on a temporary limb at the earliest reasonable moment, instead of waiting perhaps months going about on crutches while the stump consolidates. The muscles should be trained to their new work as soon as possible instead of those which will be required here-after being allowed to atrophy in the same way as those not required. A man who has got accustomed to crutches finds it difficult to do without them when the time comes for him to use an artificial limb, so the period of walking with crutches should be reduced as much as possible. A temporary artificial limb is made by moulding plaster of Paris bandages round the stump so as to make a bucket, and attaching to this a peg leg, which may consist of part of an ordinary divided crutch fixed on each side in the plaster bandages. The wearing of such a bucket assists in the shrinking and consolidation of the stump so that there is less probability of the permanent bucket requiring alteration.

Arguments sometimes used against a temporary peg leg are that it leads to an unnatural gait owing to it having a stiff knee ; that men who have once got used to a stiff knee feel insecure on a movable knee ; and it may be difficult to persuade them to take to the use of a full artificial limb which they find heavier. But Elmslie considers that if the man finds he can overcome his disability better with a peg leg there is no need to press him to use a full leg (6).

The bucket of the permanent limb is made of stiff leather with lacing in front to suit the variations in the size of the stump ; or carved out in wood, in which case it is more difficult to fit and alter when required ; or it is made in duralumin. The Roman artificial leg in the Museum of the Royal College of Surgeons, London, dating back to 300 B.C., consists of a peg leg on a wooden bucket.

The Arm.—With an artificial leg the object is to enable the wearer to walk, whatever his occupation is, but in the case of an artificial arm the object is not so simple, as it is necessary to consider the man's occupation. Does he want a strong arm to use a hammer or a spade; or does he want an arm to help in such work as typing or drawing? Every endeavour has to be made to adapt the artificial arm to the man's trade rather than to adapt the man to a fresh trade.

The Hand.—The artificial hand in all cases becomes the " left " or least used hand, and account must therefore be taken of the movements of the left hand in each trade. The variety of different movements required makes it necessary sometimes to supply an experimental appliance and vary it according to the man's own suggestions. With some artificial hands, an opening movement of the fingers is obtained by cords which pass up the arm and are attached to bands which pass over the shoulder or round the body; by raising the shoulder, or inspiring deeply, the fingers can be opened, after which they close by the action of springs. In the case of amputations through the forearm, the method introduced by Putti in Italy of leaving finger-like projections at the extremity of the stump consisting of muscle and tendons is sometimes very successful. By clamping a suitable ring round the projections to which a cord is attached movements of the artificial fingers can be obtained. A simple magnet fixed on the end of the appliance has been found useful in occupations where a succession of nails have to be driven in. The nail can be picked up and held in position by the magnet while it is driven in by the hammer. Another useful device is a box with a slotted bottom; the pointed ends of nails placed in this box, when it is shaken, fall through the slots leaving the heads of the nails uppermost; a hammer with a magnetised head can be used by a one-armed man to pick up nail after nail and drive them into wood as desired (4).

A magnetic hand, invented in Germany, consists of an electromagnet by which tools are held (8). The current is from a portable battery or from the factory supply, and contact is made by the other hand or foot. The apparatus has not come into general use as it is clumsy and requires tools specially fitted with iron handles, while the cost of the current is a considerable item.

VIII. Fitting the Work to the Worker.

Skill in surgery and ingenious mechanical appliances can do much to convert a cripple into a useful operative. But justice would not be done to the subject of reclamation or to the disabled

if attention were not drawn to the latent possibilities of fitting
the work to the worker. The instance of the magnetic hammer
given in the previous section is only one of many devices invented
by Gilbreth (4) and by Amar (3) for this purpose. Special seats
may convert legless men into useful workers. Typing machines
and cash registers may be modified and heavy hammers fitted
with special grips for use by the one-armed. In fact, what has
been said in Chapters V. and XVI., with reference to making the
pegs of occupation round for the workers to fit into, applies
doubly to the disabled. Where the will to do this exists, the
result can be attained ; and Mock states (1) that " one concern
reported that it employed all legless and one-armed men who
applied and that it had carried out this policy for five years.
To-day forty such men work here. Five of these have advanced
to the position of foreman, one to a manager. Their reasons for
favouring this type of man were purely business reasons and
can be stated as follows :—

" (1) Lessens labour turnover. These men hesitate to change
jobs more than do the able-bodied.

" (2) Make more loyal employees. They appreciate the
opportunity given them to work in a world that has heretofore
tried to place them on the scrap heap.

" (3) Lessens troubles from labour agitators because of
loyalty.

" (4) Have a greater output. They stick closer to the job,
do not move about the plant as much as one with two legs.

" (5) Are more punctual and have less absenteeism. As a
rule they take a more serious view of life, do not use alcohol,
stay home of nights, and avoid exposures that lead to
sickness.

" (6) Take a pride in their accomplishments. The reaction
from those days when they thought they were cripples makes
them strive the harder to make good. As one of them said :
' It takes a lot of extra effort at first to overcome your handicap,
and then when it is overcome this extra effort ought to push
you away ahead of the other fellow. . . . The handicapped man
who has overcome his condition and made good is never a
' cripple.' " He has overcome a difficulty, and " difficulties are
the things that show what men are." *

IX. Occupations for the Crippled.

Men who have lost a leg can obtain work more easily
than men who have lost an arm. Thus the following

* Epictetus. Bk. I., Ch. xxiv.

Table of Occupations, and the Disabilities, to which they are suited, with Maximum Periods of Training; compiled from a Record of Men who have finished their Courses.

Process.	Maximum period of training.	Disabilities.
AGRICULTURE—		
Farming	12 months.	Bullet in chest—comp. fracture of skull—fractured cranium—G.S.W. abdomen and thigh—shell-shock.
Fruit growing	12 months.	G.S.W. elbow—G.S.W. left hand.
Motor tractor driving	3 months.	G.S.W. right foot—G.S.W. buttock—neurasthenia—G.S.W. skull—phlebitis—tuberculosis—G.S.W. right shoulder—G.S.W. thigh—phthisis—defective sight—loss of two fingers—G.S.W. both thighs—asthma and bronchitis—tubercle of lung—G.S.W. left leg.
Poultry farming	6 months.	Eczema of feet—flat feet—G.S.W. left shoulder—G.S.W. head—neurasthenia—blindness—left thigh, right foot fracture—inflammation of middle ear.
Market gardening	12 months.	G.S.W. ankle—fracture of patella.
Gardening	12 months.	Epilepsy.
ARTS AND CRAFTS—		
Artistic woodwork	6 to 12 months.	Gastritis—compound fracture of jaw.
Pottery (modelling, designing, etc.)	6 months.	V.D.H. mitral disease.
Writing and Illuminating		
BAKING AND CONFECTIONERY	6 months.	Leg amputated.
BOOT AND SHOE—	6 to 12 months.	G.S.W. left foot.
Boot making and repairing	12 to 18 months.	G.S.W. right arm—amputation left thigh—amputation leg—contusion of spine—G.S.W. left leg—G.S.W. right leg—G.S.W. arm, both legs—frostbite feet—blindness—malaria—paralysis right foot—chest wound and V.D.H.—neurasthenia and V.D.H.—chronic nephritis—G.S.W. abdomen—G.S.W. head—
BRUSHMAKING	6 months.	G.S.W. left arm—neurasthenia and rheumatism.
BUILDING—		G.S.W. spine—G.S.W. right shoulder.
Builder's draughtsmen	12 months.	G.S.W. right arm—G.S.W. foot.
Carpentry	6 months.	Enteric—G.S.W. right arm—blindness—amputation right leg.
Masonry	3 years.	Leg amputated.

Occupation	Duration	Disabilities
Sign writing	6 months.	Internal injury—G.S.W. left foot—concussion of spine—left arm useless—knee wound—crippled rheumatism—toes, left arm.
Tool making	—	G.S.W. both legs.
CANE AND WILLOW—		
Basket making	1 to 2 years.	Blindness—shell-shock—osteoarthritis left knee.
Mat making	13 weeks.	Blindness.
CINEMATOGRAPHY		Rheumatism—amputation right leg—trench feet—necrosis of femur—D.A.H.—gastritis—G.S.W. scalp and right knee—amputation two legs—knee—amputation left leg—myalgia—V.D.H.—amputation right arm—nephritis—G.S.W. right knee—G.S.W. left ankle and thigh—displaced semilunar cartilage of right knee—gastritis and bronchitis—hemoptysis—chronic carrier of *Bacillus paratyphosus*—double otitis media—old fracture of metacarpal bones—cardiac and vertigo—G.S.W. left hand and arm.
COMMERCIAL	6 months.	G.S.W. right and left arms—amputation both legs—renal calculus—paralysis right arm—amputation right arm—amputation left arm and middle finger right hand—D.A.H.—aortic V.D.H. and rheumatism—G.S.W. stomach—heart disease and bronchial asthma—drop foot—amputation left leg—ulcerated stomach—contusion of back and fractured ribs—G.S.W. left shoulder—neurasthenia—tubercular hip—G.S.W. head—blind.
Book-keeping	—	Amputation right arm—left elbow.
Clerks	—	G.S.W. left arm—arthritis hip and leg.
DIAMOND CUTTING	6 months.	Loss of legs—foot paralysis—leg amputated—three fingers off—amputation right thigh—G.S.W. right arm, chest and shoulder.
DOMESTIC SERVICE—		
Caretakers and Handymen	4 months.	Right arm wound—thigh wound, leg wound—gastric trouble and neurasthenia.
ENGINEERING (ELECTRICAL)	1 to 3 years.	G.S.W. left hand—contusion of muscles of back—gas poisoning—G.S.W. right shoulder—G.S.W. right thigh—nephritis—G.S.W. head, neck, and arm—G.S.W. right elbow—fractured ribs—neurasthenia—hemiplegia—amputation right leg—dislocated left elbow—heart failure—stricture of pylorus—shrapnel wound arm—V.D.H.—G.S.W. arm—rheumatoid arthritis—G.S.W. left foot, amputation little toe—amputation both legs—albuminuria—spinal trouble—tubercle of lung—compound fracture of ulna—malaria—fractured ankle—amputation left thigh—gastritis—G.S.W. chest—emphysema—lung fibrosis, V.D.H.—blind left eye—stiff elbow—gassed—G.S.W. abdomen and side—trench feet—asthma and bronchitis—G.S.W. neck—G.S.W. face, abdomen, and buttock—enlarged kidney—deafness—D.A.H.—G.S.W. causing fits—mitral and aortic—head trepanned—tubercular hip—fractured skull—dislocation of right shoulder.

Table of Occupations and Disabilities—continued.

Process.	Maximum period of training.	Disabilities.
ENGINEERING (MARINE) . . .	—	G.S.W. face and right arm—chronic malaria—shrapnel wound back.
ENGINEERING (MECHANICAL)		
Acetylene welding . .	6 months.	G.S.W. right hip—G.S.W. head and left hand—G.S.W. left leg—G.S.W. head and V.D.H.—leg amputated.
Draughtsmanship and tracing	6 months.	Neurasthenia, paralysis of leg—heart trouble.
Motor mechanism . .	6 months.	Eczema and debility—amputation leg—G.S.W. right arm—rheumatoid arthritis—G.S.W. left arm—chronic bronchitis—G.S.W. thigh—functional right hemiplegia and shell-shock—jaw injury—abdominal adhesions—G.S.W. right ilium—pulmonary tubercular gastric ulcer—paralysed left leg—fractured cranium—G.S.W. abdomen and back—acute pneumonia—G.S.W. left thigh—trench feet—tubercle of lung—gassed—G.S.W. left foot—nephritis—epilepsy—shell shock—melancholia—loss of right eye—G.S.W. chest, groin, head—fractured arm—amputation right leg—contusion left leg.
Turning and fitting .	3 years.	G.S.W. right elbow—D.A.H.
Whitesmith and tinsmith .	6 months.	Chronic rheumatism.
FURNITURE—		
Cabinet making . .	12 months.	G.S.W. left thigh.
French polishing . .	12 months.	G.S.W. knee—emphysema.
LEATHER—		
Fancy leather goods .	6 months.	Loss of right leg—right leg amputated—right knee stiff—loss of left leg—G.S.W. right ankle—G.S.W. left hand—gassed.
MISCELLANEOUS—		
Cricket-ball making .	3 to 6 months.	Shrapnel wound in body.
Dental mechanics .	12 months.	Loss of left leg—amputation right leg.
Hairdressing . .	6 to 12 months.	Nephritis—G.S.W. forearm.
Mineral boring . .	—	V.D.H.—G.S.W. thigh—varicose veins.
Piano-making and repairing	—	Pericarditis.
Sanitary inspecting .	6 months.	G.S.W. back—left leg—ball in lung.
Toy-making . .	12 months.	Bronchitis—amputation left leg—V.D.H.
Fireman . . .	—	G.S.W. left forearm and head—amputation left forearm.
PRINTING . . .	4 years.	Shell shock—amputation left leg—G.S.W. spine—trench feet—G.S.W. sciatic nerve—G.S.W. right thigh.

Occupation	Duration	Disabilities
PROFESSIONAL—		
Chemical analysis	1 year.	G.S.W. abdomen.
Dispensing	—	Loss of right leg—G.S.W. right thigh.
Laboratory work	—	Organic heart disease.
Massage	6 months.	Blindness.
Photography	6 months.	G.S.W. right elbow.
Singing	—	Blindness.
SURGICAL APPARATUS MAKING—		Left leg amputated—right leg amputated.
Artificial limb making	—	Left leg amputated.
TAILORING	9 to 12 months (wholesale). 12 to 18 months (retail, bespoke).	Loss of right leg—G.S.W. jaw—G.S.W. left hand.
TEXTILE MANUFACTURES—		
Cotton	8 weeks.	G.S.W. knee, bullet still in.
Designing	6 months.	G.S.W. left forearm.
Roller covering	—	Amputation right leg.
Weaving	3 months.	Amputation left arm—G.S.W. back.
Wool	48 weeks.	Amputation left leg.
TRANSPORT—		
Motor drivers	6 to 12 months.	Wound right leg—myalgia—fractured right elbow—ulceration of stomach—G.S.W. hip—shell-shock—G.S.W. left hand, drop wrist, lung weak from gas—G.S.W. metacarpus and tarsus—nephritis and pulmonary tuberculosis—lost sight of one eye—G.S.W. hand and shoulder—bronchitis—duodenal ulcer—V.D.H.—gastritis and heart affection—smashed arm—head wound—elbow wound—bronchial and heart trouble—G.S.W. left buttock—G.S.W. thigh and forearm—aortic and mitral neurasthenia—chronic otitis—tuberculosis—choroiditis—G.S.W. mouth and back.
Tram driver	1 or 2 weeks.	General poisoning.
TRAINING FOR BLIND AND DEAF—		
Wood work	—	G.S.W. head—shell-shock—G.S.W. right elbow—G.S.W. left leg.

This Table, compiled from the records of training, gives some indication of occupations found suitable by actual experience to certain disabilities. It by no means pretends to be exhaustive; and no one must conclude from it that, say, cabinet making is only suitable to men with a gunshot wound in the left thigh, or hairdressing to those afflicted with nephritis or a gunshot wound in the forearm.—EDITOR OF "REVEILLE."

occupations have been adopted by men discharged from the army :—

Men who have lost a leg :—

Bootmaking.
Caretaker.
Chauffeur.
Domestic ser-
  vice.
Electrical work.
Gateman.
Groom.
Hall porter.

Industrial work
  (sundry).
Liftman.
Light duties at pithead
  (for miners).
Lodge keeper.
Milker.
Packer.
Painter.

Postal.
Printing.
Railway work, varied.
Road work.
Tailoring.
Telephone attendant.
Telegraphy.
Timekeeper.
Vanman.

Men who have lost an arm :—

Clerical.
Commissionaire.
Gateman.
Liftman.
Scholastic.

Lodge keeper.
Messenger.
Porter.
Ticket collector.
Watchman.

Telephone switchboard.
Timekeeper.
Traveller.
Ward master.
Weighman.

Men who have lost both lower limbs :—

Tailoring.
Typewriting.
Accountant.
Picture painting.

Watch and clock repair-
  ing.
Ticket and show-card
  writing.

Basket work.
Leather work and
  fancy leather work.

The table on pp. 422—425, taken from *Reveille* (12) is of interest ; it shows in greater detail the type of disability and the period of training required for learning a new occupation. *Reveille*, a monthly journal devoted to disabled ex-service men, was published during the later period of the war. It contained many interesting and valuable articles on the subject dealt with in this Chapter.

X.   Disablement from Nerve Injuries.

The disablement caused by injuries to the nerves can in many cases be removed if treated by an experienced surgeon. Nerve suture has been carried out several years after the injury with complete success. A man had his ulnar nerve severed by a bullet in the retreat from Mons in 1914 ; the wound soon healed, and he was employed in an officers' mess where he somehow escaped the travelling medical boards and the regimental medical officer. He liked his work, and was anxious to continue it, so it was not until he was demobilised in 1919 when he claimed a pension that his claw hand came under notice and he was recommended for nerve suture. It may be that he was not really anxious to have treatment which would have raised his category and sent him back to the firing line. He was operated on and his condition has considerably improved.

The success obtained with some nerves is greater than in others; thus the musculo-spiral does better than the ulnar. In some cases the ends of the nerve may be involved in callous or a mass of scar tissue, requiring a laborious dissection on the part of the surgeon to liberate the nerve and remove all the scar tissue, often a matter of two hours. The ends of the nerve may be bulbous, and it may be necessary to stretch the nerve or transpose it to get end to end suture. Such operations, which require the highest degree of skill and asepsis, can only be undertaken where there is an efficient team.

Suture of the sciatic nerve has produced very good results, so that after two or three years men have been able to jump, climb ladders, and run with no disability left at all. Success depends largely upon the accurate apposition of the different bundles of the nerve.

The public require to have a greater knowledge of what can be done in these cases. Ex-service men now understand about nerve suture and there is no difficulty in persuading them to undergo the operation; in fact, they ask for it.

XI. Defective Vision.

A person with inferior sight can carry on certain trades as well as those with perfect vision. On the other hand there are trades where the highest visual acuity is required; in consequence a man engaged in watch making or gauge testing may be disabled for his trade by a slight accident, such as would not affect the earning capacity of a farmer or a clerk.

Eyesight can therefore be graded to the different trades. Three main classes are usually adopted :—

(1) *Those trades needing ordinary sight :*—Basket makers, binders, caretakers, confectioners, domestic servants, doorkeepers, dyers, farmers, florists, gilders, grooms, glass blowers, grinders, labourers, masseurs, millers, packers, paper makers, polishers, porters, shoeing smiths, soap boilers, tanners, umbrella makers, washerwomen.

(2) *Those needing superior sight :*—Blacksmiths, bootmakers, brewers, butchers, carpenters, clerks, coopers, cutlers, drapers, dressmakers, electricians, furriers, gardeners, glaziers, miners, musicians, plumbers, postmen, tailors, tinsmiths, surgical instrument makers, turners, weavers.

(3) *Those needing maximal sight :*—Chauffeurs, diamond polishers, embroiderers, engravers, gunsmiths, jewellers, cabinet makers, lithographers, locksmiths, masons, mechanics, opticians, painters, photographers, plasterers, printers, railway servants

(engaged in the movement of trains), sailors, sculptors, ship-builders, telegraphists, watchmakers.

A man's occupation must be considered when determining the degree of disablement. As a rule the trades requiring the highest visual acuity bring in the highest wages. If a man earning high wages suffers from diminution of vision from an accident he receives compensation ; he is still able to work at a trade not requiring such good vision. If, however, his vision be diminished by disease he receives no compensation,* but he may still be able to earn a living, provided he can find suitable work.

The question arises, is the man too old to re-educate and can he be persuaded to make a fresh start in life ? By visual training it might be possible so to improve the man's vision that he could obtain work in a higher class, so that, if incapacitated by disablement in his limbs, he might be able to obtain a different class of work.

The results of visual training during the war were in many cases remarkable. After the battle of Jutland, when apparently anxiety concerning an invasion of this country ceased, a large number of young soldiers, category A 1, on the East Coast were sent overseas and replaced by men between the ages of forty and fifty of category C 1, some of whom came under the observation of the writer. Many of these men came from large industrial towns inland, where they had worked over twenty years in factories, hardly ever using their eyes for distant vision. Even going backwards and forwards to the factory they probably never required to see more than across the street. On arrival on the East Coast a large number of these men could not see the bull's eye of a target at 200 yards ; they were quite unable to distinguish ships a few miles out at sea, which was supposed to be one of their special duties, and it was as well the Admiralty maintained the coastguards for watching duties. By a system of daily visual training the vision of these men improved enor-mously, so that when they went to France twelve months later many of them had normal distant vision.

In this country a soldier who has lost the sight of both eyes receives 100 per cent. pension ; for the loss of vision of one eye he receives 50 per cent. But one man with one good eye may be able to resume his previous work and is not really disabled ; while others with one eye may be quite disabled for their previous occupation. A chauffeur with one eye cannot accurately judge distances and would be in constant danger of collision. A one-eyed man cannot be employed on scaffolding where one

* Diseases in the Schedule to Workmen's Compensation Act are here considered " accidents."

false step means a fatal fall. Employers are shy of engaging
one-eyed men ; they think that the risk of compensation is too
great. In consequence the rate of 50 per cent. is really not too
high, though there may be cases where a man's occupation is
not interfered with.

A man with one eye after about twelve months acquires by
experience a knowledge which almost replaces the sense of
" relief " he has lost. The work at St. Dunstan's has shown
what can be done to enable the blind to lead useful lives ; and
with the large number of blind civilians in the country there is
need for more of such institutions. Before the war the principal
training provided for the blind was for children blinded at birth.
There were not many places where an adult blinded by an accident
could be trained ; all institutions for the indigent blind were
entirely dependent on charity. Men who are quite blind are
found at St. Dunstan's to get on quicker than those having a
small amount of sight ; basket making, boot repairing, carpentry,
mat making, can be acquired by them in about eight months.
Blind men living and working together undoubtedly become fairly
happy, and much could be done for them by special institutions
where the buildings and grounds can be specially arranged, and
workshops and recreation rooms specially fitted for their use.
But there will always be those unfortunate ones among the
blind who are incapable of being trained and will remain a
burden to their friends or the State.

XII. Defective Hearing.

The number of people who have perfect hearing with both
ears is not large. This is probably due to damage caused in
childhood by measles, scarlet fever or adenoids. In examining
for life insurance, when the hearing of both ears is tested separately it is often found to the person's surprise that his hearing
is defective in one ear, and many claims have been made by
soldiers for deafness which has been brought on by an aggrava-
tion of an existing diseased condition, the extent of which was
not noted in the rush of examining recruits. There are several
trades in which loss of hearing gradually results, e.g., riveters
in shipyards, blacksmiths, coppersmiths, coopers, but such
men cannot be regarded as disabled. They are quite able to
carry on their trades and obtain steady advancement. There
are other occupations, such as that of a shorthand clerk, or shop
assistant, for which even a slight degree of deafness disables a
man ; here re-education for another occupation becomes a
necessity. There are occupations, on the other hand, for which

deaf people are peculiarly adapted ; an accountant, a typist, or a conveyancing solicitor may find an advantage in being able to concentrate on his work without being disturbed by noises.

The onset in nearly all forms of deafness is gradual, and if it is recognised early that the condition is one which is progressive and cannot be prevented, there is ample time for re-education. Training in lip reading for the young is useful, but with persons over forty the training is difficult ; in deaf and dumb institutions where children are taught lip reading, as well as talking on the hands, when they are by themselves they usually prefer the signs to lip reading. Lip reading requires a greater degree of concentration than is to be found in most of the working classes, and is of limited use. If the speaker happens to have a big moustache, the reader has no chance at all. If the speaker is in a bad light or a distance off, as at a theatre or public meeting, again the reader cannot make out sufficient to follow. Lip reading does, however, add to the enjoyment of cinema theatres as the performers do really say their parts and they are easy to follow under such favourable conditions.

For many it is not worth while going through the expense and trouble of lip reading if a suitable appliance can be found to aid them. Although for cases of nerve deafness no appliance is of any use, yet cases of middle ear deafness are far commoner ; for these electric ear 'phones are very satisfactory and in many cases make up the handicap. They have an advantage over ear trumpets in that both hands are free, as the 'phone is fixed on the head with a light spring.

The after-treatment of ear cases is recognised by the Ministry of Pensions as very important, and a number of aural clinics have been established where prolonged treatment can be carried out and cases kept under observation ; so that should operative interference be required it can be carried out before it is too late. In civil life one frequently comes across people with discharging ears who do not realise the importance of treatment which may prevent meningitis ; every person with a discharging ear must be made clearly to understand that neglect of treatment will result in defective hearing and that he is always running the risk of meningitis. A certain amount of treatment can be carried out by the man himself with an india-rubber syringe with a fine point, but a really satisfactory syringe for the purpose has not yet been invented. The old fashioned glass syringe with a thick bulbous end is a dangerous instrument ; there is risk in its use ; the end may block the external meatus, when the fluid forced up may drive septic material directly into the adjoining mastoid cells.

XIII. Functional Nerve Disorders.

Many so-called " shell shock " cases have never been under fire ; it is unfortunate that the name should be applied to these cases, as it is a cause of their receiving undue sympathy which delays their return to work. Owing to the need for men during the war, men who were partially mentally deficient had to be called up ; for if one man could escape service by feigning stupidity, others could do the same. It was therefore necessary to keep such men under observation and make the best possible use of them. But the strenuous life of training and the attentions of the sergeant-major were often sufficient to upset an unstable nervous equilibrium, without the greater disturbances which were required to upset the balance of normal men.

Railway spine cases, which used to come before the law courts twenty years ago for compensation claims, were undoubtedly cases of traumatic neurasthenia, but the condition was so little-recognised then, that there were usually medical men available to give evidence that the man had nothing the matter with him. Many cases of functional paralysis of a limb following genuine shell shock are now after two or three years being cured by psycho-therapeutic means. The results are striking ; it is no unusual occurrence for a man to recover the use of his hand in a few days and resume work after having regarded his hand as paralysed for about two years. Records exist of the occurrence of cases of this kind throughout the history of mankind ; they are the foundation of many miracles ; they account for the reputation attached in ancient times to such places as the great sanctuary of Æsculapius near Epidaurus (10), and in modern times to Lourdes. As a result these men are keen to resume work and are grateful for the treatment that enabled them to do so. In civilian life the severer forms of functional disturbance may not often be seen, but milder forms of neurasthenia occur, and will always present a difficult problem in getting the patients back to work. It is difficult to tell at times whether these men are genuine sufferers, and easy to regard them as loafers and shy of work. But it should be possible to employ them on graduated work in the open air for pay and gradually get them on to suitable work. The question of finding suitable work for neurasthenics is more important than training them for any occupation they may desire. A man who had been blown up in France was under hospital treatment for severe neurasthenia for eleven months ; he was discharged cured and advised to get some work on a farm. He chose to get work as a night porter at a hotel, with the result that in a fortnight he broke down again. The aftercare of severe neurasthenia to prevent relapses is important ; but there seems at present no public body in the case of civilians to assist them to appropriate work, and to help them when they are on the point of breaking down.

Nerve disorders in industrial life may not be frequently named as such, but in nearly every case of industrial convalescence an important psychological element is present retarding complete recovery. A sick craftsman (unless he happens to be in an unusually fortunate position with regard to sick and draw clubs) is an anxious man. He must resume his skilled work or surrender his social position and even slip with those dependent on him to within sight of the workhouse. An attempt, while slightly indisposed, to keep the pace expected at the factory may have precipitated the attack of dyspepsia, muscular rheumatism, or asthma from which he is diagnosed to be suffering. As recovery is delayed he sees his hold on his place becoming imperilled ; his attention centres on his symptoms and a vicious circle is started. The more he thinks of his symptoms the more pronounced they become ; the more pronounced they become, the more is his attention directed to them. The presence in industrial illness of this constant underlying anxiety is a serious influence ; it is most to be found among the better class of artizan, and less among the lower grades of labour, since those that are down fear no fall.

An assured position is the preventive measure for these cases, but, although this ideal is not practical to-day, much can be done by permitting workmen who have been away sick or are not feeling up-to-the-mark to work for short hours. Permission for such relaxation should be granted after consideration by the employment or welfare department. Action on these lines would in the long run reduce lost time and cure many obstinate cases, the nervous element in which is not fully recognised.

XIV. Disablement by Disease.

Many soldiers disabled by heart disease, neurasthenia, or nephritis are quite able to do some work, and their cases are among the most pathetic seen. They really may try to get light work, and failing to get it, as usually happens, they endeavour to make their disability last as long as possible so as to draw their treatment allowances. It would really be more economical to provide suitable occupations for these men. Many of them are so debilitated that whatever treatment they get they will be unable to follow their previous occupations. Thus a miner debilitated by severe malaria may never feel strong enough to follow his old work, but could do basket work, or cabinet making ; there are those with disease of the heart or lungs who could do half-a-day's light work at horticulture, market gardening, poultry farming, pig breeding, if such work were organised.

The case here presented for the disabled soldier equally exists for the disabled industrial worker ; here industrial service has in many cases contributed to the breakdown, *e.g.*, the miner may be disabled through nystagmus, or the sufferer from lung trouble by exposure to dust inhalation. National economy is not served by paying compensation and leaving these potential producers without any outlet for the capacity they still possess.

Tuberculosis.—The case of tuberculosis is dealt with in Chapter VI. ; colonies which have been started for reclaiming these disabled workers and providing them with a hygienic life while occupied in remunerative work suitable for each individual case, have proved a great success, and the system might be adapted to deal with other diseases. The model colony at Papworth in Cambridgeshire consists of an estate of 350 acres with a sanatorium, where men are placed on admission, and a training colony to which men pass from the sanatorium on improving in health, and learn various occupations. After six months' training the men can join the village settlement on the estate, where they get housing accommodation and the wages of the district.

Heart Cases.—The reclamation of heart cases might be on similar lines. Instead of the sanatorium there would be a hospital where the exercise tolerance of each individual would be determined and endeavour made by graduated work to improve it. Heart cases have for many years been treated by exercise, *e.g.*, walking up slopes or Swedish exercises ; but such have the disadvantage that the man is continually thinking about his disease. The various operations of gardening provide work graduated to each individual case and of sufficient interest to take a man's thoughts off himself. All grades of work can be found, from the sedentary work of pricking out seedlings in a greenhouse to digging a measured piece of ground in a certain time.

At present a man with heart disease endeavouring to resume his old work is like a fish trying to get up a weir, he tries and falls back ; but if the process were graduated, as it is sometimes for fish by a ladder, he would in many cases be able to reach and maintain the higher level.

Those who by graduated training only improve up to a certain standard could be registered for that standard and told the class of work they were fit for. They would then have the chance of joining a village settlement where suitable occupations would be found for them. As Dr. Moon states (11) : " The fact is that fairly hard work can be done by many people who suffer from heart disease, provided the hours are regular and the work more or less the same from day to day and hour to hour, while there is no undue sense of hurry in the doing of it. Anything in the nature of spurts, which may be almost an essential element in some occupations, though the work itself may not be so intrinsically heavy, should be strenuously avoided ; thus, dockers are a good instance of an occupation which involves periodical rushes, with, it may be, unduly slack intervals, and that kind of thing is bad for almost any form of heart disease, and particularly for the older and casual workers."

In such a village colony away from docks and factories, life should go on without periodical rushes.

> " Along the cool sequestered vale of life
> They kept the even tenor of their way."

Many of these heart victims after passing through the heart training hospital might prefer returning to their own homes in the towns rather than living in a village settlement. They may prefer places of entertainment and seeing their old friends ; in these cases there is not the same need of village settlements as for tuberculosis, where one object is to remove infective persons from the towns.

Sick-pay Difficulties.—The working man disabled by chronic disease receives as disablement pay 7s. 6d. a week from the National Health Insurance, and may, if he has been provident, receive a further sum from his society, but for a man with a family such sums are inadequate to maintain them with the present high prices. Yet the man is willing and able to do some light work if he can only find it. At present if a man drawing sickness pay from his society is seen to do any kind of work, such as planting potatoes in an allotment, he is at once reported and his pay stopped on the ground that he ought to be at work.

The difficulties men have in obtaining light work frequently come under notice in workmen's compensation cases, where an insurance company applies to a county court judge for the compensation to be reduced on the ground that the man can do some work. Some years ago the writer in giving evidence in such a case on behalf of an insurance company, stated that a man was fit for light work. This led the judge to remark on the uselessness of medical men coming to court and talking about light work. The man, who was a ship's fireman, followed a few minutes later into the witness box. On going up the two steps he stumbled, and to save himself, caught hold of the top of the woodwork with the hand supposed to be useless. The judge noticed this and promptly decided the case against him ; and the man, notwithstanding the judge's previous remarks, was left with a reduced compensation and the difficulty of finding light work. For him there was no transitional stage between idleness and the heavy work in a ship's stokehold. If the judge had been able to arrange for him two or three hours' digging a day for wages when he reduced the compensation, the man would have been grateful and would not have endeavoured to make the most of his injury, as the work would have enabled him to get fit to earn full wages.

Value of Occupation.—Light work with wages is the best method of overcoming the lethargic condition of mind and muscles produced by a long illness ; it restores self confidence and dispels dejection. Many disabled soldiers have had long periods of hospital treatment during which they only occupied themselves by playing cards and reading the papers. These men are difficult to get back to work ; they have lost the will to work, and their minds seem to have become clouded.

Great value comes from starting competitions in a hospital in various simple occupations, such as leather work, hearth-rug and mat making, which a man can do in bed ; the men get their minds diverted from their illness and become mentally brighter and more alert. A useful means to keep a man's will to work is to find him some suitable occupation in hospital as soon as ever he is fit for it. Such occupation might not be of any direct use to him afterwards as a means of earning a living, but by exercising his mind and his body it will produce a most beneficial effect. Something might be done perhaps by propaganda as to the advantages of training, by lectures and cinema shows to patients in hospital, distribution of illustrated pamphlets and conducting parties round workshops or farms where the disabled are employed.

Industrial Training.—A point is made in the training workshops at Loughborough of putting a man at once on productive work and of not wasting time making articles which will be thrown away. This it is found makes a man careful from the first, and, with proper supervision, is found to work well. A man is there required to put in forty-four hours a week training, and after nine to twelve months is able to work for wages as an improver, and then after another nine months to receive the full wages. That is, a cabinet maker may in eighteen months learn what an apprentice used to take six to seven years to learn. The difficulties with the trade unions are gradually being overcome, and it looks as if concentrated training in well equipped workshops would take the place of the old apprenticeship system, as was the case many years ago with the training of medical students.

Many men are anxious to avail themselves of these training facilities, but there are others who have not the necessary intelligence and grit to make a fresh start in life—" one man may take a horse to water, but twenty cannot make him drink." These men after several years of enforced idleness have lost their will to work, and present a difficult problem. Many of them, young men living with their parents, are, with their pensions, able to manage without doing any remunerative work. But what will be the position of these men ten or twenty years hence ? Another generation of trained and able bodied men will have grown up, and it will be more difficult for the disabled to get work than it is to-day, when employers who have not forgotten the promises they made at recruiting meetings are endeavouring to employ disabled men.

The question therefore arises whether the State should not on behalf, not only of the man, but also of the national welfare, insist on some form of training for the disabled, and so save, in years to come, having to maintain these men in the workhouses. A man's disablement pension is not intended to keep him in an idle state, but to make up any loss he may suffer when in competition with other workers; compensation payments for industrial disablement should be looked upon in the same light. In France, training is obligatory by law in the case of any victim of amputation who has a right to a military pension. This country has been reluctant to compel men to undergo training ; it is thought to be interfering with the liberty of the subject ; moreover, even when trained, there may be a difficulty in finding employment until the trade unions have modified their rules.

A suggestion has been made that a disabled man who refuses to undergo training should have his pension reduced in the same way as he does if he refuses treatment ; but it is well to remember the different degrees of intelligence among the working classes, and that even a reduced pension would not produce the desired effect, but rather send the lowest class begging on the streets. Some men seem born to be hewers of wood and drawers of water in every State, and to have no ambition to do any other work.

It may become necessary to establish medical boards with trade assessors to examine men not medically fit to be trained and decide what work they are fitted for. It should not be difficult for the Ministry of Labour to establish workshops and market gardens on the outskirts of our large towns to which parties of men only fit for light work could be taken by motor lorries, either for a half or a whole day.

Home Industries.—Many of the disabled may be able to work if they can do it in their own time, and for these it might be possible to arrange work in their own homes. Forty years ago in some of the villages in the Midlands, nail making by hand used to be carried on as a home industry. Each cottage had at its rear a small workshop where the man, assisted by various members of the family, carried on the trade, and often on a summer evening one would hear the villagers hammering away, having spent the heat of the day enjoying themselves. Judging from the number of public houses in these villages in those days, the men were fairly prosperous till machinery gradually killed their trade.

Among the trades suitable for home industries are tailoring, cigarette making by machine, bookbinding, watch and clock making and repairing, boot repairing, toy making, leather work, basket work, market gardening, and bee keeping. In some villages men might like to work together on a co-operative basis, and a useful war memorial would be to establish in the villages memorial workshops on the lines of the Lord Roberts Memorial Workshops. When the disabled of the recent war have passed away, there will always be those disabled in civilian life by accident or disease for whom such workshops would be useful. All available men were called up for service during the recent war ; they were graded according to their medical category and suitable work in the army was found for them.   In the industrial war we are now faced with in the world we must increase our production to the utmost by again making use of every available man ; even the disabled must be reclaimed for industry in their own interests and in the interests of the nation.

XV. Bibliography.

1. Mock, H. E.   *Industrial Medicine and Surgery.*   W. B. Saunders & Co.   1919.

2. Llewellyn, T. L.   " The Economic Aspect of Miners' Nystagmus." *The Colliery Guardian.* June 4th, 1920.

3. Amar, J. *Physiology of Industrial Organisation and the Re-employment of the Disabled.* Translated by B. Miall. London Press, Ltd.   1918.

4. Gilbreth, F. B. and L. M. *Motion Study for the Handicapped.* Geo. Routledge & Sons, Ltd.   1920.

5. Hutt, C. W. *The Future of the Disabled Soldier.* John Bale, Sons and Danielsson, Ltd.

6. Elmslie, R. C. *The After-Treatment of Wounds and Injuries.* J. and A. Churchill.

7. Chapple, W. A. " Prevention of Nerve Bulbs in Stumps." *British Medical Journal.* April 6th, 1918.

8. *The Electrical Review.* January 14th, 1916.

9. Amar, J. *Le Moteur Humain.* Translated by E. B. Daniels. Geo. Routledge & Sons, Ltd.

10. Frazer, Sir J. G. *Folk-Lore in the Old Testament*, Vol. II. Macmillan & Co., Ltd. 1918.

11. Moon, R. O. " Heart Affections in Relation to the Labour Market." *British Medical Journal.* May 8th, 1920.

12. *Reveille.* H.M. Stationery Office. February, 1919.

INDEX

THE WHITEFRIARS PRESS, LTD., LONDON AND TONBRIDGE.